THE NEW PALGRAVE

SOCIAL ECONOMICS

THE NEW PALGRAVE

SOCIAL ECONOMICS

EDITED BY

JOHN EATWELL · MURRAY MILGATE · PETER NEWMAN

W·W·NORTON

NEW YORK · LONDON

© The Macmillan Press Limited, 1987, 1989

First published in
The New Palgrave: A Dictionary of Economics
Edited by John Eatwell, Murray Milgate and Peter Newman
in four volumes, 1987

The New Palgrave is a trademark of
The Macmillan Press Limited

First American Edition, 1989
All rights reserved.

Published simultaneously in Canada by
Penguin Books Canada Ltd.
2801 John Street
Markham, Ontario L3R 1B4

ISBN 0-393-02727-9

ISBN 0-393-95852-3   PBK.

W. W. Norton & Company, Inc.
500 Fifth Avenue
New York, NY 10110

W. W. Norton & Company, Ltd.
37 Great Russell Street
London WC1B 3NU

Printed in Great Britain

1   2   3   4   5   6   7   8   9   0

Contents

Contents

General Preface

The books in this series are the offspring of *The New Palgrave: A Dictionary of Economics*. Published in late 1987, the *Dictionary* has rapidly become a standard reference work in economics. However, its four heavy tomes containing over four million words on the whole range of economic thought is not a form convenient to every potential user. For many students and teachers it is simply too bulky, too comprehensive and too expensive for everyday use.

By developing the present series of compact volumes of reprints from the original work, we hope that some of the intellectual wealth of *The New Palgrave* will become accessible to much wider groups of readers. Each of the volumes is devoted to a particular branch of economics, such as econometrics or general equilibrium or money, with a scope corresponding roughly to a university course on that subject. Apart from correction of misprints, etc. the content of each of its reprinted articles is exactly the same as that of the original. In addition, a few brand new entries have been commissioned especially for the series, either to fill an apparent gap or more commonly to include topics that have risen to prominence since the dictionary was originally commissioned.

As *The New Palgrave* is the sole parent of the present series, it may be helpful to explain that it is the modern successor to the excellent *Dictionary of Political Economy* edited by R.H. Inglis Palgrave and published in three volumes in 1894, 1896 and 1899. A second and slightly modified version, edited by Henry Higgs, appeared during the mid-1920s. These two editions each contained almost 4,000 entries, but many of those were simply brief definitions and many of the others were devoted to peripheral topics such as foreign coinage, maritime commerce, and Scottish law. To make room for the spectacular growth in economics over the last 60 years while keeping still to a manageable length, *The New Palgrave* concentrated instead on economic theory, its originators, and its closely cognate disciplines. Its nearly 2,000 entries (commissioned from over 900 scholars) are all self-contained essays, sometimes brief but never mere definitions.

Apart from its biographical entries, *The New Palgrave* is concerned chiefly with theory rather than fact, doctrine rather than data; and it is not at all clear how theory and doctrine, as distinct from facts and figures, *should* be treated in an encyclopaedia. One way is to treat everything from a particular point of view. Broadly speaking, that was the way of Diderot's classic *Encyclopédie raisonée* (1751–1772), as it was also of Léon Say's *Nouveau dictionnaire d'économie politique* (1891–2). Sometimes, as in articles by Quesnay and Turgot in the *Encyclopédie*, this approach has yielded entries of surpassing brilliance. Too often, however, both the range of subjects covered and the quality of the coverage itself are seriously reduced by such a self-limiting perspective. Thus the entry called '*Méthode*' in the first edition of Say's *Dictionnaire* asserted that the use of mathematics in economics 'will only ever be in the hands of a few', and the dictionary backed up that claim by choosing not to have any entry on Cournot.

Another approach is to have each entry take care to reflect within itself varying points of view. This may help the student temporarily, as when preparing for an examination. But in a subject like economics, the Olympian detachment which this approach requires often places a heavy burden on the author, asking for a scrupulous account of doctrines he or she believes to be at best wrong-headed. Even when an especially able author does produce a judicious survey article, it is surely too much to ask that it also convey just as much enthusiasm for those theories thought misguided as for those found congenial. Lacking an enthusiastic exposition, however, the disfavoured theories may then be studied less closely than they deserve.

The New Palgrave did not ask its authors to treat economic theory from any particular point of view, except in one respect to be discussed below. Nor did it call for surveys. Instead, each author was asked to make clear his or her own views of the subject under discussion, and for the rest to be as fair and accurate as possible, without striving to be 'judicious'. A balanced perspective on each topic was always the aim, the ideal. But it was to be sought not *internally*, within each article, but *externally*, between articles, with the reader rather than the writer handed the task of achieving a personal balance between differing views.

For a controversial topic, a set of several more or less synonymous headwords, matched by a broad diversity of contributors, was designed to produce enough variety of opinion to help form the reader's own synthesis; indeed, such diversity will be found in most of the individual volumes in this series.

This approach was not without its problems. Thus, the prevalence of uncertainty in the process of commissioning entries sometimes produced a less diverse outcome than we had planned. 'I can call spirits from the vasty deep,' said Owen Glendower. 'Why, so can I,' replied Hotspur, 'or so can any man;/ But will they come when you do call for them?' In our experience, not quite as often as we would have liked.

The one point of view we did urge upon every one of *Palgrave*'s authors was to write from an historical perspective. For each subject its contributor was asked to discuss not only present problems but also past growth and future prospects. This request was made in the belief that knowledge of the historical development of any theory enriches our present understanding of it, and so helps to construct better theories for the future. The authors' response to the request was generally so positive that, as the reader of any of these volumes will discover, the resulting contributions amply justified that belief.

Peter Newman
Murray Milgate
John Eatwell

Preface

'Whatever our definition of Economics and the economic life may be, the laws which they exhibit and obey are not peculiar to themselves, but are laws of life in its widest extent' (Philip Wicksteed, *Common Sense of Political Economy*, 1910, Book I, Chapter V).

For Rev. Wicksteed there is no 'economic motive' as such, distinct from other motives; it is 'a false category'. But there *is* a problem of wise administration of resources in general. Using a host of everyday examples, he argues that a person's allocation of time and of physical and mental effort to *all* her activities (including, for example, her prayers and her devotions) is governed by precisely the same principles as her allocation of monetary expenditure among market commodities. Admittedly, some of these problems of general administration may not be Economics at all, but he suggests that the discipline should at least include the study of 'acts of administration dealing with exchangeable things but not themselves acts of exchange', as well as the more usual 'acts of administration that directly involve exchange'.

Many of the essays collected in this volume demonstrate that modern economists interested in societal problems have successfully pursued not only Economics in Wicksteed's sense, but also his wider problem of general resource administration. Indeed, it is chiefly economists who have undertaken such wider and more sociological investigations, though there are no compelling reasons why this should be so. In any event, the economists' research has contributed sharp and fresh understanding of many social problems that at first appear to have little or no economics in them at all.

However, along with the new understanding has come misunderstanding, leading to allegations that economists working in this field are guilty of the academically modish sin of reductionism. Research that has appeared under titles like 'An Economic Theory of...', with the dots replaced by such words as 'Religion', 'Divorce', 'Extra-Marital Affairs' etc., are sometimes mistakenly seen (and not only by non-economists) as examples of the alleged 'economic motive' at work *all by itself.* They are much better seen as the workings of just one of the aspects – the 'economic aspect' – of all the motives involved in a given social situation. Looked at like this, the research is not reductionist at all but simply part of a Wicksteedian research programme into 'the laws of life in its widest extent'.

Finally, a note about the title of this volume. 'Mainstream' economics used the phrase *Social Economics* often in the past (though in several different senses), but at present it is neither in common use nor does it have a common meaning. Thus it seems appropriate as the title for a collection of articles pertaining to the use of economics in the study of society. We apologise to all those for whom it signifies something else.

The Editors

Ageing Populations

ROBERT L. CLARK

Population ageing is represented by an increase in the relative number of older persons in a population and is associated with an increase in the median age of the population. The age structure of a population is determined by its mortality, fertility, and net migration experience. Although life tables and survivorship rates date from the 17th century, the development of mathematical demography is essentially a 20th-century innovation. The techniques of mathematical demography can be used to show how the age structure of a population changes with alternative transition rates.

The importance of these transition rates is shown by the observation that in the absence of migration two arbitrarily chosen populations that are subjected to identical fertility and mortality rates will ultimately generate the same age structure. Thus, as Coale (1972, p. 3) noted, populations gradually 'forget' the past in as far as their age compositions are concerned. Of course, the population age structure may echo past irregularities for several generations before these echo effects disappear (Easterlin, 1980).

Population projections illustrate that declining fertility produces population ageing, so do decreases in mortality rates; however, fertility changes dominate the age structure of a population. For example, even if man were to become immortal, high fertility rates would produce a relatively young population. Migration can modify the age composition of a population, but non-sustained migration will have only a transitory effect on the age distribution of a population unless the migration also alters the prevailing patterns of fertility and mortality (Keyfitz, 1968, p. 94).

Concern for the economic implications of ageing populations is essentially a 20th-century phenomenon. Populations with low life expectancies and high fertility rates will have only small fractions age 65 and older. For most of human history, these were typical population characteristics. Therefore, little attention was devoted to the macroeconomic implications of ageing. In summarizing economic thinking prior to the 20th century, Hutchinson (1967, p. 346) concludes

1

that because the typical population age structure contained relatively few persons over age 65, not much attention was given to the ratio of workers to the total population. In most economic analysis, the population was simply assumed to be equivalent to labour supply.

Declining population growth occurred in Western Europe in the early part of the 20th century. The resulting ageing of populations began to attract attention. Economists focused their analyses on age structure ratios, such as the number of dependent persons (the young and old) divided by the number of persons in the population or by the number of persons of working age. Much of the research examining the economic implications of ageing populations assesses the effects of change in these dependency ratios or similar population ratios.

Dependency ratios are used to measure the relative productive potential of a population. The old-age dependency ratio generally measures the number of elderly persons at or above a certain age, say 65, divided by the number of persons of working age, say 16–64. This ratio has been widely used in economic analysis to measure the number of retired dependent persons per active member of the labour force. The old-age dependency ratio is used to illustrate the transfer of output from workers that is necessary to support retirees. This ratio rises with population ageing.

There are several problems concerning the economic interpretation of the old-age dependency ratio. First, if population ageing follows from reduced fertility, the total dependency ratio (youths plus elderly) may fall even as the old-age ratio is rising. The total cost to society of supporting the dependent populations will depend on the relative costs of maintaining the two dependent populations and the transfer mechanisms that are developed within the economic system (Sauvy, 1969, pp. 303–19). Second, the age-based dependency ratios are not perfect proxies for the ratio of inactive to active persons. Recently, some analysts have attempted to incorporate labour force participation into the dependency-ratio framework. Of course, over time, participation rates and the meaning of dependency may change. Third, significant compositional changes may occur within the elderly, youth, and working age populations. These changes have economic effects that may be as important as effects of changes in the dependency ratio itself (Clark and Spengler, 1980).

The cost of national pension systems rises with population ageing because a greater fraction of the population is receiving benefits and a smaller fraction is working and paying taxes to support the system (Munnell, 1977). This relationship has become one of the principal public policy issues associated with population ageing. The funding of pensions and the economic impact of alternative funding methods also has been subject to considerable examination. Feldstein (1974) argued that the pay-as-you-go financing of the US Social Security System substantially reduced the national savings rate. Subsequent research has produced a series of conflicting findings on this issue.

The growth of national pension systems has drawn attention to retirement ages. The impact of population ageing on pension funding requirements is exacerbated if the age of withdrawal from the labour force declines. During the past century, labour force participation rates of the elderly have fallen and the interaction of earlier retirement and population ageing has produced significant increases in income transfers to the elderly.

The changing age structure of a population may also alter the equilibrium unemployment rate and the average level of productivity in a society. Layoff and quit rates are a decreasing function of age. Since employment stability increases with age, national unemployment rates tend to decline with population ageing. Some attention has been given to the effect of ageing on productivity with emphasis on the ageing of the labour force and the ensuing slower rate of introduction of new human capital into the production process. The ability of older workers to maintain production standards has also been questioned. Data limitations preclude a definitive answer to the shape of the age-productivity profile. The macroeconomic significance of population ageing on national productivity depends on individual age-specific productivity, and any ensuing changes in investment, consumption, and savings behaviour. The net effect of these factors is unclear.

The effect of population ageing on national savings and therefore the rate of economic growth depends on age-specific savings rates and the age structure changes that occur as the population ages (Kelley, 1973). Although ageing of individuals tends to reduce their savings in old age, population ageing typically is associated with an increase in the fraction of the population in the high savings years and thus tends to stimulate increased saving and investment. The net effect of ageing on savings and growth will also depend on the cause of the population ageing. If population ageing results from slowing population growth, then the economic response to population size and rate of population growth will be observed simultaneously with the ageing effect. In general, the independent effect of population ageing will not be a major factor influencing future economic growth and development.

BIBLIOGRAPHY

Clark, R. and Spengler, J. 1980. *Economics of Individual and Population Ageing.* Cambridge: Cambridge University Press.

Coale, A. 1972. *The Growth and Structure of Human Populations: A Mathematical Investigation.* Princeton: Princeton University Press.

Easterlin, R. 1980. *Birth and Fortune.* New York: Basic Books.

Feldstein, M. 1974. Social security, induced retirement, and aggregate capital accumulation. *Journal of Political Economy* 82(5), September, 905–26.

Hutchinson, E.P. 1967. *The Population Debate.* Boston: Houghton-Mifflin.

Kelley, A. 1973. Population growth, the dependency rate and the pace of economic development. *Population Studies* 27(3), November, 405–14.

Keyfitz, N. 1968. *Introduction to the Mathematics of Population.* Reading, Mass.: Addison-Wesley.

Munnell, A. 1977. *The Future of Social Security.* Washington, DC: The Brookings Institution.

Sauvy, A. 1969. *General Theory of Population.* New York: Basic Books.

Crime and Punishment

ISAAC EHRLICH

'Economics of Crime' revives an old tradition in economic thought in its reliance on the unifying power of economic analysis to explain human behaviour and resource allocation choices both within and outside the conventional market place. Classical economists such as Beccaria, Paley, and Bentham devoted considerable attention to the explanation of crime in rational economic terms, and to the formulation of optimal rules for punishing offenders, based on utilitarian principles. Motivated, in part, by the rapid growth of reported offences in recent decades, economists have regained interest in the issue. Several studies in the 1960s, notably the seminal work by Becker (1968), have inspired the development of the 'economic approach to crime'.

The essence of the approach lies in the assumption that offenders respond to incentives, both positive and negative, and that the volume of actual offenders in the population is therefore influenced by the allocation of private and public resources to law enforcement and other means of crime prevention. For this approach to provide a useful approximation of the complicated reality of crime, it is not necessary that all those who commit specific offences respond to incentives, (nor is the degree of individual responsiveness prejudged); it is sufficient that a significant number of potential offenders so behave on the margin. By the same token, the theory does not preclude a priori any category of crime, or any class of incentives. Indeed, economists have applied this approach to a myriad of illegitimate activities, from tax evasion and violations of minimum wage laws to auto-theft, skyjacking, and murder.

THEORY. In Becker's analysis the equilibrium volume of crime was produced through the interaction between offenders and the law enforcement authority, and the focus was on propositions concerning the socially optimal probability, severity, and type of criminal sanction. Later work centred on a more complete formulation of the components of the system, especially the supply of offences, the production of law enforcement activities, and the criteria for optimal law

4

enforcement. Attempts have also been made to expand the notion and scope of the 'market' for illegitimate activities by expounding the roles played by offenders (supply), consumers and potential victims (private demand), and enforcement and prevention (government intervention), and by augmenting the relevant market equilibrium analysis.

Supply. The offender's choice is generally modelled to involve an optimal allocation of time among competing legitimate and illegitimate activities which differ in the mix of their uncertain pecuniary and non-pecuniary consequences, and offenders are presumed to act as expected-utility maximizers. The basic opportunities affecting choice are identified as the (perceived) probabilities of apprehension, conviction, and punishment, and the marginal penalties imposed ('deterrence variables'); the deterrence variables associated with related crimes; the marginal returns on competing illegal and legal activities and the risk of unemployment; and initial wealth. Entry into a specific criminal activity is shown to be related inversely to its own deterrence variables, and directly to the differential return it provides. Moreover, a one per cent increase in the probability of apprehension is shown to generate a larger deterrent effect than corresponding increases in the conditional probabilities of conviction given apprehension, and specific punishments given conviction (see Ehrlich, 1975). Essentially due to conflicting income and substitution effects, some results for active offenders are more ambiguous: a strong preference for risk may reverse the deterrent effect of sanctions (Ehrlich, 1973) and the results are even less conclusive if one assumes (as do Block and Heineke, 1975) that the length of time spent in crime, not just the moral obstacle to entering it, generates disutility. The results become less ambiguous at the aggregate level, however, as one allows for non-homogeneity of offenders due to differences in personal opportunities or preferences for crime: a more severe sanction can reduce the crime rate by deterring the entry of potential offenders even if it has little effect on actual ones.

Demand. The incentives operating on offenders often originate with, and are partially controlled by, consumers and potential victims. Transactions in illicit drugs and stolen goods, for example, are patronized by consumers who generate a direct or derived demand for the underlying offences (cf. Vandaele, 1978). But even for crimes that inflict pure harm on victims there exists an indirect (negative) demand, which is derived from a positive demand for safety. By their choice of optimal self-protective efforts through use of locks, safes, and alarms, or selective avoidance of travel, potential victims influence the marginal returns to offenders, and thus the implicit 'demand' for crime. And since optimal self-protection generally increases with the perceived risk of victimization (the crime rate), private protection and public enforcement will be interdependent.

Public intervention. Whereas crime is an external diseconomy and crime control measures are largely a public good, collective action is needed to augment individual self-protection. Public intervention typically aims to 'tax' illegal returns through the threat of punishment, or to 'regulate' offenders via incapacitation and rehabilitation programmes. All control measures are costly. Therefore, the 'optimum' volume of offences cannot be nil, but must be set at a level where the marginal cost of each measure of enforcement or prevention equals its marginal benefit.

To assess the relevant net benefits, however, one must adopt a criterion for public choice. Becker (1968) and Stigler (1970) each chose maximization of a concept of 'social income' as the relevant criterion, requiring the minimization of the sum of social damages from offences and the cost of law enforcement activities. This approach can lead to powerful propositions regarding the optimal magnitudes of probability and severity of punishments for different crimes and different offenders, or, alternatively, the optimal level and mix of expenditures on police, courts, and corrections. It reaffirms the proposition that, in equilibrium, the deterrent effect of the optimal probability of apprehension will exceed that of the conditional probabilities of conviction and of specific punishments, and it makes a strong case for the superiority of monetary fines as a deterring sanction. Different criteria for public choice, however, yield different implications regarding the optimal mix of probability and severity of punishment, as is the case when the social welfare function is expanded to include concern for the distributional consequences of law enforcement and other concepts of justice in addition to aggregate income (see Polinsky and Shavell, 1979; and Ehrlich, 1982). Furthermore, a positive analysis of enforcement must address the behaviour of the separate agencies constituting the enforcement system and the constraints of the political market. Studies which focus on the production of and demand for specific agencies, such as police and courts (see, e.g., Landes, 1971), have often adopted decision rules which deviate from the social welfare maximizing criterion.

Market equilibrium. A general equilibrium analysis of the market for offences involving the joint determination of the volume of offences and the net returns from crime in a system of interrelated markets is still at an embryonic stage. One important implication of the market model already developed is that the efficacy of deterring sanctions cannot be assessed merely by reference to the elasticity of the aggregate supply of offences, but depends on the elasticity of the private demand schedule as well. Likewise, the efficacy of rehabilitation and incapacitation programmes cannot be inferred solely from knowledge of their impact on individual offenders. It depends crucially on the elasticities of the market supply and demand schedules, as these determine the extent to which successfully rehabilitated offenders will be replaced by others responding to the prospect of higher net returns (see Ehrlich, 1981; van den Haag, 1975). A market setting has also been applied by economists to analyse various aspects of organized crime.

EMPIRICAL ANALYSES. Largely due to the paucity of theoretically relevant data, little has been done thus far to implement a comprehensive market model of illegitimate activity (but see Vandaele, 1978). In particular, few studies have sought to estimate the private demand for self-protection as part of a complete market system (see Bartel, 1975; Clotfelter, 1977). Many researchers have attempted, however, to implement a simultaneous equation model of crime and law enforcement activity consisting, typically, of three sets of basic structural equations (see Ehrlich, 1973): supply-of-offences functions linking the rate of offences with deterrence variables and other measurable incentives; production functions of law enforcement activity linking conditional probabilities of arrest, conviction, and punishment with resource inputs and other determinants of productivity; and demand-for-enforcement functions linking resource spending with determinants of public intervention. The bulk of the econometric work concerns the first two structural relationships. (For surveys see Palmer, 1977; Andreano and Siegfried, 1980; and Pyle, 1983.)

The econometric applications have been hampered by a number of methodological problems. For example, FBI crime reports are known to understate true crime rates, and related errors of measurement in estimated punishment risks may expose parameter estimation to biases and spurious correlations. The inherent simultaneity in the data requires systematic use of identification restrictions to assure consistent estimation of structural parameters. In testing offenders' responsiveness to incentives, estimates of the deterrent effect of imprisonment must be distinguished from those of its incapacitative effect. Efficient functional forms of structural equations must be selected systematically. And then there is the ubiquitous possibility that results would be biased by 'missing variables' (including links to markets for illicit drugs or handguns). While these problems have been recognized from the outset, not all studies have attempted to resolve them by applying relevant statistical remedies.

Most studies of specific offences report similar findings: probability and length of punishment are generally found to be inversely related to crime rates, and the estimated elasticities of the latter with respect to the conditional risk of apprehension are often found to exceed those with respect to the conditional risks of conviction and punishment. Crime rates are often found to be directly related to measures of income inequality and community wealth (presumably due to the link between affluence and criminal opportunities). Estimates of unemployment effects are somewhat ambiguous, however, depending, in part, on whether they are derived from time-series or cross-section data (see the survey by Freeman, 1983), and such is the case also with demographic variables. This pattern of results is derived from studies using aggregate data from different countries and locations, FBI as well as Victimization Survey statistics, and even individual crime data. There also is some evidence that police output measures are weakly responsive to additional resource inputs, although studies differ in their definitions of output and in their specifications of the relevant production functions.

Not all research, however, is consistent with the deterrence hypothesis (e.g. Forst, 1976; but see its critique by Wadycki and Balkin, 1979). Also, criticism has been raised as to the validity of the estimated deterrent effects on grounds of potential biases due to errors of measurement and the identification restrictions used (see Blumstein et al., 1978). Critics have argued that the apparent deterrent effects may mask a deterrent effect of crime on punishment variables. These issues are clearly debatable (see Ehrlich and Mark, 1977).

The applicability of the economic approach to the crime of murder, and whether the death penalty constitutes a specific deterrent have raised greater controversy. The centre of debate has been the study by Ehrlich (1975) in which the approach was found to be not inconsistent with time-series evidence (see Blumstein et al., 1978; and Ehrlich and Mark, 1977). The controversy has generated additional empirical research, some inconsistent with the deterrence hypothesis (e.g., Passell, 1975; Forst, 1977; Avio, 1979; Hoenack and Weiler, 1980) and some quite corroborative (e.g. Ehrlich, 1977; Wolpin, 1978; Phillips and Ray, 1982; Layson, 1983 and 1985).

It is early to assess the degree to which the various econometric studies on crime have produced accurate estimates of critical behavioural relationships. Some studies attempting to test the theory have not, in fact, taken sufficient account of it. Both theory and econometric design, however, must be further developed to account for missing elements of the general market model, thereby facilitating the substantive identification of structural equations and, indeed, the explanation of observed crime variations. While a consensus seems to emerge among researchers regarding the potential power of the economic approach in studying both the illegal sector of the economy and its interaction with the legal economy, future progress will greatly depend on better data.

BIBLIOGRAPHY

Andreano, R. and Siegfried, J.J. 1980. *The Economics of Crime*. Cambridge, Mass.: Schenkman.

Avio, K.L. 1979. Capital punishment in Canada: a time-series analysis of the deterrent hypothesis. *Canadian Journal of Economics*, November, 647–76.

Bartel, A.P. 1975. An analysis of firm demand for protection against crime. *Journal of Legal Studies* 4(2), June, 433–78.

Becker, G.S. 1966. Crime and punishment: an economic approach. *Journal of Political Economy* 76(2), March/April, 169–217.

Becker, G.S. and Landes, W.M. (eds.) 1974. *Essays in the Economics of Crime and Punishment*. New York: Columbia University Press.

Block, M.K. and Heineke, J.M. 1975. A labor theoretic analysis of the criminal choice. *American Economic Review* 65(3), June, 314–25.

Blumstein, A., Cohen, J. and Nagin, D. (eds.) 1978. *Deterrence and Incapacitation: Estimating the Effects of Criminal Sanctions on Crime Rates*. Washington, DC: National Academy of Science.

Carr-Hill, R.A. and Stern, N.H. 1979. *Crime. The Police and Criminal Statistics*. London: Academic Press.

Clotfelter, C.T. 1977. Public services, private substitutes, and the demand for protection against crime. *American Economic Review* 67(5), December, 867–77.

Ehrlich, I. 1973. Participation in illegitimate activities: theoretical and empirical investigation. *Journal of Political Economy* 81(3), May-June, 521–65. Reprinted with supplements in Becker and Landes (1974).

Ehrlich, I. 1975. The deterrent effect of capital punishment: a question of life and death. *American Economic Review* 65(3), June, 397–417.

Ehrlich, I. 1977. Capital punishment and deterrence: some further thoughts and additional evidence. *Journal of Political Economy* 85(4), August, 741–88.

Ehrlich, I. and Mark, R. 1977. Fear of deterrence. *Journal of Legal Studies* 6, June, 293–316.

Ehrlich, I. 1981. On the usefulness of controlling individuals: an economic analysis of rehabilitation, incapacitation and deterrence. *American Economic Review* 71(3), June, 307–22.

Ehrlich, I. 1982. The optimum enforcement of laws and the concept of justice: a positive analysis. *International Review of Law and Economics* 2(1), June, 3–27.

Fleisher, B.M. 1966. *The Economics of Delinquency*. Chicago: Quadrangle.

Forst, B.E. 1976. Participation in illegitimate activities: further empirical findings. *Policy Analysis* 2(3), Summer, 477–92.

Forst, B.E. 1977. The deterrent effect of capital punishment: a cross-state analysis of the 1960s. *Minnesota Law Review* 61(5), May, 743–67.

Freeman, R.B. 1983. Crime and unemployment. In *Crime and Public Policy*, ed. J.Q. Wilson, San Francisco: ICS.

Heineke, J.M. (ed.) 1978. *Economic Models of Criminal Behavior*. Amsterdam: North-Holland.

Hoenack, S.A. and Weiler, W.C. 1980. A structural model of murder behavior. *American Economic Review* 70(3), June, 327–41.

Landes, W.M. 1971. An economic analysis of the courts. *Journal of Law and Economics* 14(1), April, 61–107.

Layson, S. 1983. Homicide and deterrence: another view of the Canadian time-series evidence. *Canadian Journal of Economics* 16(1), February, 52–73.

Layson, S. 1985. Homicide and deterrence: a reexamination of the United States time-series evidence. *Southern Journal of Economics* 52(1), July, 68–89.

Palmer, J. 1977. Economic analyses of the deterrent effect of punishment: a review. *Journal of Research in Crime and Delinquency* 14(1), January, 4–21.

Passell, P. 1975. The deterrent effect of the death penalty: statistical test. *Stanford Law Review* 28(1), November, 61–80.

Phillips, L. 1981. The criminal justice system: its technology and inefficiencies. *Journal of Legal Studies* 10(2), June, 363–80.

Phillips, L. and Ray, S.C. 1982. Evidence on the identification and causality dispute about the death penalty. In *Applied Time Series Analysis*, ed. O.D. Anderson and M.R. Perryman, Amsterdam: North-Holland.

Polinsky, A.M. and Shavell, S. 1979. The optimal trade-off between the probability and magnitude of fines. *American Economic Review* 69(5), December, 880–91.

Pyle, D.J. 1983. *The Economics of Crime and Law Enforcement*. London: Macmillan; New York: St. Martin's Press, 1984.

Stigler, G.J. 1970. The optimum enforcement of laws. *Journal of Political Economy* 78(3), March-April, 526–35.

Tullock, G. 1967. The welfare costs of tariffs, monopolies, and theft. *Western Economic Review* 5(3), June, 224–32.

Vandaele, W. 1978. An econometric model of auto theft in the United States. In Heineke (1978).

Van den Haag, E. 1975. *Punishing Criminals*. New York: Basic Books.

Wadycki, W.J. and Balkin, S. 1979. Participation in illegitimate activities: Forst's model revisited. *Journal of Behavioral Economics* 8(2), Winter, 151–63.

Witte, A.D. 1980. Estimating the economic model of crime with individual data. *Quarterly Journal of Economics* 94(1), February, 57–84.

Wolpin, K. 1978. Capital punishment and homicide in England: a summary of results. *American Economic Review, Papers and Proceedings* 68(2), May, 422–7.

Declining Population

ROBIN BARLOW

Population decline is much less common than population growth. Looking at the geographical areas occupied by present-day nations, or by their administrative subdivisions, one sees that over the last millenium the number of years when the human population declined is almost always much exceeded by the number when it grew. Reflecting this fact, economics has devoted much more attention to the growth of population than to its decline. The preoccupation with growth, however, may be ending as more countries experience lengthy periods of reduced fertility.

Many of the economists writing on the growth of population, from Malthus to the Club of Rome, are notorious for their bleak view of the future. If population growth is a bad thing, one might be excused for thinking that its decline might be beneficial. But much of the writing on decline is equally alarmist. Does this indicate a general tendency towards pessimism in demographic commentary? Or is the model used for analysing the consequences of population change genuinely asymmetrical, in the sense that increases and decreases of population do not produce opposite effects? Or are different models being used for growth and decline?

Before considering the consequences of population decline, it is desirable first to consider the causes, because in many respects the consequences are conditioned by the causes. The population of a given geographical area can decrease because of a reduction in fertility, an increase in mortality or an increase in net emigration. Of these three factors, fertility reduction has had the least importance as a historical cause of depopulation. Most areas in the world have indeed experienced prolonged periods of fertility decline, particularly within the past 200 years, but these declines have normally been accompanied by significant reductions in mortality, and indeed many would argue that the fall in fertility has been partly a consequence of the fall in mortality, particularly infant mortality. The result has been that populations have continued to grow even when the total fertility rate (the number of live childbirths per woman during the childbearing period, assuming age-specific birth rates to stay at their current levels) has been reduced

10

by as much as 75 per cent, from a 'traditional' level of about eight to a 'modern' level of about two.

Of course, when the total fertility rate falls below the long-run replacement level, which in modern conditions of mortality is about 2.1 children per woman, the population must eventually diminish, in the absence of net immigration. However, some decades may elapse between the decline of the total fertility rate below this critical level and the subsequent decline of the population, because a pyramidal age-structure inherited from earlier regimes of high fertility can sustain the absolute number of births at a high level for several years even while age-specific birth rates are falling. In the United States, for example, the total fertility rate has been below 2.1 since 1972, but in 1984 the annual number of births was still 80 per cent greater than the number of deaths.

Increases in death rates, on the other hand, have often been so extreme and abrupt as to produce an immediate decline in population. Historically there have been three main causes of sudden increases in mortality: famine, disease and war. The three causes are not unrelated to each other. War has often caused famine, for example, and famine has caused disease. Famine, besides sometimes resulting from war and other political disorder, has been the product of natural disasters like drought and floods. Cases when disease has caused sudden increases in mortality include epidemics, like the bubonic plague in medieval Europe, and the importing of new infections into populations without immunity. A classic example of the latter is the decline of American Indian populations after their encounter with the measles, influenza, tuberculosis and other diseases brought by Europeans.

Regarding the future likelihood of these catastrophic causes of population decline, it is not easy to be optimistic, because our own 20th century provides numerous examples of such catastrophe. There have been large-scale famines leading to extensive depopulation. Probably the worst was the Chinese famine of 1959–61, caused by natural disasters and the dislocations of the Great Leap Forward. It is thought that in those years, 30 million deaths took place because of starvation (Banister and Kincannon, 1984). In the 1980s certain regions in Ethiopia and the African Sahel have been depopulated for similar reasons. As for disease, some 20th-century epidemics have reached vast proportions, in particular the influenza epidemic of 1918–19, which took 20 million lives worldwide. War and armed conflict have had even more serious depopulating effects in this century than earlier, as warring states and factions have increasingly resorted to the mass extermination of civilians. Large areas of Russia and Poland suffered population declines for this reason between 1941 and 1945, and similar declines are alleged to have occurred elsewhere during the century (Cambodia, Armenia, Uganda, Punjab).

The third cause of population decline, net emigration, is frequently encountered, but unlike mortality increases, it can often be regarded as benign. Emigration occurs in response to 'push' factors or 'pull' factors. In any individual case it is often difficult to tell whether 'push' or 'pull' is stronger, but it is certainly safe to say that in many instances, the decision to emigrate should be seen as a hopeful determination to explore new opportunities rather than as an escape from distress. Indeed, in a dynamic, expanding economy, it is to be expected that changes in demand and technology will shift the comparative advantages and disadvantages of particular regions, and that some regions will lose population to others as labour markets respond to these shifts.

At the regional or sub-national level, net emigration is often substantial enough to produce an actual decline in population. For example, in the United States between 1980 and 1983, four of the 50 states lost population, even though in all states the number of deaths during that period was less than the number of births. At the national level, net emigration is less commonly a cause of depopulation, largely because of the legal and other obstacles to international migration.

We turn now to the consequences of population decline, which, as noted above, will be found to vary according to the cause of the decline. The consequences of decline have been investigated with particular thoroughness in France, where the subject has been a matter of active political and academic discussion since the defeat of France by a more populous Germany in the war of 1870–71. In general, the tendency of the French population to stagnate has been deployed. A typical statement is found in the preamble to the Family Code of 1939, a set of pro-natalist measures adopted by the Daladier government on the eve of World War II (cited by Tomlinson et al., 1985):

> Our military and economic forces are in danger of wasting away; the country is ruining itself little by little; by contrast, the individual tax burden is increasing the whole time; each citizen is having to pay more to support the social welfare system; industry is gradually deprived of its market; land remains untilled; overseas expansion loses its momentum; and beyond our frontiers, our intellectual and artistic prestige is extinguished.

There are three themes in this bleak picture which have remained important in demographic analysis and which deserve further comment here: the increased burden of dependency said to result from a declining population, the weakening of military forces and the fall in aggregate demand.

The burden-of-dependency argument contends that in a declining population there is an increase in the ratio of dependants to workers. This causes heavier burdens on workers, both because of the increased taxes they must pay to finance public services provided to the dependent part of the population, and because of the increased levels of private consumption they must support. A fall in the rate of saving is the probable result. But there are some qualifications which should be made to this argument. First, if the population decline is due to the emigration of young adult males – a not untypical situation – there may well be an increase in the ratio of dependants to non-emigrant workers, but no corresponding additional burden on non-emigrants, since the dependants of emigrants will be supported in part by remittances.

Second, if the population decline is caused by a reduction in fertility, the rising fraction of elderly in the population will be at least partly offset by a diminishing fraction of children, with little change occurring in the ratio between all dependants and all workers (except in the very long run). The American case is illustrative. Between 1960, near the start of the current fertility decline in the United States, and 1983, the fraction of the population aged 65 or over rose from 9 per cent to 12 per cent, but the fraction aged under 18 fell from 36 per cent to 27 per cent, so that the fraction aged 18–64 actually rose from 55 per cent to 61 per cent. These numbers may even understate the real reduction in dependency burdens occurring during this period, since the fertility decline facilitated an increase in labour-force participation rates among females, reducing still further the number of dependants per worker.

While fertility declines like those occurring in the United States may not lead to much change in the ratio between all dependants and all workers, they certainly produce changes in the structure of dependency. Whether these structural changes lead to an additional fiscal burden on workers depends on the relative costs of public services for the elderly (pensions, health care) and those for children (education).

A third qualification which should be made to the burden-of-dependency argument is as follows: to the extent that the elderly finance their own consumption out of earlier saving, undertaken through a funded pension scheme or otherwise, their presence does not constitute an economic burden. For this reason and others, there is much complexity in the 'economics of ageing populations', which has become an area of active enquiry in Europe and elsewhere as anxieties have developed on such issues as the future financing of social security.

The military implications of population decline do not seem very clear, despite what French strategists have argued. A country can gain the upper hand over a more populous adversary by conscripting a larger fraction of its population, by possessing more advanced weaponry, by receiving assistance from allies, or by any of several other methods. In the 20th century there is no shortage of examples of smaller countries defeating larger (Japan against Russia in 1904, Germany against Russia in 1917, Japan against China in 1937, Israel against Egypt in 1967, Vietnam against the United States in 1975).

The aggregate-demand argument is Keynesian in nature, and suggests that in a declining population, there will be large reductions in demand for certain kinds of investment goods and consumption goods (e.g. housing and children's clothing). Weak demand in these markets could lead to a deficiency of aggregate demand and to an equilibrium with considerable unemployment. However, if there is a Keynesian problem of this nature, a Keynesian solution could also exist. Expansionary fiscal and monetary measures could in principle restore aggregate demand to its full-employment level.

There are other elements in the case against a declining population, a case developed in recent years with particular vigour by Alfred Sauvy and Julian Simon (see, for example, Dumont and Sauvy, 1984; Simon, 1981). Many of these elements are difficult to evaluate, since they concern the allegedly deleterious effects of depopulation on certain intangible characteristics of a society that are not easily measured – such as the dynamism of its artists, or its spirit of adventure, or its readiness to innovate. Also difficult to evaluate is the 'Beethoven–Einstein' argument, which says that a smaller population has a smaller probability of producing a great genius. (If that is true, perhaps such a population is also less likely to produce an evil genius on the scale of Hitler.)

Generally absent from the alarmist views on population decline is the admission that decline does have some beneficial tendencies. These may indeed be swamped by the undoubted negative tendencies, but not necessarily so. Perhaps the most powerful benefit of population decline is its immediately favourable effect on the ratio between physical resources and the labour force. In the short run, the stock of natural resources and capital is fixed, and so any reduction in labour inputs will raise the ratio of natural resources to labour, the ratio of capital to labour, the marginal product of labour, and most probably the wage rate. In the longer run, what happens to the capital-labour ratio when the labour force is diminishing is more difficult to say: the outcome depends among other things on what is happening to dependency burdens and the rate of saving. But even in the longer run, the stock of many types of utilized natural resources will be practically independent of the size of the labour force, and to that extent a smaller labour force is likely to mean a higher income per capita. To make this point, it suffices to look at the economies of Kuwait and Nigeria, which in recent years have produced roughly the same substantial volume of crude oil. But Kuwait's population is only two per cent of Nigeria's, and largely in consequence, its per capita income is about 20 times higher.

The reasoning here is the same as that employed in standard neoclassical models of migration. It is assumed that higher wages in one area will attract migrants; this movement will lower the marginal product of labour in the area of destination and raise it in the area of origin, thus narrowing wage differentials and leading to an equilibrium rate of migration. The point of interest in the present context is that declines in the labour force tend to raise output per worker, certainly in the short run and perhaps in the long run as well.

Closely related to these economic benefits from depopulation are some environmental benefits. The increase in natural resources per capita which tends to raise income per capita also tends to alleviate problems like air and water pollution, the rapid depletion of mineral resources, urban congestion and excessive use of recreational space. The environmental advantages of smaller populations have been one of the main themes of contemporary anti-natalist movements like Zero Population Growth.

In sum, it is not difficult to think of benefits as well as costs of population decline. In many of the countries now facing population decline as a result of their recent fertility history, the benefits and costs are regarded as fairly evenly balanced, or at least, 'the sense of urgency over population decline is still far from acute' (McIntosh, 1981). According to the World Bank (1984), there were 22 countries which in 1982 had a total fertility rate less than 2.1. Seventeen of these were high-income OECD countries, three were East European (East Germany, Hungary and Yugoslavia), and the others were Cuba and Singapore. In some of these countries, like France and Hungary, there is considerable anxiety about depopulation. But in others, many people seem to feel that 'smaller is better'.

14

BIBLIOGRAPHY

Banister, J. and Kincannon, L. 1984. Perspectives on China's 1982 census. Paper presented at the International Seminar on China's 1982 Population Census, Beijing.

Dumont, G.F. and Sauvy, A. 1984. *La montée des déséquilibres démographiques: quel avenir pour une France vieillie dans un monde jeune?* Paris: Economica.

McIntosh, C.A. 1981. Low fertility and liberal democracy in Western Europe. *Population and Development Review* 7(2), 181–207.

Simon, J. 1981. *The Ultimate Resource*. Princeton: Princeton University Press.

Tomlinson, R., Huss, M.M. and Ogden, P.E. 1985. France in peril: the French fear of dénatalité. *History Today* 35, April, 24–31.

World Bank. 1984. *World Development Report 1984*. New York: Oxford University Press.

Demographic Transition

ANSLEY J. COALE

The demographic transition is a specific change in the reproductive behaviour of a population that is said to occur during the transformation of a society from a traditional to a highly modernized state. The postulated change is from near equality of birth and death rates at high levels to near equality of birth and death rates at low levels. In the pre-modern state women who survive to age 50 have borne a large number of children; in the fully modernized society women bear only a small number. In a traditional society high mortality rates imply a low average duration of life; in highly modernized societies low mortality rates permit a long average duration of life.

A compilation of standard measures of current fertility and mortality in regions that the United Nations classifies as 'more developed' confirms the generalization that fertility and mortality are low in modernized populations. A measure of fertility often used by demographers is the total fertility rate (TFR), which is the average number of children that would be born (per woman) among women progressing from age 15 to age 50 subject to the birth rates at each age in the population in question. (The TFR of 1.8 in the United Kingdom in 1982 means that at 1982 rates, women would end childbearing having had an average of 1.8 births.) A measure of mortality that demographers often use is the expectation of life at birth ($e(o)$), or the average length of life of persons subject at each age to the death rates of the population in question. (The $e(o)$ of 77 females in the UK in 1982 means that women subject from birth on to 1982 death rates would survive to an average age of 77 years.) The United Nations category of 'more developed' countries includes Japan, the United States and Canada, Australia and New Zealand, the Soviet Union, and all of Europe. In 1975–80, the TFR in all of these countries except Ireland, Romania, Spain and Albania was between 1.4 and 2.5 children per woman; $e(o)$ for females was between 74 and 80 years in all but Albania, Portugal and Romania.

Modernized countries have thus arrived at a remarkably homogeneous reproductive state. Moreover, the combination of the TFR and $e(o)$ typical of these countries would produce in the long run nearly equal birth and death rates. The overall TFR in more developed countries in 1975–1980 was 2.05; female e(0) was 75.7 years. This combination would produce in the long run nearly equal birth and death rates of 12.8 and 13.6 per thousand respectively.

The demographic history as well as the current fertility and mortality levels of these modernized countries supports the generalization that their social and economic transformation has been accompanied by the postulated demographic transition. In each of the more developed countries in which TFR is low and e(o) is high, women bore at least twice as many children one or two centuries earlier; and experienced mortality leading to an average lifetime less than half the present average. In other words, much higher fertility and mortality (as implied by the transition) was characteristic of the pre-industrial era in countries now fully modernized. Because of the scarcity of valid early data on births and deaths, the evidence that birth and death rates were nearly equal in the pre-modern experience of these countries is mostly indirect. The near equality is inferred from the impossible numerical consequences that would follow the continuation for several centuries of a modest difference between the birth rate and the death rate – an average annual rate of increase of only one-half of one per cent causes a population to be multiplied by a factor of more than 12 in five centuries. Only under special circumstances such as those enjoyed by the early European settlers in North America could a pre-modern society experience any such multiplication. Populations inhabiting limited territory for hundreds of years and employing a gradually evolving technology, were limited to a low average rate of increase. Estimates of the growth of population in England show that before the Industrial Revolution, the population doubled in two centuries (from 1541 to 1741), yielding an average rate of increase of 0.35 per cent per year.

The term 'demographic transition' has wider connotations than the simple (and correct) statement that in the economically most advanced countries, fertility and morality are much lower than before modern development began. Another feature of the transition is that the decline in mortality normally preceded the decline in fertility. This sequence created a widened gap between the birth rate and death rate, a gap that was closed only after the delayed reduction in fertility again brought the two rates close together. Because of this gap, the transition includes a period of rapid growth in population.

The more important, complex, and uncertain connotation of the demographic transition is a set of hypotheses about the causal relation between industrialization (or economic development) and the reduction in fertility and mortality.

CAUSES OF THE DECLINE IN MORTALITY IN THE MORE DEVELOPED COUNTRIES. There is a disagreement among medical, social and economic historians concerning the relative role of various factors in lowering mortality in Europe beginning in the mid-18th century, a time that might be considered the first phase of the demographic transition. A number of innovations in preventive and curative medicine in the 18th and 19th centuries certainly contributed to lower mortality, including: vaccination for smallpox; the invention of anaesthesia; the discovery of the germ theory of disease and accompanying improvements in sterile conditions in surgery, and in hospitals; the pasteurization of milk; and the spread of an empirical approach to medical care so that doctors abandoned standard harmful treatments such as bleeding and purging. Specific reductions in mortality in specific areas (such as particular cities) can be identified as the result of the documented new provision of clean water or the construction of an adequate sewage system. A sustained reduction in mortality and the accompanying acceleration in population growth would not have been possible without an expanded and more regular food supply, resulting from the importation of food, from innovations in agriculture in Europe, including the introduction of new varieties of food plants from the Western Hemisphere, and from improvements in transport and extensions of markets, so that a local crop failure need no longer cause a rise in death rates. Improved diets may also have contributed to lower mortality. Also cited is a change in personal habits, such as more frequent bathing, and washing of hands and clothing.

Increases in $e(o)$ since World War I, and especially after World War II, have been derived from the increasingly scientific basis of medical practice. Research has identified the causes of many diseases; medical technology has created the first really effective treatment (chemotherapy and antibiotics) for bacterial diseases and effective vaccines have been found for many viral diseases not susceptible to drug therapy.

In a broad sense, all of these factors contributing to reduced mortality are a natural part of modern industrialization, which both depended on and fostered the growth of modern science, and its application to agriculture, transportation, manufacturing, communications, and indeed almost every facet of life, naturally including medicine.

CAUSES OF THE TRANSITIONAL DECLINE OF FERTILITY. The first 'transitional' reductions in fertility large enough to affect national birth rates occurred in France and the United States – beginning within a decade or two of 1800. Since the United States was known for its rapid rate of increase and high birth rate (because it combined the moderately high marital fertility of European populations with much earlier marriage than in Western Europe), the early beginning of a decline in American fertility was not much noticed, especially since births were not registered, and the decline could only be inferred indirectly from changes in age composition. The decline in French fertility was well recognized; by 1900 the birth rate in France was only 22 per thousand, and the TFR only 2.8, low levels not attained until the 1920s or later in other European countries. Indeed, the generalization that the decline of mortality occurred before the decline in fertility applies very poorly to the French transition; throughout the 19th century, the fall in the birth rate closely paralleled the fall in the death rate. As a result the increase in the population of France was much less than in other major European countries. The slow growth of population was a matter of great concern in France, where it was blamed for the decline in the power of France relative to Germany, as exemplified in the outcome of the Franco-Prussian war.

18

French social scientists were the first to propose explanations of the modern decline in fertility. Arsène Dumont, writing before 1900, attributed the reduction in the birth rate to what he called 'social capillarity' (Dumont, 1890). He explained that in democratic societies where there are opportunities for social and economic advancement, a small family provides an opportunity for improvement in position. The small family rises in social and economic level, just as fluid rises in a small diameter tube, or capillary. In traditional societies, the opportunity for advancement is absent, and so is the incentive to have a small family. A French economist, Leroy-Beaulieu, expressed before World War I surprisingly modern-sounding views about why fertility was low in advanced societies (Leroy-Beaulieu, 1913). He said that in primitive societies expenditures of money and effort on children are limited, that children begin work at an early age and are soon contributing more to the family than they consume. In an advanced civilization child labour is outlawed, education is compulsory, and the emancipated young make many trying demands on their parents. Fertility is depressed by social ambition and the desire for comfort and luxury. Emancipated women find marriage less attractive, and may find a professional career competitive with maternity.

From the 1920s to the 1950s, Warren Thompson, C.P. Blacker, Frank Notestein and Kingsley Davis developed full and systematic statements of the typical changes in reproductive behaviour during industrialization, introduced the term demographic transition, and provided additional hypotheses to explain the fall in fertility (Thompson, 1930; Blacker, 1947; Notestein, 1953; Davis, 1945). Prominent among these is the decline in mortality itself. Lower death rates increase the size of family to be supported, and diminish the number of births needed to attain a given target number of children who survive to adulthood. Another factor suggested was the introduction of new forms of support for the aged (pensions, insurance policies and savings accounts), institutions that substituted for the traditional support of aged parents by their children, and thus reduced one of the incentives for childbearing.

The transition theorists disproved the conjectures of some biologists, who suggested that modern urban women had less reproductive capacity than their ancestors. (Clinical research showed that urban American women not practising contraception conceived at a rate as high as colonial Americans.) They also provided evidence that much of the restriction in fertility was attained by folk methods of contraception (especially *coitus interruptus*), with the implication that the transition in fertility had not been the result, primarily, of the invention of new contraceptives (although these inventions also contributed to the decline). In short, the decline in fertility had been to a large degree a change in the motivation to bear children, as suggested earlier by the pre-World War I French writers.

RECENT RESEARCH ON THE DEMOGRAPHIC TRANSITION. Since about 1960 both historical studies and theoretical analysis have broadened, but seldom simplified, our knowledge of transitional changes in fertility and mortality. An important contribution is Louis Henry's concept of *natural fertility* (Henry, 1961). In analysing fertility rates in different populations in which there is little or no practice of contraception, Henry found large variations in the level of fertility among married women. These variations are caused by differences in the duration and intensity of breastfeeding (which delays the resumption of ovulation and lengthens the interval between births); by taboos on intercourse while a mother is nursing; or by periodic separation of spouses. The distinctive characteristic of *natural fertility* is that behaviour of the sort described above that lengthens interbirth intervals is not parity specific; that is, the behaviour is practised after the first birth as well as after the fifth or sixth. Parity is the state of having borne a certain number of children; a six parity woman is one who has had six births. On the other hand, *controlled fertility* occurs when married couples alter their behaviour to reduce their fertility after a certain number of children have been born.

Various evidence fron contemporary less developed countries (and from historical research, including the analysis of parish registers and genealogies in the pre-modern stage of more developed countries) shows that under pre-modern conditions, marital fertility is and has been little affected by parity-related restriction. Modern evidence includes interview responses about the practice of contraception in less developed countries; historical evidence is mostly in the form of the age pattern of marital fertility, which has a characteristic structure of continued relatively high rates to higher ages when fertility is natural.

In pre-modern societies with long established traditions governing marriage and reproduction, the level of fertility has usually been surprisingly moderate. In Western Europe before 1800, marital fertility was rather high; if marriage had been early and universal, the total fertility rate would have been between eight and nine children. In fact, marriage was late (23 to 28 years average age at first marriage for women) and many remained single at age 50 (10–20 per cent). The actual TFR, therefore, was as low as four to five and a half children. In many non-European traditional societies marriage was early and universal; but marital fertility was moderate, being checked by various non-parity-related restrictions. Thus the TFR of rural China in about 1930 was only 5.5, and the TFR of India in 1901–1911 was only about 6.2, instead of the eight or higher that would have occurred with Asian marriage patterns and European maritial fertility rates.

Moderate fertility rather than very high fertility has evident advantages for a long-enduring traditional society. The combination of fertility and mortality that such a society experiences determines the average rate of increase, which cannot be very different from zero over a long period. A TFR of eight would produce a rate of increase of two per cent annually if e(o) were 30 years; at this rate of increase, the population would be multiplied by 1,000 in 350 years! Thus a TFR of over eight years would be sustainable only if e(o) were less than 20 years. The TFR of 5.5 in China produces a zero rate of increase in combination with an e(o) of 25 years, just about the mortality of the rural Chinese population. By maintaining customs that restricted fertility (late marriage, or prolonged nursing) traditional societies could achieve a more favourable mortality level, and have more resilience in the face of disaster, or more success in competing with rivals.

Fertility reduction as part of the demographic transition has consisted essentially of the replacement of moderate 'natural' fertility in the pre-modern era by very low controlled fertility achieved by contraception in the highly modernized state.

The circumstances under which the European decline in fertility began and under which it continued have been the subject of an extended research project centred since 1963 at the Office of Population Research at Princeton University. Its strategy is to construct indexes of fertility in all (or nearly all) of the 700 provinces of Europe from as early as data permit until a major decline in marital fertility (characteristically of fifty per cent or more) had occurred, and to collect and analyse information on the concurrent changing social and economic conditions in the different provinces (Coale and Watkins, 1986).

The project was undertaken to provide a firmer and more extensive foundation for generalizations concerning the demographic transition. It has undermined or strongly qualified previously accepted interpretations of the decline in fertility, in addition to suggesting a number of additional factors related to the decline.

The timing of the reduction in fertility is one of the surprises that this project provided. The decline began in France many decades before a sustained reduction in marital fertility was initiated in other European populations. Some of the French *départements* in which the reduction began no later than 1800 contain mostly peasant populations with low levels of literacy and high infant mortality. England, the acknowledged pioneer in the Industrial Revolution, having the highest proportion living in cities in Europe, did not begin to reduce fertility at an especially early date; later, for example, than Belgium or Switzerland, in each of which the proportion of the labour force in agriculture was twice as high, and the fraction living in cities only half as great as in England.

The research on fertility in Europe did not establish a checklist of characteristics (a threshold) that would serve as a sure indication that fertility reduction was about to begin. Reduction began under various conditions, in rural populations with little education, and high mortality, as well as in the expected context of highly literate populations with mostly non-agricultural occupations. It revealed a frequent geographic clustering of similar trends and levels of fertility. Adjacent provinces sharing the same language or ethnic origin were often alike in fertility even though different in educational levels, infant mortality and the proportions living in cities. At the same time, adjacent provinces that had a different cultural background (suggested, say, by a differing language or dialect) were not alike in fertility.

Low fertility or early decline is found in provinces in which voting patterns indicate secularized attitudes; for example, marital fidelity was already low in 1911 in Italy in provinces that 60 years later voted in favour of more liberal divorce laws. High fertility and late decline is found in provinces in which household industry (small-scale agriculture and handicrafts) was especially prevalent.

THE DEMOGRAPHIC TRANSITION IN LESS DEVELOPED COUNTRIES. In the 1940s, the authors of the demographic transition foresaw a postwar period of very rapid growth in the poorer parts of the world (those now labelled as less developed by the United Nations). They predicted what was later referred to as the 'population explosion' before it began. This foresight was derived from their interpretation of earlier demographic changes in Europe and other industrialized areas. Improvement in living conditions would reduce mortality in the poorer countries; fertility would at first remain high, as it had in most of the richer countries, because customs that maintain moderately high fertility are slow to change.

These forecasts underestimated the acceleration of growth in the less developed countries (ldc's), partly because unprecedented progress in low-cost curative and preventive medicine made possible unprecedented reductions in mortality, even in countries in which other forms of social and economic progress were slight. Until the 1960s, only a few areas had experienced a quantitatively important reduction in fertility, but in the 1970s a fall of a sufficient magnitude in fertility has occurred in a sufficient fraction of the less developed world to reduce the overall rate of increase, despite continuing reductions in mortality.

As in the demographic transition in Europe, the association in the less developed countries between changing fertility and specific features of social and economic progress is complex. Differences in traditional beliefs and customs appear to play a part in determining whether or not the rate of childbearing falls, in addition to such differences as education and per capita income. In several areas with a culture that derives from China – Singapore, Hong Kong, Taiwan, and South Korea – there have been reductions of 50 per cent or more in the total fertility rate. Social and economic development has been very rapid in these same areas. The TFR in Singapore is now lower than the average in more developed countries. In per capita income, life expectancy, energy consumption and educational attainment, Singapore has surpassed the poorer countries among those classified as more developed. It can thus be considered an instance of exceptionally rapid attainment of more developed status, including the current mortality and fertility levels typical of such status.

The sequence of fertility and mortality levels in other less developed countries is less consistent with the demographic transition. Kuwait had a per capita income ($20,000) nearly double that in the United States; 76 per cent of persons of appropriate age are enrolled in secondary school, the population is 91 per cent urban, and e(o) for females is 75 years; but the TFR is 5.7. In China per capita income is estimated at 310 dollars, 44 per cent of the appropriate age group is enrolled in secondary school, the population is 21 per cent urban, and e(o) for females is about 69 years; but the TFR is about 2.5. The Central Asian Republics of the Soviet Union constitute an instance of a population in which educational attainment at least through primary school is nearly universal among women under 40, and mortality is low, yet rural fertility remains very high.

In short, there are examples of populations that have reduced fertility while still low in income and rural in residence, and of others that have retained high fertility while making extraordinary gains in life expectancy, income, and education.

A high enough degree of modernization is accompanied by the full demographic transition; it is a sufficient condition for very low fertility and mortality, but not a necessary one. Religion and social tradition influence how resistant a population may be to reduced fertility as modernization occurs; information campaigns, expansion of family planning clinics, and incentives can speed the process.

BIBLIOGRAPHY

Blacker, C. 1947. Stages in population growth. *Eugenics Review* 39(3), October, 88–102.

Coale, A. 1979. The use of modern analytical demography by T.R. Malthus. *Population Studies* 33(2), July, 329–32.

Coale, A. and Watkins, S. (eds) 1986. *The Decline of Fertility in Europe.* Princeton: Princeton University Press.

Davis, K. 1945. The world demographic transition. *Annals of the American Academy of Political and Social Science* 237, January, 1–11.

Dumont, A. 1890. *Dépopulation et civilisation. Etude démographique.* Paris: Lecrosnier and Babe.

Henry, L. 1961. Some data on natural fertility. *Eugenics Quarterly* 8(2), June, 81–91.

Landry, A. 1934. *La révolution démographique.* Paris: Sirey.

Leroy-Beaulieu, P. 1913. *La question de la population.* Paris: F. Alcan.

Notestein, F. 1953. Economic problems of population change. *Proceedings of the Eighth International Conference of Agricultural Economists.*

Thompson, W. 1930. *Population Problems.* New York: McGraw Hill.

Discrimination

PETER MUESER

Discrimination may be said to occur in a market where individuals face terms of trade that are determined by personal characteristics which do not appear directly relevant to the transaction. Most concern has centred on differential treatment by race or ethnic group, and by sex. The primary focus has been on the labour market and housing market, with research motivated, in large part, by controversy over the role of government in maintaining or eliminating observed differentials.

The first extensive literature on the economics of discrimination dates to the equal pay controversy in Britain beginning before the turn of the century, focusing on the lower wage of women. Although interest in the economics of pay differentials by sex abated in the two decades following World War II, many aspects of the more recent theory appeared in this literature. The modern development of systematic models of economic discrimination began with the publication of Gary Becker's *The Economics of Discrimination* (1957). With the passage of laws prohibiting discrimination in the US, Britain and other countries in the 1960s and 1970s, research in the area has again grown.

MARKET DISCRIMINATION AND PERSONAL PREFERENCES. Becker's (1957) treatment took market discrimination to be the result of personal tastes of participants, providing a simple, closed model with a variety of testable implications. Earnings differentials, and discrimination in housing and other markets stem from the attempts of owners, workers and customers to avoid contact or interaction with certain groups.

Consider the first the influence of employer preferences. Rather than maximizing profits, employers maximize a utility that incorporates the personal characteristics of employees. If employers prefer to hire workers from group A rather than group B and are willing to sacrifice profits to do so, they may be said to have discriminatory tastes. Where such employers dominate the market, the relative wages of group B workers must adjust downward if any are to be hired, and the

24

resulting difference equals the pecuniary value of the employed preference. Where there are variations in taste among employers, relative wages are determined by the shape of the taste distribution, and the proportion of A and B workers to be hired.

Employees may also be taken to have discriminatory preferences over the group membership of their co-workers. If discriminating workers and members of the group they shun are perfect substitutes in production, employers have an incentive to provide separate facilities for groups, but no wage differential between groups will occur. In order for such preferences to cause wage differentials, the technology of production must preclude complete separation. For example, if it is necessary for supervisors to interact with assembly line workers, and supervisors prefer one group of workers to another, an employer who has no taste for discrimination and faces a competitive labour market will hire members of both groups only if their wages differ correspondingly.

Customers' tastes may also influence market wages in the absence of employer preferences. The extension of this approach to a variety of markets is clear. Housing discrimination would occur if owners required a premium in order to sell or rent to individuals in certain groups. However, in markets for goods, in contrast to services, no appreciable price differential could survive unless restrictions on resale were binding.

In any of these cases, some market participants may have a taste for discrimination without market differentials occurring if there are sufficient number of non-discriminating participants to interact with the disliked group. One obvious source of non-discriminating participants is fellow group members. If groups are equally represented among employers, various kinds of workers, and customers, complete segregation can occur without economic loss to any group. Preferences against trading with those outside one's own group can only affect terms of trade where groups have different resources or skills. The formal model is, however, silent on the source of such differences.

COMPETITION AND DISCRIMINATORY PREFERENCES. It is widely argued that, in the long run, competition in markets for output and capital will drive out discriminating employers. Since discrimination by race and sex has long existed, this result has frequently been taken as grounds for rejecting the model (Arrow, 1972). In fact, this conclusion follows only from a particular version of the model, in which the taste for discrimination imposes a direct utility loss on the employer for each employee hired from the disliked group. Since non-discriminating employers suffer no such utility loss, under free competition, where they can expand production or buy out discriminators, they will take over the market. This need not be the case. A polar example has been termed nepotism, in which preferences for hiring one group act much like a net subsidy for the employer. In this case, those with the strongest discriminatory preferences ultimately dominate the market.

In general, discriminating employers earn lower money profits than those who do not discriminate, but this does not imply that under competition they will be driven from the market. Foregone profits must be recognized as consumption expenditures, and, so long as employer resources are sufficient to permit any consumption, there is no inconsistency between perfect competition and the existence of stable, long-run wage differentials stemming from employer preferences.

While market discrimination may survive competition, restrictions on competition will often result in more severe discrimination. In a competitive market, any market differential translates into a pecuniary cost that the discriminating employer must pay. But where prices do not equalize supply and demand, the employer's cost of discrimination may decline.

An effective minimum wage or, during times of economic decline, a wage that is downwardly rigid, allows the employer to hire both more productive workers and those most preferred without paying a higher wage. In contrast, if wages do not adjust immediately in an economic upturn, the cost of discrimination will increase.

Where a union successfully bargains for wages above the competitive level, discriminatory hiring, on the basis of either employers' or union members' preferences may take place at lower cost. In fact, discrimination against blacks by unions in the US was explicit and widespread until the 1930s, but by the 1960s union representation for blacks and whites was nearly identical. Black representation has been greatest in industrial unions, where unionization often hinges on the ability to organize both black and white workers, and proportionally lowest in craft unions, where unions frequently exercise power by limiting membership. Despite the historically high level of union discrimination, it appears to have contributed relatively little to observed black-white wage differentials in the US.

The cost of discrimination to firms may decline where there are restrictions on profit maximization. Those who manage non-profit organizations, regulated monopolies or government bureaucracies will devote more resources to improving their own working conditions; unless faced with direct constraints, they will be more likely to exercise personal preferences in the kinds of workers they hire (Alchian and Kessel, 1962).

Finally, in markets with search costs, discrimination may occur even if there are sufficient non-discriminating participants to trade with members of the disliked group, since the appropriate matching cannot occur.

DISCRIMINATION AS EXPLOITATION. It is frequently asserted that discrimination is engaged in because it is profitable. In general, there is some level of discrimination by members of any group that will improve the terms of trade so as to increase their money incomes. Discrimination by white employers, under some conditions, may increase the incomes of whites by increasing both employer profits and the earnings of white workers. Similarly, tastes that restrict blacks and women to certain kinds of jobs may increase money income both for employers and white male employees.

If discriminators' preferences are taken seriously, however, the impact of discriminatory preferences on money income is irrelevant. Although Becker's original treatment calculated such welfare effects, like any such comparison it required an arbitrary normalization to compare individuals with differing preferences. Changes in money income due to discrimination can be taken to represent group welfare if discriminatory behaviour does not reflect actual personal preference. However, individual incentives in a competitive market can no longer explain discrimination, since those who discriminate least receive the greatest gains. It is necessary that some process exist by which the group enforces its will on individual choices. Exploitation must have its roots in a social or political process.

Historically, there is no question that the enactment of discriminatory laws and provision of unequal public services has often represented the exploitation of groups with little political power. J.S. Mill (1869) argued that limitations on women's legal rights and the restrictions they faced in entering certain occupations, were part of a policy to provide men both with higher earnings in the labour market and greater authority over their wives at home. The history of governmental action regarding blacks in America since the Civil War is replete with examples of policies designed to benefit whites with political power at the expense of blacks.

Despite the government's often central role in furthering dominant group interests, there are clearly other channels by which groups exercise influence. An ethnic group is generally bound together by an ideology that dictates members' actions in a wide variety of contexts. Although some members may internalize such ideology, compliance is enforced by systems of social norms and sanctions within the group. The process by which such systems develop is not well understood, although it has been shown that discriminatory norms may be self-enforcing once established (Akerlof, 1976). Nonetheless, it is clear empirically that economic relations among groups, and their relations within the power structure, are critical in determining group ideology and, in turn, individual actions.

For example, it is a recurrent observation that severe ethnic or racial antagonism often can be traced to the point at which groups first find themselves competing in the labour market. Some writers have argued that all discrimination by race or ethnic group can be traced to such a dynamic, in which groups mobilize political and economic resources to further their material interests. The goal of such action is seen to be the exclusion of the competing group from the labour market or, failing this, the creation of a caste system providing the dominant group with preferential treatment (Bonacich, 1972).

As a rule, it is among lower income groups that racism appears most virulent and associated violence most common. In part, this reflects the fact that racism is a source of power to those groups whose alternatives are limited. In some measure, social norms, personal animosity and collective violence substitute for political power and state action.

In contrast to the assumption of the preference-based model, the treatment here implies that discriminatory preferences cannot be taken as exogenous. Tastes, or apparent tastes, may develop to further group interests. This is not to say that individual actions are ever completely determined by group interest, even where these are unambiguous. Within the most tightly structured groups, for example where ethnic identity is strong, discriminatory collusion against outsiders relies heavily on the availability of explicit policing mechanisms. Where individual behaviours are difficult to observe, and the benefits of violating collusive rules are great, discrimination will be less successful.

It must be stressed that many of the conclusions of the taste-based model may apply even where groups' interests play a critical role in shaping individuals' actions. For example, the model tells us that if white workers who compete with black workers merely refuse to work with them, white workers obtain no net gain in income. It is only through the adoption of discriminatory practices by employers that white workers realize gains.

STATISTICAL DISCRIMINATION. Participants in a market have an incentive to consider personal characteristics if these provide information that is relevant to the exchange but costly to obtain by other means. Statistical discrimination occurs where an ascribed characteristic serves this function. The widely accepted use of sex in markets for various kinds of insurance is an obvious example. Markets for credit and rental housing have similar structures, as does the market for labour. Initial screening is particularly critical in hiring for entry level positions in firms with internal labour markets, where a firm often undertakes extensive worker training, and implicit contracts limit the employer's ability to adjust wages in accord with realized productivity.

Some labour market analysts have attempted to limit the term statistical discrimination to contexts in which an employer distinguishes groups that do not differ in average productivity (Aigner and Cain, 1977). For example, where an employer favoured men over women because women were more likely to quit after receiving firm-specific training, this would not be labelled discrimination. In contrast, statistical discrimination would be said to occur if an employer screened by race in jobs where expected ability was critical, because he was unable to judge the abilities of blacks. Such a distinction becomes muddied when it is recognized that matching the worker to the job is part of the productive process.

In certain respects, observed patterns of employment for women and blacks are consistent with statistical discrimination. Both are seriously under-represented in jobs offering extended promotion ladders, and, historically, firms often explicitly reserved for white males the training that prepared an employee for promotion.

Since such persistent statistical discrimination results from the efficient use of information, the basis of wage differentials would seem to rest on pre-market influences, not market dynamics. However, it is possible that group differences are themselves the result of employer expectations. Assume employers believe that members of a particular group have lower levels of the skills necessary for success in screened jobs. In so far as performance is ultimately rewarded for those placed in screened positions, members of this group, because they are less likely to be hired into such positions, will have reduced incentives to invest in relevant skills. Any one employer who hired members of that group into these positions would find workers to be less productive, so beliefs would be confirmed.

In addition to a number of technical conditions (Arrow, 1972), in order for such a 'self-fulfilling prophecy' to be stable, the actions of a single firm must not alter individual incentives. If it were possible for a firm to contract with individuals to fill positions prior to the point when they acquire such skills, individuals who entered contracts, whatever their group membership, would face the same incentives to obtain skills, and the vicious circle would be broken. The acquisition of such skills must therefore occur well in advance of the point that individual workers and firms can easily enter into agreements. Differences in socialization by sex, or cultural differences by race or ethnic group, if in response to disparate treatment in the labour market, could reflect this kind of vicious circle.

EXPLAINING MARKET DIFFERENTIALS. Earnings for women have been appreciably below those of men in almost all societies, past and present. Differences in levels of market participation and other observable personal attributes explain only a portion of the differential. Historically, some of the difference may be identified with governmental or institutional discrimination. Nevertheless, the enactment of laws in many countries prohibiting discrimination in the 1960s and 1970s have had little effect on the overall distribution of wages by sex. There is no obvious way to identify the impact of discrimination in explaining observed differences. Any unobserved direct market discrimination may induce differences in labour market participation and measurable pre-market factors, yet any unmeasured differences between men and women that are not due to discriminatory treatment, may also contribute to the wage differential.

Women have historically performed the bulk of household work and child care, participating in the labour market less continuously and less intensively than have men. Given this division of labour within the family, women who expect to marry have less incentive to develop skills requiring continuous labour market participation. Non-discriminating employers may simply pay women less because they have not invested in those skills that are most valuable in the market.

How the earnings gap is viewed must depend partly on the source of the family's division of labour. If it results from market discrimination, or social norms constructed to benefit dominant males, it may be analysed in terms of the models of discrimination. However, such a division is also consistent with joint optimization by husband and wife: if the bearing and rearing of children are even weakly complementary, it is efficient for the family to have the women specialize in both these non-market tasts. Sex-typed socialization would then merely reflect preparation for anticipated roles.

That perfect equality would occur in the absence of all labour market discrimination seems unlikely. Nonetheless, unless there are strong sanctions, employers have an incentive to practise statistical discrimination, magnifying whatever sex differences would occur in its absence.

The labour market disadvantages suffered by many ethnic and racial groups is similarly open to interpretation. Thomas Sowell (1981) has argued that cultural differences between arriving immigrant groups and blacks in the US are more important in explaining their economic progress than the levels of discrimination they faced. While it is clear that cultural factors are critically important, the

29

degree to which these or other pre-market differences explain observed earnings differentials is unclear. The theory implies that discrimination will be most common and most damaging against groups with low levels of resources, those who would be disadvantaged in its absence.

For blacks in the US, slavery and subsequent governmental discrimination induced shortfalls in human resources that would have limited black achievement under the best of conditions. Nonetheless, up through the 1960s, measured pre-market differences explained only a modest portion of observed earnings differentials. Although unobserved pre-market differences may have played a role, given the pervasiveness of explicit market discrimination, it seems likely that discrimination further depressed the black position. To what degree labour market differences that persist despite the prohibition of discrimination since 1965 – most notably in rates of unemployment – are due to unmeasured pre-market differences, possibly associated with statistical discrimination, or to other market discrimination, is an open question.

BIBLIOGRAPHY
Akerlof, G. 1976. The economics of caste and of the rat race and other woeful tales. *Quarterly Journal of Economics* 90(4), November, 599–617.
Aigner, D. and Cain, G. 1977. Statistical theories of discrimination in labor markets. *Industrial and Labor Relations Review* 30(2), January, 175–87.
Alchian, A. and Kessel, R. 1962. Competition, monopoly, and the pursuit of pecuniary gain. In *Aspects of Labor Economics*, NBER Special Conference Series, Princeton: Princeton University Press.
Arrow, K. 1972. Models of job discrimination. In *Racial Discrimination in Economic Life*, ed. A. Pascal, Lexington, Mass.: D.C. Heath.
Becker, G. 1957. *The Economics of Discrimination*. 2nd edn, Chicago: University of Chicago Press, 1971.
Bonacich, E. 1972. A theory of ethnic antagonism: the split labor market. *American Sociological Review* 37, October, 547–59.
Mill, J.S. 1869. *The Subjection of Women*. New York: Stokes, 1911.
Sowell, T. 1981. *Ethnic America: A History*. New York: Basic Books.

Distributive Justice

EDMUND S. PHELPS

Social justice is justice in all of the relationships occurring in society: the treatment of criminals, children and the elderly, domestic animals, rival countries, and so forth. Distributive justice is a narrower concept for which another name is economic justice. It is justice in the economic relationships within society: collaboration in production, trade in consumer goods, and the provision of collective goods. There is typically room for mutual gain from such exchange, especially voluntary exchange, and distributive justice is justice in the arrangements affecting the distribution (and thus generally the total production) of those individual gains among the participants in view of their respective efforts, opportunity costs, and contributions.

In earlier times the discussion of distributive justice tended to focus upon the obligations of the individual toward those with whom he or she had exchanges. So an employer was expected to be just or not to be unjust, and the problem was to demarcate employer injustice. With the rise of governments capable of redistribution and the spread of economic liberalism, the focus shifted to the distributional obligations of the central government. Let enterprises and households pursue their self interests while the government attends to distribution (within the limits of its just powers). Distributive justice is largely about redistributive taxation and subsidies. The latter may take many forms such as public expenditures for schooling and vocational training (beyond the point justified only by the Pareto principle from the status quo ante) as well as cash subsidies for the employment of labour or low-wage labour (whether paid to employer or employee).

Note that the so-called negative income tax, whatever the claims for or against it as a tool of social justice, does not appear to be an instrument for distributive justice unless restricted somehow to those participating (more than some threshold amount?) in the economy (and thus in the generations of the gains to be (re)distributed). In any case, it will not be discussed here, although some propositions about subsidies apply also to the negative tax.

The suggestion that distributive justice might (at least in principle) require subsidies, not merely tax concessions or tax forgiveness for the working poor, tends to raise the eyebrows of some and accounts for the fact that distributive justice raises the hackles of a few. As long as the Iroquois and the Sioux have no contact, there are no gains to be distributed and distributive justice does not apply; if they are let free to engage in bilateral inter-tribal exchanges, however, the payment of a subsidy to pull up the wage of the lowest earners, who are Sioux, say, would come partly or wholly at the expense of the Iroquois. Now some commentators object to the notion that the Sioux, whose exchanges with the Iroquois are entirely voluntary and all of whom have benefited (or could have), we may suppose, might deserve an additional payment from the Iroquois, perhaps through some supra-tribal authority. Ayn Rand (1973), for example, argues that it is one thing to require of a poor person a fare for riding a bus with empty seats that the other riders can finance out of the benefits they receive from the bus – she has no qualms about such a free ride – and another thing for the poor reason to tax the other riders. But she has got the economics wrong in the application of her (actually rather Rawlsian) ethical premise. Up to a point, a subsidy to the poorest-earning group (the Sioux in the above example) would leave the others (the Iroquois) still with a net gain – a gain after the tax needed to pay the subsidy. This is because of diminishing returns: When the group of Sioux workers is added to the fixed pool of Iroquois' labour and land, the extra product added by the first arrivals – and, more generally, the average of the extra products added by the succession of Sioux workers – is larger than the extra product resulting from the last of these workers, which is the 'marginal product' of Sioux labour; the Iroquois could afford a subsidy equal to the excess of the average extra product over the marginal product. Correctly applied, then, the Randian objection is to a gain-erasing or, at any rate, a gain-reversing subsidy, not to *any* subsidy whatsoever.

Another objection to the concept of distributive justice and to the admissibility of subsidies argues that if these notions were sound it would make sense, by analogy, to apply them to marriage allocation, to the matching of husbands and wives; since we never hear of such applications the ideas are presumably unsound. Of course, it would strike us as novel and foreign to see a proposal for a tax on marriage with Iroquois men and a subsidy to marriage to Sioux men on the ground that the former were apparently more attractive to women (from either tribe) and the resulting inequality of benefits unjust and demanding correction. But the reasons might be other than the supposed unacceptability of the ideas of distributive justice. Maybe the impracticability of deciding on the taxes and subsidies stands in the way. Perhaps a marriage subsidy would be demeaning while employment subsidies would not, being graduated or even a flat amount per hour. Yet the key observation may be that, although there is economic exchange here and although racial discrimination or racial prejudices could cause real injustices, the Sioux and Iroquois men in this example are not cooperating for mutual gain and so no problem about the just division of such gains can arise; they are competing, or contesting, for partners, not forming partnerships with one another. Thus distributive justice cannot apply here.

The terms offered to the working poor, as already implied, is the locus classicus to which notions of distributive justice have been applied. However, two other arenas in which issues of justice are being fought out should be mentioned. One of these is the problem of intergenerational justice. It was first addressed in a celebrated paper in 1928 by Frank Ramsey, who adopted as the criterion of optimality the standard associated with utilitarianism – the sum of utilities over time. This conception of intergenerational justice encountered difficulties when in the 1960s it was applied to optimum saving of a society in which the population is to grow without bound, although that odd demographic case may have put utilitarianism to an unfair (and absurb) test. In 1970 John Rawls struggled with the problem of intergenerational justice in a famously problematic section of his, only to conclude that '...the difference principle [i.e., Rawls's maximin or, more accurately, leximin principle] does not apply to the savings problem. There is no way for later generations to improve the situation of the least fortunate first generation.' This seems to say that intergenerational justice, if there is such a thing, is not a problem of distributive justice, since there is no cooperation for mutual gain among generations, not even between adjacent ones in the chain. But the premise that the current generation cannot be helped by succeeding generations appears, on the face of it, to be a slip in Rawls's economics. In a closed economy, we can help fuure generations by providing them with more capital – even in an open economy enjoying perfect capital mobility, we can provide them with social overhead capital that the world capital market would not provide (or not so cheaply) – and, if overlapping with us, they can help us by meeting consumption claims we make through our issue of public debt and pension entitlements. Thus distributive justice does apply here, with a precision fit. What Rawls may be interpreted to mean is that if, being the least fortunate owing to heaven-sent technological discoveries over the future, the present generation were permitted to invest nothing (not even gross of depreciation!) – rather as we can imagine the poorest in the static problem to begin by sullenly asking for equality – the future generations could not bribe the present one to do something in their mutual interest – unlike the static problem in which the rich can explain the benefits of trickle-down. But in fact the next generation *can* bribe the present one with some old-age consumption in return for some investment. It may be conjectured that a maximin-optimal growth path would still exist in a model along the lines of the Phelps-Riley model notwithstanding the introduction of technological progress.

The other arena in which we find a debate over distributive justice is the international trade field. When a giant nation trades with a small number of pygmy countries, not large enough even in the aggregate to influence relative prices in the giant state, the latter receive all the gains from trade and the former gets nothing and loses nothing; this is exactly the Rawlsian maximin solution if perchance the pygmy countries are poorer (in some suitably defined way) than the giant. But if these tiny countries 'spoil the market', worsening their terms of trade in the course of exporting to and importing from the giant, because they are not of negligible size at least in the aggregate, then the Rawlsian solution is not obtained by the free market. The recent North–South problem of which the 'Southern' countries complain can be understood as the tendency of the 'Northern' countries that are already the richest countries, such as the North American and European countries, to retain the gain from trade resulting from the aforementioned change in the terms of trade caused by the 'Southern' countries through their trade with the 'Northern' ones. The 'Southern' countries believe justice to require that the 'Northern' countries arrange to give back that gain through some appropriate international transfer mechanism.

There are able and serious philosophers who would be happy to see distributive justice left to the economists. In fact, the history of philosophy has been seen as a process of divesting itself of a sub-field as soon as it could thrive independently. Likewise, there are economists who would leave the subject to philosophers. But, whichever group receives the lion's share of the contract to work on it, it seems that the economics (as well as philosophy) of the problems being studied is an essential element of the subject. In this sense and for this reason, the necessary cross listing notwithstanding, distributive justice is an important field under economics.

BIBLIOGRAPHY

Phelps, E.S. and Riley, J.G. 1978. Rawlsian growth: dynamic programming of capital and wealth for intergeneration 'maximin' justice. *Review of Economic Studies* 45(1), February, 103–20.

Ramsey, F.P. 1928. A mathematical theory of saving. *Economic Journal* 38, December, 543–59.

Rand, A. 1973. Government financing in a free society. In *Economic Justice*, ed. E.S. Phelps, Harmondsworth: Penguin.

Rawls, J. 1970. *A Theory of Justice*. Oxford: Oxford University Press; Cambridge, Mass.: Harvard University Press.

Domestic Labour

S. HIMMELWEIT

The term domestic labour entered economic vocabulary in the early 1970s as a result of feminist interest in criticizing and expanding economic categories to incorporate women's activities. Both mainstream and critical traditions in economics tried to grapple with the problem of how to account for the difference between men's and women's position on the labour market. One approach was to relate women's lesser training and skills in paid employment to competing demands made on (married) woman's time by domestic commitments, with a tacit, though unexplained, acceptance that for women paid employment has to fit into time left over after the allocation of that needed for domestic labour, while for men it is the other way round. It is only by the addition of such an assumption that the analysis of domestic labour can be said to have had anything to say about *women*.

Neoclassical economists have seen domestic labour as one of three competing claims on people's time, the others being paid work and leisure. A household maximizes 'its' utility, which is a function of the consumption goods bought with income received from paid work by members of the household, the direct consumption of the products of time spent in domestic labour and a variety of ways of spending remaining leisure time (Becker, 1965). Women have a comparative advantage to men in domestic labour over paid work and so one or other partner should specialize; either a women should not take paid employment or her husband should do no housework. Even if there is no instrinsic different between men and women initially, specialized human capital can be acquired in each type of labour, so it makes sense for a division of labour to take place and for at most only one member of a household to work both in the home and outside. This is taken to explain both why the majority of domestic labour is performed by women and also why women work shorter hours in paid employment than men, accumulate less market-oriented training and skills, and have broken employment histories.

Two criticisms can be mounted of this approach. The first is that the comparative advantage itself needs explanation. At an individual level it can be accounted for by the lower relative earnings of women. But the outcome of individual household choices cannot, without circularity, then in turn be used to explain women's inferior earnings by the lesser time spent in the labour market acquiring appropriate human capital. At best such an approach can account for the division between houseworkers and paid workers, and if combined with an assumption that sex is used as a screening mechanism by employers, a form of rational statistical discrimination, why one sex as a whole will be more likely to constitute the houseworkers and the other the employees. But to explain why sex presents itself as a variable by which to screen, and why it is the *female* sex that constitutes the homeworkers, recourse must be made to biological differences in aptitude, an acceptable fall-back to some, but not to those who wish to show the power of the neoclassical economic approach to explain everything, nor to the feminist movement whose claims that a woman's place was socially rather than *naturally* in the home had led to the initial interest in the question.

The second criticism poses more fundamental problems for this type of analysis. The concept of a household's 'utility function' is a very shaky one. Individualism, upon which neoclassical economics is based, takes individuals as the only actors and decision makers, rejecting thereby, for example, the marxist notion of class interests and forces. The idea of a household utility function cannot therefore be entertained unless either all members of the household have identical preferences concerning the allocation of resources and leisure time among themselves or some rule for aggregating diverse preferences is adopted. Quite apart from the difficulty of devising such a rule which satisfies fairly minimal criteria to ensure that household preferences represent some meaningful aggregate of those of its members (Samuelson, 1956; Arrow, 1951), there is little evidence that households, rather than individuals, make decisions at all. Indeed, feminists would argue that such an approach obscures one of the key questions it was supposed to illuminate: differential power and thus an unequal division of labour within the household (Pahl, 1980).

This problem can be overcome by assuming one member of the household is sufficiently powerful, well-endowed and altruistic that all other members of the household are or aspire to be 'his' beneficiaries (Becker, 1974). Then the interest of all family members are served by the maximization of family income and the whole family can behave as one single decision-making unit. The assumptions of this model, which might seem appropriate only to an idealized picture of a Victorian patriarchal family, are necessary in order to avoid oligopolistic decision making, and even then care has to be taken to ensure that paterfamilias is not driven into a corner solution, whereupon the unity of the family breaks down.

Marxist approaches criticize neoclassical analyses for failing to take account of the different social relations involved in wage and housework. The categories of marxist analysis are particularly appropriate to the analysis of unequal power relations, making marxism seem to some feminists more likely to offer a useful approach. The marxist notion of exploitation is based upon the characterization of *specific* forms of surplus extraction. The attempt to analyse domestic labour in these terms would therefore illuminate power relations within the household, without falling into the trap of conflating housework with paid labour, by recognizing its relations of production, not just its product, to be specific.

Accounts which characterized domestic labour as a separate mode of production came both from writers claiming to be orthodox marxists, extending rather than revising Marx's work, and from others who saw themselves more as using parts of Marx's mode of analysis to criticize and reformulate orthodox Marxism. Of the latter group Christine Delphy, for example, argued that there is a transhistorical family mode of production in which wives' labour power is exploited by their husbands and which has coexisted with and outlasted the modes of production Marx described (Delphy, 1970). Harrison, on the other hand, sees the domestic mode of production as a specific subordinate counterpart to a capitalist mode of production unchanged from that of traditional marxist analysis.

Other accounts rejected the characterization of domestic labour as a separate mode of production on the grounds that a mode of production must be capable of independent self-perpetuation, since the term was used for the characterization of whole societies. The notion of a social formation encompassing two or more modes of production articulated with each other, while appropriate to the analysis of transition between modes, was not appropriate to the continued mutually dependent symbiotic relationships which exists between housework and wage work for capital. The alternative was to extend the notion of the capitalist mode of production to include housework (Gardiner, Himmelweit and Mackintosh, 1975). That extension was needed because the transformation of the wage into reproduced labour power is a process requiring labour and taking place under specific relations of production, and not the unproblematic natural process that Marx took it to be (O'Brien, 1981).

The effect within marxist theory of characterizing housework as a separate mode of production is to make housewives a class, exploited through performing surplus labour above the amount needed to reproduce their own labour power. This surplus was appropriated, according to different versions, either by their husband directly or transferred through lowering the value of his labour power to the capitalist who employed him. But if housework was seen as part of the capitalist mode of production, a housewife's class position, like that of anyone else, would be determined by her access to the means of production, and for most women that would put them in the working class along with their husbands.

Another area of dispute was whether domestic labour should be seen as value and/or surplus value producing. Some argued that it did produce value, because it produced the commodity labour power (Dalla Costa, 1973). In so far as the housewife worked longer hours than that needed to reproduce her own labour she also produced surplus value. Against this it could be argued that the housewife by producing use-values needed to reproduce labour power did not thereby make labour power her product, any more than the baker, butcher or obstetrician did (Seccombe, 1975). Labour power is an attribute of a living human being and is not, *pace* Marx, a commodity like any other in that it is not directly produced by labour at all. In that case the labour that a housewife expands is use-value but not value creating, and therefore *a fortiori* not surplus value creating.

The dispute as to whether domestic labour counted as productive labour turned upon the same issue, since within the capitalist mode of production labour is productive, according to the Marxist definition, if and only if it produces surplus value. Those who argued that domestic labour produced surplus value could therefore also claim that it was productive labour. But against this could be put Marx's own demonstration that productive labour must, to produce surplus value, take place between two exchanges: in the first labour power is bought for a wage, in the second the product is sold. Domestic labour requires neither exchange and therefore is technically outside the classification into productive and unproductive labour, which applies only to wage labour (Fee, 1976).

The 'domestic labour debate' as it became known failed to answer the question to which it was addressed: what is the material basis of women's oppression? To do so, it would have had to do more than classify domestic labour using the existing categories of Marxist analysis. By using those developed for the study of wage labour for capital it fell into a similar trap to the neoclassical approach.

The neoclassical approach failed to recognize that the different social relations under which domestic labour went on rendered the use of the theory of utility maximization developed to model market decision-making inappropriate. The assumptions needed in order that the division of labour within the home could be set up as a soluble decision-making problem had to turn the gender-divided household into a homogeneous single decision-making unit. Divisions within the household disappeared and its individual members became indistinguishable by anything that could be remotely related to gender except by recourse to some form of biological reductionism. Circularity is a common problem with utility analysis and in this case the only way to avoid it was by appeal to supposed biological differences, the very suppositions which feminists had rejected as insufficient to explain the social construction of gender-divided work patterns.

Marxism can escape the charge of circularity because its method is a historical one. Circularity thus becomes recast as the reproduction through time of the conditions which give rise to a gender-divided society. But ultimately marxism fell into the same trap. Although it did recognize that domestic labour and wage labour go under different relations of production, it failed to give those different relations any constructive effect, seeing domestic labour as simply labour that did not have all the attributes of waged labour for capital. To have got further it would have been necessary to relate the analysis of domestic labour to the sex of those who performed it and to its fundamental characteristic of being labour involved in *reproduction* rather than just another form of production (Himmelweit, 1984).

BIBLIOGRAPHY

Arrow, K.J. 1951. *Social Choice and Individual Values.* Cowles Commission Monograph No. 12, New York: John Wiley & Sons.

Becker, G. 1965. A theory of the allocation of time. *Economic Journal* 75, September, 493–517.

Becker, G. 1974. A theory of social interactions. *Journal of Political Economy* 82(6), November-December, 1063–93.

Dalla Costa, M. 1973. Women and the subversion of the community. In *The Power of Women and the Subversion of the Community.* 2nd edn, Bristol: Falling Wall Press.

Delphy, C. 1970. The main enemy. *Partisans* (Paris), Nos. 54–55.

Fee, T. 1976. Domestic labour: an analysis of housework and its relation to the production process. *Review of Radical Political Economy* 8(1), Spring, 1–8.

Gardiner, J., Himmelweit, S. and Macintosh, M. 1975. Women's domestic labour. *Bulletin of the Conference of Socialist Economists* 4(2). Reprinted in *On the Political Economy of Women*, CSE Pamphlet No. 2, London: Stage One, 1976.

Harrison, J. 1973. The political economy of housework. *Bulletin of the Conference of Socialist Economists* 3(1), Winter, 35–52.

Himmelweit, S. 1984. The real dualism of sex and class. *Review of Radical Political Economics* 16(1), 167–83.

O'Brien, M. 1981. *The Politics of Reproduction.* London: Routledge & Kegan Paul.

Pahl, J. 1980. Patterns of money management within marriage. *Journal of Social Policy* 9(3), July, 313–35.

Samuelson, P.A. 1956. Social indifference curves. *Quarterly Journal of Economics* 70(1), February, 1–22.

Seccombe, W. 1975. Domestic labour – reply to critics. *New Left Review* 94, November/December, 85–96.

Entitlements

HILLEL STEINER

In the strong sense, an entitlement is something owed by one set of persons to another. The thing owed is either a performance of a certain kind, such as a dental extraction, or a forbearance from interfering from some aspect of the title-holder's activity or enjoyment, such as not trespassing on someone's land. Strong entitlements imply the presence of a right in the person entitled and a corresponding or *correlative* obligation in the person owing the performance or forbearance. Typically, the person entitled is further vested with ancillary powers to waive the obligation or, alternatively, to initiate proceedings for its enforcement. A secondary (and contested) instance of a strong entitlement arises with respect to the position of a third-party beneficiary of a right-obligation relation between two other parties, such as the beneficiary of an insurance policy. Third parties usually lack powers of waiver and enforcement, for it is not strictly to them that fulfilment of the obligation is owed.

A weaker form of entitlement may be said to pertain to those of a person's activities which, while not specifically protected by obligations in others not to interfere, are nevertheless indirectly and extensively protected by their other forbearance obligations. Thus, while persons may be under no obligation specifically to allow someone to use a pay telephone, they probably do have forbearance obligations with respect to assault, theft, property damage, etc., the joint effect of which is to afford some high (but incomplete) degree of protection to someone using a pay telephone. However, such an entitlement amounts to less than the full protection afforded by a right inasmuch as it does not, for example, avail against anyone who may already be using that telephone.

Beyond strong and weak entitlements, one may also possess many largely unprotected liberties. These consist in those activities from which one has no obligation to refrain but with which, equally, no direct or extensive indirect claims to non-interference. So, broadly speaking, persons' strong entitlements may be construed as conjunctively constituting their spheres of ownership, while their weak entitlements and their unprotected liberties constitute the fields of activity within which they exercise the powers and privileges of ownership. Normally, it is persons' strong entitlements that are of primary normative concern, with weak entitlements and unprotected liberties being determined residually.

Entitlements may be either legal or moral. Sets of legal entitlements tend to reflect the multifarious demands of various customs, moral principles, judicial decisions and state policy. A set of moral entitlements, on the other hand, is commonly derived from some basic principle embedded in a moral code. The nature of this derivation varies with the type of code involved. In many single-value codes (such as utilitarianism), entitlements are instrumental in character: whether and what sort of an obligation is owed, by one person to another, depends upon the relative magnitude of the contribution that fulfilment of that obligation would make to realizing that value. Changing causal conditions of maximization warrant alterations in the content and distribution of entitlements. Codes containing a plurality of independent values characteristically generate entitlements from a principle of justice. The set of entitlements thus derived possesses intrinsic and not merely instrumental value, though its normative status depends upon the ranking of justice in relation to the code's other values. In such codes, the chief distinction between moral obligations that (like kindness) are not correlative to any entitlement and those of justice that are, lies in the fact that only the latter are waivabe and permissibly enforceable.

Much of the philosophical treatment of entitlements is located in discussions of rival theories of justice. These theories differ according to the various norms they propose for determining who owes what to whom. Endorsing the classical formal conditions of justice – 'rendering to each what is due to him' and 'treating like cases alike' – they diverge widely in their interpretations of what is due to a person and what count as like cases. Procedural and substantive criteria that have been offered for determining individuals' entitlements include: relative need, productivity, equal freedom, equal utility, personal moral worth, interpersonal neutrality, personal inviolability, initial contract and so forth. As is immediately obvious, the nature and distribution of the entitlements mandated by each of these criteria are by no means self-evident, and their identification thus requires supplementary postulates that are variously drawn from psychological theories, from theories of moral and rational choice, and from conceptual analyses of the criteria themselves. It is also true that not all of these criteria are mutually exclusive: given a plausible set of premises, some can be derived from others.

There are other dimensions, apart from their distributive norms, in which theories of just entitlements differ. Some of these differences are logically implied by the nature of the norms themselves, while others are independent of them. One such dimension is the kinds of object to be distributed in conformity with a proposed criterion. Proffered items include all utility-producing goods, means of production, natural resources, the rents of superior skills or talents, and even human body parts. What one may do with the things to which one has strong entitlements – what weak entitlements and unprotected liberties one possesses – is largely a function of the sorts of thing to which others are strongly entitled. The intricate structure of permissibility, jointly formed by the rights one has against others and the rights others have against oneself, constitutes the fields of activity within which each person exercises those rights. It thereby also determines the respective spheres of market, state and charitable activities.

A third differentiating dimension is the range of subjects to be counted as having entitlements. Generally accepting the membership of all adult human beings in the class of title-holders, theories differ over whether their distributive norms extend to minors, members of other societies, deceased persons (in respect of bequest), persons conceived but not yet born (in respect of abortion), persons not yet conceived (in respect of capital accumulation and environmental conservation) and non-human animals. Again, the nature and interpretation of a theory's distributive criterion often work to delimit its class of title-holders.

In the light of this multiplicity of differentiating dimensions, the classification – let alone assessment – of theories is no simple task. One, but by no means the only, important respect in which many of them can be compared is in terms of the scope they allow for unconstrained individual choice. Thus theories might be ranged along a spectrum from those that prescribe only an initial set of entitlements (permitting persons thereafter to dispose of these as they choose), to those that require constant enforceable adjustment of the content and distribution of entitlements to conform to certain norms. However, even this way of arraying competing theories is somewhat underspecified, inasmuch as it fails to capture the varied ramifications of the restrictions implied by different initial entitlements.

Hence it is an open question as to where on this spectrum one would locate theories that (via a unanimity requirement) construe each person's initial entitlement as a veto on a social or constitutional contract. Such an entitlement may in turn be derived from some interpretation of equal freedom, personal inviolability or interpersonal neutrality. Or it may itself be taken as an intuitively acceptable foundational postulate for deriving a more complex set of entitlements. Whether an initial contract theory is permissive or restrictive of wide individual choice depends upon its account of the terms of that contract. The derivation of these terms usually proceeds from some conception of human nature – of human knowledge and motivation – along with some meta-ethical theory about the nature of moral reasoning. Contractual terms generated by these premises may extend only to the design of political institutions, thereby leaving the determination of individuals' substantive entitlements to the legislative process. Alternatively, such contracts may stipulate a set of basic individual rights that are immune to legislative encroachment. In either case, the resultant scope for individual choice remains underdetermined. In the first case it depends upon the extent of legislation, while in the second it depends upon the size and nature of the stipulated set of rights. Laws and constitutional rights imply both restrictions on each person's conduct but also, *ipso facto*, restrictions on the extent of permissible interference with others' conduct.

Dispensing with the initial contract device and hypothetical unanimous agreement, some theories derive a set of entitlements directly (non-procedurally) from a substantive foundational value. Among such theories, one type assigns entitlements according to the differential incidence of some stipulated variable in the population of title-holders. Need and productivity are particularly prominent variables in this field, often acquiring their normative import from the values of welfare equalization and maximization. Clearly, applications of these distributive criteria respectively presuppose accounts of essential human requirements and of economic value. Although, for such theories, any shift in the incidence of the stipulated variable occasions a corresponding adjustment of entitlements, the issue of whether this adjustment must be imposed or occurs spontaneously partly turns on the model of interactive behaviour employed. In general, models indicating spontaneous adjustment generate that conclusion by ascribing dominance to altruistic (need) or income-maximizing (productivity) behaviour. To the extent that these ascriptions are empirically unrealistic, such theories mandate enforceable restrictions on the scope for individual choice.

Another type of directly derived (non-contract-based) entitlement set is drawn from foundational values like equal freedom, personal inviolability or interpersonal neutrality, which, by definition, are of uniform non-differential incidence in the population of title-holders. Varying interpretations of these concepts tend nonetheless to converge on the Kantian injunction that persons must be treated as ends in themselves and, more specifically, that no person's ends may be systematically subordinated to those of another. Here the theoretical task is to design a set of entitlements that is independent of any particular conception of 'the good' – independent of particular preferences and (other) moral values – and that is such as to ensure that the consequences of persons' actions, whether harmful or beneficial, are not imposed on others. A typical, though by no means invariable, structural feature of such an entitlement set is its extensive use of a threefold classiciation of things in the world as selves, raw natural resources and objects which are combinations of these. While title-holders are each vested with ownership of themselves (their bodies and labour), such theories often contain some sort of egalitarian constraint on individual entitlements to raw natural resources. The precise form of this constraint determines the nature of the encumbrances that may be imposed on the ownership of objects in third category. But since these encumbrances exhaust the restrictions on what persons may do with what they own, such theories are presumed to allow considerable scope for individual choice.

It is hardly worth remarking that many theories of entitlement combine aspects of the three types outlined above. The assessment of competing theories – a complex task, as stated previously – commonly consists in testing for internal coherence and in appraising the interpretations placed on core concepts in the theory. Thus, if it is supposed that the moral principle underpinning a set of entitlements is that of justice, and that justice is analytically linked to the concept of rights, there is room for dispute as to whether the first (initial contract) and second (needs, productivity) types of theory are properly viewed as theories of entitlement. A distinctive normative feature of rights is that they are held non-contingently to confer an element of individuated discretion on their owners. It is unclear whether possession of a veto in a collective-choice procedure amounts to a sufficiently individuated sphere of discretion. On the other hand, the entitlements generated by considerations of need or productivity, while sufficiently individuated, appear to lack any necessarily discretionary character. A difficulty besetting the first and third types of theory arises with regard to the notion of initial entitlements. Specifically, it seems clear that the identification of each person's initial entitlement – either in a collective-choice procedure or under an egalitarian constraint on natural resource ownership – cannot be interpreted as an historically 'one-off' determination, in the face of an undecidable number and size of partially concurrent future generations. These are among the more salient problems commanding attention in current work on theories of entitlement.

BIBLIOGRAPHY
Buchanan, J.M. 1974. *The Limits of Liberty*. Chicago: University of Chicago Press.
Demsetz, H. 1964. Toward a theory of property rights. *American Economic Review, Papers and Proceedings* 57, 347–59.
Dworkin, R. 1981. What is equality? *Philosophy and Public Affairs* 10, 185–246 and 283–345.
Hohfeld, W.N. 1919. *Fundamental Legal Conceptions*. New Haven: Yale University Press.
Lyons, D. (ed.) 1979. *Rights*. Belmont: Wadsworth Publishing Company.
Nozick, R. 1974. *Anarchy, State and Utopia*. Oxford: Blackwell; New York: Basic Books.
Rawls, J. 1971. *A Theory of Justice*. Cambridge, Mass.: Harvard University Press; Oxford: Oxford University Press, 1972.
Sen, A.K. 1981. Rights and agency. *Philosophy and Public Affairs* 11, 3–39.
Steiner, H. 1987. *An Essay on Rights*. Oxford: Blackwell.

Envy

PETER J. HAMMOND

Envy is a deadly sin, but then so is avarice or greed, and greed seems not to trouble economists. Envy does, however, perhaps because it is an externality. Different economists have also used the term in different senses. Veblen (1899) avoids the word 'envy', but one feels that some of the pleasure of conspicuous consumption may come from the malicious belief that it induces envy in others. Brennan (1973) uses the term 'malice' to indicate negative altruism – a distaste for the income of others – and 'envy' to indicate that the marginal disutility of another's income increases as their income increases. For other concepts of envy, see Nozick (1974) and Chaudhuri (1985).

Most economists now use the word 'envy' in a narrow technical sense due to Foley (1967), who was much more interested, however, in finding an adequate concept of 'equity'. First, however, one should turn to Rawls (1971), whose *Theory of Justice* has 12 pages of very pertinent discussion.

RAWLS ON ENVY AND JUSTICE. Rawls (1971) defines envy in a way which he attributes to Kant, and he is careful to distinguish 'envy' from 'jealousy', which can be thought of as a protective response to envy:

> we may think of envy as the propensity to view with hostility the greater good of others even though their being more fortunate than we are does not detract from our advantages. We envy persons whose situation is superior to ours... and we are willing to deprive them of their greater benefits even if it is necessary to give up something ourselves. When others are aware of our envy, they may become jealous of their better circumstances and anxious to take precautions against the hostile acts to which our envy makes us prone. So understood envy is collectively disadvantageous: the individual who envies another is prepared to do things that make them both worse off, if only the discrepancy between them is sufficiently reduced (p. 532).

This is in section 80, on 'the problem of envy' in which Rawls asks whether his theory of justice is likely to prove impractical because 'just institutions... are likely to arouse and encourage these propensities [such as envy] to such an extent that the social system becomes unworkable and incompatible with human good' (p. 531). This is a positive question; a normative one arises when one recognizes the possibility of 'excusable envy' because 'sometimes the circumstances evoking envy are so compelling that, given human beings as they are, no one can reasonably be asked to overcome his rancorous feelings' (p. 534). In the following section 81, on 'envy and equality', Rawls argues carefully that his 'principles of justice are not likely to arouse excusable... envy... to a troublesome extent' (p. 537). Thereafter, he discussed the conservative contention 'that the tendency to equality in modern social movements is the expression of envy' (p. 538), and Freud's lamentable suggestion that an egalitarian sense of justice is but an adult manifestation of childish feelings of envy and jealousy. Recently, indeed, a particular progressive tax in West Germany has been labelled an 'envy tax' (*Neidsteuer*), as noted by Bös and Tillmann (1985). Anyway, Rawls is careful to distinguish 'rancorous' envy from the justifiable feelings of resentment at being treated unjustly. While envy may often form the basis of an appeal to justice, the claims that all appeals to justice rely on envy often fail to distinguish envy from resentment. I shall return to this later.

EQUITY AS ABSENCE OF 'ENVY'. More recently, however, 'envy' has acquired a precise technical sense in economic theory, following the (apparently independent) lead taken by Feldman and Kirman (1974) and by Varian (1974) in analysing a concept of 'equity' due to Foley (1967, p. 75). Apparently Foley was the first to use the term 'envy' in this sense, though only informally: Feldman, Kirman and Varian include it in their titles.

Consider any allocation (x_g^i) ($g = 1$ to n; $i = 1$ to m) of n goods to each of m individuals. Suppose these individuals have preferences represented by ordinal utility function $U^i(x^i)$ ($i = 1$ to m) of each individual i's own (net) consumption vector x^i. Then individual i is said to *envy* j if $U^i(x^j) > U^i(x^i)$, so that i prefers j's allocation to his own. Notice that this is a purely technical definition; it tells us nothing about i's emotional or psychological state, whether i is unhappy because he prefers what j has, or whether i's 'envy' makes him want to harm j. There is no sin in this unemotional economists' concept of envy, but no particular ethical appeal either. Indeed, it might be better to say that 'i finds j's position to be *enviable*', to minimize the suggestions of emotion.

Nevertheless, Foley was concerned to introduce a concept of equity of welfare which overcomes the deficiencies of equality of after-tax income – deficiencies which are obvious when there are different public goods in different areas, different preferences for leisure as against consumption, and different needs as well. Thus Foley proposes the absence of 'envy' as a test of whether an allocation is equitable. Formally, (x_g^i) is *equitable* is $U^i(x^i) \geqslant U^i(x^j)$ for all pairs of individuals i and j.

Foley (1967) was careful to qualify this test. First, lifetime consumption plans must be considered so that the prodigal do not envy the higher later consumption enjoyed by the thrifty. Second, as he says:

if a gas station attendant has the desire to be a painter but not the ability, it may be necessary to make the painter's life very unattractive in other ways before the gas station attendant will prefer his own; so unattractive, perhaps, that the painter will envy the attendant while the attendant is still envying him. These cases must be interpreted flexibly; either equivalents to the talents must be postulated which the gas station attendant does possess, or reasonable alternatives framed that abstract from the glamour and prestige of certain activities (p. 75).

Foley (1967, p. 76) concludes his discussion of 'equity' as follows:

If tastes differ greatly, there is very little gained by the analysis since a very wide range of allocations will meet the equity criterion. The definition is offered only as a tentative contribution to a difficult and murky subject and concludes the sketchy discussion this paper will make of welfare economics.

FAIRNESS AND OTHER EXTENSIONS OF EQUITY. In a one-good problem of dividing a cake, procedures for achieving 'fair' allocations, without envy and with no cake wasted, were discussed in works such as Steinhaus (1948, 1949), and Dubins and Spanier (1961) before Foley. Fairness with many goods was considered by Schmeidler and Vind (1972), by adding Pareto efficiency to the requirement that nobody should envy anybody else's *net trade vector* (as opposed to the consumption vector, which includes the endowment). Pazner and Schmeidler (1974) and Varian (1974) then came up with examples of economies with production in which there are no fair allocations, because Pareto efficiency requires skilled workers to supply more hours of labour than unskilled workers, and tastes are such that no allocation of consumption then avoids envy. Feldman and Kirman (1974) considered reducing the degree of envy, whereas Pazner and Schmeidler (1978) weakened the notion of equity to 'egalitarian' equivalence, – finding an allocation (x_g^i) in which each individual i is indifferent between x^i and a consumption in an 'egalitarian' allocation $(\bar{x}_g^i)$ with $\bar{x}^i$ independent of i. Of course, in this egalitarian allocation there is no envy. These later developments all seem like attempts to rescue a dubious notion of equality without giving up first-best Pareto efficiency, even though that is surely unattainable anyway in economies with private information.

ENVY AND RESENTMENT RECONSIDERED. In the definition of envy, each individual i compares the consumption vector x^j of another with his own, x^i, using i's own utility function U^i. But $U^i(x^j) > U^i(x^i)$ is insufficient for i's envy to be excusable, in Rawl's sense. Indeed, if x^j is preferable for i because j has some special needs met, i's envy is quite unjustifiable. As Sen (1970, ch. 9) points out in his discussion of Suppes's (1966) grading principles of justice, comparisons of x^j and x^i must allow for differences in tastes, needs, and so on. Thus the appropriate comparison in determining what is inequitable is rather whether $U^j(x^j) > U^i(x^i)$. If this is true, we might say that i *resents* j. Absence of resentment then requires all individuals to have equal utility levels; of course, this requires interpersonal comparisons of utility levels, of the kind used to make decisions 'in an original position', behind the 'veil of ignorance', before each individual knows his tastes. The technical sense of envy defined earlier differs from this technical notion of resentment precisely because it ignores the original position; not surprisingly, then, envy has no moral force, whereas resentment may well have.

Complete absence of resentment in this sense is probably too strong; but one should look for there to be no resentment in the weaker sense that no individual can legitimately feel treated unjustly by the institutions that determine his welfare. That, of course, reverts to Rawls (1971), though not necessarily to his particular concept of justice.

BIBLIOGRAPHY

Bös, D. and Tillmann, G. 1985. An 'Envy Tax': theoretical principles and applications to the German surcharge on the rich. *Public Finance/Finances Publiques* 40, 35–63.

Brennan, G. 1973. Pareto desirable redistribution: the case of malice and envy. *Journal of Public Economics* 2, 173–83.

Chaudhuri, A. 1985. Formal properties of interpersonal envy. *Theory and Decision* 18, 301–12.

Dubins, L.E. and Spanier, E.H. 1961. How to cut a cake fairly. *American Mathematical Monthly* 68, 1–17.

Feldman, A. and Kirman, A. 1974. Fairness and envy. *American Economic Review* 64, 995–1005.

Foley, D.K. 1967. Resource allocation and the public sector. *Yale Economic Essays* 7, 45–198.

Nozick, R. 1974. *Anarchy, State, and Utopia.* Oxford: Blackwell; New York: Basic Books.

Pazner, E. and Schmeidler, D. 1974. A difficulty in the concept of fairness. *Review of Economic Studies* 41, 441–3.

Pazner, E. and Schmeidler, D. 1978. Egalitarian equivalent allocations: a new concept of economic equity. *Quarterly Journal of Economics* 92, 671–87.

Rawls, J. 1971. *A Theory of Justice.* Cambridge, Mass.: Harvard University Press; Oxford: Clarendon Press, 1972.

Schmeidler, D. and Vind, K. 1972. Fair net trades. *Econometrica* 40, 637–42.

Sen, A.K. 1970. *Collective Choice and Social Welfare.* San Francisco: Holden-Day.

Steinhaus, H. 1948. The problem of fair division. *Econometrica* 16, 101–4.

Steinhaus, H. 1949. Sur la division pragmatique. *Econometrica* 17, 315–19.

Suppes, P. 1966. Some formal models of grading principles. *Synthèse* 16, 284–306.

Varian, H.R. 1974. Equity, envy and efficiency. *Journal of Economic Theory* 9, 63–91.

Veblen, T. 1899. *The Theory of the Leisure Class.* New York: Macmillan and Viking, 1967.

Equality

JAMES S. COLEMAN

The very use of the term 'equality' is often clouded by imprecise and inconsistent meanings. For example, 'equality' is used to mean equality before the law (equality of treatment by authorities), equality of opportunity (equality of chances in the economic system), and equality of result (equal distribution of goods), among other things. These different meanings often conflict, and are almost never wholly consistent. See Hayek (1960, p. 85; 1976, pp. 62–4) for a discussion of equality before the law and equality of result, and Rawls (1971) for a discussion of equality of opportunity within a theory of distributive justice. Elsewhere I have discussed the difference between equality of opportunity and equality of result in education (Coleman, 1975). See also Pole (1978) for a detailed examination of the changing conceptions of equality in American history.

Some order can be brought into the confusion among the different use of the term 'equality' by first conceiving of a system that constitutes an abstraction from reality. The system consists of:

(a) a set of positions which have two properties:
    (i) when occupied by persons, they generate activities which produce valued goods and services;
    (ii) the persons in them are rewarded for these activities, both materially and symbolically;
(b) a set of adult persons who are occupants of positions;
(c) children of these adults;
(d) a set of normative or legal constraints on certain actions.

What is ordinarily meant by equality under the law has to do with (b), (c), and (d): that the normative or legal constraints on actions depend only on the nature of the action, and not on the identity of the actor. That is, the law treats persons in similar positions similarly, and does not discriminate among them according to characteristics irrelevant to the action.

What is ordinarily meant by equality of opportunity has to do with (a), (b), and (c): that the processes through which persons come to occupy positions give an equal chance to all. More particularly, this ordinarily means that a child's opportunities to occupy one of the positions (a) do not depend on which particular adults from set (b) are that child's parents. What is ordinarily meant by equality of result has to do with (a.ii): that the rewards given to the position occupied by each person are the same, independent of the activity.

These three conceptions, equality under the law, equality of opportunity, and equality of result can also be seen as involving different relations of the State to the inequalities that exist or spontaneously arise in ongoing social activities. Equality before the law implies that the laws of the State do not recognize distinctions among persons that are irrelevant to the activities of the positions they occupy, but otherwise make no attempt to eliminate inequalities that arise. Equality of opportunity implies that the State intervenes to insure that inequalities in one generation do not cross generations, that children have opportunities unaffected by inequalities among their parents. Equality of result implies a continuous or periodic intervention and redistribution by the State to insure that the inequalities which arise through day-to-day activities are not accumulated, but are continuously or periodically eliminated.

The relations between the first two kinds of equality differ according to how close a society is to a legally minimalist society or a legally maximalist society. In a society that is legally minimalist, equality before the law is compatible with a high degree of inequality of opportunity – depending on the distribution of opportunity provided by other institutions in society, such as the family. In a legally maximalist society, in which many functions of traditional institutions have been taken over by institutions that are creatures of the State (e.g., functions of the family taken over by the public school), equality before the law implies a high degree of equality of opportunity. Only in a society in which the law was far more intrusive than found anywhere, and children were taken from their families to be raised 'with equal opportunity' by the State, could it be said that equality before the law would coincide with equality of opportunity.

The relation between equality of opportunity and equality of result is somewhat different, for it implies two different kinds of interventions of the State. Equality of opportunity implies intervention to provide each person with resources that give equal 'chances' to obtain the material and symbolic rewards that arise from productive activity, while equality of result implies intervention in the distribution of these rewards, to provide each person with equal *amounts*. The two concepts become indistinguishable only when the State intervenes to insure that each position (in (a) above) provides the same set of material and symbolic rewards; and in such a circumstance, 'opportunity' loses meaning altogether.

IS EQUALITY 'NATURAL'? There are certain philosophical positions that take equality of result as a 'natural' point, from which all others are deviations. Isaiah Berlin probably states this as well as any other

No reason need be given for... an equal distribution of benefits for that is 'natural', self evidently right and just, and needs no justification, since it is in some sense conceived as being self justified... The assumption is that equality needs no reasons, only inequality does so; that uniformity, regularity, similarity, symmetry,... need not be specially accounted for, whereas differences, unsystematic behavior, changes in conduct, need explanation and, as a rule, justification. If I have a cake and there are ten persons among whom I wish to divide it, then if I give exactly one tenth to each, this will not, at any rate automatically, call for justification; whereas if I depart from this principle of equal division I am expected to produce a special reason. It is some sense of this, however latent, that makes equality an idea which has never seemed intrinsically eccentric... (1961, p. 131).

This quotation describes a view with which Berlin does not necessarily identify himself. In the same paper, he states that 'equality is one value among many... it is neither more nor rational than any other ultimate principle... rational or non-rational'. It is, however, the position implicitly taken by John Rawls in his *Theory of Justice*, for the book is addressed to the question, 'When can inequalities (of result) be regarded as just?' Rawls's answer can be paraphrased as 'Only those inequalities are just which make the least well off person better off than that person would be (other things being equal) in the absence of the inequalities'.

Whether equality of result is 'natural' or not, and whether the position of Berlin and Rawls is correct or incorrect, would appear to depend on how the distribution of goods occurs: If goods are initially the property of a single central source (e.g., 'the State'), then Berlin's position and that of Rawls appear correct. If all rights and resources originate with the State (or with the king, as in early political theory), than an equal distribution has some claim to be seen as natural. (If, for example, the revenue from oil discovered on public lands is a major component of GNP, as in some Middle Eastern states, equal distribution constitutes a natural point.) But if goods are seen to arise from the activities of a set of independent actors each with certain initial property rights, and each with a certain amount of zeal and skill, 'equality' (meaning equality of result) is hardly natural, and is inconsistent with the distribution of property rights including rights to the fruits of one's own activity.

EQUALITY, ENVY AND RESENTMENT. The idea of equality as 'natural' appears also to derive in part from the ubiquity of envy and resentment in society, with the demand for 'equality' as an expression of these feelings which carries legitimacy. A number of sociologists have pointed to this connection. For example, Simmel writes (1922, translated in Schoeck, 1969, p. 236–7):

Characteriscally, no one is satisfied with his position in relation to his fellow beings, but everyone wishes to achieve a position that is in some way an improvement. When the needy majority experiences the desire for a higher standard of living, the most immediate expression of this will be a demand for equality in wealth and status with the upper ten thousand.

Simmel follows with an anecdote: at the time of the 1848 revolution, a women coal-carrier remarked to a richly dressed lady, 'Yes, madam, everything's going to be equal now; I shall go in silks and you'll carry coal'.

Helmut, Schoeck, in an extensive examination of the role of envy in society, argues that

> social philosophers have largely failed to see how little the individual is concerned with being *equal* to someone else. For very often his sense of justice is outraged by the very fact that he is denied the measure of inequality which he considers to be right and proper (1969, p. 234).

Feelings of envy and resentment constitute a challenge to the existing distribution of *rights* in society, between those held collectively and those held individually. In particular, it is a challenge to the existence of individual property rights. The centrality of property rights for conceptions of equality is seen most clearly in neoclassical economic theory, which assumes a distribution of property rights among a set of independent actors, accompanied by a free market. (See Meade, 1964, for a discussion of property rights and the market in relation to equality.) It is to economic theory that I now turn.

THE ROLE OF 'EQUALITY' IN ECONOMY THEORY. The concept of 'equality' has no place in positive economic theory. In this it is unlike the concept of 'liberty', for economic theory is predicated on the assumption of liberty, that is, free choice (subject only to resource constraints) among alternative actions. There is, in the concept of free choice, however, something closer to the idea of equality before the law than to equality of opportunity, and closer to the latter than to equality of result. Equality of result implies a distribution process that is the antithesis of the market.

But normative economics, that is, welfare economics, makes up for the absence of 'equality' from positive economic theory, for the idea of equality of result is a part of the very atmosphere surrounding welfare economics. The question of what policies will maximize social welfare is not often answered directly in terms of equality in the distribution of valued goods, but the idea seems always to hover nearby. The most direct expression of the central importance of equality in welfare economics was probably that of Pigou (1938; see also Bergson, 1966, ch. 9) who reasoned that because money, like everything else, had declining marginal utility, and thus a dollar was worth much less to a person when he had a million others than when it was the only one he had, then the maximum of social welfare could only be achieved when incomes were made equal. (Neither Pigou nor any other welfare economist followed this implication with actual policy recommendations for equality of income, thus raising the question: if the criterion is correct, then why not recommend implementing it?)

The rock on which Pigou's argument is often regarded as foundering is that of interpersonal comparison of utility. To move from the relative importance for one person of a dollar when he is rich and when he is poor to its relative importance to different persons is a move which, as has been often reiterated, cannot be justified on positive grounds. Perhaps the most widely quoted statement to this effect is that of Lionel Robbins (1938):

> But, as time went on, things occurred which began to shake by belief in the existence between so complete a continuity between politics and economic analysis... I am not clear how these doubts first suggested themselves; but I well remember how they were brought to a head by my reading somewhere – I think in the work of Sir Henry Maine – the story of how an Indian official had attempted to explain to a high-caste Brahmin the sanctions of the Benthamite system. 'But that,' said the Brahmin, 'cannot possibly be right – I am ten times as capable of happiness as that untouchable over there.' I had no sympathy with the Brahmin. But I could not escape the conviction that, if I chose to regard men as equally capable of satisfaction and he to regard them as differing according to a hierarchial schedule, the difference between us was not one which could be resolved by the same methods of demonstration as were available in other fields of social judgment... 'I see no means,' Jevons had said, 'whereby such comparison can be accomplished.'

Edgeworth expressed the same point, 'The Benthamite argument that equality of means tends to maximum happiness, presupposes a certain equality of natures; but if the capacity for happiness of different classes is different, the argument leads not to equal, but to unequal distribution' (1897, p. 114).

Such arguments are ordinarily taken as conclusive within the domain of economics, and with their acceptance, the very programme of welfare economics – not to speak of the foundations for a policy designed to bring equality – is emasculated.

A philosopher might argue, of course, that there is no logical difference between the comparison of utilities of two persons and the comparison of utilities of one person at two different times. Neither, by this argument, is warranted. See, for example, Parfit (1984).

However, Pigou's conclusion has, quite apart from problems of interpersonal comparison of utility, another deficiency. It assumes that each person is an island, and contributes nothing to the welfare of others, nor has his welfare contributed to by others. Yet it is the essence of social and economic systems that there is interdependence, that one person's activities do affect the welfare of others, whether intended or not. One person spends money on loud radios that cause disturbance, while another plants flowers that others enjoy. Or one uses income for training which is productive, benefiting general welfare, while another uses income on drink and becomes an alcoholic, requiring public-expense hospitalization.

But if this is so, then maximization of welfare one time period into the future would require that these interdependencies be taken into account. Maximization would occur only if resources were distributed among persons in accordance with the positive impact of their activities on those events which bring welfare to others. But in general persons do not capture the full benefits of their welfare-generating activities, nor do persons pay the full cost of their welfare-diminishing activities.

The matter can also be seen as a problem in input-output economics: What current allocation of resources among productive activities (i.e., among positions in the system as described earlier) will achieve some desired distribution of final consumption? If the aim is to maximize the sum of final consumption ('maximizing welfare'?), it is quite unlikely that either the current allocation necessary to achieve that, or the distribution of final consumption itself, will approach equality. Even if the desired final distribution is equality, and even if that is achievable within the system of activities, it is highly unlikely that the allocation at time O necessary to achieve that at time t will be equal. And it may well be that the only distribution in time O that would achieve equality at time t would do so at a low level of welfare, with each having less than if there were inequality at time t resulting from a different distribution at time O. If Pareto optimality is taken as a self-evident necessary condition for optimal policies, then because of the processes described above, a criterion of equal distribution (either initially or subsequently) would violate the condition. This suggests that Rawls's question was misdirected, and should have been 'when (assuming non-violation of constitutional rights) is *equality* of distribution justified?' and should have been answered, 'Only when there is no unequal distribution that would subsequently make each better off.'

Thus even if Pigou's point that maximizing welfare requires equalizing marginal utilities is accepted, and noncomparability of utilities is ignored, the policy implication of equalizing incomes appears shortsighted in the extreme. Another way of seeing so is by use of Robert Nozick's Wilt Chamberlain example, an example designed to argue against theories of distributive justice which, like that or Rawls, use the resulting distribution of goods ('end state theories', to use Nozick's term) as a criterion.

> Now suppose that Wilt Chamberlain is greatly in demand by basketball teams, being a great gate attraction. (Also suppose contracts run only for a year, with players being free agents.) He signs the following sort of contract with a team: In each home game, twenty five cents from the price of each ticket of admission goes to him. (We ignore the question of whether he is 'gouging' the owners, letting them look out for themselves.) The seasons starts, and people cheerfully attend his team's games; they buy their tickets, each dropping a separate twenty five cents for their admission price into a special box with Chamberlain's name on it. They are excited about seeing him play; it is worth the total admission price to them. Let us suppose that in one season one million persons attend his home games, and Wilt Chamberlain winds up with $250,000, larger even than anyone else has. Is he entitled to this income? (Nozick, 1974, p. 161).

Thus as Nozick points out, an equal distribution at one point will lead to an unequal distribution at a later point, due to the very system of activities through which persons satisfy their interests.

There are only three ways to prevent this, all of which, carried to their limit, can be shown to reduce welfare. One is to prevent the economic exchange through which persons spend their quarters as they see fit, for such exchanges may lead to a large accumulation in the hands of the Wilt Chamberlains.

A second is to attack the system of activities itself, the system which generates that matrix of coefficients that transform equality into inequality – that is, shutting down professional basketball, which redistributes income from those with low incomes to those with high incomes. The third way is to allow the exchange, but then to tax the high incomes back down to equality. This effectively eliminates the activity, because if income is an incentive to carry out the activity that is paid for, the Wilt Chamberlains lose all incentive to carry out the activity.

Indeed, unless there is a perfect positive correspondence of those activities which are intrinsically pleasurable with those which produce benefits for others, and a perfect negative correspondence with those that produce harm for others, the absence of any extrinsic incentives will lower the welfare for all. The more interrelated the activities of individuals, the greater the reduction in social welfare when extrinsic incentives are absent.

It is true that taxation which is not carried to the limit, but is merely 'progressive', does not eliminate the incentive for activities that bring high income, for these activities continue in societies that have progressive taxation. But this taxation may lead to underprovision of welfare-generating activities. That is, efficiency may be sacrificed to achieve some distributional goals. The potential conflicts between efficiency and equality are discussed in the literature on optimal taxation (e.g., Atkinson and Stiglitz, 1980, part II). (A device which is informally used in social systems to reduce the disincentive effect of regimes of taxation and redistribution that shift incomes in the direction of equality is the attachment of social stigma to the receiving of income thus redistributed, for example, stigma associated with being 'on welfare'. The existence of this stigma constitutes a means of informally reconstituting the differential incentives that are reduced by redistribution.)

All three approaches to preventing inequalities from arising out of equality give, at their extreme, the same result: elimination of the very system of activities that generates welfare in the first place; for it is these activities which not only generate welfare, but also transform equality at one time into inequality at a later time.

Thus it becomes clear that the source of inequalities is embedded in the very matrix of social and economic activities through which individuals increase the welfare of themselves and one another. If, through technology for example, this matrix changes in such a way that individuals' satisfaction of wants is more concentrated in a few hands (e.g., by the invention and development of television), then inequalities will necessarily increase.

More generally, the degree of inequality seems related to the degree of interdependence in this matrix of social and economic activities. In a social system that has very low interdependence (e.g., a social system composed largely of subsistence farmers, a condition that was once the case for nearly all societies), the welfare of each in future periods depends largely on his own initial distribution of resources (including zeal and skill). If that distribution is near equality, then near equality is perpetuated into the future, modified only by random events. More important, even if the initial distribution is unequal, the low interdependence of the system of activities means that these inequalities (also modified by random events) are merely carried forward into the future. In a system with a high degree of interdependence, however, there are a great many configurations which constitute 'inequality-generating' activity structures. In such activity structures, initial distribution of equality will lead to highly unequal distributions. This inequality in turn will lead in the next generation to inequality of opportunity, constrained only by random processes or explicit policies towards non-inheritance of position, i.e., toward equality of opportunity. (In a system in which attention to basketball was directed not to televised professional teams, but to games of the local high school, both the material and nonmaterial rewards among basketball player would be more equally distributed. There would be a greater equality of results, which would arise not through a change in the set of persons (b), the distribution of children (c), or the normative and legal constraints (d), but only through a change in the distribution of positions.)

Does this mean that there tends to be a negative relation between the interdependence of activities in a social system (and thus the total social product) and the equality with which the activities of the system distribute the product? If so, this is a discouraging result for those who would prefer a social system in which incomes are not increasingly unequal, for it specifies an opposition between two goals both regarded as desirable.

This question has two parts, a within-generation part and a between-generation part. Within generations, it appears likely that there is a negative relation, that increased interdependence does, except in an unlikely activity structure, increase inequality. It is possible that this negative relation is responsible for the rise in redistributive actions of governments as interdependence of economic activities increase.

Between generations, the answer would appear to hinge largely upon the relative rates of increase of interdependence of activities and of equality of opportunity (i.e., non-inheritance of position). The latter can occur through regression to the mean as well as through explicit policy intervention (see Becker and Tomes, 1986, for a discussion). If equality of opportunity increases more slowly than interdependence of activities, then (except for unlikely configurations of the activity matrix) there will be a decrease in equality of result among lineages of persons. If equality of opportunity increases more rapidly than the increase in interdependence of activities, there will be an increase in equality of result among lineages, even with a decrease in equality of result within generations.

Altogether, there has been little investigation of the matters discussed above, that is, just how the structure of social and economic activities itself affects inequalities. Such investigations would lead toward taking work on equality partly out of the realm of normative theory, bringing it partly into the realm of positive theory.

BIBLIOGRAPHY

Atkinson, A.B. and Stiglitz, J.E. 1980. *Lectures on Public Economics*. New York: McGraw-Hill.

Becker, G. and Tomes, N. 1986. Inequality, human capital, and the rise and fall of families. In *Approaches to Social Theory*, ed. S. Lindenberg, J. Coleman, and S. Nowak, New York: Russell Sage.

Bergson, A. 1966. *Essays in Normative Economics*. Cambridge, Mass.: Harvard University Press.

Berlin, I. Equality. In *Justice and Social Policy*, ed. F.A. Olafson, Englewood Cliffs: Prentice Hall, 131.

Coleman, J. 1975. What is meant by 'an equal educational opportunity'? *Oxford Review of Education* 1(1), 27–9.

Edgeworth, F.Y. 1897. *Papers Relating to Political Economy*. London: Macmillan for the Royal Economic Society, 1925; New York: B. Franklin, 1963.

Hayek, F.A. 1960. *The Constitution of Liberty*. Chicago: University of Chicago Press.

Hayek, F.A. 1976. *Law, Legislation and Liberty*, Vol. 2. Cambridge: Cambridge University Press; Chicago: University of Chicago Press, 1978.

Meade, J.E. 1964. *Efficiency, Equality and the Ownership of Property*. London: Allen & Unwin.

Nozick, R. 1974. *Anarchy, State and Utopia*. Oxford: Blackwell; New York: Basic Books.

Parfit, D. 1984. *Reasons and Persons*. Oxford: Oxford University Press.

Pigou, A.C. 1938. *Economics of Welfare*. 4th edn, New York: Macmillan.

Pole, J.R. 1978. *The Pursuit of Equality in American History*. Cambridge: Cambridge University Press; Berkeley: University of California Press.

Rawls, J. 1971. *A Theory of Justice*. Cambridge, Mass.: Harvard University Press; Oxford: Clarendon Press, 1972.

Robbins, L. 1938. Interpersonal comparisons of utility. *Economic Journal* 48, 635–41.

Schoeck, H. 1969. *Envy: A Theory of Social Behavior*. New York: Harcourt, Brace and World.

Simmel, G. 1962. *Soziologie*. 2nd edn, Munich and Leipzig: Duncker & Humblot.

Extended Family

OLIVIA HARRIS

It has long been assumed that extended families are typical of pre-capitalist or non-capitalist societies, while the nuclear family form is the product of industrialization and urbanization. Modernization theories, deriving ultimately from 19th-century thinkers such as the French social reformer Frédéric Le Play (e.g., 1871), and finding different forms of expression in the Chicago School of urban sociology (e.g., Wirth, 1938) and Parsonian functionalism (e.g., Parsons and Bales, 1955), was articulated in a moderate form by W. Goode:

> Whenever the economic system expands through industrialisation, family patterns change. Extended kinship ties weaken, lineage patterns dissolve, and a trend toward some form of the conjugal system generally begins to appear – that is, the nuclear family becomes a more independent kinship unit (1963, p. 6).

While Goode himself recognizes that the conjugal family was prevalent in Western Europe long before the Industrial Revolution and limits himself to stating how functionally suited it is to the industrial system, it has long been assumed that the nuclear family emerged as a result of the development of capitalism (e.g., Tawney, 1912). How this supposed transformation is interpreted depends on ideological positions: for those critical of the effects of capitalism the extended family evokes a world of solidarity and human values, while for the opposite tradition which finds its decisive expression in liberalism as a political doctrine, the extended family serves to maintain dependency between kin and to prevent the development of the entrepreneurial spirit.

What is meant by the extended family? The term is ambiguous in the same way as the concept of the family itself: that is, it can refer either to a *co-resident group*, consisting of a wider group of kin than the single nuclear family, or to a network of genealogically and affinally related kin who cooperate and interact closely. However, in either case it is used especially to contrast with the dissolving of kin ties and their replacement by various types of voluntary association and contractual ties, which are said to be typical of capitalist society.

The extended family is frequently defined by the criterion of co-residence, not only because large residential groupings contrast so strikingly with the small units of Western capitalist society, but also because there is a normative assumption contained within the word 'family' that close kin *should* share their resources and if possible live together.

However, even the criterion of co-residence is not as clear-cut as might at first appear (Goody, 1972). Available historical and anthropological evidence reveals that there are many different ways in which kin can share domestic space, from maintaining virtually independent budgets, to operating as a close-knit single economic unit with a strong head (usually known as a 'patriarch'). Moreover, while most authors try to maintain a distinction between the terms family and household, the terms frequently become elided or confused. The word family of course derives from the Latin *familia*, which referred to a whole complex household enterprise, including slaves. This broader definition of 'family' was only restricted to genealogical kin from the beginning of the 19th century (Flandrin, 1976, pp. 4–10). The ambiguity arises from the contemporary ideology that co-resident domestic groups (i.e. households) *should* be based on close kin relationships, and that the intimacy, cooperation and pooling of resources found within a household are only appropriate between close kin. More specifically, Western familial ideology assumes that the co-resident kin group is the social unit within which sharing and pooling take place, while exchange takes place *between* households (Harris, 1982).

Such assumptions have two problems: first, that they render us blind to the presence within households of people who are not related to the household core, that is, servants, lodgers and others. This has had damaging consequences for European family history, which only in recent years has begun to appreciate the significance of what is clearly a major pattern of European family organization and domestic life (Macfarlane, 1970; Harris, 1982; Smith, 1984). Secondly, such assumptions place undue emphasis on the individual household unit, at the expense of adequate consideration of movement and cooperation *between* households or their members.

Apart from methodological problems, the view that extended families are 'pre-capitalist' while the nuclear family is typical of capitalism has turned out to be inaccurate even for English history and the early development of capitalism. Macfarlane has recently summarized a large body of historical research to argue that the English peasant economy was not based on extended families from at least the 13th century. English rural society was mobile, with a developed market in land and labour; children were as likely to work as servants for a wage and buy land when they reached maturity, as to inherit a family farm (Macfarlane, 1978). Moreover, a study of 19th-century Lancashire proposed that industrial-ization actually *increased* the number of extended (i.e. three-generation) house-holds (Anderson, 1971; see also Tilly and Scott, 1978; Hareven, 1982).

On a more general level, the work of Laslett and his associates has used extensive historical demographic research to argue that 'the nuclear family predominates numerically almost everywhere, even in underdeveloped parts of the world' (Laslett, 1972, p. 9). Laslett's arguments were particularly directed against the orthodoxy established by Le Play that the three-generational 'stem family' (*famille souche*) was the dominant family form of the European peasantry, derived from factors such as the inalienability of the land belonging to a particular house and patriline, the buying out of siblings by a chosen successor, and extensive provisions for retirement.

Certain difficulties can be found with Laslett's influential and important arguments; in particular, Berkner (1972) has demonstrated the existence of stem families in 18th-century Austria by emphasizing an essential feature of households ignored by Laslett, namely that they change over time in accordance with individual life cycles and mortality rates. Thus, even in areas where the 'stem family' is the basic principle of organization, only a minority of actual households will conform to this type. This approach has been extended by Wolf (1984) to include the notion of 'family cycle' in a discussion of rural Taiwan in the 20th century. Others have argued Laslett's use of the 'community' as his basic unit of analysis is inappropriate, since there are significant variations between households according to class and socio-economic position. Overall there is a problem in assessing how far majority household forms in terms of *statistical frequency* reflect what each society considers to be the ideal. The discrepancy can be illustrated by contemporary industrial Britain, where research has revealed that a surprisingly large percentage of households do not conform to the ideal nuclear family type, for all that it is enshrined in legislation, welfare policies and religious belief (McIntosh, 1979). The problems are obviously magnified when we turn to scanty historical data.

In recent years, detailed historical research on European families has revealed a complexity and variation that modifies Laslett's early argument but also refuses any simple correlation of family types with particular modes of production, economic stages, or even countries. Even regarding England, opinions differ as to how far and in what circumstances the nuclear family was the dominant type; taking a broader European perspective, Anderson summarizes the debate as follows:

> the European pre-industrial household was a regionally diverse one with England, northern France, North America and possibly the Low Countries... being unique in both their low proportion of complex households and their overall homogeneity of household patterns. By contrast, areas of much greater complexity predominated in the east and south... while in Northern Europe a more locally diverse pattern was found (1980, p. 29).

Various explanations have been proposed for variation in household and family forms; the influence of different systems of distributing productive property has rightly been considered of major importance. Goody (1976) offers a global theory of the formation of domestic groups in terms of land distribution which in turn he derives from agricultural technology (see also Goody, Thirsk and Thompson,

1976). However, it is too general to be applicable to the understanding of local variations; a recent exhaustive discussion of the evidence from English history from 1250 to 1800 concludes that it would be hard to maintain that the relationship between landed property and the family's development cycle was the sole or even the most important determinant of rural family forms (Smith, 1984, p. 86).

In modernization theories, one of the structural explanations for the replacement of the extended family by the nuclear or conjugal family was precisely the shift away from agrarian production with land as the basic means of subsistence, to an industrial system in which the majority owned no means of production except their own labour power. However, some have argued that the organization of labour can be a major determinant of household size in peasant societies. Conversely, studies of proto-industrialization and factory production show how family ties can be strengthened and household size increased in order to maximize cooperation and the pooling of labour (Anderson, 1971; Medick, 1976). The same pattern can be documented outside of Europe in different contexts: some of the classic examples of large extended family households, for example, the Indian joint family, or the Japanese *dozuku*, have shown remarkable resilience in adapting to the various processes of urbanization and industrialization (Yanagisako, 1979; see also Smith, Wallerstein and Evers, 1984).

Large, extended family households, although not as generally found in pre-capitalist societies as was once supposed, do occur in many different contexts. However, there are major problems of definition. Is it really appropriate to include within a single category an Amazonian longhouse (*maloca*) inhabited by a variety of agnatically related families who cooperate in consumption, and the famous Balkan *zadruga*, where an older man might run a unit consisting of up to fifty people, all his direct descendants, who operate as a single production unit?

Thus the whole notion of the extended family household needs substantial modification, whether one considers its historical distribution, its determinants, or its status as an individual unit.

In the broader sense of extended family as a network of kin, too, debates centre on how far such kin ties are typical of 'pre-capitalist' societies, and how far they disintegrate with the development of capitalism. Shorter (1975) presents a provocative version of the modernization thesis, arguing that the 'modern family' is private and more independent of wider kin and social ties than the 'traditional' family. But there is substantial disagreement: students of European history cite evidence to argue that neighbourhood ties have long been more significant in everyday life than kin ties (e.g., Macfarlane, 1970). Goody (1983) argues that European family structures are unusual in this respect, because of policies of the early Church to proscribe marriage between close kin. Conversely, case studies from the nations of the economic periphery, and of non-European migrant groups in metropolitan regions, indicate how suited extended family networks are to business success (e.g., the classic studies for West Africa of Cohen, 1969, and Okali, 1983). Overall, the emphasis of modernization theories on linear change determined by the economy cannot be sustained, both because the pattern supposed to be typical of industrial society is found much earlier in European history, and because it is tied too closely to a supposed functional fit with industrial production. With the current restructuring of the world economy away from industry, we can expect extended family forms to thrive in many economic situations.

BIBLIOGRAPHY

Anderson, M. 1971. *Family Structure in Nineteenth Century Lancashire.* Cambridge: Cambridge University Press.

Anderson, M. 1980. *Approaches to the History of the Western Family 1500–1914.* London: Macmillan.

Berkner, L. 1972. The stem family and developmental cycle of the peasant household: an eighteenth-century Austrian example. *American Historical Review* 77, 398–418.

Flandrin, J-L. 1976. *Families in Former Times.* Trans., Cambridge: Cambridge University Press, 1979.

Goode, W. 1963. *World Revolution and Family Patterns.* New York and Glencoe, Ill.: Free Press.

Goody, J. 1972. The evolution of the family. In *Household and Family in Past Time*, ed. P. Laslett and R. Wall, Cambridge: Cambridge University Press.

Goody, J. 1976. *Production and Reproduction: A Comparative Study of the Domestic Domain.* Cambridge: Cambridge, University Press.

Goody, J. 1983. *The Development of the Family and Marriage in Europe.* Cambridge: Cambridge University Press.

Goody, J., Thirsk, J. and Thompson, E.P. (eds) 1976. *Family and Inheritance.* Cambridge: Cambridge University Press.

Hareven, T. 1982. *Family Time and Industrial Time.* Cambridge: Cambridge University Press.

Harris, O. 1982. Households and their boundaries. *History Workshop Journal* 13, 143–52.

Laslett, P. 1972. Introduction. In *Household and Family in Past Time*, ed. P. Laslett and R. Wall, Cambridge: Cambridge University Press.

Le Play, F. 1871. *L'organization de la famille selon le vrai modèle signalé par l'histoire de toutes les races et de tous les temps.* Paris.

Macfarlane, A. 1970. *The Family Life of Ralph Josselin.* Cambridge: Cambridge University Press.

Macfarlane, A. 1978. *The Origins of English Individualism.* Oxford: Basil Blackwell.

McIntosh, M. 1979. The welfare state and the needs of the dependent family. In *Fit Work for Women*, ed. S. Burman, London: Croom Helm.

Medick, H. 1976. The proto-industrial family economy. *Social History* 1(3), 291–315.

Netting, R., Wilk, R. and Arnould, E. (eds) 1984. *Households. Comparative and Historical Studies of the Domestic Group.* Berkeley: University of California Press.

Parsons, T. and Bales, R. 1955. *Family. Socialization and Interaction Process.* Glencoe, Ill.: Free Press.

Shorter, E. 1975. *The Making of the Modern Family.* New York: Basic Books.

Smith, J., Wallerstein, I. and Evers, H.D. (eds) 1984. *Households and the World Economy.* California: Sage Publications.

Smith, R. (ed.) 1984. *Land, Kinship and Life Cycle.* Cambridge: Cambridge University Press.

Tawney, R.H. 1912. *The Agrarian Problem of the Sixteenth Century.* London: Longmans; New York: Harper, 1967.

Tilly, L. and Scott, J. 1978. *Women, Work and Family.* New York: Holt, Rinehart & Winston.

Wirth, L. 1938. Urbanism as a way of life. *American Journal of Sociology* 44, July, 1–24.

Wolf, A. 1984. Family life and the life cycle in rural China. In Netting, Wilk and Arnould (1984).

Yanagisako, S. 1979. Family and household: the analysis of domestic groups. *Annual Review of Anthropology* 8, 161–205.

Family

GARY S. BECKER

In virtually every known society – including ancient, primitive, developing, and developed societies – families have been a major force in the production and distribution of goods and services. They have been especially important in the production, care, and development of children, in the production of food, in protecting against illness and other hazards, and in guaranteeing the reputation of members. Moreover, parents have frequently displayed a degree of self-sacrifice for children and each other that is testimony to the heroic nature of men and women.

Of course, families have radically changed over time. The detailed kinship relations in primitive societies traced by anthropologists contrast with the predominance of nuclear families in modern societies, where cousins often hardly know each other, let alone interact in production and distribution. The obligations in many societies to care for and maintain elderly parents is largely absent in modern societies, where the elderly either live alone or in nursing homes.

Nevertheless, families are still much less prominent in economic analysis than in reality. Although the major economists have claimed that families are a foundation of economic life, neither Marshall's *Principles of Economics*, Mill's *Principles of Political Economy*, Smith's *Wealth of Nations* nor any of the other great works in economics have made more than casual remarks about the operation of families.

One significant exception is Malthus's model of population growth. Malthus was concerned with the relation between fertility, family earnings, and age at marriage, and he argued that when economic circumstances are less favourable couples usually do (or should) marry later. However, this important insight (see Wrigley and Schofield, 1981, for evidence that prior to the 19th century, marriage rates in England did increase when earnings rose) had no cumulative effect on the treatment of the family by economists.

During the last 40 years, economists have finally begun to analyse family behaviour in a systematic way. No aspect of family life now escapes interpretation with the calculus of rational choice. This includes such esoteric subjects as why some contraceptive techniques are preferred to others, and why polygamy declined, as well as more 'traditional' subjects such as what determines age at marriage, number of children, the amount invested in the human capital of children, and the amount spent by children on the care of elderly parents. This essay sets out the 'economic approach' to various aspects of family behaviour. Detailed discussion of particular aspects can be found in the bibliography.

I FERTILITY. Let us start with the Malthusian problem: how is the number of children, or fertility, of a typical family determined? Crucial to any discussion is the recognition, taken for granted by Malthus, that men and women strongly prefer their own children to children produced by others. This preference to produce one's children eventually helped stimulate economists to recognize that families, and households more generally, are important producers as well as consumers.

The desire for own children means that the number of children in a family is affected by supply conditions. Supply is determined by knowledge of birth control techniques, and by the capacity to produce children, as related to age, nutrition, health, and other variables.

The demand side emerges through maximization of the utility of a family that depends on the quantity of children (n) and other commodities (z), as in

$$U = U(n, z). \tag{1}$$

Utility is maximized subject not only to household production functions for children and other commodities, but also to constraints on family resources. Money income is limited by wage rates and the time spent working, and the time available for household production is limited by the total time available. These constraints are shown by the following equations where λ is the marginal utility of family income. The total net cost of rearing a child (Π_n) equals the value of the goods and services that he consumes, plus the value of the time spent on him by family members ($\Sigma w_i(t_{n_i})$), minus his earnings that contribute to family resources.

$$\left.\begin{array}{l} p_n n + p_z z = \sum w_i t_{wi} + v \\ t_{n_i} + t_{z_i} + t_{w_i} = t \end{array}\right\} \text{ all } i \in f, \tag{2}$$

where t_{w_i} is the hours worked by the ith family members, w_i is his or her hourly wage, v is non-wage family income, t_{n_i} and t_{z_i} are the time allocated to children and other commodities by the ith member, and t is the total time available per year or other time unit.

By substituting the time constraints into the income constraint, one derives the family's full income (S):

$$\left(p_n + \sum w_i t_{n_i}\right)n + \left(p_z + \sum w_i t_{z_i}\right)Z = \sum w_i t + v = S, \qquad \Pi_n n + \Pi_z Z = S. \tag{3}$$

If utility is maximized subject to full income, the usual first order conditions follow:

$$\frac{\partial U}{\partial n} = \lambda \Pi_n, \tag{4}$$

and

$$\frac{\partial U}{\partial Z} = \lambda \Pi_z, \tag{5}$$

The basic theorem of demand states that an increase in the relative price of a good reduces the demand for that good when real income is held constant. If the qualification about income is ignored, then, in particular, an increase in the relative price of children would reduce the children desired by a family. The net cost of children is reduced when opportunities for child labour are readily available, as in traditional agriculture. This implies that children are more valuable in traditional agriculture than in either cities or modern agriculture, and explains why fertility has been higher in traditional agriculture (see the evidence in Jaffe, 1940; Gardner, 1973).

Production and rearing of children have usually involved a sizeable commitment of the time of mothers, and sometimes also that of close female relatives, because children tend to be more time intensive than other commodities, especially in mother's time (i.e. in equation (3), $p_n/\Pi_n < p_z/\Pi_z$). Consequently, a rise in the value of mother's time would reduce the demand for children by raising the relative cost of children. In many empirical studies for primitive, developing, and developed societies, the number of children has been found to be negatively related to various measures of the value of mother's time (see e.g. Mincer, 1962; Locay, 1987).

Women with children have an incentive to engage in activities that are complementary to child care, including work in a family business based at home, and sewing or weaving at home for pay. Similarly, women who are involved in complementary activities are encouraged to have children because children do not make such large demands on their time. This explains why women on dairy farms have more children than women on grain farms: dairy farming inhibits off-farm work because that is not complementary with children.

During the past one hundred years, fertility declined by a remarkable amount in all Western countries; as one example, married women in the US now average a little over two live births compared with about five-and-a-half live births in 1880 (see US Bureau of the Census, 1977). Economic development raised the relative cost of children because the value of parents' time increased, agriculture declined, and child labour became less useful in modern farming. Moreover, parents substituted away from number of children toward expenditures on each child as human capital became more important not only in agriculture, but everywhere in the technologically advanced economies of the 20th century (for a further discussion, see Becker, 1981, ch. 5).

II 'QUALITY' OF CHILDREN. The economic approach contributes in an important way to understanding fertility by its emphasis on the 'quality' of children. Quality refers to characteristics of children that enter the utility functions of parents, and has been measured empirically by the education, health, earnings, or wealth of children. Although luck, genetic inheritance, government expenditures, and other events outside the control of a family help determine child quality, it also depends on decisions by parents and other relatives.

The quality and quantity of children interact not because they are especially close substitutes in the utility function of parents, but because the true (or shadow) price of quantity is partly determined by quality, and vice versa. To show this, write the utility function in equation (1) as

$$U = U(n, q, Z),$$
(6)

where q is the quality of children. Also write the family budget equation in equation (3) as

$$\Pi_n n + \Pi_q q + \Pi_c nq + \Pi_z Z = S,$$
(7)

where Π_n is the fixed cost of each child, Π_q is the fixed cost of a unit of equality, and Π_c is the variable cost of children.

By maximizing utility subject to the family income constraint, one derives the following first order conditions:

$$\frac{\partial U}{\partial n} = \lambda(\Pi_n + \Pi_c q) = \lambda \Pi_n^*,$$
(8)

$$\frac{\partial U}{\partial q} = \lambda(\Pi_q + \Pi_c n) = \lambda \Pi_q^*,$$
(9)

$$\frac{\partial U}{\partial Z} = \lambda \Pi_z.$$
(10)

Quantity and quality interact because the shadow price of quantity (Π_n^*) is positively related to the quality of children, and the shadow price of quality (Π_q^*) is positively related to the quantity of children.

To illustrate the nature of this interaction, consider a rise in the fixed cost of quantity (Π_n) that raises the shadow price of quantity (Π_n^*), and thereby reduces the demand for quantity. A reduction in quantity however, lowers the shadow price of quality (Π_q^*), which induces an increase in quality. But the increase in quality, in turn, raises further the shadow price of quantity, which reduces further the quantity of children, which induces a further increase in quality, and so on until a new equilibrium is reached. Therefore, a modest increase in the fixed cost of quantity could greatly reduce the quantity of children, and greatly increase their quality, *even when quantity and quality are not good substitutes in the utility function.*

The interaction between quantity and quality can explain why large declines in fertility are usually associated with large increases in the education, health, and other measures of the quality of children (see the evidence in Becker, 1981, ch. 5). It also explains why quantity and quality are often negatively related among families: evidence for many countries indicates that years of schooling and the health of children tend to be negatively related to the number of their siblings (see e.g. De Tray, 1973; Blake, 1981).

The influence of parents on the quality of their children links family background to the achievements of children, and hence links family background to inequality of opportunity and intergenerational mobility. Sociologists have dominated discussions of intergenerational mobility, but in recent years economists have emphasized that the relation between the occupations, earnings, and wealths of parents and children depends on decisions by parents to spend time, money, and energy on children. Economists have used the concepts of investment in human capital and bequests of nonhuman wealth to model the transmission of earnings and wealth from parents and children (see e.g. Conlisk, 1974; Loury, 1981; Becker and Tomes, 1986). These models show that the relation between say the earnings of parents and children depends not only on biological and cultural endowments 'inherited' from parents, but also on the interaction between these endowments, governing expenditures on children, and investments by parents in the education and other human capital of their children.

III ALTRUISM IN THE FAMILY. I have followed the agnostic attitude of economists to the formation of preferences, and have not specified how quality of children is measured. One analytically tractable and plausible assumption is that parents are altruistic toward their children. By 'altruistic' is meant that the utility of parents depends on the utility of children, as in

$$U_p = (z_p, U_1, \ldots, U_n),$$ (11)

where z is the consumption of parents, and U_i, $i = 1, \ldots, n$ is the utility of the ith child.

Economists have generally explained market transactions with the assumption that individuals are selfish. In Smith's famous words,

> It is not from the benevolence of the butcher, the brewer, or the baker, that we expect our dinner, but from their regard to their own interest. We address ourselves, not to their humanity but to their self-love, and never talk of our own necessities but of their advantage.

The assumption of selfishness in market transactions has been very powerful, but will not do when trying to understand families. Indeed, the main characteristic that distinguishes family households from firms and other organizations is that allocations within families are largely determined by altruism and related obligations, whereas allocations within firms are largely determined by implicit or explicit contracts. Since families compete with governments for control over resources, totalitarian governments have often reached for the loyalties of their subjects by attacking family traditions and the strong loyalties within families.

The preference for *own* children mentioned earlier suggests special feelings toward one's children. Sacrifices by parents to help children, and vice versa, and the love that frequently binds husbands and wives to each other, are indicative of the highly personal relations within families, that are not common in other organizations (see also Ben-Porath, 1980; Pollak, 1985).

Although altruism is a major integrating force within families, the systematic analysis of altruism is recent, and many of its effects have not yet been determined. One significant result has been called (perhaps infelicitously) the Rotten Kid theorem, and explains the coordination of decisions among members when altruism is limited. In particular, if one member of a family were sufficiently altruistic toward other members to spend time or money on each of them, they would have an incentive to consider the welfare of the family as a whole, *even when they are completely selfish.*

The proof of this theorem is simplest when the utility of an altruist (called the 'head') depends on the combined resources of all family members. Consider a single good (x) consumed by all members: the head and n beneficiaries (not only children but possibly also a spouse and other relatives). The head's utility function can be written as

$$U_h = U(x_h, x_1, \ldots, x_n). \tag{12}$$

The budget equation would be

$$x_h + \sum_{i=h}^{n} g_i = I_h, \tag{13}$$

where I_h is the head's income, g_i is the gift to the ith beneficiary, and the price of x is set at unity. With no transactions costs, each dollar contributed would be received by a beneficiary, so that

$$x_i = I_i + g_i, \tag{14}$$

where I_i is the income of the ith beneficiary. By substitution into equation (13),

$$x_h + \sum x_i = I_h + \sum I_i = S_h. \tag{15}$$

The head can then be said to maximize the utility in (12), subject to family income (S_h).

To illustrate the theorem, consider a parent who is altruistic toward her two children, Tom and Jane, and spends say $200 on each. Suppose Tom can take an action that benefits him by $50, but would harm Jane by $100. A selfish Tom would appear to take that action if his responsibility for the changed circumstances of Jane were to go undetected (and hence not punished). However, the head's utility would be reduced by Tom's action because family income would be reduced by $50. If altruism is a 'superior good', the head will reduce the utility of each beneficiary when her own utility is reduced. Therefore, should Tom take this action, she would reduce her gift to him from $200 to less than $150, and raise her gift to Jane to less than $300. As a result, Tom would be made worse off by his actions.

Consequently, a selfish Tom who anticipates correctly the response from his parent will not take this action, even though the parent may not be trying to 'punish' Tom because she may not know that Tom is the source of the loss to Jane and the gain to herself. This theorem requires only that the head know the outcomes for both Tom and Jane and has the 'last word' (this term is due to Hirshleifer, 1977).

The head has the 'last word' when gifts depend (perhaps only indirectly) on the actions of beneficiaries. In particular, if gifts to the ith beneficiary depend both on his income and on family income, as in

$$g_i = \psi_i(S_h) - I_i, \qquad \text{with} \quad \frac{d\psi_i}{dS_h} > 0 \qquad (16)$$

then by substitution into equation (14),

$$x_i = I_i + g_i = \psi(S_h). \qquad (17)$$

The head would then have the 'last word' because x_i would be maximized by maximizing S_h; for further discussion of the Rotten Kid theorem, see Becker (1981, ch. 5), Hirshleifer (1977), and Pollak (1985).

Although this theorem is applicable even when beneficiaries are envious of each other or of the head, it does not rule out conflict in families with altruistic heads. Sibling rivalry, for example, is to be expected when children are selfish because they each want larger gifts from the head, and each would try to convince the head of his or her merits. Conflict also arises when several members are altruistic to the same beneficiaries, but not to each other. For example, if parents are altruistic to their children but not to each other, each benefits when the other spends more on the children. Married parents might readily work out an agreement to share the burden, but divorced parents have more serious conflict. Noncustodial parents (usually fathers) fall behind in their child support payments partly to shift the burden of support to custodial parents (see the discussion in Weiss and Willis, 1985).

Altruism provides many other insights into the behaviour of families. For example, an efficient division of labour is possible in altruistic families without the usual principal-agent conflict because selfish as well as altruistic members consider the interests of other members. Or contrary to some opinion, bequests and gifts to children are not perfect substitutes even in altruistic families. Bequests not only transfer resources to children but also give parents the last word, which induces children to take account of the interests of elderly parents (see Becker, 1981, ch. 5; and also Bernheim, Schleiffer and Summers, 1986). Moreover, if public debt or social security were financed by taxes on succeeding generations that are anticipated by altruistic parents who make bequests, they would raise their bequests to offset the higher taxes paid by their children. Such compensatory reactions negate the effect of debt or social security on consumption and savings (see the detailed analysis in Barro, 1974).

IV THE SEXUAL DIVISION OF LABOUR. A sharp division of labour in the tasks performed by men and women is found in essentially all societies. Women have had primary responsibility for child care, and men have had primary responsibility for hunting and military activity; even when both men and women engaged in agriculture, trade, or other market activities, they generally performed different tasks (see the discussion in Boserup, 1970).

Substantial division of labour is to be expected in families, not only because altruism reduces incentive to shirk and cheat (see section III), but also because of increasing returns from investments in specific human capital, such as skills that are especially useful in child rearing or in market activities. Specific human capital induces specialization because investment costs are partially (or entirely) independent of the time spent using the capital. For example, a person would receive a higher return on his medical training when he puts more time into the practice of medicine. Similarly, a family is more efficient when members devote their 'working' time to different activities, and each invests mainly in the capital specific to his or her activities (see Becker, 1981, 1985; for developments of this argument outside families, see Rosen, 1981).

The advantages of a division of labour within families do not alone imply that women do the child rearing and other household tasks. However, the gain from specialized investments implies the traditional sexual division of labour if women have a comparative advantage in childbearing and child rearing, or if women suffer discrimination in market activities. Indeed, since a sexual division of labour segregates the activities of men and women, and since segregation is an effective way to avoid discrimination (see Becker, 1981), even small differences in comparative advantage, or a small amount of discrimination against women, can induce a sharp division of labour.

Until recently, the sexual division of labour in Western countries was extreme; for example, in 1890, less than five per cent of married women in the United States were in the labour force. In 1981, by contrast, over 50 per cent even of married women with children under six were in the labour force (see Smith and Ward, 1985). However, the occupations of employed men and women are still quite different, and women still do most of the child rearing and other household chores (see *Journal of Labor Economics*, January 1985).

The large growth in the labour force participation of married women during the 20th century is mainly explained by the economic development that transformed Western economies. Substitution toward market work was induced by the rise in the potential earnings of women (see Mincer, 1962). Moreover, the growth in clerical jobs and in the services sector generally, gave women more flexibility in combining market work and child rearing (see Goldin, 1983). In addition, the large decline in fertility during this period (see section I) greatly facilitated increased labour force participation by married women. The converse is also true, however, because the rise in participation of women discouraged child-bearing.

V DIVORCE. Since women specialize in child care, they have been economically vulnerable to divorce and the death of their mates. All societies recognized this vulnerability by requiring long term contracts, called 'marriage', between men and women legally engaged in reproduction. In Christian societies, these contracts often could not be broken except by adultery, abandonment or death. In Islam and Asia they could be broken for other reasons as well, but husbands were required to pay compensation to their wives when they divorced without cause.

The growth of divorce during this century in Western countries has been remarkable. Essentially no divorces were granted in England prior to the 1850s (see Hollingsworth, 1965), whereas now almost 30 per cent of marriages there will terminate by divorce, and the fraction is even larger in the United States, Sweden and some other Western countries (see US Bureau of the Census, 1977). What accounts for this huge growth in divorce over a relatively short period of time?

The utility-maximizing rational choice perspective implies that a person wants to divorce if the utility expected from remaining married is below the utility expected from divorce, where the latter is affected by the prospects for remarriage; indeed, most persons divorcing in Western countries now do remarry eventually (see e.g. Becker, Landes and Michael, 1977). This simple criterion is not entirely tautological because several determinants of the gain from remaining married can be evaluated.

Some persons become disappointed because their mates turn out to be less desirable than originally anticipated. That new information is an important source of divorce is suggested by the large fraction occuring during the first few years of marriage. Although disappointment is likely to be involved in most divorces, the large growth in divorce rates, especially the acceleration during the last 20 years, is not to be explained by any sudden deterioration in the quality of information. Instead, we look to forces that reduced the advantages from remaining in an imperfect marriage.

The strong decline in fertility over time discouraged divorce because the advantages from staying married are greater when young children are present. Conversely, fertility declined partly because divorce became more likely since married couples are less likely to have children when they anticipate a divorce (see Becker, Landes and Michael, 1977, for supporting evidence). The rise in labour force participation of married women also lowered the gain from remaining married because the sexual division of labour was reduced, and women became more independent financially. At the same time, the labour force participation of married women increased when divorce became more likely since married women want to acquire skills that would raise their incomes if they must support themselves after a divorce.

Legislation certainly eased the legal obstacles to divorce, but empirical investigations have not found significant permanent effects on the divorce rate (see e.g., Peters, 1983). Moreover, economic analysis suggests that even no-fault divorce and other radical changes in divorce legislation would not significantly affect the rate of the divorce because bargaining between husbands and wives about the terms of staying married or divorcing offsets even sharp changes in divorce laws.

To show this, let income by I_h^d and I_w^d respectively, if h and w decide to divorce, and I_h^m and I_w^m, respectively, if they remain married. The budget equation is

$$x_h^d + x_w^d = I_h^d + I_w^d = I^d \tag{18}$$

when divorced, and

$$x_h^d + x_w^m = I_h^m + I_w^m = I^m \tag{19}$$

when married. I suggest that the decision to divorce is largely independent of divorce laws, and depends basically on whether $I^d \gtreqless I^m$, because both h and w can be made better off by divorce when $I^d > I^m$ and by remaining married when $I^m > I^d$.

Consider, for example, a comparison between unilateral or no-fault divorce, and divorce only by mutual consent. Assume that the husband appears to gain from divorce ($I_h^d > I_h^m$), but the apparent loss to the wife is greater, so that $I^d < I^m$. If divorce were unilateral, he might be tempted to seek a divorce even when she would be greatly harmed. However, she could change his mind by offering a bribe (b_h) that would make both of them better off by staying married:

$$x_h^m + b_h > I_h^d, \qquad \text{and} \qquad I_w^m - b_h > I^d. \tag{20}$$

This bribe is feasible because $x_h^m + x_w^m = I^m > I^d$. He would then prefer to remain married, even if he could divorce without her consent. Note that they would also decide to remain married if divorce required mutual consent because at least one of them must be made worse off by divorce.

Divorce rates have been affected less by legislation that has regulated the conditions for divorce than by legislation that has affected the gains from divorce. For example, aid to mothers with dependent children and negative income taxes encourage divorce by providing poorer women with child support and 'alimony' (see Hannan, Tuma and Goeneveld, 1977).

VI MARRIAGE. Marriages can be said to take place in a 'market' that 'assigns' men and women to each other or to remain single until better opportunities come along. An optimal assignment in an efficient market with utility-maximizing partipants has the property that persons not assigned to each other could not be made better off by marrying each other.

In all societies, couples tend to be of similar family background and religion, and are positively sorted by education, height, age, and many other variables. The theory of assignments in efficient markets explains positive assortative mating by complementarity, or 'superadditivity', in household production between the traits of husbands and wives. Efficient assignments also partly explain altruism between husbands and wives: persons 'in love' are likely to marry because, at the detached level of formal analysis, love can be considered one source of 'complementarity'.

Associated with optimal assignments are imputations that determine the division of incomes or utilities in each marriage. Equilibrium incomes have the property that

$$I_{ii}^m + I_{ii}^f = I_{ii}, \tag{21}$$

and

$$I_{ii}^m + I_{ij}^f \geqslant I_{ij}, \qquad i \neq j, \tag{22}$$

where I_{ij} is the output from a marriage of the ith man (m_i) to the jth women (f_j), and I_{ii}^m and I_{jj}^f are the incomes of m_j and f_j, respectively. The inequality in equation (22) indicates that $\{ii\}$ is an optimal assignment because m_i and $f_j, j \neq i$, could not be made better off by marrying each other instead of their assigned mates (f_i and m_j, respectively). Equilibrium incomes include dowries, bride prices, leisure and 'power' (further discussion can be found in Becker, 1974, 1981; the analysis of optimal assignments in Gale and Shapley, 1962; and Roth, 1984, is less relevant to marriage because equilibrium prices – i.e. incomes – are not considered).

Many of the forces in recent decades that reduce the gain from remaining married (see section V) have also raised the gain from delaying first marriage and remarriage. These include the decline in fertility and the rise in labour force participation of married women. The reduced incentive to marry in Western societies is evident from the rapid increase in the number of couples living together without marriage, and in the number of births to unmarried women. Nevertheless, even in Scandinavia, where the trend toward cohabitation without marriage has probably gone furthest, married persons are still far more likely to remain together and to produce children than are persons who cohabit without marriage (for Swedish evidence, see Trost, 1975).

VII SUMMARY AND CONCLUDING REMARKS. Families are important producers as well as spenders. Their primary role has been to supply future generations by producing and caring for children, although they also help protect members against ill health, old age, unemployment, and other hazards of life.

Families have relied on altruism, loyalty, and norms to carry out these tasks rather than the contracts found in firms. Altruism and loyalty are concepts that have not been utilized extensively to analyse market transactions, and our understanding of their implications is only beginning. Yet a much more complete and understanding is essential before the behaviour and evolution of families can be fully analysed.

Firms and families compete to organize the production and distribution of goods and services, and activities have passed from one to the other as scale economies, principal-agent problems, and other forces dictated. Agriculture and many retailing activities have been dominated by family firms that combine production for the market with production for members. Presumably, such hybrid organizations are important when altruism and loyalty are more effective than contracts in organizing market production (see Becker, 1981, ch. 8; Pollak, 1985), and when the production and care of children complements production for the market.

Families in Western countries have changed drastically during the past thirty years; fertility declined below replacement levels, the labour force participation of married women and divorce soared, cohabitation and births to unmarried women became common, many households are now headed by unmarried women with dependent children, a large fraction of the elderly either live alone or in nursing homes, and children from first and second, sometimes even third, marriages frequently share the same household.

Nevertheless, obituaries for the family are decidedly premature. Families are still crucial to the production and rearing of children, and remain important protectors of members against ill-health, unemployment, and many other hazards. Although the role of families will evolve further in the future, I am confident that families will continue to have primary responsibility for children, and that altruism and loyalty will continue to bind parents and children.

BIBLIOGRAPHY

Barro, R.J. 1974. Are government bonds net wealth? *Journal of Political Economy* 82(6), November-December, 1095–117.

Becker, G.S. 1974. A theory of marriage: Part II. *Journal of Political Economy* 82(2), part II, S11–26.

Becker, G.S. 1981. *A Treatise on the Family*. Cambridge, Mass.: Harvard University Press.

Becker, G.S. 1985. Human capital, effort, and the sexual division of labor. *Journal of Labor Economics* 3(1), Part II, 533–58.

Becker, G.S., Landes, E.M., and Michael, R.T. 1977. An economic analysis of marital instability. *Journal of Political Economy* 85(6), December, 1141–87.

Becker, G.S. and Tomes, N. 1986. Human capital and the rise and fall of families. *Journal of Labor Economics* 4(2, Part 2), S1–39.

Ben-Porath, Y. 1980. The F-connection: families, friends, and firms and the organization of exchange. *Population and Development Review* 6(1), 1–30.

Bernheim, B.I., Schleiffer, A. and Summers, L.H. 1986. Bequests as a means of payment. *Journal of Labor Economics* 4(3), Part 2, S151–82.

Blake, J. 1981. Family size and the quality of children. *Demography* 18(2), 421–42.

Boserup, E. 1970. *Woman's Role in Economic Development*. London: Allen & Unwin; New York: St. Martin's Press.

Conlisk, J. 1974. Can equalization of opportunity reduce social mobility? *American Economic Review* 64(1), March, 80–90.

De Tray, D.N. 1973. Child quality and the demand for children. *Journal of Political Economy* 81(2), Pt II, Mar-Apr, S70–95.

Gale, D. and Shapley, L.S. 1962. College admissions and the stability of marriage. *American Mathematical Monthly* 69(1), January, 9–15.

Gardner, B. 1973. Economics of the size of North Carolina rural families. *Journal of Political Economy* 81(2), Part II, March-April, S99–122.

Goldin, C. 1983. The changing economic role of women: a quantitative approach. *Journal of Interdisciplinary History* 13(4), 707–33.

Hannan, M.T., Tuma, N.B. and Groeneveld, L.P. 1977. Income and marital events: evidence from an income maintenance experiment. *American Journal of Sociology* 82(6), 611–33.

Hirshleifer, J. 1977. Shakespeare vs. Becker on altruism: the importance of having the last word. *Journal of Economic Literature* 15(2), 500–502.

Hollingsworth, T.H. 1965. *The Demography of the British Peerage*. Supplement to *Population Studies* 18(2).

Jaffe, A.J. 1940. Differential fertility in the white population in early America. *Journal of Heredity* 31(9).

Locay, L. 1987. *Population Density of the North American Indians.* Cambridge, Mass.: Harvard University Press.

Loury, G.C. 1981. Intergenerational transfers and the distribution of earnings. *Econometrica* 49(4), 843–67.

Malthus, T.R. 1798. *An Essay on the Principle of Population.* Reprinted, London: J.M. Dent, 1958; New York: Modern Library, 1960.

Marshall, A. 1890. *Principles of Economics.* London: Macmillan; 5th edn. New York: Macmillan, 1946.

Mill, J.S. 1848. *Principles of Political Economy, with some of their applications to Social Philosophy.* Reprinted, New York: Colonial Press, 1899.

Mincer, J. 1962. Labor force participation of married women. In *Aspects of Labor Economics,* Princeton: Princeton University Press.

Peters, E. 1983. The impact of state divorce laws on the marital contract: marriage, divorce, and marital property settlements. Discussion Paper No. 83–19. Economics Research Center/NORC.

Pollak, R.A. 1985. A transactions cost approach to families and households. *Journal of Economic Literature* 23(2), 581–608.

Rosen, S. 1981. Specialization and human capital. *Journal of Labor Economics* 1(1), 43–9.

Roth, A. 1984. The evolution of the labor market for medical interns and residents: a case study in game theory. *Journal of Political Economy* 92(6), 991–1016.

Smith, A. 1776. *An Inquiry into the Nature and Causes of the Wealth of Nations.* Reprinted, New York: Modern Library, 1937.

Smith, J.P. and Ward, M.P. 1985. Time series growth in the female labor force. *Journal of Labor Economics* 3(1), Part II, 559–90.

Trost, J. 1975. Married and unmarried cohabitation: the case of Sweden and some comparisons. *Journal of Marriage and the Family* 37(3), 677–682.

US Bureau of the Census, 1977. *Current Population Reports.* Series P-20, No. 308, Fertility of American Women: June, 1976.

Weiss, Y. and Willis, R. 1985. Children as collective goods and divorce settlements. *Journal of Labor Economics* 3(3), 268–92.

Wrigley, E.A. and Schofield, R.S. 1981. *The Population History of England 1541–1871.* Cambridge, Mass.: Harvard University Press.

Fertility

RICHARD A. EASTERLIN

At the aggregate level, human reproduction is the ultimate source of an economic system's labour input and of the consumers who constitute the principal destination of the economy's output. At the individual level, children are an important source of satisfaction that compete with alternatives for the limited parental resources of time, energy and money available. Despite this, reproductive behaviour has traditionally been omitted from economic theorizing, and even in the past three decades has gained only a marginal foothold.

Possibly the hesitancy of economic theory to address the determinants of childbearing reflects a sensitivity to reality. Several empiricial regularities involving the relation of fertility to income have posed a formidable challenge to theoretical interpretation. First, there is the long-term trend. In an historical epoch when real income per capita and, in consequence, real consumption of almost all goods has risen at unprecedented rates for a century or more in developed countries, births per couple over the reproductive career have fallen from levels often as high as six or more to two or less. Second, the cross-sectional relation between fertility and income within countries has been found to be variable and often lacks any significant association. Third, over the business cycle a positive association between fertility and income has typically been observed. Moreover, in a number of developed countries in the post-World War II period there was an unprecedented and unanticipated 'baby boom' of a decade or more in duration followed by an almost equally startling 'baby bust'.

It is often the case that new policy concerns stimulate economic theory, and this is clearly so with regard to fertility behaviour. Although unusually low fertility in the developed countries in the Great Depression had led to some experimentation with economic incentives to childbearing, the major policy stimulus by far was the emergence in the post-World War II era of the so-called 'population problem' as a presumed obstacle to economic growth in the less-developed world. Could measures be designed to lower reproduction rates in high-fertility societies and thus reduce rates of population growth? Concern with this issue spurred a number of economists to take a fresh look at fertility behaviour.

The contemporary economic theory of fertility dates from work by Harvey Leibenstein (1957) and Gary S. Becker (1960), which sought in somewhat different ways to assimilate the explanation of fertility behaviour to the economic theory of household demand (Leibenstein (1974) and Keeley (1975) give a good review of this early history). In 1965 Becker extended his analysis to incorporate the emerging concepts of household production theory and the allocation of time (Becker, 1965; Lancaster, 1971). For a decade or so this line of work, which came to be known as the Chicago–Columbia approach, dominated the economic theory of fertility. Among the more influential contributions were those made by Mincer (1963), Nerlove (1974) and Willis (1973). A volume edited by T.W. Schultz (1974) and a survey article and subsequent book by T.P. Schultz (1976, 1981) brought together a number of attempts to apply this approach empirically to the experience of developed and less-developed countries. A valuable commentary on the evolution of this work appears in Ben-Porath (1982).

Throughout much of this period, a second line of work was in progress that came to be dubbed the 'Pennsylvania' model (Sanderson, 1976, 1980; Behrman and Wolfe, 1984). Although this work largely accepted the Chicago–Columbia view as far as it went, it sought to broaden the model to include theoretical and empirical considerations that figured prominently in the sociological and demographic literature on fertility. One set of considerations related to taste influences on the demand for children, particularly of what economists would term a 'relative income' nature (Ben-Porath, 1975; Easterlin, 1969; Leibenstein, 1975). Good theoretical expositions of the demand for children, reflecting taste considerations as well as those in the Chicago–Columbia model, are given by Lindert (1978) and Turchi (1975). The other set of considerations relates to 'natural fertility' or so-called 'supply' factors (Easterlin, 1978; Tarbarrah, 1971). A formal statement of what came to be termed the 'supply–demand' approach was published in 1980 (Easterlin, Pollak and Wachter, 1980). In 1983 an interdisciplinary National Academy of Sciences panel adopted the supply–demand framework in surveying the literature on determinants of fertility in developing countries (Bulatao and Lee, 1983). (As shall become clear, in this theory supply and demand are not used in the usual economic sense.)

Recent work points to some convergence of the two lines of work. Scholars working in the Chicago–Columbia tradition have introduced into their work intergenerational influences which can be likened to the taste influences of the Pennsylvania model (Becker and Tomes, 1976), and have also started investigating supply factors (Michael and Willis, 1976; Rosenzweig and Schultz, 1985). But the two schools remain sufficiently distinct, especially in their interpretation of the empirical regularities described above, to warrant separate discussion. Using the empirical regularities as the framework for the discussion, the following aims to indicate for the non-specialist the principal ideas on each side, their relations to each other, and their bearing on the interpretation of each of the empirical regularities mentioned. Needless to say, there is also variability within each school as well as work not easily classified under either head.

THE SECULAR DECLINE IN FERTILITY. Over the long term, growth in real per capita income has everywhere been accompanied by a decline in child-bearing from levels sometimes averaging as high as six or more births per woman to around two or less. In seeking to explain this development, as in understanding fertility behaviour more generally, the Chicago–Columbia model focuses on changes in the demand for children.

A simple economic model analogous to that for the demand for any economic good, the original starting point for economic theorizing on fertility, would see the number of children demanded as varying directly with household income (assuming children are a 'normal' good), directly with the price of goods relative to children, and inversely with the strength of tastes for goods relative to children. In the Chicago–Columbia approach price and income are the explanatory variables featured, and especially price. The explanation of the secular fertility decline provides a typical illustration. The decline is seen as due to a decrease in the demand for children brought about by socio-economic development. This decrease in demand, in turn, is ascribed to a strong negative effect associated with an increase in the relative price of children that outweighs a weak positive effect from higher income. The most common explanation of the increased relative price of children focuses on the opportunity cost of the wife's time. In keeping with the household production function concept, children are seen as requiring inputs of goods and time, and the price of children, as depending, accordingly, on the prices of these inputs. Typically, the input of the wife's time in childbearing and raising is the central focus, and the assumption is made that children are more time-intensive with regard to the wife's time than other forms of consumption. The opportunity cost of the time input into children is then seen as increasing secularly as the wife's opportunity cost, proxied by her schooling, rises (Willis, 1973). Other factors increasing the relative price of children are sometimes cited, such as the price of labour relative to capital, the prices of other child inputs, or a systematic change in the 'quality' of children demanded, where quality is identified with the quantities of inputs of time and goods into a child (Lindert, 1980, 1983; T.P. Schultz, 1979; T.W. Schultz, 1974). All of these are seen as working via a negative impact on the demand for children, as in the case of the opportunity cost of a wife's time.

Several objections based on empirical studies have been raised to a purely demand interpretation of the secular fertility decline. For one thing, a phase of increasing fertility has often preceded the secular fertility decline (Dyson and Murphy, 1985); is this to be taken as implying an initial period of increasing demand for children? Then, too, there are indications of low fertility in some sub-Saharan African societies, apparently associated with venereal disease. How is this to be treated in a demand-oriented theory? Perhaps most important, demographic surveys of contemporary premodern populations have repeatedly turned up evidence of what demographers call a 'natural fertility' regime, the absence of any attempt deliberately to limit fertility among almost all segments of the population, aside from some elite groups (Coale, 1967; Henry, 1961). If parents are choosing the number of children they have in accordance with a demand model, how is one to explain the fact that so few are doing anything to control their fertility? It seems unlikely that unregulated fertility would assure that most couples would have just as many children as they want and no more, and thus result almost uniformly throughout a population in no practice of family size limitation.

To deal with questions of this type the Pennsylvania model stresses two factors as fertility determinants in addition to the demand for children: (1) the potential supply of children, the number of surviving children parents would have if they did not deliberately limit fertility; and (2) the costs of fertility regulation, including both subjective (psychic) drawbacks and objective costs, the time and money required to learn about and use specific techniques.

The introduction of supply considerations is the most distinctive feature of the Pennsylvania model. (Regulation costs are sometimes treated in Chicago–Columbia models although usually subordinated to demand.) The most obvious example of the importance of a supply constraint in determining observed fertility is the case of a couple that has fecundity problems and is consequently unable to produce as many children as it wants. True, child adoption is a logical option in such a case, but empirically this practice is of quite limited significance. Clearly, a supply constraint due to sterility would explain the African case mentioned above. Aside from sterility problems, however, the production of children is kept down significantly in almost all pre-modern societies by various types of behaviour that have unperceived consequences for fertility (a phenomenon conceptually designated 'unperceived jointness' by Easterlin, Pollak and Wachter, 1980). The most important types of behaviour in this regard are deferment of sexual unions beyond menarch, which reduces exposure to intercourse and prolonged breast feeding, which has the effect of delaying the return of ovulation after a birth. Also, because the subject of parents' demands is not births *per se*, but surviving children, high infant and child mortality in pre-modern societies further restricts the supply of children.

The Pennsylvania model suggests two possible reasons for 'natural fertility' behaviour. First, there is the possibility of excess demand. If in most households in a pre-modern society the supply of children were less than demand, then parents would have as many children as they could. In such a situation there would be a general absence of any practice of deliberate family size limitation, and differences in observed fertility would be determined by the circumstances responsible for differences in supply.

Even if supply exceeded demand, however, deliberate family size limitation would not necessarily occur, because of the costs attaching to the various techniques of fertility control. If, for example, the disutility attaching, say, to abstinence or withdrawal, exceeds the disutility of an excess number of children, and no other contraceptive practices are known, then a couple's observed fertility would again be governed by its supply. Thus the Pennsylvania model identifies two cases in which rational behaviour would be consistent with an absence of deliberate fertility regulation – (a) an excess demand condition, and (b) high perceived costs of fertility regulation.

In interpreting the secular fertility decline, the Pennsylvania model envisages a typical pre-modern society as starting from a condition of unregulated fertility due to either or both of the circumstances just mentioned, and moving to a situation of algebraically increasing excess supply, as supply increases and demand decreases (though not necessarily concurrently) with socio-economic development. The increase in supply might reflect a decrease in breastfeeding that raises natural fertility, improved child survival, or both. The decreased demand might be due to a rise in the relative cost of children, as in the Chicago–Columbia model, or an anti-natal shift in tastes due to education or the introduction of new consumer goods (Behrman and Wolfe, 1984; Easterlin, 1978). If the disutility associated with an excess supply of children remains less than the disutility associated with use of contraception, then fertility will remain uncontrolled and an increase in actual fertility, reflecting the growth of natural fertility, will be observed. Such circumstances could account for a phase of increasing fertility prior to the secular fertility decline. Eventually, however, as excess supply continues to rise, the pressures for adoption of deliberate control will prevail, and observed fertility will decline. Lower costs of fertility regulation due, say, to better contraceptive knowledge or improved contraceptive availability, might also contribute to the shift to lower fertility, although it is unlikely that this factor in itself could explain an initial phase of increasing fertility.

Thus, the supply–demand approach sees the supply of children and regulation costs, as well as demand, as factors that may significantly influence observed fertility in pre-modern societies and in the early stages of the secular fertility decline. Eventually, however, as modernization progresses, most households shift to a position of substantial potential excess supply and increasingly perceive costs of fertility regulation as low. Because of this, demand influences become increasingly dominant in determining fertility, although these influences may reflect taste changes in addition to anti-natal price effects (cf. Mueller and Short, 1983). Thus, in contemporary developed societies, both schools emphasize demand as the principal influence determining fertility, although they differ with regard to the underlying determinants of demand that are considered most important.

In recent work by some members of the Chicago–Columbia school, a supply–demand mode has also been adopted, but sharp conceptual differences from the Pennsylvania model remain (Schultz, 1981; Rosenzweig and Schultz, 1985). In the Chicago–Columbia model, supply is determined solely by biological factors and all behavioural factors operate through demand. In contrast, in the Pennsylvania model, supply is constrained by behaviour that has the unintentional effect of limiting fertility. Particularly at issue is the extent to which considerations of family size enter into individual decisions on marriage-timing, length of breastfeeding, and consumption. Based on motivational data from sample surveys as well as behavioural data of various types, the Pennsylvania model assumes such decisions to be taken largely independently of family size concerns. The positivist methodology of the Chicago–Columbia school leads to rejection of this evidence, and to a theoretical conception that stresses on *a priori* grounds the endogeneity to the fertility decision of marriage-timing and breastfeeding behaviour. In the Pennsylvania model it is the behavioural influences on supply that are principally responsible for constraining fertility to the extent that it may fall short of demand in pre-modern societies. Aside from cases of physiological sterility, the supply concept of the Chicago–Columbia school would be unlikely to constrain fertility effectively; hence their supply–demand model largely preserves their emphasis on demand conditions as the determinant of observed fertility behaviour in all times and places.

THE CROSS-SECTIONAL RELATION BETWEEN FERTILITY AND INCOME. As has been mentioned, cross-sectional empirical studies of the relation between fertility and income yield mixed results, and this is so even after controlling for numerous other variables (Mueller and Short, 1983; Simon, 1974). Sometimes the direction of relationship is positive, sometimes negative; sometimes the relationship is significant, sometimes not significant. Because economists of both schools working in the fertility area intuitively accept that children are a normal good, these empirical findings have provoked an extensive research for explanation, and, in particular, for price or taste factors that might vary systematically with income level. This search has again involved rather different types of emphasis by the Chicago–Columbia and Pennsylvania schools.

Consistent with the interpretation of the secular fertility decline, the variable stressed most frequently by the Chicago–Columbia school has been the opportunity cost of a wife's time, a variable first brought to the fore by Mincer (1963). The idea is that husbands with higher permanent income are likely to have spouses with higher education and thus higher market wage rates. A general increase in the potential earnings of both sexes would then lead to a substitution effect against children due to the wife's higher wage rate that offsets a positive income effect from the husband's wage rate. Because of the absence of wage rates for nonworking wives, empirical tests of this hypothesis have usually used wife's education as a proxy for the opportunity cost of wife's time (T.W. Schultz, 1974).

A second line of explanation in the Chicago–Columbia approach stressed by Becker himself and differing from the price-of-time argument emphasizes the association between what is called 'child quality' and income (Becker and Lewis, 1974). In this case the variation with income of the quantities of child inputs, rather than their prices, is the focus. The basic idea is that as parents' income increases, they are assumed to want to increase child inputs and thus to spend more, on the average, on their children, just as they are expected to want to spend more on themselves. This positive association between desired expenditures per child and parental income causes children to be more expensive for wealthier parents than poorer ones, and is presumed to offset the positive effect of income *per se* on the demand for children.

Although the Pennsylvania school does not reject the plausibility of these hypotheses, it offers yet another one, again influenced by the demographic work of sociologists, as in the supply–demand approach. In this case, the analysis builds on the sociological notion that one's economic socialization experience early in the life cycle plays an important part in forming one's material tastes. It is assumed that the material environment surrounding young persons in the course of their upbringing leads to the formation of a socially defined subsistence level that they wish to achieve on reaching adulthood (Ahlburg, 1984; Easterlin, 1973). Only to the extent that actual income exceeds this subsistence constraint would a couple feel free to embark on family formation. Assuming that young adults with higher income come from more affluent backgrounds, then the expected positive effect of higher income on the demand for children would be offset by the higher goods aspirations of wealthier compared with poorer couples (Easterlin, 1969).

Recently there has been some convergence in the two views. On the one hand, the Chicago–Columbia school has introduced consideration of what is called 'child endowments', stressing the effect of one's family of origin on fertility behaviour, as in the Pennsylvania model (Becker, 1981; Becker and Tomes, 1976; Nerlove, 1974). On the other hand, the Pennsylvania school has added to its conception concern with parents' desires for expenditures on their children as well as for themselves (Easterlin, 1976). Both schools typically argue that because of such systematic correlates of changing income, the cross-sectional observed relation of income and fertility is uncertain. Leibenstein (1974, 1975) takes a stronger stance, asserting on *a priori* grounds that negative taste changes associated with higher income offset positive income effects and cause a negative association between income and fertility. The argument is that a higher status household must more than proportionately increase its expenditures on 'status goods' in order to maintain its relative life style and economic status.

Much of the theorizing regarding the cross-sectional income–fertility relationship assumes that the same arguments would apply in both pre-modern and developed societies. Development of the supply–demand model by the Pennsylvania school has led to reconsideration of this proposition. If, in pre-modern societies, fertility is largely determined by supply conditions, whereas in developed countries it is largely determined by demand factors, there is obviously no reason to expect the same relation between income and fertility (Behrman and Wolfe, 1984). Indeed, a systematic shift in the relation of income to fertility might be observed, as the dominant determinants shifted from supply to demand (Crimmins et al., 1984). To illustrate, from a supply viewpoint, in a pre-modern society higher income might lead to better nutrition and thereby higher fecundity of a wife, or to shorter breastfeeding as baby food substitutes become available and affordable. For both reasons the ability to produce children would be positively related to income. If a natural fertility regime prevailed, then such supply effects might yield a positive relation between observed fertility and income. With the progress of modernization and a growing predominance of demand factors in fertility determination, this initial positive cross-sectional association might change to a non-significant or (on Leibenstein reasoning) even a negative relationship. The possibility that supply factors might dominate the cross-sectional income–fertility relationship in developing countries has not been considered by the Chicago–Columbia school, presumably because of their more restricted concept of supply.

FLUCTUATIONS. Economic theorizing about fertility fluctuations has focused primarily on the experience of the developed countries, and particularly the United States. The protracted postwar baby boom and bust, from a low in the 1930s to a peak in the 1950s and then a new 1970s trough, has attracted most attention; shorter-term business cycle fluctuations, much less.

The interpretation of the United State baby boom and bust advanced by the Pennsylvania school is a relative income one that builds on the arguments about taste formation described in the preceding section (Easterlin, 1973, 1980). The basic idea is that the cohorts that were in the family forming ages in the late 1940s and 1950s were raised under the economically deprived circumstances of the Great Depression and World War II. As a result, the material aspirations formed during their economic socialization experience were low. Their labour market experience, however, was quite favourable, because of the combined circumstances of a prolonged post-World War II economic expansion and the relative scarcity of young workers, the latter echoing the unprecedently low fertility of the 1920s and 1930s. In consequence, these cohorts enjoyed high relative income, that is, high income relative to their material aspirations, and this led to earlier marriage and child-bearing, higher completed family size, and the baby boom that lasted through the late 1950s.

The circumstances of the subsequent cohorts tended to be the reverse – declining relative income, postponed marriage and childbearing, lower completed family size – adding up to a baby bust. On the one hand, these cohorts had formed high material aspirations as a result of their upbringing in the boom circumstances following World War II. On the other, their own labour experience was much less favourable, partly because of some slackening in the growth of aggregate demand, and partly because of a sharply increased relative supply of workers in family forming ages, itself a consequence of the prior baby boom.

As the foregoing suggests, the relative income hypothesis can, with some restrictive assumptions, be translated into a relative cohort size hypothesis. If one assumes fairly stable growth in aggregate demand and a largely closed economy, then variations in the earnings of younger compared with older workers would be dominated by variations in the relative supply of younger workers. A relatively small cohort of young adults would cause a narrowing of the shortfall of younger workers' incomes compared with older; a relatively large cohort would cause a widening of the gap. Taking older workers' incomes as a proxy for the material aspirations formed by young adults when in their parents' homes, one obtains the same type of relative income mechanism engendering fertility movements that was just described. This relative cohort size variant has been used to demonstrate the possibility of a self-generating fertility cycle (Lee, 1974; Samuelson, 1976).

In contrast to the taste formation influences emphasized in the Pennsylvania model, the Chicago–Columbia interpretation of the baby boom and bust builds on a price-of-time argument similar to that used in explaining the secular fertility decline (Butz and Ward, 1979). An increase in husband's income is thought to have a positive effect on fertility; an increase in the wife's wage rate, a negative effect due to the price-of-time effect. In the baby boom period, it is argued, the labour market for women relative to men, as indexed by wage rate movements for the two sexes, was comparatively weak; thereafter the labour market for women expanded commensurately with that for men. Thus, in the baby boom period, men's wage rates rose while women's remained relatively flat; hence a net positive impact on fertility prevailed, reflecting the dominant effect of men's compared with women's wage rate changes. Thereafter, women's wage rates rose commensurately with men's, and a negative effect dominated, due to the higher absolute magnitude of the elasticity of fertility with respect to women's wage rates than men's. The result of the disparate changes in men's and women's wages before and after 1960 was thus an upswing in fertility followed by a downswing. Young women's labour force participation moved inversely with fertility in the two periods, reflecting the differing pull of women's wage rates.

Several critiques of the econometric techniques used in this analysis have appeared (Kramer and Neusser, 1984; McDonald, 1983). Also, the movement in labour force participation of older women does not fit easily into the argument. This is because older women, who are highly substitutable for younger women in most jobs, showed a marked rise in labour force participation before 1960, the period when the female labour market was presumably weak, and then much slower growth after 1960, when the female labour market was presumably stronger. In addition, the Chicago–Columbia view implies that the more favourable movement in women's wages after 1960 would have shortened birth intervals (Mincer and Polachek, 1974), whereas the opposite, in fact, occurred. Nevertheless, the Butz–Ward analysis remains the prevailing interpretation advanced by adherents of the Chicago–Columbia school. Some analysts have found that a combination of the Pennsylvania and Chicago–Columbia models is superior to either alone (Devaney, 1984; Lindert, 1978).

The Pennsylvania and Chicago–Columbia models have quite different implications for the future of fertility fluctuations. The Pennsylvania model suggests that a growing scarcity of younger workers in the 1980s and 1990s, echoing the baby bust of the 1960s and 1970s, is a factor making for a turnaround in the relative income of young adults and thus for an upturn in fertility. In contrast, the Chicago–Columbia view envisages further fertility declines on the assumption that women's wages are likely to continue to rise commensurately with men's.

The two models also differ in their predictions regarding variations in fertility over the business cycle. The Pennsylvania model anticipates a positive association of the type traditionally observed (Ben-Porath, 1973). Because of the importance of historical evidence in forming tastes, one would expect tastes to remain largely invariant in periods as short as the usual business cycle. Variations in actual earnings associated with the business cycle might therefore be expected to lead to corresponding variations in fertility as income expectations were revised.

In contrast, the Chicago–Columbia analysis suggests that the short-term association between fertility and income varies with the proportion of females in the labour force. The reasoning is that the relative importance of the negative effects of women's wage changes versus the positive effect of men's wage changes will be greater, the larger the proportion of women in the labour force. Hence, as the proportion of women at work rises, the more sensitive does fertility become to fluctuations in women's wage rates. Based on the uptrend in women's labour force participation, the Chicago–Columbia model thus foresees the emergence of counter-cyclical fertility fluctuations. When women's wage rates are high, as in a boom period, the price-of-time effect will pull them into the labour market and consequently reduce fertility; when wage rates are low, the reverse will occur. This mechanism is claimed to have operated during the business cycles of the 1970s.

CONCLUSION. This survey has aimed at highlighting some of the principal differences between the two leading schools of economic theorizing about reproductive behaviour, as manifested in the interpretations offered of trends, fluctuations and cross-sectional variations in the income–fertility relationship. As the survey demonstrates, the evolution of theorizing on reproductive behaviour has been away from a simple economic model of demand emphasizing income and market price variables toward the recognition of additional constraints on behaviour. Perhaps more than in any other area of economic analysis, the constraint of time inputs has come to the forefront, both the amounts of time required in childbearing and childrearing and the prices at which these inputs should be valued. This interest has stimulated fruitful empirical inquiries by economists into the use of time within the household. Also, explicit attention has been paid to the constraint on one's behaviour arising from the way that prior experience shapes one's tastes. Thus, attention has been directed to the way that one's experience in one's family of origin and one's socialization experience more generally may shape adult preferences with regard to material aspirations and family size. In this area, economists have sometimes pushed beyond the conceptual speculations of sociologists to formulate specific empirical models of taste formation. Finally, recognition has emerged of the constraint on 'consumption' of children arising from production possibilities within the household. Whether because of biological or behavioural attributes, a couple may be unable to produce as many children as demanded, and its observed consumption would thus reflect this rationing constraint.

As the foregoing discussion shows, the introduction of these new behavioural constraints has arisen from growing awareness by economists of the intractability of empirical evidence on reproductive behaviour, and a resultant attempt to accommodate within economic analysis conceptual contributions from related disciplines. Although some progress in understanding reproductive behaviour has been made, there is still no single generally accepted theory of reproductive behaviour, and no consensus on the interpretation of the empirical regularities described above. However, if it is true that scientific breakthroughs frequently occur at the juncture of different disciplines, fertility theory is undoubtedly one of the frontiers of economic theory beckoning for more intensive exploration.

BIBLIOGRAPHY

Ahlburg, D.A. 1984. Commodity aspirations in Easterlin's relative income theory of fertility. *Social Biology* 31(3/4), Fall/Winter, 201–7.

Becker, G.S. 1960. An economic analysis of fertility. In *Demographic and Economic Change in Developed Countries*, Universities–National Bureau Conference Series No. 11, Princeton: Princeton University Press.

Becker, G.S. 1965. A theory of the allocation of time. *Economic Journal* 75, September, 493–517.

Becker, G.S. 1981. *A Treatise on the Family*. Cambridge, Mass.: Harvard University Press.

Becker, G.S. and Lewis, H.G. 1974. Interaction between quantity and quality of children. In *The Economics of the Family*, ed. T.W. Schultz, Chicago: University of Chicago Press.

Becker, G.S. and Tomes, N. 1976. Child endowments and the quantity and quality of children. *Journal of Political Economy* 84(4), Part 2, August, S143–S162.

Behrman, J.R. and Wolfe, B.L. 1984. A more general approach to fertility determination in a developing country: the importance of biological supply considerations, endogenous tastes and unperceived jointness. *Economica* 51, August, 319–39.

Ben-Porath, Y. 1973. Short-term fluctuations in fertility and economic activity in Israel. *Demography* 10(2), May, 185–204.

Ben-Porath, Y. 1975. First generation effects on second generation fertility. *Demography* 12(3), August, 397–405.

Ben-Porath, Y. 1982. Economics and the family – match or mismatch? A review of Becker's 'A Treatise on the Family'. *Journal of Economic Literature* 20(1), March, 52–64.

Bulatao, R.A. and Lee, R.D. (eds) 1983. *Determinants of Fertility in Developing Countries: A Summary of Knowledge*. New York: Academic Press.

Butz, W.P. and Ward, M.P. 1979. The emergence of counter-cyclical US fertility. *American Economic Review* 69(3), June, 318–28.

Coale, A.J. 1967. The voluntary control of human fertility. *Proceedings of the American Philosophical Society* 111(3), June, 164–9.

Crimmins, E.M., Easterlin, R.A., Jejeebhoy, S.J. and Srinivasan, K. 1984. New perspectives on the demographic transition: a theoretical and empirical analysis of an Indian state, 1951–1975. *Economic Development and Cultural Change* 32(2), January, 227–53.

Devaney, B. 1984. An analysis of variations in U.S. fertility and female labor force participation trends. *Demography* 20(2), May, 147–61.

Dyson, T. and Murphy, M. 1985. The onset of fertility transition. *Population and Development Review* 11(3), September, 399–440.

Easterlin, R.A. 1969. Towards a socioeconomic theory of fertility: a survey of recent research on economic factors in American fertility. In *Fertility and Family Planning: A World View*, ed. S.J. Behrman, Leslie Corsa, Jr. and R. Freedman, Ann Arbor: University of Michigan Press.

Easterlin, R.A. 1973. Relative economic status and the American fertility swing. In *Family Economic Behavior: Problems and Prospects*, ed. E.B. Sheldon, Philadelphia: Lippincott.

Easterlin, R.A. 1976. Population change and farm settlement in the northern United States. *Journal of Economic History* 36(1), March, 45–75.

Easterlin, R.A. 1978. The economics and sociology of fertility: a synthesis. In *Historical Studies of Changing Fertility*, ed. C. Tilly, Princeton: Princeton University Press.

Easterlin, R.A. 1980. *Birth and Fortune*. New York: Basic Books.

Easterlin, R.A., Pollak, R.A. and Wachter, M.L. 1980. Toward a more general economic model of fertility determination: endogenous preferences and natural fertility. In *Population and Economic Change in Developing Countries*, ed. R.A. Easterlin, Chicago: University of Chicago Press.

Henry, L. 1961. La fécondité naturelle: observations – théorie – résultants. *Population* 16(4), October/December, 625–36.

Keeley, M. 1975. A comment on 'An Interpretation of the Economic Theory of Fertility'. *Journal of Economic Literature* 13(2), June, 461–7.

Kramer, W. and Neusser, K. 1984. The emergence of countercyclical U.S. fertility: note. *American Economic Review* 74(1), March, 201–2.

Lancaster, K.J. 1971. *Consumer Demand: A New Approach*. New York: Columbia University Press.

Lee, R. 1974. The formal dynamics of controlled populations and the Echo, the Boom and the Bust. *Demography* 11(4), November, 563–85.

Leibenstein, H. 1957. *Economic Backwardness and Economic Growth*. New York: John Wiley.

Leibenstein, H. 1974. An interpretation of the economic theory of fertility: promising path or blind alley? *Journal of Economic Literature* 12(2), June, 457–79.

Leibenstein, H. 1975. The economic theory of fertility decline. *Quarterly Journal of Economics* 89(1), February, 1–31.

Lindert, P.H. 1978. *Fertility and Scarcity in America*. Princeton: Princeton University Press.

Lindert, P.H. 1980. Child costs and economic development. In *Population and Economic Change in Developing Countries*, ed. R.A. Easterlin, Chicago: University of Chicago Press.

Lindert, P.H. 1983. The changing economic costs and benefits of having children. In *Determinants of Fertility in Developing Countries: A Summary of Knowledge*, Vol. 1, ed. R. Bulatao and R.D. Lee, New York: Academic Press.

McDonald, J. 1983. The emergence of countercyclical US fertility: a reassessment of the evidence. *Journal of Macroeconomics* 5(4), Fall, 421–36.

Michael, R.T. and Willis, R.J. 1976. Contraception and fertility: household production under uncertainty. In Conference on Research in Income and Wealth, *Household Production and Consumption*, New York: National Bureau of Economic Research.

Mincer, J. 1963. Market prices, opportunity costs, and income effects. In *Measurement in Economics*, ed. C. Christ et al., Stanford: Stanford University Press.

Mincer, J. and Polachek, S. 1974. Family investments in human capital: earnings of women. In *The Economics of the Family*, ed. T.W. Schultz, Chicago: University of Chicago Press.

Mueller, E. and Short, K. 1983. Effects of income and wealth on the demand for children. In *Determinants of Fertility in Developing Countries: A Summary of Knowledge*, Vol. 1, ed. R. Bulatao and R.D. Lee, New York: Academic Press.

Nerlove, M. 1974. Household and economy: toward a new theory of population and economic growth. *Journal of Political Economy* 82(2), Part II, March/April, S200–S218.

Rosenzweig, M.R. and Schultz, T.P. 1985. The demand for and supply of births: fertility and its life cycle consequences. *American Economic Review* 75(5), December, 992–1015.

Samuelson, P.A. 1976. An economist's non-linear model of self-generated fertility waves. *Population Studies* 30(2), July, 243–7.

Sanderson, W.C. 1976. On two schools of the economics of fertility. *Population and Development Review* 2(3–4), September/December, 469–77.

Sanderson, W.C. 1980. Comment. In *Population and Economic Change in Developing Countries*, ed. R.A. Easterlin, Chicago: University of Chicago Press.

Schultz, T. 1976. Determinants of fertility: a micro-economic model of choice. In *Economic Factors in Population Growth*, ed. A.J. Coale, New York: Halstead Press.

Schultz, T.P. 1979. Current developments in the economics of fertility. In *International Union for the Scientific Study of Population: Economic and Demographic Change: Issues for the 1980's*, Proceedings of the Conference, Helsinki 1978, Vol. 3, Liège: IUSSP, 27–38.

Schultz, T.P. 1981. *Economics of Population*. Reading, Mass.: Addison-Wesley Co.

Schultz, T.W. (ed.) 1974. *The Economics of the Family*. Chicago: University of Chicago Press.

Simon, J.L. 1974. *The Effects of Income on Fertility*. Chapel Hill: University of North Carolina Press.

Tabarrah, R.B. 1971. Toward a theory of demographic development. *Economic Development and Cultural Change* 19(2), January, 257–77.

Turchi, B.A. 1975. *The Demand for Children: The Economics of Fertility in the United States*. Cambridge, Mass.: Ballinger.

Willis, R.J. 1973. A new approach to the economic theory of fertility behavior. *Journal of Political Economy* 81(2), Part II, March/April, S14–S64.

Full Employment

G.D.N. WORSWICK

An expression which came into general use in economics after the Depression of the 1930s, full employment applies to industrially developed economies in which the majority of the economically active are the employees of firms or public authorities as wage and salary earners.

There has always been some unemployment in the course of development of capitalist economies and views have differed as to its causes and as to the extent to which it was a matter of public concern. In the first path of the 20th century three principal strands of thought about unemployment can be distinguished. Firstly, the followers of Marx believed that cycles were an integral part of capitalist development and would lead to ever deepening crisis: the attempt to evade this by colonial expansion would only lead to conflict between imperialist powers. A second group of analysts paid particular attention to the measurement and dating of business cycles, distinguishing cycles of different periodicity, but they did not, as a rule, offer systematic theories. The third strand consisted of those economists who argued that in capitalist economies, if the forces of the market were left to work themselves out, there would always be a tendency towards an equilibrium, in modern parlance towards full employment.

Table 1 shows average rates of unemployment in six developed countries for various periods of the 20th century. National estimates of unemployment are obtained either by sample survey or as the by-product of administration, such as a system of unemployment insurance. There are many problems in counting both the numbers unemployed and the labour force, whose ratio is to constitute the 'rate' of unemployment. There have been attempts to standardize rates obtained in different countries by different methods and over different periods. The figures in Table 1, taken from Maddison (1982) and OECD *Main Economic Indicators* are thought to be reasonably comparable. Only in two cases was it feasible to give estimates before World War I. We have four countries for the interwar years and all six after 1950. It will be seen that in the Depression years 1930–34 the average rates of unemployment were far higher than in any earlier

Table 1   *Unemployed as a Percentage of the Total Labour Force*

	France	Germany	Japan	Sweden	U.K.	U.S.A.
1900–1913	—	3	—	—	4.3	4.7
1920–1929	—	3.8	—	3.1	7.5	4.8
1930–1934	—	12.7	—	6.3	13.4	16.5
1935–1938	—	3.8	—	5.4	9.2	11.4
1950–1959	1.4	5.0	2.0	1.8	2.5	4.4
1960–1969	1.6	0.7	1.3	1.7	2.7	4.7
1970–1979	3.7	2.8	1.6	2.0	4.3	5.4
1980–1984	7.9	6.1	2.4	2.8	11.8	8.2

Sources: 1900–1979 A. Maddison, *Phases of Capitalist Development*, Oxford University Press, 1982. 1980–1984 OECD. *Main Economic Indicators*, Paris. (In the overlapping years 1975–1979 there are small discrepancies between Maddison and OECD for Germany and UK. The latest OECD figures were adjusted to be consistent with Maddison.)

period in the 20th century and that even in the later 1930s the rates remained abnormally high except in Germany.

The time was ripe for a theory which could account for the persistence of large-scale unemployment and it was provided by John Maynard Keynes in *The General Theory of Employment, Interest and Money* (1936), which the author himself said was all about 'my doctrine of full employment'. The self-equilibrating tendencies expounded by those whom Keynes called 'classical' economists did not necessarily function in the manner prescribed for them and capitalist economies could get stuck with persistent unemployment. According to orthodox theory, unemployment should entail falling wages which would eliminate any 'involuntary' unemployment. Similarly, interest rates would fall, bringing about a recovery of investment. Keynes argued that money wages might by 'sticky', and even if they were not, falls in money wages would not entail corresponding falls in real wages, since prices would also fall. As to rates of interest, there was no guarantee that such falls as could occur would give a strong enough impetus to recovery. The analysis points clearly to the idea, which others developed more explicitly, that fiscal policy, that is, the adjustment of the budget balance between revenue and expenditure, could prove a more powerful lever to bring about full employment.

Within less than ten years, the British wartime coalition government, in a famous White Paper, had accepted 'as one of their primary aims and responsibilities' the maintenance of 'a high and stable level of employment', and other governments, in Australia, Canada and Sweden, for instance, made similar affirmations. Article 55 of the United Nations Charter called on members to promote 'higher standards of living, full employment, and conditions of economic and social progress and development'. This remarkable change in public policy cannot be attributed simply to the 'Keynesian Revolution' in economic thought. More powerful was the observation that twice in a generation full employment had only been realized in war. How far the new principles were responsible for the performance of economies in the postwar period is a disputed question. The facts are that for the twenty-five years after 1945 the growth rates of productivity in European countries were much higher, and the average levels of unemployment much lower than they had ever been. Fluctuations in output and employment were smaller than in the past. A group of OECD experts reporting in 1968 said that the results of using fiscal policy to maintain economic balance had been encouraging, though there was room for further improvement. In the United States, the government's attitude towards the new ideas was initially somewhat cooler. By its own past standards, productivity growth was not exceptional, and unemployment, though much lower than in the Depression, was much the same as in the 1920s and before 1914. The Keynesian battle was not truly joined in the USA until the 1960s. In the majority of countries, the era of exceptional growth and full employment came to an end in the early 1970s, since when longer spells of high unemployment have been experienced.

Full employment does not mean zero unemployment. There can be dislocations where large numbers of workers are displaced from their present employment, and time is needed before new workplaces can be created. This can happen at the end of a war, or following some major technological change. Apart from such special cases, regular allowance must be made for frictional and seasonal unemployment. Policy would not aim, therefore, at zero but at the elimination of unemployment attributable to demand deficiency. Governments targeting full employment would like to know the level of measured unemployment to which this corresponds. Three attempts to answer this question deserve mention. (1) The definition given by Beveridge (1944) was that the number of unemployed (U) should equal the number of unfilled vacancies (V). When U is very high, we would expect to find V low, and vice versa. If, over a number of fluctuations, U and V trace out a fairly stable downward sloping curve, we could pick the point on it where $U = V$ as indicating full employment. (2) Phillips (1958) claimed that for Britain there was a good statistical relationship between the level of unemployment and the rate of change of money wages. By choosing the level of unemployment deriving zero wage inflation, or when labour productivity was rising, the slightly higher level delivering zero price inflation, we could pinpoint full employment. (3) Friedman (1968) objected that in the long run there was no trade-off between unemployment and inflation: instead he argued that there was a 'natural' rate of unemployment, such that if the actual level was pushed below this, there would be not only inflation, but accelerating inflation. If this theory could be substantiated, one could choose the 'non-accelerating inflation rate of unemployment' (NAIRU) as the target. It is evident that the usefulness of each of the above approaches turns on the closeness and stability of the statistical relationship actually observed. Experience in different countries has varied, and the British evidence should be regarded as illustrative. For the period from the early 1950s to the later 1960s econometric analysis produced reasonably stable relationships for all three approaches, yielding estimates of the full employment level of unemployment of the order of 2–3 per cent. But in the 1970s any stability of the Phillips curve crumbled, and estimates of NAIRU shot up from below two to over ten per cent, but without any clear indication of the institutional or structural changes which must have occurred to bring about so large a shift in so short a time. The UV relationship did not escape entirely unscathed either, but a plausible story can be told in terms of an outward shift of the UV curve. Brown (1985) reckoned that the United States, the United Kingdom and France suffered increases in the imperfections of the labour market in the period from the early 1960s to 1981 which might account in full employment $(U = V)$ conditions for extra unemployment of two per cent or less. It would seem that the substantial rises in unemployment, especially in Europe, in the 1970s and 1980s can only be accounted in a smaller part by a rise in 'full employment' unemployment and that a greater part denotes a shortfall below it.

If the growth of output of developed economies after 1945 was exceptional, so also was the rate of price increase: in Britain, for example, such a sustained and substantial rise (3–4 per cent a year on average) had not been seen in peacetime for more than two centuries. Some countries had faster rises, but, in most cases, there was no clear sign of acceleration. A marked change of gear in price inflation occurred between the 1960s and 1970s, precipitated by two large cost impulses. Around 1969 there was in many countries a distinct surge in wage increases which Phelps Brown (1983) has called 'the Hinge' and in 1973 there was the first of the great OPEC oil price rises. Confronted with these spontaneous boosts in costs, the authorities had to choose between allowing their consequences to be worked out within the bounds of the existing monetary and fiscal stance and adjusting that stance to accommodate them, which would mean that final prices would also jump. They began increasingly to opt for the former course. In doing so they received intellectual support from the first wave of the 'monetarist' counter-revolution against the now orthodox Keynesian demand management. Firstly, it was said that to push unemployment below the 'natural rate' would cause accelerating inflation. In any case, too little was known about the structure of the economy, in particular its time lags, for fine tuning to be a sensible policy. Better to adopt simple rules, such as fixed targets for the growth of the supply of money, which would keep inflation under control, and output and employment would adjust to the level indicated by the 'natural rate' of unemployment. Later developments in the new classical economics went further and denied altogether the possibility that governments, by loan financed expenditure, for instance, could effect lasting changes in employment. Instead, it was suggested, the only way to bring down unemployment was to reduce the monopoly power of trade unions, and to take other steps to free labour markets, such as abolishing minimum wage legislation and reducing unemployment benefit. Though not supported by any substantial body of evidence, these new ideas undoubtedly helped to persuade central banks to adopt fixed monetary targets, or rules, and after the second OPEC price rise in 1979, most governments followed restrictive monetary policies with more severe budgets. Calculations of 'constant employment' budget balances show a tightening equivalent to several percentage points of GNP in some cases, especially in Europe where unemployment rose considerably after 1980. On the other hand the United States broke ranks in 1983, allowing both actual and 'constant employment' deficits to rise, and it was the one major economy to experience falling unemployment.

If there is little evidence of a unique 'natural rate' of unemployment, it is nevertheless clear that to bring down a cost-induced inflation by demand restriction may involve high unemployment for a great many years. A wide range of 'income policies' has been attempted, and others canvassed, to secure that firms and workers would settle for lower prices and wages than they would seek if they were acting alone, provided others would do the same. It is unlikely that full employment of the kind experienced in Europe in the 1950s and 1960s could return without the aid of such policies. Throughout the great postwar expansion world trade grew at an unprecedented rate. Fixed exchange rates, with permission to change parities if needed, worked well enough for most countries to maintain their external balance. However, the Bretton Woods system crumbled and was succeeded by generally floating exchange rates, while at the same time controls over capital movements were begin dismantled. Exchange rates came to be determined as much by capital movements as by trade, and they can diverge widely and for long periods from any level suggested by purchasing power parity. Thus full employment is also seen to depend increasingly on the joint action of all, or of a large number, of countries.

Employment policy has been linked with the welfare state in contradictory ways. On the one hand, higher unemployment is tolerated on the grounds that welfare provision mitigates the economic hardship involved: on the other hand, higher welfare costs are perceived as a growing burden on economies with high unemployment.

BIBLIOGRAPHY

Beveridge, W. 1944. *Full Employment in a Free Society*. London: George Allen & Unwin.

Brown, A.J. 1985. *World Inflation since 1950*. Cambridge: Cambridge University Press.

Friedman, M. 1968. The role of monetary policy. *American Economic Review* 58(1), March, 1–17.

Keynes, J.M. 1936. *The General Theory of Employment, Interest and Money*. London: Macmillan; New York: Harcourt, Brace.

Maddison, A. 1982. *Phases of Capitalist Development*. Oxford: Oxford University Press.

OECD. 1968. *Fiscal Policy for a Balanced Economy*. Paris: Organization for Economic Cooperation and Development.

Phelps Brown, E.H. 1983. *The Origins of Trade Union Power*. Oxford: Clarendon Press.

Phillips, A.W. 1958. The relation between unemployment and the rate of change of money wage rates in the United Kingdom. *Economica* 25, November, 283–99.

Gender

FRANCINE D. BLAU

The term gender has traditionally referred, as has sex, to the biological differences between men and women. More recently a movement has arisen both in social science writings and in public discourse to expand this definition to encompass also the distinctions which society has erected on this biological base, and further to use the word gender in preference to sex to refer to this broader definition. In this essay, we describe the relationship of this expanded concept of gender to economic theory.

Historically, gender has not been perceived to be a central concept in economic analysis, either among the classical and neoclassical schools or among Marxist economists. However, as the force of current events has thrust gender-related issues to the fore, economists have responded by seeking to analyse these issues. The outcome of this process has been not only a better understanding of the nature of gender differences in economic behaviour and outcomes, but also an enrichment of the discipline itself.

While, as noted above, the mainstream of economic analysis paid scant attention to gender-related issues, the 19th century campaign for female suffrage did focus some attention on gender inequality. Among classical economists, J.S. Mill (1878) eloquently argued for the 'principle of perfect equality' (p. 91) between men and women. Not only did he favour equality of the sexes within the family, but also women's 'admissibility to all the functions and occupations hitherto retained as the monopoly of the stronger sex'. He also expressed the belief 'that their disabilities elsewhere are only clung to in order to maintain their subordination in domestic life' (p. 94). In the Marxist school, Engels (1884) tied the subjection of women to the development of capitalism and argued that women's participation in wage labour outside the home, as well as the advent of socialism, was required for their liberation. The belief in emancipating effects of a fuller participation in employments outside the home was shared not only by Mills and Engels, but also by such contemporary feminist writers as Gilman (1898).

The passage of time has proved these views oversimplified. As Engels and Gilman correctly foresaw, there has been an increase in the labour force participation of women, particularly of married women, in most of the advanced industrialized countries. This has undoubtedly altered both the relationship between men and women and the very organization of society in many ways. However, while women's labour force participation has in many instances risen dramatically, it nonetheless remains the case that the types of jobs held by men and women, as well as the earnings they receive, continue to differ markedly.

The contribution of modern neoclassical analysis, which comprises the main focus of this essay, has been to subject to greater scrutiny and more rigorous analysis both women's economic roles within the family and the causes of gender inequality in economic outcomes. We examine each of these areas below. However, the interrelationships between the family and the labour market, most importantly the consequences of labour market discrimination against women for their roles and status in the family, have tended to be neglected. Nonetheless, the possible existence of such feedback effects is an important issue which is also considered here.

TIME ALLOCATION IN THE FAMILY CONTEXT. Prompted in part by their desire to understand the causes of the rising labour force participation of married women in the post-World War II period, economists extended the traditional theory of labour supply to consider household production more fully. The consequence was not only a better understanding of the labour supply decision, but also the development of economic analyses of the related phenomena of marriage, divorce and fertility.

The traditional theory of labour supply. The traditional theory of labour supply, also known as the labour–leisure dichotomy, was a simple extension of consumer theory. In this model, individuals maximize their utility, which is derived from market goods and leisure, subject to budget and time constraints. Where an interior solution exists, utility is maximized when the individual's marginal rate of substitution of income for leisure is set equal to the market wage.

Since in this model all time not spent in leisure is spent working, a labour supply (leisure demand) function may be derived with the wage, non–labour income, and tastes as its arguments. The well-known results of consumer theory are readily obtained. An increase in non–labour income, all else equal, increases the demand for all normal goods including leisure, inducing the individual to consume more leisure and to work fewer hours (the income effect). An increase in the wage, *ceteris paribus*, has an ambiguous effect on work hours due to two opposing effects. On the one hand, the increase in the wage is like an increase in income and in this respect tends to lower work hours due to the income effect. On the other hand, the increase in the wage raises the price (opportunity cost) of leisure inducing the individual to want to consume less of it, i.e., a positive substitution effect on work hours.

The theory sheds light on the labour force participation decision when it is realized that a corner solution will arise if the marginal rate of substitution of income for leisure at zero work hours is greater than the market wage. In this case, the individual maximizes utility by remaining out of the labour force. The impact of an increase in the wage is unambiguously to raise the probability of labour force participation, since, at zero work hours, there is no off-setting income effect of a wage increase.

Household production and the allocation of time. While the simple theory is sufficient for some purposes, it has limited usefulness for understanding the determinants of the gender division of labour in family and the factors influencing women's labour force participation, both at a point in time and trends over time. The key to addressing these issues is a fuller understanding and analysis of the household production process.

The first step in this direction was taken by Mincer (1962) who pointed out the importance, especially for women, of the three-way decision among market work, non-market work and leisure. He argued that the growth in married women's labour force participation was due to their rising real wages which increased the opportunity cost of time spent in non-market activities. But since, during the same period, the real wages of married men were also increasing, this must mean that the substitution effect associated with women's own real wage increases dominated the income effect associated with the growth in their husbands' real wages. While this part of the analysis could be accommodated in the framework of the traditional model, the next question Mincer raised could not. Why should the substitution effect dominate the income effect for women when such time series evidence as the declining work week suggested a dominance of the income effect over the substitution effect for men? The answer, according to Mincer, lay in women's responsibility for non-market production. The opportunities for substituting market time (through the purchase of market goods and services) are greater for time spent in home work than for time spent in leisure. Thus, since married women spend most of their non-market time on household production while men spend most of their on leisure, the substitution effect of a wage increase would be larger for married women than for men.

Becker (1965) advanced this process considerably by proposing a general theory of the allocation of time to replace the traditional theory of labour supply. In this and other work (summarized in Becker, 1981), he laid the foundations of what has become known as the 'new home economics', and spearheaded the development of economic analyses of time allocation, marriage, divorce and fertility. Interestingly, while Mincer opened a window on household production by distinguishing non-market work from leisure where the traditional labour supply theory had not done so, Becker was able to provide a further advance by again eliminating the distinction. However, while in the traditional labour supply model all non-market time is spent in leisure, in Becker's model all non-market time is spent in household production.

Specifically, Becker assumes that households derive utility from 'commodities' which are in turn produced by inputs of market goods and non-market time. It is interesting to note that Becker's 'commodities', produced and consumed entirely in the home, are the polar opposite of Marx's (1867) 'commodities', produced and exchanged in the market. Examples of Becker's commodities range from sleeping, which is produced with inputs of non-market time and of market goods like a bed, sheets, a pillow and a blanket (and in some cases, perhaps, a sleeping pill); to a tennis game that is produced by inputs of non-market time combined with tennis balls, a racquet, an appropriate costume, and court time; to a clean house produced with inputs of non-market time and a vacuum cleaner, a bucket and a mop, and various cleaning products.

In this model the production functions for the commodities are added to the constraints of the utility maximization problem. Utility can still be expressed as a function of the quantities of market goods and non-market time consumed; however, market goods and non-market time now produce utility only indirectly through their use in the production of commodities. Relative preferences for market goods versus home time depend on the ease with which the household can substitute market goods for non-market time in consumption and production. Substitution in consumption depends on their preferences for 'goods intensive' commodities – those produced using relatively large inputs of market goods in comparison to non-market time – relative to 'time intensive' commodities – those produced using relatively large inputs of non-market time in comparison to market goods. Substitution in production depends on the availability of more goods-intensive production techniques for producing the same commodity.

The usefulness of these ideas may be illustrated by considering the relationship of children to women's labour force participation. Children (especially when they are small) may be viewed as a time-intensive 'commodity'. Traditionally, it has been the mother who has been the primary care-giver. Moreover, while it is possible to substitute market goods and services for home time in caring for children (in the form of babysitters, day care centres, etc.), these alternative production techniques tend to be costly and it is sometimes difficult to make suitable alternative arrangements (in terms of quality, scheduling, etc.). Thus, at a point in time, the probability that a woman will participate in the labour force is expected to be inversely related to the number of small children present. Over time, the increase in women's participation rates has been associated with decreases in birthrates, as well as increases in the availability of various types of child care facilities, formal and informal. Changes in social norms (Brown, 1984) making it more acceptable to substitute for the time of parents in the care of young children may also have been a factor, although it is difficult to know, in this case as in others, the extent to which attitude change precedes or follows change in the relevant behaviour.

The relationship between labour force participation and fertility is reinforced by the impact of the potential market wage on women's fertility decisions. Greater market opportunities for women have increased the opportunity cost of children (in terms of their mothers' time inputs) and induced families to have fewer of them. Similarly, the greater demand for alternative child care arrangements (also due to the increased value of women's market time) has made it profitable for more producers to enter this sector.

The gender division of labour. In our discussion of children, we simply assumed that women tend to bear the primary responsibility for child care. However, the gender division of labour in the family is also an issue which the new home economics addresses. According to Becker (1981), the division of labour will be dictated by comparative advantage. To the extent that women have a comparative advantage in household and men in market production, it will be efficient for women to specialize to some extent in the former while men specialize in the latter. In this view, the increased output corresponding to this arrangement constitutes one of the primary benefits to marriage. Thus, women's increasing labour force participation is seen to have reduced the gains from marriage thereby contributing to the trend towards higher divorce and lower marriage rates.

The notion that, where families are formed, it is generally efficient and thus optimal for one member, usually the wife, to specialize to some extent in household production, while the husband specializes entirely in market work, has important consequences for women's status in the labour market. As we shall see in greater detail below, human capital theorists expect such a division of labour to lower the earnings of women relative to men, due to work force interruptions and smaller investments in market-oriented human capital. For this and other reasons, it is important to consider in greater detail whether such specialization is indeed as desirable for the family as the model suggests, and, by implication, whether it is apt to continue into the future. There are three points to be made in this regard.

First, such a division of labour may not be as advantageous for women as it is for men (Ferber and Birnbaum, 1977; Blau and Ferber, 1986). Thus, even if such a specialization is efficient in many respects, it may not maximize the family's utility. Indeed, when there are conflicts of interest or even pronounced differences in tastes between the husband and wife, the concept of the family utility function itself becomes less meaningful, since the way in which the preferences of family members can meaningfully be aggregated to form such a utility function has not been satisfactorily specified.

What are the disadvantages to women of their partial specialization in household production? First, in a market economy, such an arrangement makes them to a greater or lesser degree economically dependent on their husbands (see also Hartmann, 1976). This is likely to reduce their bargaining power relative to their husbands' in family decision-making, as well as to increase the negative economic consequences for them (and frequently for their children) of a marital break-up. In the face of recent increases in the divorce rate, such specialization has become a particularly risky undertaking. Second, as more women come to value their careers in much the same way as men do, both in terms of achievement and earnings, their specialization in housework to the point where it is detrimental to their labour market success is not apt to be viewed with favour by them. The utility-maximizing family will take these disadvantages into account in conjunction with the efficiency gains of specialization in allocating the time of family members.

If specialization is indeed considerably more productive than sharing of household responsibilities, it may be possible for this higher output to be used in part to compensate women for the disadvantages detailed above. However, it is likely that the gains to such specialization will shrink over time relative to the disadvantages of such an arrangement. As women anticipate spending increasingly more of their working lives in the labour market, their investments in market-oriented capital may be expected to continue to grow and their comparative advantage in home work relative to men to decline. Moreover, as the quality of the opportunities open to women in the labour market continues to improve, the disadvantages of specialization in home work in the form of foregone earnings and possibilities for career advancement will also rise. Thus, greater sharing of household responsibilities between men and women is likely to become increasingly prevalent, even if women in general retain a degree of comparative advantage in household production for some time to come.

A second point to be made with regard to women's specialization in household production is that comparative advantage does not comprise the only economic benefit to family or household formation (Ferber and Birnbaum, 1977; Blau and Ferber, 1986). Families and households also enjoy the benefits of economies of scale in the production of some commodities, as well as the gains associated with the joint consumption of 'public' goods. These benefits of collaboration would be unaffected by a reduction in specialization, even if those based on comparative advantage would be diminished. Other benefits of marriage or household formation may actually be increased by a more egalitarian division of household responsibilities. For example, two-earner families are in a sense more diversified and thus enjoy greater income security than families which depend on only one income. It may also be the case that the enjoyment derived from joint consumption is enhanced when the members of a couple have more in common, as when both participate in market and home activities. Thus, the incentives of couples to adhere to the traditional division of labour in order to enjoy the economic benefits of marriage may not be as strong as suggested when only the gains to comparative advantage are considered.

Finally, it is important to point out that women's comparative advantage for household production may stem not only from the impacts of biology and gender differences in upbringing and tastes, but also from the effect of labour market discrimination in lowering women's earnings relative to men's. Decisions based to some extent on such market distortions are not optimal from the perspective of social welfare even though they may be rational from the perspective of the family. The importance of such feedback effects are considered in greater detail below.

GENDER DIFFERENCES IN LABOUR MARKET OUTCOMES. We turn now to the contribution of economic analysis to an understanding of the causes of gender inequality in economic outcomes. Here, the consideration of gender issues has been accommodated principally through the development of new and interesting applications of existing theoretical approaches. The particular challenge posed to the theories by women's economic status is the existence of occupational segregation as well as earnings differentials by sex. Occupational segregation refers to the concentration of women in one set of predominantly female jobs and of men in another set of predominantly male jobs. The reasons for such segregation and its relationship to the male–female pay differential are two key questions to be addressed.

As in the case of the analysis of women's roles in the family, the catalyst for the development of these approaches was provided by external events. Some moderate degree of interest in this issue was generated in England by the World War I experience. Pursuant to the war effort, there was some substitution of women into traditionally male civilian jobs, although not nearly to the degree that there would be during World War II. Questions of the appropriate pay for women under these circumstances arose and stimulated some economic analyses of the gender pay differential – all of which gave a prominent causal role to occupational segregation. These included the work of Fawcett (1918) and Edgeworth (1922) (which provided the antecedents for Bergmann's (1974) overcrowding model, discussed below) and Webb (1919).

The analysis of gender differentials in the labour market received another impetus in the early 1960s, this time in the United States, with the development of the women's liberation movement and the passage of equal employment opportunity legislation. Two broad approaches to the issue have since evolved. First is the human capital view which lays primary emphasis on women's own voluntary choices in explaining occupation and pay differences. Second are a variety of models of labour market discrimination which share the common characteristic of placing the onus for the unequal outcomes on differential treatment of equally (or potentially equally) qualified men and women in the labour market. While these two approaches may be viewed as alternatives, it is important to point out that they are in fact not mutually exclusive. Both may play a part in explaining sex differences in earnings and occupations and the empirical evidence suggests that this is the case (see, e.g., Treiman and Hartmann, 1981). Indeed, as we shall see, their effects are quite likely to reinforce each other. We now consider each of these approaches in turn.

The human capital explanation. The human capital explanation for gender differences in occupations and earnings, developed by Mincer and Polachek (1974), Polachek (1981) and others, follows directly from the analysis of the family described above. It is assumed that the division of labour in the family will result in women placing greater emphasis than men on family responsibilities over their life cycle. Anticipating shorter and more discontinuous work lives as a consequence of this, women will have lower incentives to invest in market-oriented formal education and on-the-job training than men. Their resulting smaller human capital investments will lower their earnings relative to those of men.

These considerations are also expected to produce gender differences in occupational distribution. It is argued that women will choose occupations for which such investments are less important and in which the wage penalties associated with work force interruptions (due to the skill depreciation that occurs during time spent out of the labour force) are minimized. Due to their expected discontinuity of employment, women will avoid especially those jobs requiring large investments in firm-specific skills (i.e. skills which are unique to a particular enterprise), because the returns to such investments are reaped only as long as one remains with the firm. The shorter expected job tenure of women in comparison with that of men is also expected to make employers reluctant to hire women for such jobs, since employers bear some of the costs of such training. Thus, to the extent that it is difficult to distinguish more from less career-oriented women, the former may be negatively affected (see the discussion of statistical discrimination below).

More recently, Becker (1985) has further argued that, even when men and women spend the same amount of time on market jobs, women's homemaking responsibilities can still adversely affect their earnings and occupations. Specifically, he reasons that since child care and housework are more effort intensive than are leisure and other household activities, married women will spend less effort than married men on each hour of market work. The result will be lower hourly earnings for married women and, to the extent that they seek less demanding jobs, gender differences in occupations.

Thus, the human capital analysis provides a logically consistent explanation for gender differences in market outcomes on the basis of the traditional division of labour by gender in the family. An implication generally not noted by those who have developed this approach is that, to the extent that the human capital explanation is an accurate description of reality, it serves to illustrate graphically the disadvantages for women of responsibility for (specialization in) housework which we discussed above. To the extent that gender differences in economic rewards are not fully explained by productivity differences, we must turn to models of labour market discrimination to explain the remainder of the difference.

Models of labour market discrimination. As noted earlier, models of discrimination were developed to understand better the consequences of differences in the labour market treatment of two groups for their relative economic success. The starting point for models of labour market discrimination is the assumption that members of the two groups are equally or potentially equally productive. That is, except for any direct effects of the discrimination itself, male and female labour (in this case) are perfect substitutes in production. This assumption is made not because it is necessarily considered an accurate description of reality, but rather because of the question which discrimination models specifically address: why do equally qualified male and female workers receive unequal rewards? Such models may then be used to explain how discrimination can produce pay differentials between men and women in excess of what could be expected on the basis of productivity differences.

Theoretical work in this area was initiated by Becker's (1957) model of racial discrimination. Becker conceptualized discrimination as a taste or personal prejudice. He analysed three cases, those in which the tastes for discrimination were located in employers, co-workers and customers, respectively. As Becker pointed out, for such tastes to affect the economic status of a particular group adversely, they must actually affect the behaviour of the discriminators.

One may at first question, whether such a model is as applicable to sex as to race discrimination in that, unlike the case of racial discrimination, men and women are generally in close contact within families. However, the notion of socially appropriate roles, not explicitly considered by Becker, both sheds light on this question and establishes a link between his theory and occupational segregation. Thus, employers may be quite willing to hire women as secretaries, receptionists or nursery school teachers but may be reluctant to employ them as lawyers, college professors or electricians. Co-workers may be quite comfortable working with women as subordinates or in complementary positions, but feel it is demeaning or inappropriate to have women as supervisors or as peers. Customers may be happy to have female waitresses at a coffee shop, but expect to be served by male waiters at an elegant restaurant. They may be delighted to purchase women's blouses or even men's ties from female clerks, but prefer their appliance salesperson, lawyer or doctor to be a man. Such notions of socially appropriate roles are quite likely a factor in racial discrimination as well.

Employers with tastes for discrimination against women in particular jobs will be utility rather than profit maximizers. They will see the full costs of employing a woman to include not only her wages but also a discrimination coefficient ($d_r \geqslant 0$) reflecting the pecuniary value of the disutility caused them by her presence. Thus, they will be willing to hire women only at lower wages than men ($w_f = w_m - d_r$). If men are paid their marginal products, employer discrimination will result in women receiving less than theirs. When employers differ in their tastes for discrimination, the market-wide discrimination coefficient will be established at a level which equates supply and demand for female labour at the going wage. Thus the size of the male–female pay gap will depend on the number of women seeking work, as well as on the number of discriminatory employers and on the magnitude of their discrimination coefficients.

One of the particular interesting insights of Becker's (1957) analysis is that profit-maximizing employers who do not themselves have tastes for discrimination against women will nonetheless discriminate against them if their employees or customers have such prejudices. Male employees with tastes for discrimination against women will act as though their wage is reduced by $d_e (\geqslant 0)$, their discrimination coefficient, when they are required to work with women. Thus, they will consent to be employed with women only if they receive a higher wage – in effect a compensating wage differential for this unpleasant working condition.

The obvious solution to this problem from the employer's point of view is to hire a single-sex work force. If all employers followed such a strategy, male and female workers would be segregated by firm, but there would be no pay differential. Yet, as Arrow (1973) has noted, employers who have made a personnel investment in their male workers, in the form of recruiting, hiring or training costs, may not find it profitable to discharge all their male employees and replace them with women, even if the latter become available at a lower wage. While such considerations cannot explain how occupations initially become predominantly male, it can shed light on one factor – the necessity of paying a premium to discriminatory male workers to induce them to work with women – contributing to the perpetuation of that situation. Further, where women do work with discriminating male workers, a pay differential will result.

Some extensions of Becker's (1957) analysis of employee discrimination are also of interest. Bergmann and Darity (1981) point out that employers may be reluctant to hire women into traditionally male jobs because of adverse effects on the morale and productivity of the existing male work force. Given the replacement costs discussed above this would be an important consideration. As Blau and Ferber (1986) note, employee discrimination may also directly lower women's productivity relative to that of men. For example, since much on-the-job training is informal, if male supervisors or coworkers refuse or simply neglect to instruct female workers in these job skills, women will be less productive than men workers. Similarly, the exclusion of women from informal networks and mentor-protégé relationships in traditionally male occupations can diminish their access to training experiences and even to the information flows needed to do their jobs well.

Customer discrimination can also reduce the productivity of female relative to male employees. Customers with tastes for discrimination against women will act as if the price of a good or service provided by a woman were increased by their discrimination coefficient, $d_c (\geqslant 0)$. Thus, at any given selling price, a female employee will bring in less revenue than a male employee. Women either will not be hired for such jobs or will be paid less. The potential applicability of this model is not only to conventional sales jobs. In our 'service economy', a large and growing number of jobs entail personal contact between workers and customers/clients.

Models based on the notion of tastes for discrimination are consistent with occupational segregation, but do not necessarily predict it. If wages are flexible, it is altogether possible that such discrimination will result in lower pay for women, but little or no segregation. However, if discriminatory tastes against women in traditionally male pursuits (on the part of employers, employees and/or customers) are both strong and prevalent, women may tend to be excluded from these areas. On the other hand, even if such segregation occurs, it may or may not be associated with gender pay differentials. In the presence of sufficient employment opportunities in the female sector, equally qualified women may earn no less than men.

The relationship between occupational segregation and earnings differentials is further clarified in Bergmann's (1974) overcrowding model. If for whatever reason – labour market discrimination or their own choices – potentially equally qualified men and women are segregated by occupation, the wages in male and female jobs will be determined by the supply and demand for labour in each sector. Workers in male jobs will enjoy a relative wage advantage if the supply of labour is more abundant relative to demand for female than for male occupations. Such 'crowding' of female occupations can also widen differentials between male and female jobs that would exist in any case due to women's smaller human capital investments or to employers' reluctance to invest in their human capital.

Perhaps the most serious question that has been raised about the Becker analysis, particularly of the case of employer discrimination, is its inability to explain the persistence of discrimination in the long run. Assuming that tastes for discrimination vary, the least discriminatory firms would employ the highest proportion of lower-priced female labour. They would thus have lower costs of production and, under constant returns to scale, could in the long run expand and drive the more discriminatory firms out of business (Arrow, 1973).

This issue has provided the rationale, at least in part, for the elaboration of alternative models of discrimination, including the statistical discrimination model discussed below. Others, not considered here, have emphasized non-competitive aspects of labour markets (e.g. Madden, 1973). However, this criticism of the Becker model is a double-edged sword in that it has led some economists to doubt that labour market discrimination is responsible, in whole or part, for gender inequality in economic rewards. Yet it is important to recognize that the phenomenon which we seek to understand is intrinsically complex. From this perspective it is not surprising that no easy solution has been found to the question of why discrimination has persisted. Similarly, the various models of discrimination, each emphasizing different motivations and different sources of this behaviour, need not be viewed as alternatives. Rather, each may serve to illuminate different aspects of this complex reality.

As noted above, models of statistical discrimination were developed by Phelps (1972) and others to shed light on the persistence of discrimination. They do so by imputing a motive for employer discrimination which, in an environment of imperfect information, is consistent with profit maximization. Statistical discrimination occurs when employers believe that, all else equal, women are on average less productive or less stable workers than men. The common perception that women are more likely to quit their jobs than men would be an example of this.

As in the employer taste for discrimination model, statistical discrimination would cause employers to prefer male workers and to be willing to hire women only at a wage discount. A difference is, however, that in this case male and female workers are not perceived to be perfect substitutes. Further, if women are viewed as less stable workers, there will tend to be substantive differences between male and female jobs, with the former emphasizing firm-specific skills to a greater extent. This is essentially the picture painted by the dual market model (Piore, 1971; Doeringer and Piore, 1971). In this view, women tend to be excluded from the 'primary sector', jobs requiring firm-specific skills and thus characterized by relatively high wages, good promotion opportunities and low turnover rates, and to find employment in the 'secondary sector', comprised of low paying, dead-end jobs in which there tends to be considerable turnover.

Like the human capital model, the notion of statistical discrimination provides a link between women's roles in the family and gender differences in market outcomes. However, the connection is in terms of differences in the treatment of men and women, rather than differences in the choices they make.

One crucial issue is of course whether employers' perceptions are indeed correct. If they are, as Aigner and Cain (1977) have pointed out, then in some sense labour market discrimination as conventionally defined does not exist: women's lower wages are due to their lower productivity. Nonetheless, the employer's inability to distinguish between more and less career-oriented women certainly creates an inequity for the former vis-à-vis their male counterparts.

On the other hand, employer perceptions may be incorrect or exaggerated. Differentials based on such erroneous views undoubtedly constitute discrimination as economists have defined it. However, as Aigner and Cain (1977) have persuasively argued, gender differentials based on employers' mistaken beliefs are even less likely to persist in the long run than those based on employers' tastes for discrimination. Nonetheless, in times of rapid changes in gender roles, there may be considerable lags in employers' perceptions. Employers' incorrect views could also magnify the impact of employee or customer discrimination, as when such discrimination is either less extensive or more susceptible to change than employers believe.

A potentially more powerful role for statistical discrimination is provided in models which allow for feedback effects, for example Arrow's (1973) model of perceptual equilibrium. In this case, men and women are assumed to be potentially perfect substitutes in production, but employers believe that, for example, women are less stable workers (Arrow, 1976). They thus allocate women to jobs where the cost of turnover is minimized and women respond by exhibiting the unstable behaviour employers expect. The employers' assessments are correct *ex post*, but are in fact due to their own discriminatory actions. This equilibrium will be stable even though an alternative equilibrium is potentially available in which women are hired for jobs which are sufficiently rewarding to inhibit instability. More generally, any form of discrimination can adversely affect women's human capital investments and labour force attachment by lowering the market rewards to this behaviour (see also, Blau, 1984; Blau and Ferber, 1986; Ferber and Lowry, 1976; and Weiss and Gronau, 1981).

CONCLUSION. We have considered the contributions of neoclassical economic theory to our understanding of women's labour supply decisions, the gender division of labour within the family, and male–female differences in labour market outcomes. With the introduction of feedback effects, the separate strands of neoclassical theory analysing women's economic roles in the family and their labour market outcomes may be more tightly woven together. The causation runs not only from women's roles within the family to their resulting economic success, as human capital theorists emphasize, but also from their treatment in their labour market to their incentives to invest in market-oriented human capital and to participate in the labour force continuously. Thus, even a small amount of discrimination at an early stage of the career can have greatly magnified effects over the work life. While it is unlikely that labour market discrimination created the traditional division of labour between men and women in the family, it could certainly help to perpetuate it.

However, it is also the case that increasing opportunities for women in the labour market create powerful incentives to reduce gender differences in family roles and in labour market behaviour. At the same time, women's increased attachment to the labour force, due not only to these increased opportunities but also to changes in household technology and in tastes, may be expected to increase their market productivity and hence their earnings directly, and also to reduce statistical discrimination against them. Similarly, the movement of women into traditionally male jobs has the potential not only to increase the wages of those who become so employed, but to reduce overcrowding and increase wages in female jobs as well. Thus, just as a fuller understanding of the interrelationships between women's roles in the family and their status in the labour market helps us to understand the persistence of gender inequality in economic outcomes, it also enables us to appreciate how changes in either one of these spheres, or both, can induce a mutually reinforcing process of cumulative change. Recent signs of progress in reducing the pay gap in many of the advanced industrialized countries may well signal the beginnings of such a process.

In our emphasis upon the interdependence of women's status within the family and the labour market, we have in some respects returned to our starting point, for this conclusion bears a close resemblance to the views of the 19th-century observers which we reviewed at the outset. However, it is also clear that neoclassical economic theory has enhanced our understanding of the causes of gender differences in both the family and the labour market, as well as allowing us to comprehend better the links between the two sectors.

BIBLIOGRAPHY

Aigner, D. and Cain, G. 1977. Statistical theories of discrimination in labor markets. *Industrial and Labor Relations Review* 30(2), January, 175–87.

Arrow, K. 1973. The theory of discrimination. In *Discrimination in Labor Markets*, ed. O. Ashenfelter and A. Rees, Princeton: Princeton University Press.

Arrow, K. 1976. Economic dimensions of occupational segregation: comment I. *Signs* 1(3), Part II, 233–7.

Becker, G. 1957. *The Economics of Discrimination*. 2nd edn, Chicago: University of Chicago Press, 1971.

Becker, G. 1965. A theory of the allocation of time. *Economic Journal* 75, September, 493–517.

Becker, G. 1981. *A Treatise on the Family*. Cambridge, Mass.: Harvard University Press.

Becker, G. 1985. Human capital, effort, and the sexual division of labor. *Journal of Labor Economics* 3(1), January, 533–58.

Bergmann, B. 1974. Occupational segregation, wages and profits when employers discriminate by race or sex. *Eastern Economic Journal* 1, April/July, 103–10.

Bergmann, B. and Darity, W., Jr. 1981. Social relations in the workplace and employer discrimination. *Proceedings of the Thirty-Third Annual Meeting of the Industrial*

Relations Research Association. ed. B.D. Dennis, New York: Industrial Relations Research Association, 155–62.

Blau, F. 1984. Discrimination against women: theory and evidence. In *Labor Economics: Modern Views,* ed. W. Darity, Boston: Kluwer-Nijhoff Publishing.

Blau, F. and Ferber, M. 1986. *The Economics of Women, Men, and Work.* Englewood Cliffs, NJ: Prentice-Hall.

Brown, C. 1984. Consumption norms, work roles, and economic growth. Paper presented at the conference on Gender in the Workplace, Washington, DC: Brookings Institution, November.

Doeringer, P. and Piore, M. 1971. *Internal Labor Markets and Manpower Analysis.* Lexington, Mass.: D.C. Heath and Co.

Edgeworth, F. 1922. Equal pay to men and women for equal work. *Economic Journal* 32, December, 431–57.

Engels, F. 1884. *The Origin of the Family, Private Property and The State.* New York: International Publishers, 1972.

Fawcett, M.G. 1918. Equal pay for equal work. *Economic Journal* 28, March, 1–6.

Ferber, M. and Birnbaum, B. 1977. The 'new home economics': retrospects and prospects. *Journal of Consumer Research* 4(1), June, 19–28.

Ferber, M. and Lowry, H. 1976. The sex differential in earnings: a reappraisal. *Industrial and Labor Relations Review* 29(3), April, 377–87.

Gilman, C. 1898. *Women and Economics: a study of the economic relation between men and women as a factor of social evolution.* New York: Harper & Row, 1966.

Hartmann, H. 1976. Capitalism, partriarchy and job segregation by sex. *Signs* 1(3), Part II, 137–69.

Madden, J. 1973. *The Economics of Sex Discrimination.* Lexington, Mass.: D.C. Heath and Co.

Marx, K. 1867. *Capital: A Critique of Political Economy,* Vol. I. New York: International Publishers, 1967.

Mill, J.S. 1869. *The Subjection of Women.* 4th edn, London: Longmans, Green, Reader & Dyer, 1878; New York: Stokes, 1911.

Mincer, J. 1962. Labor force participation of married women. In *Aspects of Labor Economics,* National Bureau of Economic Research, Princeton: Princeton University Press.

Mincer, J. and Polachek, S. 1974. Family investments in human capital: earnings of women. *Journal of Political Economy* 82(2), Part II, S76–S108.

Phelps, E. 1972. The statistical theory of racism and sexism. *American Economic Review* 62(4), September, 659–61.

Piore, M. 1971. The dual labor market: theory and implications. In *Problems in Political Economy: an urban perspective,* ed. D. Gordon, Lexington, Mass.: D.C. Heath and Co.

Polachek, S. 1981. Occupational self-selection: a human capital approach to sex differences in occupational structure. *Review of Economics and Statistics* 63(1), February, 60–69.

Treiman, D. and Hartmann, H. (eds) 1981. *Women, Work, and Wages: equal pay for jobs of equal value.* Washington, DC: National Academy Press.

Webb, B. 1919. *The Wages of Men and Women: should they be equal?* London: Fabian Bookshop.

Weiss, Y. and Gronau, R. 1981. Expected interruptions in labour force participation and sex-related differences in earnings growth. *Review of Economic Studies* 48(4), October, 607–19.

Gifts

C.A. GREGORY

A gift, according to the *Concise Oxford Dictionary*, is a 'voluntary transference of property; thing given, present, donation'. For most economists, especially those familiar only with industrial capitalist economies, that is all that need be said on the matter: it is obvious what gift exchange is and there is nothing to be explained. The only problem the phenomenon of exchange poses for the economist is that of 'value' and this arises in the context of commodity exchange.

For the anthropologist, however, the phenomenon of exchange poses questions about the nature of gift exchange. These lie at the centre of the discipline and the topic has been the subject of much theoretical debate. Anthropologists stress that while gifts appear to be voluntary, disinterested and spontaneous, they are in fact obligatory and interested. It is this underlying obligation that anthropologists seek to understand: What is the principle whereby the gift received has to be repaid? What is there in the thing given that compels the recipient to make a return?

It is clear that the one economic category – exchange – means fundamentally different things to different people and that these contrary perceptions of the exchange process have given rise to quite distinct theoretical traditions. The reasons for this are to be found in the historical conditions which gave rise to the development of the academic disciplines of economics and anthropology. The history of economic thought must be understood with reference to the development of mercantile and industrial capitalism in Europe; the development of anthropological theorizing, on the other hand, must be situated in the context of the imperialist expansion of European capitalism and especially the colonial consquest of Africa and the Pacific towards the end of the 19th century. The fact that economists have been preoccupied with commodity exchange whilst anthropologists have been primarily concerned with gift exchange simply reflects the fact that the modern European economy is organized along very different lines from the indigenous economies of Africa, the Pacific and elsewhere. The data anthropologists have collected from these countries over the past one hundred years has revolutionized our understanding of tribal economy and the theory of the gift; their theoretical reflections on this data constitutes a major contribution to the theory of comparative economic systems and also to the theory of development and underdevelopment. This anthropological literature takes us far beyond the superficial dictionary definition of the gift and raises important questions about the seemingly unrelated issue of shell money; interestingly it also bring us back to the original meaning of the word as 'payment for a wife' and 'wedding' found in *The Oxford Dictionary of English Etymology*.

Anthopological accounts of gift giving first began appearing towards the end of the 19th century; by the end of World War I a large quantity of data had been collected. The most spectacular accounts came from the Kwakiutl Indians of the northwest coast of America and from the Melanesian Islanders of the Milne Bay District of Papua New Guinea. Among the Kwakiutl vast amounts of valuable property (mainly blankets) are ceremonially destroyed in a system called 'potlatch' (Boas, 1897). In the potlatch system the prestige of an individual is closely bound up with giving: a would-be 'big man' or 'chief' is constrained to give away or to destroy everything he possesses. The principles of rivalry and antagonism are basic to the system and people compete with one another, each trying to outgive the other in order to gain prestige. The status and rank of individuals and clans is determined by this war of property. In Papua New Guinea, the classic home of competitive gift exchange, the instruments of 'gift warfare' are food (Young, 1971) and shells of various shapes and sizes (Leach and Leach, 1983). These are not destroyed but transacted by status seekers according to complicated sets of rules which we are only now beginning to understand. Most Papua New Guinea societies are without any form of ascribed status and the egalitarian ideology of these societies means that competitive gift giving is primarily concerned with the maintenance of equal status rather than dominance. Staying equal is, as Forge (1972) has pointed out, an extremely onerous task requiring continual vigilance and effort: perfect balance is impossible to achieve as the temporal dimension of gift exchange necessarily introduces status inequalities. Perhaps the most complicated gift exchange system in Melanesia is the Rossel Island 'monetary system'. This was first described by Armstrong (1924) and has recently been restudied by Liep (1983). On Rossel Island there are two kinds of 'shell money' *ndap* and *ko*. A single unit of *ndap* is a polished piece of *spondylus* shell a few millimetres thick, having an area varying from 2 to 20 square centimetres and roughly triangular in shape. A single unit of *ko* consists of ten pieces of *chama* shell of roughly the same size and thickness with a small hole in the centre for binding them together. Each shell group contains some forty-odd hierarchical divisions. What is unusual about these divisions is that they have rank rather than value, that is, they are ordinally related rather than cardinally related. For example, the relationship of a big *ndap* shell to a small one is analogous to that between an ace of hearts and a two of hearts rather than that between a dollar and a cent.

The publication of Armstrong's (1928) ethnography of Rossel Island and Malinowski's (1922) now classic description of an inter-island gift exchange system called *kula* sparked off a debate about the nature of 'shell money' which still rages today. This debate is kept alive not from an antiquarian interest in 'archaic' money systems but because these gift exchange systems are still flourishing despite their incorporations into the world capitalist economy (MacIntyre and Young, 1982; Gregory, 1980, 1982). On Rossel Island, for example, not only are the *ndap* and *ko* shell still transacted as gifts according to the complicated rules of old, but the demand for Rossel Island *chama* shells for use in the flourishing *kula* gift exchange system of neighbouring islands has transformed Rossel Island into a major commodity producer and exporter of *chama* shells (Liep, 1981; 1983).

These facts raise conceptual questions about the difference between gift exchange and commodity exchange, and theoretical and empirical questions about the nature of the interaction between them. Neoclassical economics answers these questions within a framework that employs the universalist and subjectivist concept 'goods', a category which, by definition, cannot explain the particularist and objective nature of gift and commodity exchange (Gregory, 1982). A 'gift' therefore becomes a 'traditional good' and highly questionable psychological criteria are used to distinguish this from a 'modern good'. For example, Einzig argues that 'the intellectual standard' of people in tribal societies 'is inferior and their mentality totally different from ours' (1948, p. 16); Stent and Webb (1975, p. 524) argue that 'traditional' consumers in Papua New Guinea are on the bliss point of their indifference curves. A further difficulty economists have with the problem of contrasting economic systems -and this is not restricted to neoclassical economic thought – is the habit of beginning an argument with an analysis of barter in an 'early and rude state of society'. The barter economies of these theories are figments of a Eurocentric imagination that bear no resemblance at all to actual tribal economies. Economic anthropologists have been making this point for over fifty years but without much success (Malinowski, 1922, pp. 60–61; Polanyi, 1944, pp. 44–5). What is needed, then, is an empirically based theory of comparative economy. The foundations of such a theory were laid by Marx (1867) but the rise to dominance of neoclassical theory precluded any further development of the theory of comparative economy within the economics discipline. The theoretical advances have come from without and have been made by anthropologists, sociologists and economic historians.

The outstanding contribution to the 20th-century literature is undoubtedly Mauss's *The Gift: Forms and Functions of Exchange in Archaic Societies*, first published in French in 1925 as 'Essai sur le don, forme archaique de l'echange' in Durkheim's journal, *L'Année Sociologique*. Mauss (1872–1950) was Durkheim's nephew and became a leading figure in French sociology after his uncle's death. His essay on the gift is a remarkable piece of scholarship. Not only did he survey all extant ethnographic data on gift giving from Melanesia, Polynesia, northwest America and elsewhere, he also examined the early literature from Ancient Rome, the Hindu classical period and the Germanic societies. His essays conclude with a critique of western capitalist society by drawing out the moral, political, economic and ethnic implications of his analysis.

The key to understanding gift giving is apprehension of the fact that things in tribal economies are produced by non-alienated labour. This creates a special bond between a producer and his/her product, a bond that is broken in a capitalist society based on alienated wage-labour. Mauss's analysis focused on the 'indissoluble bond' between things and persons in gift economies and argued that 'to give something is to give a part of oneself' (1925, p. 10). Gifts therefore become embodied with the 'spirit' of the giver and this 'force' in the thing given compels the recipient to make a return. This does not exist in our system of property and exchange which is based on a sharp distinction between things and persons, that is, alienation (1925, p. 56). The wage-labourer in a capitalist society gives a 'gift' which is not returned (1925, p. 75). Capitalism for Mauss then was a system of non-reciprocal gift exchange; a system where the recipients of a gift were under no obligation to make a return gift.

This analysis of the wage-labour contract under capitalism has a Marxian ring about it. However, Mauss was no revolutionary and he drew very different policy conclusions from his analysis of the wage-labour relation. He argued for a welfare capitalism where the state, through its social legislation, provided recompense to the workers for their gifts.

A feature of Mauss's work, and indeed a feature of much early theorizing about the gift, was the evolutionary framework within which the ethnographic data was analysed. The tribal economies studied by anthropologists were seen as living fossils from European pre-history, hence the use of terms such as 'archaic' and 'primitive'. These early theorists, then, were only concerned with the intellectual contribution this data could make to the study of comparative economy. To the extent that they were concerned with the welfare of living people it was the welfare of their European countrymen and women; they were not concerned with policies for the development of tribal peoples.

The other outstanding theorist in this evolutionary tradition was another Frenchman, Claude Lévi-Strauss. His theory of the gift is contained in his *The Elementary Structures of Kinship* (1949). Like Mauss's *The Gift*, Lévi-Strauss's book is an encyclopaedic survey of the ethnographic literature. Its central focus is marriage. In line with a long tradition in anthropology he conceptualizes this as an exchange of women. However, Lévi-Strauss's innovation is to argue that women are the 'supreme gift' and that the incest taboo is the key to understanding gift exchange. The virtual universal prohibition on marriage between close kin, he argues, is the basis of the obligation to give, the obligation to recieve, and the obligation to repay.

Lévi-Strauss's theory is an analytical synthesis of literally thousands of ethnographic accounts from the Australian Aborigines, the Pacific and Asia. The original or most elementary form of gift exchange, according to Lévi-Strauss, is 'restricted' exchange where the moieties of a population exchanged sisters at marriage; the second form is 'delayed' exchange where a women is given this generation and her daughter returned the next; the most advanced form is 'generalized' exchange where one clan gives women to another clan but never receives any in return, the closure of the system being brought about by a circle of giving. In the movement from one state to another, extra spheres of gift exchange are developed as symbolic substitutes for women. These are needed to maintain the ever widening marriage alliances brought about by the shift from restricted to generalized exchange. This movement from marriage to exchange is an aspect of an opposing movement from exchange to marriage. Lévi-Strauss sees a continuous transition from war to exchange, and from exchange to intermarriage as effecting a transition from hostility to alliance, and from fear to friendship.

Lévi-Strauss's theory has attracted considerable critical attention and has been described by his principal opponent as 'in large measure fallacious' (Leach, 1970, p. 111). Whatever its shortcomings his theory nevertheless manages to establish the important link between gift giving and the social organization of kinship and marriage. In other words, he has established a relationship between the obligation to give and receive gifts and the biological and social basis of human reproduction.

While Lévi-Strauss was developing his theory of the gift, an economic historian, Karl Polanyi, was approaching the problem from an altogether different perspective in his classic study, *The Great Transformation* (1944). His problem was the analysis of the emergence of the 'self-regulating market' and in order to grasp the 'extraordinary assumptions' underlying such a system he developed a theory of comparative economy based on ethnographic and historical evidence.

Polanyi correctly identified the Smithian 'paradigm of the bartering savage', which is accepted as axiomatic by many social scientists, as a barrier to an adequate understanding of non-market economy. In a tribal economy, notes Polanyi, the propensity to truck, barter and exchange does not appear: there is no principle of labouring for remuneration, the idea of profit is banned and giving freely is acclaimed a virtue. How, then, is production and distribution ensured, he asks. Polanyi devoted only ten pages of his book to answering this question but his insights have had a significant impact on anthropological thought (see e.g. Dalton and Kocke, 1983). Tribal economy, he argued, is organized in the main by two principles; *reciprocity* and *redistribution*. Reciprocity works mainly in regard to the sexual organizations of society, that is, family and kinship, and it is that broad principle which helps to safeguard both production and family sustenance. Redistribution refers to the process whereby a substantial part of all the produce of the society is delivered to the chief who keeps it in storage. This is redistributed at communal feasts and dance when the villagers entertain one another as well as neighbours from other districts.

Reciprocity and redistribution are able to work because of the institutional patterns of *symmetry* and *centricity*. Tribes, says Polanyi, are subdivided along a symmetrical pattern and this duality of social organization forms the 'pendant' on which the system of reciprocity rests. (Lévi-Strauss's restricted exchange model of gift exchange also presupposes dual social organization.) The institution of territorial centricity forms the basis of redistribution.

To these two principles, Polanyi adds a third – *householding*, production for use with *autarky* as its basis – and argues that all economic systems known to us up to the end of feudalism were organized on either the principle of reciprocity, or redistribution, or householding, or some combination of the three. These made use of the patterns of symmetry, centricity and autarky, with custom, law, magic and religion cooperating to induce the individual to comply with the rules of behaviour.

Capitalism, in Polanyi's view, implies the wholesale destruction of these principles and the establishment of free markets in land, money and labour run according to the profit principle. Like Marx, Polanyi sees the emergence of free wage-labour as a commodity as the crucial defining characteristic of capitalism. Labour was the last of the markets to be organized in England and both Marx and Polanyi saw the enclosure movements, especially those at the time of the industrial revolution, as central to this process. Polanyi is more precise in his historiography however. He sees the Poor Law Reform of 1834, which did away with the final obstruction to the functioning of a free labour market, as the beginning of the era of the self-regulating market.

Postwar developments in the theory of the gift have built on the foundations laid by Mauss, Lévi-Strauss and Polanyi. The influential contributions of Godelier (1966, 1973), Meillassoux (1960, 1975) and Sahlins (1972) in particular are heavily indebted to these theorists whose ideas they attempt to develop in the light of Marx's theory of comparative economy. Recent empirical research (e.g. Strathern, 1971; Young, 1971; Leach and Leach, 1983) has provided, and will continue to provide, the basis for new comparative insights into the theory of the gift (Forge, 1972).

An important postwar development in the theory of the gift has been the analysis of the impact of colonization and capitalist imperialism on tribal societies.

For the early contributors to this literature the problem was how to explain the process of destruction brought about by capitalism. Paul Bohannan (1959), an American anthropologist with fieldwork experience in West Africa, developed a theory of the impact of money on a tribal economy based on Polanyi's ideas. Commodity exchange, according to Polanyi, is a 'uni-centric economy' because of the nature of 'general purpose money' which reduces all commodities to a common scale. In a tribal society, by way of contrast, the economy is 'multi-centric': there are multiple spheres of exchange, each with 'special purpose' money that could only circulate within that sphere. Among the Tiv of West Africa, for example, there were three spheres of exchange. The first sphere contained locally produced foodstuffs, tools and raw materials; the second sphere contained non-market 'prestige' goods such as slaves, cattle, horses, prestige cloth (*tuguda*) and brass rods; the third sphere contained the 'supreme gift', women. Bohannan's argument was that the general purpose money introduced by the colonial power reduced all the various spheres to a single sphere, thereby destroying them.

Bohannan's theory was applied to the analysis of the impact of colonization in other parts of the world, Papua New Guinea among others (e.g. Meggitt, 1971). While Bohannan's theory makes an important conceptual advance in comparative economy it is now recognized that his theory of the impact of colonization has a number of shortcomings as a description of what happened in West Africa (see Dorward, 1976); furthermore, it does not post the problem to be explained. Today, it is now realized, the problem is not, 'How was the tribal gift economy destroyed?' but rather, 'Why has it flourished under the impact of colonization?'

Take the famous potlatch system, for example. The establishment of a canning industry in the area in 1882 led to a rapid increase in the per capita income of the Kwakiutl, a rapid increase in the number of blankets that could be purchased, and hence a rapid increase in the number of blankets given away in potlatch ceremonies. Before the canning industry was established the largest potlatch consisted of 320 blankets, but during the period 1930–1949 potlatch ceremonies involving as many as 33,000 blankets were recorded (Codere, 1950, p. 94). This rapid growth in potlatch occurred despite the institution in 1885 of a law prohibiting the ceremonies. The system has not retained its pristine form, however. Legal and other influences have brought about a variety of outward changes in form but the original purpose of the system still persists: the presentation of a claim to a specific social status (Drucker and Heizer, 1967. pp. 47–52).

In Papua New Guinea, to take another example, the establishment of one of the world's largest copper mines in Bougainville has stimulated a flourishing import of shells into the island. The shells are manufactured by the Langalanga people of western Malaita in the Solomon Islands some 1550 kilometres away. The mine has given the people of Bougainville income earning opportunities unavailable to other islanders and they are able to outbid other purchasers for the Langalangan shells. The Langalangans, for their part, have oriented all their production away from local purchasers to the Bougainville market. In Bougainville the shells are used mostly by the Siwai people who give them as marriage gifts and traditional gift exchanges involving land and pigs; they are also used as ornaments (see Connell, 1977).

This symbiosis between commercialization and gift exchange is found elsewhere in Papua New Guinea. The famous *kula* gift exchange system in the Milne Bay District still persists despite more than one hundred years of colonization (Leach and Leach, 1983). Milne Bay is now something of an economic backwater, its heyday of commercial development being the gold mining era early in this century. Labour is probably one of the area's most important exports today. These migrants maintain close contact with their villages and often send home money, some of which is channelled into *kula* transactions. The migrants, who are senior public servants, entrepreneurs, and politicians, also take their culture with them to the urban areas. The result is that the *kula* ring now extends to Port Moresby, where Mercedes cars and telephones have replaced outrigger canoes and conch shell horns as the principal means of communication.

There is some empirical evidence that appears to contradict the theses that gift exchange has effloresced under the impact of colonization. Prior to the European colonization of West Africa and India these countries were part of a flourishing international cowrie-shell economy. The shells (*cyprae moneta*) were produced in the Maldive Islands of the Indian Ocean and were shipped to West Africa and India where they were used primarily as instruments of exchange but also for religious and ornamental purposes (Heimann, 1980). The cowrie shells were an important and profitable item of international trade in the mercantile era. They were purchased very cheaply in the Maldives – where they grow in great profusion – and exported to India or Europe. The merchants of Europe re-exported them to West Africa where they used them to purchase slaves.

This international shell economy, which had persisted for many centuries, began to collapse around the middle of the 18th century. The supply of shells began to increase rapidly and their price began to fall. For example, in 1865, 1636 tons of cowries were imported into Lagos; by 1878 imports totalled 4472 tons, which was the peak; ten years later imports had fallen to a mere ten tons. Cowrie shell prices (measured in pounds sterling) collapsed over this period. In 1851 two thousand cowries cost 4s. 9d. but by 1876–79 the price had fallen to 1s. 0d. (Hopkins, 1966; Johnson, 1970). By the beginning of the 20th century cowrie shells were no longer current; their place had been taken by the fiat money of the respective colonial government.

This evidence of the destructive impact of colonization only appears to contradict the 'efflorescence of gift exchange' thesis however. The reality is otherwise and the evidence demonstrates the point that exchange is a social relationship which varies depending upon the political and historical context. Objects, such as shells, have many uses, and the historical fact that they have been used as instruments of gift exchange here, as objects of commodity exchange there, and as currency in other places has caused great confusion in the literature. The issue is further confused by the fact that in contemporary Papua New Guinea for example, a shell may be used in all three roles during the same day. The issue can be clarified somewhat by inquiring into the primary role of an exchange object and situating this historically and comparatively in terms of the mode of reproduction of a society. The uniqueness of a place such as Papua New Guinea becomes apparent from this perspective. Papua New Guinea, unlike West Africa or India, was not part of an international mercantile economy prior to European colonization, and as a result commercial exchange transactions were a subordinate and insignificant part of total exchange. Pre-colonial India and West Africa, on the other hand, were highly commercialized: land and labour were freely transacted as commodities with gold and silver commodity monies being used as the principal instruments of exchange. The colonization of West Africa transformed it from being a stateless commodity economy to a state controlled one. This involved a suppression of the stateless commodity monies and their substitution by state fiat money. In India a similar process occurred as the British Government established strong centralized administrative control over numerous weak, corrupt princely states. The destruction of the cowrie shell economy must be seen as part of this process of transition from stateless commodity money to state fiat money. Cowries were the small change of gold and silver. The relationship of cowries to gold and silver, then, finds its counterpart in the relationship of pennies to shillings and pounds. However, whereas the relationship between gold and cowries is determined by production conditions and changes from day to day, the relationship between pounds and pennies is set by government decree and never changes. Where a stable government exists, and the value of money remains constant, it is obvious that a merchant or consumer will prefer to use the latter.

The shells used in West Africa and India, then, were used primarily as instruments of commodity exchange and the term 'shell money' is correct in this context. However, the shells used in the exchange systems of Melanesia and elsewhere were not used as the small change of commodity monies in pre-colonial times. They were used primarily as instruments of gift-exchange and the term 'shell gifts' is more appropriate in this context. Colonization has resulted n the efflorescence of gift-exchange in Melanesia because the colonial state brought an end to tribal warfare and facilitated a transition from fighting with weapons to fighting with gifts. These gifts take the form of women, shells, food and even money nowadays. These gifts do not involve a 'voluntary transference of property' as the *Oxford English Dictionary* would have it. They are the results of obligations imposed on people struggling to achieve status and wealth in a situation where indigenous systems of land tenure, kinship and marriage are being incorporated into an international economic and political order, over which tribespeople and peasants have little control.

BIBLIOGRAPHY

Armstrong, W.E. 1924. Rossel Island money: a unique monetary system. *Economic Journal* 34, 423–9.

Armstrong, W.E. 1928. *Rossel Island: An Ethnological Study*. Cambridge: Cambridge University Press.

Boas, F. 1897. *Kwakiutl Ethnography*. Ed. H. Codere, Chicago: University of Chicago Press, 1966.

Bohannan, P. 1959. The impact of money on an African subsistence economy. *Journal of Economic History* 19(4), 491–503.

Codere, H. 1950. *Fighting with Property*. New York: Augustin.

Connell, J. 1977. The Bougainville connection: changes in the economic context of shell money production in Malaita. *Oceania* 48(2), December, 81–101.

Dalton, G. and Köcke, J. 1983. The work of the Polanyi group: past, present and future. In S. Ortiz (ed.), 1983.

Dorward D.C. 1976. Precolonial Tiv trade and cloth currency. *The International Journal of African Historical Studies* 9(4), 576–91.

Drucker, P. and Heizer, R.F. 1967. *To Make My Name Good: A Reexamination of the Southern Kwakiutl Potlatch*. Los Angeles: UCLA Press.

Einzig, P. 1948. *Primitive Money*. London: Eyre and Spottiswoode.

Forge, A. 1972. The Golden Fleece. *Man* 7(4), 527–40.

Godelier, M. 1966. *Rationality and Irrationality in Economics*. London: New Left Books, 1972.

Godelier, M. 1973. *Perspectives in Marxist Anthropology*. Cambridge: Cambridge University Press, 1977.

Gregory, C.A. 1980. Gifts to men and gifts to god: gift exchange and capital accumulation in contemporary Papua. *Man* 15(4), 626–52.

Gregory, C.A. 1982. *Gifts and Commodities*. London: Academic Press.

Heimann, J. 1980. Small change and ballast: cowry trade and usage as an example of Indian Ocean economic history. *South Asia* 3(1), 48–69.

Hopkins, A.G. 1966. The currency revolution in south-west Nigeria in the late nineteenth century. *Journal of the Historical Society of Nigeria* 3(3), 471–83.

Johnson, M. 1970. The cowrie currencies of West Africa. *Journal of African History* 11(1), 17–49; 11(3), 331–53.

Leach, E.R. 1970. *Lévi-Strauss.* London: Fontana.

Leach, J.W. and Leach E. (eds) 1983. *The Kula.* Cambridge: Cambridge University Press.

Lévi-Strauss, C. 1949. *The Elementary Structures of Kinship.* Trans., London: Eyre and Spottiswoode, 1969.

Liep, J. 1981. The workshop of the Kula: production and trade of shell necklaces in the Louisade Archipelago. *Folk og Kultur* 23, 297–309.

Liep, J. 1983. Ranked exchange in Yela (Rossel Island). In J.W. Leach and E. Leach (eds), *The Kula*, Cambridge: Cambridge University Press.

MacIntyre, M. and Young, M. 1982. The persistence of traditional trade and ceremonial exchange in the Massim. In *Melanesia: Beyond Diversity*, ed. R.J. May and Hank Nelson, Canberra: Australian National University.

Malinowski, B. 1922. *Argonauts of the Western Pacific.* New York: E.P. Dutton.

Marx, K. 1867. *Capital.* Vol. 1: *A Critical Analysis of Capitalist Production.* Moscow: Progress Publishers, n.d.; New York: International Publishers, 1967.

Mauss, M. 1925. *The Gift.* London: Routledge and Kegan Paul, 1974.

Meggitt, M.J. 1971. From tribesman to peasants: the case of the Mae-Enga of New Guinea. In *Anthropology in Oceania*, ed. L.R. Hiatt and C.J. Jayawardena, Sydney: Angus and Robertson.

Meillassoux, C. 1960. Essai d'interprétation du phénomène économique dans les sociétés traditionelles d'auto-subsistance. *Cahiers d'Etudes Africaines* 4, 38–67.

Meillassoux, C. 1975. *Maidens, Meal and Money.* Cambridge: Cambridge University Press, 1981.

Ortiz, S. (ed.) 1983. *Economic Anthropology: Topics and Theories.* New York: University Press of America.

Polanyi, K. 1944. *The Great Transformation.* New York: Rinehart.

Sahlins, M. 1972. *Stone Age Economics.* Chicago: Aldine.

Stent, W.R. and Webb, L.R. 1975. Subsistence, affluence and market economy in Papua New Guinea. *Economic Record* 51, 522–38.

Strathern, A.J. 1971. *The Rope of Moka.* Cambridge: Cambridge University Press.

Young, M.W. 1971. *Fighting with Food: Leadership, Values and Social Control in a Massim Society.* Cambridge: Cambridge University Press.

Health Economics

VICTOR R. FUCHS

Health economics is an applied field in which empirical research predominates. It draws its theoretical inspiration principally from four traditional areas of economics: finance and insurance, industrial organization, labour, and public finance. Some of the most useful work employs only elementary economic concepts but requires detailed knowledge of health technology and institutions. Policy-oriented research plays a major role, and many important policy-relevant articles are published in journals read by physicians and others with direct involvement in health (e.g. Enthoven, 1978).

The systematic application of economic concepts and methods to the health field is relatively recent. In a comprehensive bibliography of health economics based on English language sources through 1974 (Culyer, Wiseman and Walker, 1977), fewer than 10 per cent of the entries are dated prior to 1963. In that year a seminal article by Arrow (1963) discussed many of the central theoretical problems, and a few years later a major monograph based on modern econometric methods appeared (M.S. Feldstein, 1967).

The literature prior to 1963, thoroughly reviewed by Klarman (1965), was primarily institutional and descriptive. Significant contributions include discussions of US medical care institutions (Davis and Rorem, 1932; Ginzberg, 1954; Somers and Somers, 1961), mental illness (Fein, 1958), public health (Weisbrod, 1961), and the British National Health Service (Lees, 1961). The first US conference on health economics was held in 1962 (Mushkin, 1964), the first international conference in 1973 (Perlman, 1974), and the first widely adopted textbook did not appear until 1979 (P. Feldstein, 1983).

The field divides naturally into two distinct, albeit related, subjects: the economics of health *per se*, and the economics of medical care. The latter has received much more attention from economists than the former, but it is useful to consider health first because the demand for medical care is, in part, derived from the demand for health, and because many of the theoretical and empirical problems in the economics of medical care arise because of difficulties in measuring, valuing, and analysing health.

HEALTH. *Concepts, measures, and valuation.* Health is multidimensional. With the exception of the dichotomy between life and death, there is no completely objective, invariant ordering across individuals or populations with respect to health. Health can be defined according to criteria such as life expectancy, capacity for work, need for medical care, or ability to perform a variety of personal and social functions. Economists' attempts to measure and analyse differences in health across individuals and populations have typically focused on mortality (especially age-specific and age-adjusted death rates), morbidity (as evidenced by symptoms or diagnosed illnesses), or self-evaluations of health status. There have also been several attempts to take account simultaneously of mortality, morbidity, and health-related limitations by weighting years of life according to illness and disability.

Despite claims that health is more important than any other goal and that human life is priceless, economists note that individuals make tradeoffs between health and other goals and that the valuation of health (including life itself) is necessary for the rational allocation of scarce resources. The two leading approaches to the valuation of human life are 'discounted future earnings' and 'willingness to pay'. Rice (1966) estimated the costs of various illnesses as the sum of direct expenditures for medical care, the foregone earnings attributable to morbidity, plus the cost of premature death, which is assumed to be equal to the present value of future earnings. Willingness to pay is usually defined as the amount of money an individual would require (pay) in exchange for an increase (decrease) in the risk of death. This approach is preferred on theoretical grounds (Schelling, 1968; Mishan, 1971; Jones-Lee, 1974), but difficult to estimate empirically. Two oft-quoted studies that infer the value of life from risk-related wage differentials differ five-fold in their estimates (Thaler and Rosen, 1976; Viscusi, 1978).

The determinants and consequences of variations in health. Health is sometimes modelled as a dependent and sometimes as an independent variable, although frequently causality runs in both directions. Health has been studied as a function of medical care, income, education, age, sex, race, marital status, environmental pollution, and personal behaviours such as cigarette smoking, diet, and exercise. Grossman (1972) developed a model of the *demand* for health – both as a consumption commodity that enters directly into utility and as an investment commodity that contributes to the production of other goods and services. In his model, variables such as age and schooling affect the optimal level of health by changing its shadow price. Most studies that make health the dependent variable take a *production function* approach (Auster, Leveson and Sarachek, 1969) with health depending on income, medical care, education, and other inputs.

There is a strong positive correlation between income and health among less developed countries, but, *ceteris paribus*, the relationship tends to disappear at higher levels of income. This may reflect a high income elasticity of demand for other goods and services that adversely affect health, or may result from stress or other harmful side effects of earning more money. Also, as the average level of income rises, those diseases that stem from poverty tend to disappear and those that are not related to income form an increasing share of the burden of illness.

Advances in medical care such as the introduction of antibiotics have had significant effects on mortality and morbidity, but holding constant the state of medical science, the marginal effect of an increase in the quantity of medical care on health appears to be small in developed countries. Elimination of financial barriers to care, as in the British National Health Service, has not been accompanied by a reduction in the traditional mortality differentials across social classes. In all countries health is strongly correlated with years of schooling, but the explanation is not firmly established. Education may increase the efficiency with which individuals produce health. Alternatively, some third variable, such as time preference, may simultaneously affect schooling and health (Farrell and Fuchs, 1982). Marital status and health are strongly correlated (more so for men than for women), but the causality probably runs both ways. Other interesting correlations include those between wife's education and husband's health, and between parents' education and children's health.

Health has frequently been used as an independent variable to explain labour force participation, particularly at older ages. Not only do retired persons frequently cite poor health as the reason for retirement, but current workers who report a health limitation are more likely to withdraw from work in subsequent years. Health status has also been used to explain wages, productivity, school performance, fertility, and the demand for medical care. The results are often sensitive to the particular measure of health that is used, but the direction of effect generally confirms *a priori* predictions.

Health as a commodity. Health is both an intermediate commodity that affects production and a final commodity that affects utility directly. When health is included in the utility function several questions arise. Do standard theories regarding risk aversion and time discounting with respect to income apply equally to health? How is the marginal utility of income affected by changes in health levels? Both income and health are, in part, exogenously determined by initial endowments, and these endowments are likely to be positively correlated. The endogenous aspects of income and health are subject to many forces, some that may produce positive correlation and some the reverse. Although utility is a function of health, there can be a considerable difference between maximizing health (as measured, say, by life expectancy) and maximizing utility. The value of a given reduction in the probability of death (as evidenced by willingness to pay) is higher when the probability is high than when it is low. Thus programmes to treat the seriously ill at high cost per death averted are often preferred to preventive programmes that avert deaths at lower costs.

Many health problems have a significant genetic component, while others are attributable to unfavourable experiences during the foetal period, at delivery, or in childhood. The resulting heterogeneity among individuals poses a variety of problems for analysis and policy. Unobserved heterogeneity can bias inferences about the effects of health interventions, especially in studies based on non-experimental data (Rosenzweig and Schultz, 1982). For instance, if people born with weak hearts are less inclined to exercise vigorously, the true effect of exercise on heart disease may be less than that inferred from observational studies. When heterogeneity is observable, the problem becomes primarily one of incorporating both efficiency and distributional considerations into policy analysis. Whose health should be considered in setting standards for air pollution or occupational safety? Under what circumstances should persons in poor health be required to pay actuarially fair health-insurance premiums?

The externalities associated with health have attracted considerable discussion. Analysis of the benefits of vaccination or the costs of pollution is fairly straightforward, but other externalities are less conventional. Individuals may derive utility from knowing that the poor sick among them are receiving medical care. They could attempt to achieve this through voluntary philanthropy, but the amount purchased is likely to be less than socially optimal because each individual's contribution would maximize private utility, ignoring the effects on others (Pauly, 1971). These health-centred philanthropic externalities are sometimes invoked to explain the widespread subsidization of medical care for the poor through national health insurance or other institutional arrangements in preference to general income redistribution.

MEDICAL CARE. Medical care accounts for more than 10 per cent of gross national product in the United States and approximately that much in several other developed countries. By contrast, restraints on input prices and quantities result in about a 6 per cent share in the United Kingdom. The effect on health of such wide variation in medical care expenditures is not clear. Governments in all countries play a large role as regulators, subsidizers, direct buyers, or producers of medical care. Economists have paid considerable attention to the reasons for and consequences of these governmental interventions. One useful way of categorizing economic research on medical care is to relate it to the older, better established areas of specialization that furnish most of the concepts used in health economics. Some studies, to be sure, draw their inspiration from and enrich more than one area.

Finance and insurance. Risk aversion and uncertainty about future health create a demand for health insurance (Arrow, 1963; Phelps, 1973). Once insurance is in place, moral hazard leads to over-utilization of medical care (Pauly, 1968). These two observations have generated a huge amount of research on the role of health insurance in health services (Rosett, 1976). The effect of insurance on the demand for care is better understood than is the demand for insurance itself. The usual risk aversion story, for example, cannot explain why many people purchase policies that cover the first dollar of expenditure but have a ceiling beyond which expenditures are not covered.

Asymmetry in information about potential demand for medical care creates another analytical and policy problem for insurance markets. When the consumer knows a great deal more about his health status and preferences than does the insurance company, adverse selection can lead to a breakdown in the free market in insurance. Group insurance is a typical solution, with participation achieved by compulsion, direct subsidies, or indirect subsidies via the tax system. Compulsory health insurance is also advocated to deal with the free rider problem. The possibility of free riders implies that even countries without explicit national insurance have public or private programmes that provide some kind of implicit universal coverage.

Many research methods, including a large-scale prospective controlled experiment (Newhouse et al., 1981) have been used to study the effect of insurance on the demand for care. As a result, few empirical propositions in economics have been as well established as the downward slope of the demand curve for medical care. Nevertheless, precise estimates of price elasticity (net of insurance) are difficult to obtain, in part because the features of some insurance policies – deductibles, varying coinsurance rates, and limits on indemnity payments – imply that the consumer faces a variable price under uncertainty (Keeler, Newhouse et al., 1977).

One solution to the risk aversion/moral hazard dilemma is for insurance to be provided in the form of contingent claims. For each identifiable condition the insured would be covered for care up to the point where the marginal benefit equals the marginal cost. Consumers, when well, may prefer that type of contract, but once sick they will want any care that has positive marginal benefit. Furthermore, the physician may want to provide care up to the point where marginal benefit is zero. The insurer's task is to enforce the tighter standard on the patient and the physician. This will often require some deception or nonprice rationing which patients can try to offset by strategic behaviour. The resulting loss of trust and less than candid exchange of information between patient and physician can adversely affect the production of care.

Industrial organization. Probably the largest range of problems and the largest volume of research in health economics falls in the area of industrial organization. There are many different, though related, industries to study: for example, physicians' services, hospitals, drugs, nursing homes, dental care. The topics covered range from licensure and regulation (Peltzman, 1973) to price discrimination (Kessel, 1958) and nonprice rationing (Friedman, 1978) to technological innovation and diffusion (Russell, 1979). Organization in the narrow sense of the term is of considerable interest because of the admixture of public, private nonprofit, and for-profit hospitals, and because the modes of physician practice range from solo fee-for-service to huge groups of salaried physicians. Behaviour inside the organization is particularly important in analysing nonprofit hospitals (the dominant form of organization in the United States) because the trustees, the administrator, the attending physicians, and the house staff all have considerable power and frequently have different objectives.

Medical care is, in many respects, the quintessential service industry. First, it is extremely difficult to measure output. As a result, standard economic accounts show little or no gain in productivity over time despite large expenditures for research and development and rapid technological change. Second, the consumer frequently plays a major role in the production process. This means not only that the value of the patient's time is part of the cost of care, but that the patient's knowledge, skill, and motivation, and the level of trust between patient and physician can affect the outcome of the care process. Third, the physician often knows a great deal more than the patient does about the patient's need for various types of care. This asymmetry of information has been used to explain the unwillingness of most societies to rely solely on competitive market forces to insure appropriate behaviour by physicians. Fourth, because output cannot be stored and short-run supply is relatively inelastic, productivity is sensitive to changes in demand. The stochastic nature of the demand for hospital care results in excess capacity and the problem is exacerbated by systematic variation in demand according to day of week and month of year.

Despite the difficulty of measuring output, numerous estimates of hospital short-run and long-run cost functions have been made (Lave and Lave, 1970). In the short run, marginal cost is below average cost in most hospitals. Long-run average cost tends to fall with increasing size until about 200 beds and then tends to be constant with a possible rise after a size of about 500 beds. Most researchers have defined output as a day of care or as a hospital admission. Standardization for patient mix can only be done incompletely, and failure to measure the effects of care on health is a serious limitation. To be sure, changes in health are only one aspect of output. A consideration fraction of resources in hospitals and nursing homes is devoted to *caring* for people who are in pain or who are disabled, regardless of whether their health status is (or even can be) improved. Also, a significant fraction of physicians' time is devoted to providing information and validation independently of any intended or actual effect on health status.

The problem of measuring output also increases the difficulty of analysing the demand for care. Additional complications result from the possibility that physicians may shift the patient's demand (Sloan and Feldman, 1978; Evans, 1974). Some economists concede that physicians have the power to shift demand, but believe that it is sufficiently and uniformly exploited so that further shifting can be ignored. Others argue that the amount of shifting varies with exogenous changes in the physician/population ratio. This follows from a model in which physicians maximize utility as a function of income, leisure, and 'correct practice'. The empirical evidence is consistent with this model (Fuchs, 1978), but it is consistent with other explanations as well.

Perhaps less controversial is the proposition that physicians can and do change their patients' demand for hospital care. One example of this is in the United States is the lower hospital utilization by patients enrolled in prepaid group practice plans such as Kaiser Permanente (Luft, 1981). Patients pay a single annual premium for total care regardless of the quantity of services used; physicians typically receive a salary or a share of the net income after the hospital and other costs have been paid. An even more spectacular change in hospital utilization emerged when Medicare (the US publicly funded insurance for the elderly) changed from retrospective cost-reimbursement to prospective payment per admission in a particular diagnosis-related group. In just two years the average length of stay of patients 65 years of age and older in short-term general hospitals fell 12 per cent without any change in conventional demand variables.

The demand for care usually increases as health worsens, but not always. For instance, an elderly person who is in good general health may demand a variety of surgical interventions for specific problems such as hip replacement or lens implantation; a person of the same age who is in bad health may not.

Problems in measuring output imply problems in measuring price. An alternative approach to the estimation of price change is to measure change in the total cost of treating a defined illness or medical condition. A price index calculated by this method was found to rise more rapidly than the conventional medical care price index (Scitovsky, 1967), possibly as a result of unmeasured changes in output. Technological advances may have increased the cost of care by making it possible for the physician to do more things for the patient.

Economic research on drugs falls into two main categories that reflect differing policy concerns in the United States before and after the 1962 Kefauver-Harris Amendments to the Pure Food and Drug Act. Prior to the amendments, attention was focused on price fixing, price discrimination (manufacturers' prices vary in several ways, depending upon the type of customer), and on alleged socially wasteful expenditures for product differentiation. Since 1962 economic research has shifted to the volume and character of innovation. A decrease in the flow of new drugs has been attributed to the increased cost of satisfying regulatory requirements (Grabowski et al., 1978). Despite the questions raised by economists regarding the net benefit of tighter controls, other countries have tended to follow the policy direction set by the United States in 1962.

In recent years in the United States and many other countries, the major health policy questions have revolved around efforts to contain the cost of care. Most economists have argued for greater reliance on market mechanisms and less on regulation (Zeckhauser and Zook, 1981), but an intricate web of social, political, and economic considerations seems to preclude a pure laissez-faire approach to health (Fuchs, 1974).

Labour economics. Much of the research on the economics of *health* comes out of labour economics, especially the human capital branch. Concerning medical care, labour economists have been primarily interested in the demand and supply of various health occupations. Numerous studies of the earnings of physicians have mostly confirmed the results of a pioneering study (Friedman and Kuznets, 1945) that physicians, on average, realize an excellent return on their investment in medical education. Research on choice of speciality and location, however, does not support any simple model of physicians as income maximizers. Some specialities appear to have more intrinsic appeal than others, and the wide geographical variation in the physician/population ratio in the United States is not primarily the result of variation in fees or income. Changes in physician distribution by speciality or location, however, do conform closely to predictions based on standard utility maximization (Newhouse et al., 1982).

Research on nurses in the United States has focused heavily on an alleged persistent 'shortage'. One explanation is that the principal employers of nurses – hospitals – have monopsony power (Yett, 1975). Faced with rising supply curves, hospitals equate the marginal cost of nurses with their marginal revenue product and set the wage on the supply curve. The 'shortage' simply reflects the fact that the hospital administrator would like to hire more nurses at the going wage, but has no incentive to raise the wage.

Public finance. Ever since Bismarck introduced compulsory health insurance to Germany in 1883, the financing of health care has been of increasing concern to governments and to economists who specialize in public finance. Even in the United States, the last major holdout against national health insurance, government pays directly for about 42 per cent of all health-care expenditures, and pays indirectly for an appreciable additional share through tax exemptions and allowances. Numerous reasons have been offered as to why governments pay for health care, but each has its shortcomings.

All explanations that are health related (e.g., 'health is a right', 'the government has an obligation to reduce or eliminate class differentials in mortality') are suspect because in Bismarck's time there was virtually no connection between medical care and health, and even today the connection at the margin is highly circumscribed. The explanation that medical care is a 'merit' good seems circular. Governments are said to subsidize 'merit' goods, but the only way to identify them is by the presence of government subsidies. The standard externality-public good explanation applies to the prevention and treatment of communicable diseases, but this accounts for only a small fraction of health care. Subsidies in other industries such as agriculture or the merchant marine can frequently be explained by pressure from producers, but government subsidies for health care have usually been opposed by the producers of care.

Subsidies for health care are frequently defended on the grounds that it is unfair to allow the distribution of health care to be determined by the distribution of income. Many economists counter by saying it would be more efficient to redistribute income and then let the poor decide how much of the increase they want to devote to health care and how much to other goods and services. The crux of the problem seems to be that the amount of redistribution that society wants to make to an individual may depend on the individual's need for care. The greater the need, the greater society's willingness to redistribute. It may be more efficient to combine the determination of need with the redistribution via the delivery of care than to separate the functions.

One special problem arises in this field from the proposition that in order to reduce inequality, governments should limit the amount of care that individuals can obtain. This view is virtually inescapable once a government is committed to equality in health care and constrained to keep the health budget within limits set by general budgetary considerations. No country can afford to provide health care for all its citizens up to the point where the marginal benefit is zero.

Economists spend a great deal of time deploring the fact that no country shows much interest in evaluating the outcome of medical care. It might be more fruitful to try to explain why this is so. No doubt part of the answer is that evaluation is very difficult, but part may be related to the symbolic and political role that medical care plays in modern society. When governments, insurance companies, or employers promise to finance all necessary and appropriate care, they typically have to introduce implicit constraints to keep from going bankrupt. A thorough evaluation would make these constraints explicit and could create a great deal of dissatisfaction.

Future research. Because health economics is predominantly applied and policy-oriented, future research will undoubtedly be influenced by the changing nature of health problems and by developments in medical science. Thus, it is reasonable to expect to see more attention to the health problems of the elderly – chronic illness and the need for long-term care. Among the non-elderly, health problems stemming from substance abuse are large and growing in importance. The new understanding of the role of genetic factors in disease creates dramatic opportunities for screening and intervention, but these opportunities will pose problems of enormous complexity for analysis and policy. The gap between what is technically possible and what is economically feasible will probably widen; thus, the demand for guidance concerning the efficiency and equity implications of alternative health policies is likely to grow. Further development of health economics as an established field of inquiry will help to meet that demand.

BIBLIOGRAPHY

Arrow, K.J. 1963. Uncertainty and the welfare economics of medical care. *American Economic Review* 53(5), December, 941–73.

Auster, R., Leveson, I. and Sarachek, D. 1969. The production of health, an explanatory study. *Journal of Human Resources* 4, Fall, 412–36.

Culyer, A.J., Wiseman, J. and Walker, A. 1977. *An Annotated Bibliography of Health Economics.* London: Martin Robertson; New York: St. Martin's Press, 1977.

Davis, M.M. and Rorem, C.R. 1932. *The Crisis in Hospital Finance.* Chicago: University of Chicago Press.

Enthoven, A.E. 1978. Consumer-choice health plan. *New England Journal of Medicine* 298, 23 March and 30 March.

Evans, R.G. 1974. Supplier-induced demand: some empirical evidence and implications, In *The Economics of Health and Medical Care*, ed. M. Perlman, London: Macmillan.

Farrell, P. and Fuchs, V.R. 1982. Schooling and health: the cigarette connection. *Journal of Health Economics* 1(3), December, 217–30.

Fein, R. 1958. *Economics of Mental Illness.* New York: Basic Books.

Feldstein, M.S. 1967. *Economic Analysis for Health Service Efficiency.* Amsterdam: North-Holland.

Feldstein, P. 1983. *Health Care Economics.* 2nd edn, New York: John Wiley & Sons.

Friedman, B. 1978. On the rationing of health services and resource availability. *Journal of Human Resources* 13 (Supplement), 57–75.

Friedman, M. and Kuznets, S. 1945. *Income from Independent Professional Practice*, General Series No. 45, New York: National Bureau of Economic Research.

Fuchs, V.R. 1974. *Who Shall Live? Health, Economics, and Social Choice*. New York: Basic Books.

Fuchs, V.R. 1978. The supply of surgeons and the demand for operations. *Journal of Human Resources* 13 (Supplement), 35–56.

Ginzberg, E. 1954. What every economist should know about health and medicine. *American Economic Review* 44(1), March, 104–19.

Grabowski, H.G., Vernon, J.M. and Thomas, L.G. 1978. Estimating the effects of regulation on innovation: an international comparative analysis of the pharmaceutical industry. *Journal of Law and Economics* 21(1), April, 133–63.

Grossman, M. 1972. *The Demand for Health: A Theoretical and Empirical Investigation*. New York: National Bureau of Economic Research.

Jones-Lee, M. 1974. The value of changes in the probability of death or injury. *Journal of Political Economy* 82(4), July-August, 835–49.

Keeler, E.B., Newhouse, J.P. et al. 1977. Deductibles and demand: a theory of the consumer facing a variable price schedule under uncertainty. *Econometrica* 45(3), April, 641–55.

Kessel, R.A. 1958. Price discrimination in medicine. *Journal of Law and Economics* 1(2), October, 20–53.

Klarman, H.E. 1965. *The Economics of Health*. New York: Columbia University Press.

Lave, J.R. and Lave, L.B. 1970. Hospital cost functions: estimating cost functions for multi-product firms. *American Economic Review* 60(3), June, 379–95.

Lees, D.S. 1961. *Health Through Choice*. Hobart Paper No. 14, London: Institute of Economic Affairs.

Luft, H.S. 1981. *Health Maintenance Organizations: Dimensions of Performance*. New York: John Wiley & Sons.

Mishan, E.J. 1971. Evaluation of life and limb: a theoretical approach. *Journal of Political Economy* 79(4), 687–705.

Mushkin, S.J. (ed.) 1964. *The Economics of Health and Medical Care*. Ann Arbor: University of Michigan Press.

Newhouse, J.P. et al. 1981. Some interim results from a controlled trial of cost sharing in health insurance. *New England Journal of Medicine* 305, 17 December, 1501–7.

Newhouse, J.P. et al. 1982. Does the geographical distribution of physicians reflect market failure? *Bell Journal of Economics* 13(2), Autumn, 493–505.

Pauly, M.V. 1968. The economics of moral hazard: comment. *American Economic Review* 58(3), June, 531–6.

Pauly, M.V. 1971. *Medical Care at Public Expense, A Study in Applied Welfare Economics*. New York: Praeger.

Peltzman, S. 1973. An evaluation of consumer protection legislation: the 1962 drug amendments. *Journal of Political Economy* 81(5), September-October, 1049–91.

Perlman, M. (ed.) 1974. *The Economics of Health and Medical Care*. London: Macmillan.

Phelps, C. 1973. *The Demand for Health Insurance: A Theoretical and Empirical Investigation*. Santa Monica: The Rand Corporation, No. R-1054–OEO.

Rice, D.P. 1966. Estimating the Cost of Illness. Washington, DC: USDHEW, Public Health Service Publication, 947–6.

Rosenzweig, M.R. and Schultz, T.P. 1982. The behavior of mothers as inputs to child health: the determinants of birth weight, gestation, and rate of fetal growth. In *Economic Aspects of Health*, ed. V.R. Fuchs, Chicago: University of Chicago Press.

Rosett, R.N. (ed.) 1976. *The Role of Health Insurance in the Health Services Sector.* New York: National Bureau of Economic Research.

Russell, L.B. 1979. *Technology in Hospitals.* Washington, DC: Brookings.

Schelling, T.C. 1968. The life you save may be your own. In *Problems in Public Expenditure Analysis*, ed. S.B. Chase, Washington, DC: Brookings.

Scitovsky, A.A. 1967. Changes in the costs of treatment of selected illnesses, 1951–65. *American Economic Review* 57(4), December, 1182–95.

Sloan, F., and Feldman, R. 1978. Competition among physicians. In *Competition in the Health Care Sector: Past, Present, and Future*, ed. W. Greenberg, Washington, DC: Federal Trade Commission.

Somers, H.M. and Somers, A.R. 1961. *Doctors, Patients, and Health Insurance.* Washington, DC: Brookings.

Thaler, R. and Rosen, S. 1976. The value of saving a life: evidence from the labor market. In *Household Production and Consumption*, ed. N.E. Terleckyj, New York: National Bureau of Economic Research.

Viscusi, K.W. 1978. Labour market valuations of life and limb: empirical evidence and policy implications. *Public Policy* 26(3), Summer, 359–86.

Weisbrod, B.A. 1961. *Economics of Public Health.* Philadelphia: University of Pennsylvania Press.

Yett, D.E. 1975. *An Economic Analysis of the Nurse Shortage.* Lexington, Mass.: Heath.

Zeckhauser, R. and Zook, C. 1981. Failures to control health costs: departures from first principles. In *A New Approach to the Economics of Health Care*, ed. Mancur Olson, Washington, DC: American Enterprise Institute for Public Policy Research.

Household Production

RICHARD A. BERK

Even a casual survey of recent developments in neoclassical economics will reveal a self-conscious intellectual imperialism. Substantive areas traditionally the private preserve of other social science disciplines have experienced significant incursions: fertility, voting behaviour, crime, education, and others. But perhaps the most visible and influential expansion of neoclassical economics has been into the formation, functioning, and dissolution of families. Under the banner of the 'new home economics', conventional utility maximization with fixed preferences claims to provide explanations for an enormous variety of decisions made by households and their members.

There is little doubt that these developments have gained a number of adherents. Among economists, much of this success can be attributed to the obvious appeal of creatively moving a well-known theoretical apparatus to a novel setting. But, there have also been converts from outside economics. For them, perhaps more important than the merits of a new home economics is the absence of persuasive alternatives; the new home economics is effectively directed at the soft underbellies of other social-science disciplines.

In particular, family sociology has conventionally applied conceptual frameworks placing instrumental activities in the market and expressive activities in the home (e.g. Blood and Wolf, 1960). It does not occur to most sociologists, therefore, to think about households as 'productive', nor to see household activities as the concrete manifestation of production functions; home life is about affect. In addition, many sociologists are inductively inclined, preferring to work up from data not down from theory. Their literature, as a result, is rich in facts that are not easily placed under a single theoretical rubric; perhaps knowing more has meant knowing less.

DO FAMILIES REALLY OPTIMIZE? General criticisms of utility maximization are well known and need not be reviewed here (e.g. Hollis and Nell, 1975; Leibenstein, 1976; Lesourne, 1977; Simon, 1978). For at least two reasons, however, utility maximization may be especially problematic within the family setting.

130

First, all neoclassical economic perspectives on households require that households optimally allocate their resources. This assumption has to be supported in part with the argument that inefficient households either will not form or will not survive (Becker, 1981, pp. 40–2, 66–82, 219–36); households form and dissolve within a 'marriage market', which performs the same functions as any other free market.

However, as Blaug (1980, p. 119) has observed in a somewhat different context,

> to survive, it is only necessary to be better adapted to the environment that one's rivals, and we can no more establish from natural selection that surviving species are perfect than we can establish from economic selection that surviving firms are profit maximizers.

At best, therefore, only family partnerships better suited to the environment need survive; the survivors are not required to be optimally adapted. In other words, the assumption of optimization cannot be justified by recourse to market forces.

Second, there is some scepticism about whether families can adjust quickly to a changing environment. Schultz (1974, p. 6) observes,

> The typical family that we observe, especially in rich countries, lives in an economy in which economic conditions are and have been changing substantially over time. As these changes occur, thinking in terms of economics, there are presumably responses – responses in the age at which marriage occurs, responses in spacing and number of children, and responses in the amount of family resources devoted to investment in children. Furthermore, before these families have fully adjusted and have arrived at an equilibrium with respect to any given economic change, additional and unexpected changes will have occurred. Thus, the families we observe are seldom, if ever, in a state of economic equilibrium.

WHOSE WELLBEING IS BEING MAXIMIZED? Almost all neoclassical perspecticves on the family assume that the decision-making unit is the family as a whole, and that there is a single household utility function. In the face of considerable skepticism (e.g. Nerlove, 1974; Mancer and Brown, 1980; McElroy and Horney, 1981; Witte, Tauchen and Long, 1984), Becker's use of 'altruism' (1981, pp. 172–201) is perhaps the best justification.

However, according to Ben-Porath (1982, p. 54), Becker's formulation requires some very strong assumptions, such as perfect information, despite powerful incentives for household members not to reveal accurately how well off they are. In a similar manner, Pollak (1985, p. 599) argues that Becker's results do not depend on altruism per se, but on 'implicit assumptions about power, or equivalently, about the structure of the bargaining game'. Perhaps most important, there is lots of evidence that *ongoing* conflict and coercion characterize a significant number of households. For example, one is a very long way from a single utility function when a recent report from the United States Attorney General's Office asserts (Hart, 1984, p. 11),

Battery is a major cause of injury to women in America. Nearly a third of female homicide victims are killed by their husbands or boyfriends. Almost 20 percent of all murders involve family relationships. Ascertainable reported cases of child abuse and neglect have doubled from 1976 to 1981. In addition to one million reported cases of child maltreatment, there may be another million unreported cases. Untold numbers of children are victims of sexual abuse, and uncounted older persons suffer abuse.

WHAT ABOUT JOINT PRODUCTION? Given the linear budget constraint, Pollak and Wachter (1975) point out that joint production is effectively excluded from the recent neoclassical approaches to the family. Thus, it is impossible to obtain psychic gratification and a concrete household commodity from the same household activity (e.g. cooking a meal). Berk and Berk (1983, p. 388) observe that joint production could be incorporated with a nonlinear budget constraint, but *additional assumptions* would have to be made. For example, one would need to specify through the appropriate elasticities how responsive to changes in family money income each of the joint products happened to be. It is very unlikely that data could be found to inform meaningfully such an exercise.

The key question, therefore, is whether joint production is common, and what little research that exists (e.g. Berk and Berk, 1979, pp. 237–250), coupled with everyday experience, suggests that it is widespread. One has only to introspect a bit about the nature of child care.

ARE THERE CONSTANT RETURNS TO SCALE? The assumption of constant returns to scale also create difficulties. In recent statements (e.g. Becker, 1981), household commodities are rather general entities such as prestige, health, esteem and the like. There is no reason to assume that for these outputs, constant returns to scale hold. Indeed, common experience suggests quite the opposite.

For example, doubling the amount of food one ingests will affect one's health in rather different ways depending on how much food one ordinarily ingests. For malnourished individuals, a rather dramatic improvement in health will probably be seen. For well-fed individuals, little improvement will result, and depending on the kind of food eaten, health could actually decline. In short, the linear budget constraint is once again inappropriate so that the usual formulations of the household production function no longer yields signed results. And again, the use of a nonlinear budget constraint requires new assumptions that are very unlikely to have any meaningful justification.

WHAT ABOUT TRANSACTION COSTS? Despite an explicit interest in household production, the recent neoclassical economics of the household so abstracts the production process that it becomes difficult to recognize the daily activities in which we all engage. Berk (1980, p. 136) has observed, 'One of the ironies of the New Home Economics is that with all the talk about the household production function, scant attention is paid to the actual production processes implied'. More recently, Pollak (1985, p. 582), has noted that

Since neoclassical economics identifies firms with their technologies and assumes that firms operate efficiently and frictionlessly, it precludes any serious interest in the economizing properties and internal structure and organization of firms. The new home economics, by carrying over this narrow neoclassical view from firms to households, thus fails to exploit fully the insight of the household production approach.

Pollak goes on to propose a transactions cost approach to households in which the family is conceptualized as a governance structure rather than a preference ordering. Special emphasis is placed on how families are able to provide incentives to their members and monitor their performance. For example, because important instrumental and expressive activities are carried out in the same setting, families are able to apply rewards and punishments not readily available to other institutions. Yet at the same time, the intermingling of economic and personal relationships means that quarrels initiated in one sphere may carry over into another. Whatever the merits of Pollak's perspectives, they emphasis how much of family life has been lost in the neoclassical abstraction.

MODEL SPECIFICATION IN EMPIRICAL WORK. The ultimate validation of any theory must come from how it performs in the empirical world. By and large, the empirical work done to date within the new home economics has been roughly consistent with theoretical predictions. However, the effects of key variables are often very small and/or statistically indistinguishable from zero (e.g. Layard and Mincer, 1985). More important, as Pollak asserts (1985, p. 584), 'because of the central role of unobservable variables (e.g., preferences, household technology, genetic endowments), the new home economics view of the family does not lead simply or directly to a model capable of empirical implementation'.

For example, it is one thing to 'hold constant' the role of *a priori* preferences when extracting the essentials for theory development, but quite another to omit sound measures of tastes from one's econometric models (Berk and Berk, 1983, pp. 380–1). Unless the omitted taste variables are uncorrelated with either the outcome variable or the explanatory variables that are included, biased estimates will result. Hence, even when statistical results appear consistent with economic theory, it is not clear what has been demonstrated. And to date, the empirical literature has typically failed to introduce reasonable measures of family members' preferences.

CONCLUSIONS. Given the current state-of-the-art, economists probably ask far too much of their theories. Nowhere is this more true that in the recent applications of neoclassical microeconomiccs to families. In the search for signed results, enormous simplifications and abstractions have been introduced. One is left with a perspective that if taken literally will probably fail.

First, the requisite assumptions, if accepted at face value, make the theory of dubious relevance for most households. Consequently, one is in practice reduced to arguing about how closely the theory approximates reality, and almost any empirical findings may be dismissed. If, for example, in certain developing countries women's labour force participation does not respond in expected ways to increases in market wages, one may simply claim that the market economy is insufficiently mature.

Second, many of the theory's key concepts are typically unobserved in practice and perhaps even unobservable in principle. This means that all empirical efforts are undermined by errors in variables and model misspecification. Once again, therefore, virtually any empirical finding may be discarded. For example, if women with more education spend fewer hours caring for their children than women with less education, it may be that one is witnessing the substitution effects (via greater market wages) predicted by economic theory. Alternatively, with greater education comes a preference for market activities. Or, women who already prefer market activities to home activities obtain more education. However, *all* of these interpretations may be easily dismissed. Neither the going, occupationally specific wage nor preferences for market activities are directly measured.

In contrast, the sensitizing role of recent efforts by neoclassical economists to understand family life has been extraordinarily useful. The new home economics force one to address seriously the nature of household production and the degree to which concepts from neoclassical economics can be instructive. In other words, we are told where to look and given some initial tools to aid in that process. These are major accomplishments.

BIBLIOGRAPHY

Becker, G.S. 1981. *A Treatise on the Family*. Cambridge: Harvard University Press.

Ben-Porath, Y. 1982. Economics and the family – match or mismatch? *Journal of Economic Literature* 20(1), March, 52–64.

Berk, R.A. 1980. The new home economics: an agenda for sociological research. In *Women and Household Labor*, ed. S.F. Berk, Beverly Hills, California: Sage.

Berk, R.A. and Berk, S.F. 1979. *Labor and Leisure at Home*. Beverly Hills: Sage Publications.

Berk, R.A. and Berk, S.F. 1983. Supply-side sociology of the family: the challenge of the New Home Economics. In *Annual Review of Sociology*, Vol. 9, Palo Alto, California: Annual Reviews Inc.

Blaug, M. 1980. *The Methodology of Economics*. Cambridge: Cambridge University Press; New York: Cambridge University Press.

Blood, R.O. and Wolf, D.W. 1960. *Husbands and Wives: The Dynamics of Married Living*. New York: Macmillan.

Hannan, M.T. 1982. Families, markets and social structure. *Journal of Economic Literature* 20(1), March, 65–72.

Hart, W.L. 1984. *Attorney General's Task Force on Family Violence*. Washington, DC: US Department of Justice.

Henderson, J.M. and Quandt, R.E. 1980. *Micro-economic Theory: A Mathematical Approach*. 3rd edn, New York: McGraw Hill.

Hollis, M. and Nell, E. 1975. *Rational Economic Man*. Cambridge: Cambridge University Press.

Layard, R. and Mincer, J. (guest eds.) 1985. Trends in women's work, education and family building. *Journal of Labor Economics* 3(1), January, i–iii.

Leibenstein, H. 1976. *Beyond Economic Man*. Cambridge: Harvard University Press.

Lesourne, J. 1977. *A Theory of the Individual for Economic Analysis.* New York: North Holland.

McElroy, M.B. and Horney, M.J. 1981. Nash – bargained household decisions: toward a generalization of the theory of demand. *International Economic Review* 22, June, 333–49.

Mancer, M. and Brown, M. 1980. Marriage and household decision-making. *International Economic Review* 21, February, 31–44.

Nerlove, M. 1974. Toward a new theory of population and economic growth. In *Economics of the Family*, ed. T.W. Schultz, Chicago: University of Chicago Press.

Pollak, R.A. 1985. A transaction cost approach to families and households. *Journal of Economic Literature* 23(2), June, 581–608.

Pollak, R.A. and Wachter, M.L. 1975. The relevance of the household production function and its implications for the allocation of time. *Journal of Political Economy* 83(2), April, 255–77.

Schultz, T.W. 1974. Fertility and economic values. In *Economics of the Family*, ed. T.W. Schultz, Chicago: University of Chicago Press.

Simon, H.A. 1978. Rationality as process and as product of thought. *American Economic Review* 68(2), May, 1–16.

Witte, A.D., Tauchen, H.V. and Long, S.K. 1984. Violence in the family: a non-random affair. Working paper no. 89, Department of Economics, Wellesley College, October.

Human Capital

SHERWIN ROSEN

Human capital refers to the productive capacities of human beings as income producing agents in the economy. The concept is an ancient one, but the use of the term in professional discourse has gained currency only in the past twenty-five years. During that period much progress has been made in extending the principles of capital theory to human agents of production. Capital is a stock which has value as a source of current and future flows of output and income. Human capital is the stock of skills and productive knowledge embodied in people. The yield or return on human capital investments lies in enhancing a person's skills and earning power, and in increasing the efficiency of economic decision-making both within and without the market economy. This account sketches the main ideas, and the bibliography is necessarily restrictive. For additional detail and alternative interpretations, the reader should consult the surveys by Blaug, Rosen, Sahota and Willis, which also present complete bibliographies.

Differences in form between human and non-human capital are of less import for analysis than are differences in the nature of property rights between them. Ownership of human capital in a free society is restricted to the person in whom it is embodied. By and large a person cannot, even voluntarily, sell a legally binding claim on future earning power. For this reason the exchange of human capital services is best analysed as a rental market transaction. Quantitative analysis is restricted to the income and output flows that result from human capital investments: wage payments and earnings flows are viewed as the equivalent of rentals of human capital value, because a person cannot sell asset claims in himself. Even the long-term commitments found in enduring employment relationships are best viewed as a sequence of short-term, renewable rental contracts. By contrast, the legal system places many fewer restrictions on the sale and voluntary transfer of title to non-human capital. In fact, substantial activity on non-human capital asset markets is a hallmark of an enterprise system of organization.

Flexibility must be maintained, however, in these distinctions, which are not

136

always hard and fast. The institution of slavery was the primary example of a transferable property right in human capital. To be sure, the involuntary elements of slavery are essential, but even voluntary systems have not been unknown. Similarly, indentured servitude was an example of a legally enforceable long-term contractual claim on the human capital services of others. And in many societies today there are severe legal restrictions on transfer of title to non-human capital: the chief example is collective and state ownership of non-human capital in planned economies.

BACKGROUND. Classical economics maintained a tripartite distinction among the factors of production, Land, Labour and Capital; whereas the modern economics is much less rigid in these divisions. Viewed from the perspective of supply, factors of production, whatever their form, can be increased and improved at some cost. To the extent that these improvements involve weighing future benefits against current costs, the principles of capital theory are applicable.

William Petty, the early actuary and national income accountant, is generally credited with the first serious application of the concept of human capital, when in 1676 he compared the loss of armaments, machinery and other instruments of warfare with the loss of human life. Elements of such comparisons survive to the present day. However, Adam Smith set the subject on its main course. *The Wealth of Nations* identified the improvement of workers' skills as a fundamental source of economic progress and increasing economic welfare. It also contained the first demonstration of how investments in human capital and labour market skills affect personal incomes and the structure of wages. Alfred Marshall stressed the long-term nature of human capital investments, and the role of the family in undertaking them. He also pointed out that non-monetary considerations would play a unique role in these decision because of the dual nature of workers as factors of production and as consumers of their work environments. The distinguished actuary and scientist Alfred Lotka provided the first quantitative application of human capital in collaboration with Dublin, calculating the present value of a person's earnings to serve as guidelines for the rational purchase of life insurance. J.R. Walsh made the first cost imputation of human capital value. Frank Knight focused upon the role of improvements in society's stock of productive knowledge in overcoming the law of diminishing returns in a growing economy.

These early contributions stand as landmarks. However, the impetus for rapid progress in this area came from the quantitative revolution in economics after World War II, when extensive data sources revealed certain systematic regularities. The first of these stems from economists' interest in understanding the nature and sources of economic growth and development in the 1950s and 1960s. Detailed calculations by national income accountants showed that conventional aggregate output measures grow at a more rapid pace than aggregate measures of factor inputs. A fundamental conservation law in economics would be violated unless the explained 'residual' was identified with (unexplained) technical change. Research associated with T.W. Schultz and Edward Denison attributed much of the measured residual to improvements in factor inputs. Schultz adopted an all-inclusive concept of human capital. At its heart lay secular improvements in worker's skills based on education, training and literacy; but he also pointed to sources of progress in improved health and longevity, the reduction in child mortality and greater resources devoted to children in the home, and the capacity of a more educated population to make more intelligent and efficient economic calculations. John Kendrick systematically pursued the empirical implications of these ideas and demonstrated that the rate of return on these inclusive human capital investments is of comparable magnitude to yields on non-human capital. This line of research as a whole proves that an investment framework is of substantial practical value in accounting for many of the sources of secular economic growth.

Another parallel strand of development arose from professional interest in the nature and determinants of the personal distribution of income and earnings. This problem was propelled, in addition, by substantial public interest in the problem of poverty and prospects for redistributing resources to the poor. Empirical bases for this inquiry were, and continue to be, supported by extensive personal survey instruments (such as Census and allied records) that have become widely available in the post-war period. Much of this work has focused on the role of education and training as important determinants of personal wealth and income. Herman Miller's updating and elaboration of Dublin and Lotka's calculation found a strong and systematic relationship between education and personal economic success, a finding that has been replicated many times in virtually every country where data are available to make the calculations.

The fundamental conceptual framework of analysis for virtually all subsequent work in this area was provided by Gary Becker, who not only organized the emerging empirical observations but also provided a systematic method for seeking new results and implications of the theory. Practically every idea in his book has been pursued at length in the research of the past two decades. Following Schultz's lead, Becker organized his theoretical development around the rate of return on investment, as calculated by comparing the earnings streams in discounted present value on alternative courses of actions. Rational agents pursue investments up to the point where the marginal rate of return equals the opportunity cost of funds. Hence, conditional on the sources of financing investments through the market and family resources, there is a tendency for rates of return to be equated at the margin. This theory of *supply* of human capital implies empirically refutable restrictions on intertemporal and interpersonal differences in the patterns of earnings and other aspects of productivity. In focusing on the development of a person's skills and earning capacity over the life cycle, human capital theory has evolved as a theory of 'permanent income' and wealth.

Becker also made a distinction between human capital that is specific to its current employment in a firm, and that which has more general value over a broader set of employments. The concept of firm-specific capital is closely allied with organizational capital, a person's contribution to a specific organization, the value of which is lost and must be reproduced by costly investment when the employment relationship is terminated. General human capital represents skills that are not specifically tied to a single firm and whose employment can be transferred from one firm to another without significant loss of value. This distinction has proved valuable for analysing the determinants of turnover and firm-worker attachments and its ramifications are still being pursued. For example, the concept of firm-specific capital underlies the transactions cost basis for recent research on labour market and other contracts.

THE RATE OF RETURN. The connection between the rate of return on investment in human capital and observable earnings is illustrated by Smith's discussion of the relative earnings of physicians and other professional workers. A person who contemplates entering one of these fields must look forward to a long period of training and costly personal investment before any income is forthcoming. Furthermore, the long training period cuts into the period of actual practice and reduces the period of positive earnings. Consequently earnings must *compensate* for the cost and effort required to practice the trade: if they did not, fewer people would find it attractive to enter.

The compensatory nature of earnings on prior investments, equivalent to a rate of return, is the fundamental insight of human capital theory. First, it points to the opportunities foregone by an action as a fundamental cost of undertaking it. Thus the direct tuition and other costs of education are only one component of the true cost. The fact that the person defers entering the market and gives up a current source of earnings is also properly counted as a cost. Second, the focus on the intertemporal and life-cycle nature of these decisions leads to a much different concept of income and inequality than simply examining current earnings. Human capital theory suggests that the distributions of *lifetime earnings* and human capital *wealth* are the keys to analysing the distribution of economic welfare, because earnings are the result of prior investments.

Two methods are widely used to calculate the return on human capital investments. Consider one alternative, call it the null alternative, which yields an earnings flow of $x_0(t)$. Consider another alternative, call it the investment alternative, which yields an earnings flow of $x_1(t)$. For example, in the leading case $x_0(t)$ is the expected flow of earnings in year t if one terminates education after high school graduation and $x_1(t)$ is the earnings that can be expected if one continues on to college. The time index t commences as of high school graduation, so $x_1(t)$ will typicall show a phase (during the period of college attendance) of much smaller values than does $x_0(t)$. However, in later life $x_1(t)$ is generally larger than $x_0(t)$. This is precisely the investment content of the decision to continue school: there is a current cost in terms of income foregone, but a deferred benefit in terms of greater earnings prospects in the future. Write the difference $z(t) = x_1(t) - x_0(t)$. Then $z(t)$ shows a systematic pattern of negative values when t is small and positive values when t is large; $z(t)$ is increasing from negative to positive in between. Observed earnings in the two choices allows calculation of the internal rate of return, defined as the rate of interest which equates the present discounted value of the two earnings streams. If i is the internal rate, then $\Sigma z(t)/(1+i)' = 0$.

Of course, it is not possible to observe earnings in the path not taken. A person either stops school or continues on the next level. In practice, the calculation is made by using observed average earnings of college graduates at different ages as an estimate of $x_1(t)$ and using the observed average earnings of high school graduates as an estimate of $x_0(t)$. The typical calculation produces an estimate of i in the neighbourhood of 10 per cent, comparable to the rate of return on investment in physical capital. Hanoch presents the most complete treatment of this problem. Remarkably, rates of return on education in the vicinity of 10 per cent are found in a wide variety of countries and economic institutions.

Another method of calculation, first presented by Jacob Mincer, brings out the economic aspects of these estimates more clearly. Suppose a person contemplates a level income in amount $y(s)$ over the life work-life cycle if s years of schooling are undertaken. If schooling is productive we must have that $y'(s) = dy/ds$ is positive, that is, anticipated earnings must be increasing in years of schooling. The present discounted value of wealth associated with some choice s, from the point of view of the present time, is simply

$$W(s) = y(s) \int_s^n e^{-rt}\, dt,$$

where the index of integration runs from s, the time the person completes school and enters the market, to n, the time the person retires. Since n is large, we may take the approximation.

$$W(s) = y(s) \int_s^\infty e^{-rt}\, dt = y(s)\, d^{-rs}/r.$$

Assume that the schooling decision is made to maximize human capital wealth $W(s)$. Then differentiating with respect to s, the first order condition $[y'(s) - ry(s)]e^{-rs} = 0$, or $y'(s)/y(s) = r$. y'/y is nothing other than the marginal internal rate of return on investment in schooling, so schooling is chosen such that its marginal internal rate equals the rate of interest. This rule, similar to the economic problem of when to cut a tree or uncork the wine, is one that maximizes lifetime consumption prospects for the person.

Now extend this argument to many people. In an economy with many similar individuals making schooling choices, all would choose the same value of s, satisfying $d\log y(s)/d\log s = r$. Since there would be no differences in schooling choices among them occupations and jobs that required either more or less education would go unfilled, and the labour market would not clear. Yet, if we observe that in the market equilibrium different people choose different amounts of schooling, with some actually choosing more education and some actually choosing less, then the market earnings on jobs with different schooling requirements must adjust so that the marginal condition is an identity for all possible values of s. That is, people must be indifferent as to how much education they choose. Viewing the marginal condition as a differential equation in y and s and integrating yields the *restriction* $y(s) = y_0 e^{rs}$, where y_0 is the earnings of a person without any schooling. Substituting this back into the definition of $W(s)$, we have

$$W(s) = y_0 e^{rs} \int_s^\infty e^{-rt} \, dt = y_0/r$$

is *independent of s*. Writing $W(s) = W$ to reflect this fact, we have $y(s) = (rW)e^{rs}$, and $\log y(s) = \log(rW) + rs$. Think of this last expression as a regression equation. Then after adjusting the income data for age and experience, a regression of the log of income on years of school yields an estimate of the marginal internal rate of return to education (r) as the regression coefficient on schooling. The constant term in the regression estimates 'earning capacity' $\log(rW)$.

The economic logic underlying this development clearly shows the compensatory nature of the returns to schooling and its relationship to the theory of supply. The equilibrium earnings–schooling function is an equalizing difference on the foregone opportunity and other costs of attending school. If people are alike, earnings must rise with schooling to cover direct and indirect costs. Otherwise no one would be inclined to undertake these investments. Notice that in this example, income differences are equalized on cost at every point and that the human wealth (W) is the same for all. Thus there is inequality of earnings, but complete equality of human capital wealth or life cycle earnings. Restricting attention to inequality in the observed distribution of earnings would give a highly misleading indication of inequality in the true distribution of economic welfare in this case.

This simple decision problem provides a convenient and powerful conceptual framework around which much of the research in this area has been organized. The value of this framework was first demonstrated by Becker, who expanded it to include interpersonal differences in abilities and talents and in family circumstances. Interpersonal differences in the rate of interest r, are identified with financial constraints on human capital investments associated with family background and related factors. A person confronting a higher rate of interest would be unable to finance human capital investments on favourable terms and would therefore rationally choose to invest less than a person who was able to borrow at lower rates. Similarly, there may be interpersonal differences in talents among people. Some may be more skilled in learning, which makes schooling effectively cheaper for them, or they may have natural talents which either complement or substitute for schooling in producing earning capacity.

Considerations such as these lead to an identification problem in the schooling–earnings relationship observed *across* different individuals (see Rosen, 1977, for elaboration; also Willis). To begin, let us isolate the effects of family background and financial constraints by restricting attention to a subset of individuals with the same natural talents and abilities. Then differences in school choices within this group would be provoked by corresponding differences in family backgrounds and financial constraints. The reason for this goes back to the institutional feature of human capital assets noted above, that a person cannot sell an asset claim to future earning power. Thus human capital does not serve as collateral for investments in anywhere near the same way as title to physical capital does for non-human investment. A house, for example, serves as collateral for a mortgage. If the purchaser defaults on the mortgage then the creditor gains title to the house, which can then be sold to settle the debt. Non-transferable titles to human capital make this kind of arrangement impossible for personal investments. Relaxing these kind of constraints is, of course, the fundamental economic logic behind the public provision of education in most countries throughout the world. But since direct tuition and related costs are only a part of the true costs of schooling, the importance of foregone earnings costs suggests that financial constraints would still remain a factor in educational decision-making. As Marshall noted, the social and economic status of the family play an important role in educational choices.

From the point of view of econometric estimation, observing a subset of the population where abilities are roughly constant, but where financial constraints dictate different schooling choices allows identification of the schooling–earnings relationship for that ability level. This in turn enables the analyst to calculate the social rate of return on investment, and to determine empirically the effect on personal and aggregate wealth of social policies that relax the financial constraints. Earnings of otherwise similar people who were less constrained serve as excellent estimates of the true earnings prospects for more constrained individuals.

Extensive empirical investigation of the connection between schooling, earnings, and family background shows a very strong and systematic relationship between parents' socioeconomic status and background and the school quality and completion levels of their children (e.g. Griliches, 1970, 1977). This is prima facie evidence of financial constraints on educational choices, though it does not rule out other routes by which family background affects a person's economic success, such as complementary investments in the home in child care and quality. These studies also indicate a direct connection between family background and earnings given the schooling choices of children. The causal link between these direct effects of family background and earnings remain to be established. It could reflect common but unobserved variance components across generations within families, such as unobserved ability; and also unmeasured factors, such as school quality and the quality of parental inputs, that are correlated with family background. Whatever their source, these direct linkages are numerically small compared with the effect of schooling itself on earnings. Most of the effect of family background on economic success works through its effects on the educational decisions of children and through that to economic success as measured by income and earnings. The direct effect on income, while persistent and significant, is quantitatively small.

SOME APPLICATIONS. Perhaps the main policy area where these ideas on financial constraints are important is in public provision of training and 'manpower' development programmes for the poor. The logic of these policies rests on the proposition that a person's income in a market economy reflects the quantity of resources that the person controls and the value of these resources. People who are permanently poor have less skills and also less valuable skills than the non-poor. So an attractive policy to help eliminate poverty is to give them more and better resources through education and training. The rate of return has been widely used for programme evaluation. For if the social return to investment in subsidized training is less than the rate of return on other forms of social investment, then programmes emphasizing direct monetary and other transfers to the poor are better bets for society overall than devoting resources to skill enhancement. There now exists a voluminous literature on manpower programme evaluation along these lines, largely stemming out of the social programmes what were instituted in the 1960s and 1970s in the United States. The evidence is mixed. While many examples of successful programmes can be found, the prevailing assessment among experts is that the average programme has not been clearly successful (Ashenfelter, 1978). This empirically based conclusion suggests that the underlying causes of poverty are more complicated than simple family constraints on resources which thwart human capital investments. Lack of motivation, discrimination, ability, low quality prior education and insufficient investments in children in the home, as well as constraints on financing are among many of the possibilities that present themselves as causal factors in reducing personal investments in human capital.

The changing role of women in the workplace and in the home has refocused current professional interest on the role of families in determining economic success of children. While these intergenerational connections between the wealth and economic status of parents and their children have long been recognized as a key element in the question of poverty and the size distribution of income, these aspects have only been linked to human capital theory in very recent years. Again, the impetus for this interest lies in the empirical findings summarized above, and also in some that have come from unexpected quarters, namely the economic success of immigrants and their children.

Recent work by Barry Chiswick (1978) has established a systematic empirical pattern for many immigrant groups into the United States. Chiswick finds that members of the first generation of immigrants earn less than comparable native born citizens in the first two decades of their life in the US. At that point their incomes reach parity with native born citizens and beyond it actually surpass the incomes of the native population. More remarkably, the sons of these immigrants – the members of the second generation – earn incomes which exceed those of the sons of native born workers. However, by the third generation there is parity, and the effects of foreign-born status wash out. While certain aspects of Chiswick's findings remain controversial and are being studied at length, they support the 'melting pot' view of economic life in the US. There is obviously substantial interest and importance in examining similar phenomena in other countries.

The chief theoretical work in the intergenerational transmission of wealth and economic status through families is contained in the research of Becker and Tomes. This work directly addresses intergenerational linkages through preferences and attitudes of parents toward their children, through natural hereditary transfers of ability and through discretionary transfers of resources through the generations. This work is the most complete theoretical description of the intergeneration distribution of wealth available so far. Inheritability of abilities is known from statistical theory to imply a regression-toward-the-mean phenomenon. Thus the fortunes of one generation are not only linked by direct transfers of non-human wealth and human capital investments, but also by inherited traits. These two forces interact in the intergenerational transmission mechanism. The economic fortunes of generations are more closely linked the greater the degree of inheritability of ability and the greater the propensity of parents to invest in their children's human capital. The effects of good fortune in one generation spills over to the next through the transfer mechanism. Interestingly, it may spill over to several subsequent generations. Thus regression toward the mean may occur only after several generations rather than after only one. When borrowing constraints are imposed on this structure even more persistence is implied because low income families do not have sufficient resources to invest in their children, whose incomes as parents are smaller than they would otherwise be. These issues are important for understanding social and economic mobility, and only recently have data become available to study them empirically. In the end this may be one of the most important developments in human capital theory.

ABILITY BIAS. The other major area where considerable research progress has been made is the role of ability in determining economic success. In terms of the decision model above, interpersonal differences in ability shift the earnings–schooling relationship. More able persons earn more at a given level of schooling than the less able, so the observed income-schooling relationship does not necessarily represent the returns available to a given person. Thus consider a group of individuals who have the same financial resources (the same value of r in the term discussion above). If ability is complementary with schooling then the rate of return to schooling will be larger for the more able and they will choose to invest more. A person observed choosing less education rationally does so because the personal return is relatively small under these circumstances. Comparing the earnings of persons who choose less education with those of persons choosing more education leads to a biased assessment of the returns due to differences in their abilities. This 'ability bias' issue has been examined in much detail.

The basic issue was originally posed by Becker, using the discounted earning stream comparisons presented above. If $x_0(t)$ is the earnings stream of people who stop school after high school completion and $x_1(t)$ is the earning stream of those who continue to college, then $x_1(t)$ is likely to be a biased estimate of the earnings prospects of high school graduates had they continued on to college. In so far as their average ability is lower than college graduates, their earnings had they chosen to continue on to college are likely to be smaller than $x_1(t)$. Similarly, the higher average abilities of college going persons makes it probable that $x_0(t)$ is a downward biased measure of what they would have earned had they stopped their education after high school graduation. Thus comparing $x_1(t)$ with $x_0(t)$ yields an upward biased estimate of the rate of return to education for either group.

In order to correct this bias it is necessary to purge the earnings data of the direct effects of ability. Several methods have been proposed, and most find that the effect of ability biases in rate of return calculations is positive but relatively small (Griliches). The fundamental reason for this is due to a finding of Welch, that while the direct effect of measured ability on earnings is positive (given schooling), its numerical effect is quite small. Even a person whose measured ability is one standard deviation above the mean receives, on average, an income that is only a few percentage points above average.

Most of the research in this area has concentrated on indexes of ability associated with IQ and other measures meant to predict school performance. However, predictors of school performance and grades are not necessarily good predictors of economic success. The most sophisticated studies employ factor analytic statistical models, in which measured abilities embodied in IQ scores and the like serve only as indicators of underlying and unobserved 'true' abilities. These studies show that 'raw' rate of return estimates unadjusted for ability differences overstate 'true' rate of return calculations by only a few percentage points. The rate of return to schooling remains substantial, and of comparable magnitude to that on other forms of investment even after ability adjustments have been made.

Most of this ability-bias research assumes that ability can be captured statistically as a single factor (in the statistical sense). However, some recent work is based on a multiple-factor view of ability in which there are different dimensions and components (Willis and Rosen, 1978). This multi-factor framework is familiar from the theory of comparative advantage in economics. A unidimensional specification of ability only allows for absolute advantage, where a person who is more able in one thing is necessarily more able in everything else. By contrast, a comparative advantage specification allows for both absolute and relative advantages. A person may be very talented in all things (absolute advantage), but may also be relatively more talented in some things than others. Furthermore, absolute advantage may not be so important. A great musician is not necessarily adept at non-musical activities such as accounting; and the typical accountant may well have no more than the average musical ability in the entire population. An extension of the model above shows that people would naturally select themselves into those occupations and educational categories that exploit their comparative advantage. Thus those who choose to specialize their human capital investments in musical activities would be likely to have more natural talent for it than the population at large. Similarly, those who learn the plumbing trade would be likely to have more mechanical ability than those who make some other choice. These types of selection problems gain research interest because

145

educational and occupational choices are closely linked. While much important work remains to be done in this area, available evidence is at least consistent with the existence of comparative advantage and occupational selection. If so, the overall ability bias in simple rate of return calculations is likely to be relatively small.

The question of ability bias and selection comes up in a quite different manner in the literature on educational screening and signalling (Spence, 1973). In its most extreme form, the signalling literature maintains the hypothesis that education has no direct effect on improving a person's skills, but rather serves as an informational device for identifying more and less talented people. This model rests on a unidimensional view of ability and also on the suppositions that direct observation of a person's ability and productivity is very costly and that a person knows much more about his own abilities than other persons do. In these circumstances, education serves as a signal of ability if the more able can purchase the educational signal on more favourable terms than the less able. For then education and ability are highly correlated, and the higher income earned by those with more schooling is supported in equilibrium by their higher ability-productivity.

Several points must be made in this connection. The first is, that taken on its own terms, the signalling and human capital models have very similar implications for the rational choice of schooling. In fact they appear to be econometrically indistinguishable on the basis of income and schooling data alone. The chief difference is a normative one, that schooling has little social value when it serves as a signal, and has much social value when it produces real human capital. Second, the data reveal considerable 'noise' in the schooling–earnings relationship. An investigator does very well when a third of the total variance in earnings can be 'explained' in the analysis of variance sense by observable personal factors such as education, experience, ability measures, family background and other factors. The schooling–earnings relationship is very strong in the sense of population averages, but the error in prediction is very large for any given person. Large personal prediction errors dull the value of education as a signal. This fact also suggests that education is a personally risky investment. Third, when the signalling model is expanded, it does not necessarily imply that educational signals are socially unproductive. Education may have significant social value in identifying naturally talented people if there is social value in classification and sorting. For example, there may be significant interactions among workers in an organization. If so, then the organization must be structured to choose the optimal *distribution* of talent within it; for example, it may be socially beneficial for the most talented people to work together. In so far as the educational system serves to classify people for these purposes, it is producing a form of human capital (information in this case) which has both private and social value. Finally, the value of education in assisting persons to find their niche in the overall scheme of the economy, precisely because they do not know so much about themselves, has never been quantified.

SIGNALLING AND INFORMATION. A definitive empirical study capable of distinguishing signalling and human capital views of investment in education is yet to be produced in spite of many attempts to do so. Most work in this area has floundered on the fact that the two views imply very similar equilibrium implications about the observed relationship between earnings and schooling, so that if any real progress is to be made, future investigations will have to look elsewhere. A promising area is to examine the direct effects of education on productivity (and not on income alone). Much research has been done on educational production functions, which have an obvious bearing on these linkages and how a different form of education might affect them. For example, some evidence suggests that preschool training can overcome the adverse effects of a poor home environment in educational success. Hanushek (1977) reviews the literature on educational production.

Surprisingly few studies have attempted to examine the schooling–productivity linkage directly, probably because data on personal productivity measures are hard to find, but those few that have managed to do so have found some very impressive results. Griliches reviews the issues at the aggregate level. However, the sharpest results have arisen in agriculture, a sector which has shown an enormous and sustained growth in productivity for at least five decades. The rate of return to education among farmers is substantial. Since most of these persons are self-employed and sell their produce in impersonal, competitive markets, it is difficult to make an *a priori* case that signalling plays any significant role in their educational decisions. Moreover, detailed study shows how these returns come about. More educated farmers control larger resources in the form of larger farms. It is possible that there is a common connection with family background and wealth. However, available evidence suggests that these farmers are also much more efficient in their techniques of production, and that their education is used primarily to keep them informed of recent technological changes in agricultural production, which they adopt with greater frequency and with quicker response. The case that education makes farmers more efficient processors of new information is very well made in the work of Welch (1976, 1978). Schultz indicates that similar findings would apply to much of agricultural production throughout the world, and broadens the argument to make it more generally applicable to all walks of life.

NON-MONETARY CONSIDERATIONS. Another potential source of bias in rate of return calculations arises from the limitations of earnings data. Using expected discounted earnings as the choice criterion is a first order approximation to a more complete formulation. Discounted expected *utility* is the ideal choice index, because an employment relationship is a tie-in between the productive services rendered by human capital skills on the one hand, and the consumption of non-pecuniary aspects of the work environment on the other. The imputed monetary equivalent value of these job-consumption items should be added to earnings in a complete calculation. The same is true of the skills that are utilized outside of the market sector, such as in home production (see Michael, 1982).

That individuals may differ in their tastes for employment of alternative forms of human capital leads to the existence of rents in human capital valuations. Furthermore, the evidence suggests that on-the-job consumption values increase with education and skill. Jobs which require more schooling are likely to be more desirable on *both* monetary and non-monetary grounds (this evidence is reviewed in Rosen, 1986). Economic theory suggests that some portion of earning capacity would be 'spent' on more desirable and more amenable jobs. To the extent that the value of work amenities increase with schooling, observed earnings are a downward biased estimates of total earnings for the more educated, and measured rates of return are downward biased.

These issues are most sharply drawn in the treatment of hours worked in rate of return calculations. For example, if observed earnings alone are used in the calculations, groups such as physicians are found to exhibit large rates of return on their medical education, whereas groups such as teachers are found to earn much lower returns. But physicians work very long hours, perhaps as much as 40 per cent more than the typical worker, whereas teachers work far fewer hours than most other workers; they do not work in the summer, for instance. It is necessary to make judgements about the imputed value of leisure to deal adequately with these differences. If leisure is valued at the wage rate, the proper calculation refers to 'full' income at a common hours-worked standard. Similar considerations apply to growth accounting calculations: The secular increase in embodied skills and human capital has been accompanied by a secular decrease in working hours among the employed population. The imputed value of the quantity and quality of increased 'leisure' should be counted in a measure of welfare Also, using only market transactions as a basis for calculation conceals the significant value of human capital in home production among those groups, especially women, whose activities have shifted between the non-market and market sectors.

OCCUPATIONAL CHOICE. The discussion so far has concentrated on the role of formal schooling in human capital production. A small but important literature has used these ideas to analyse occupational choice, especially among the professions. The first, and still significant work in this area is due to Friedman and Kuznets, who set the general framework in terms of wealth maximization and rate of return calculations on entry into law, medicine and dentistry. Subsequent literature, of which the work of Freeman is especially notable, has applied modern time-series statistical methods to these problems, concentrating especially on the role of income prospects in attracting or repelling new entrants into a profession.

The human capital perspective suggests that longer term income prospects should play an important role in occupational decisions of the young and that short-term and transitory fluctuations should be of lesser consequence because they have small impact on expected lifetime wealth. Nevertheless, a central finding in this literature is that current market conditions have large effects on occupational choice, and that supply to a specific occupation is relatively elastic with respect to current wages. The effects of long-term prospects have been much more difficult to isolate empirically, depending as they do on specific formulations of expectations and the connections between future earnings expectations and current and past realizations. In so far as a person is 'locked in' to a profession after choosing it, economic theory suggests that long-term expectations should be the primary determinant of choice. The finding that current prospects are highly significant in these choices suggests considerable mobility and recalibration of choices after training. For example, many lawyers use their skills outside the formal practice of law, and in complementary ways in the business sector more generally. However, the nature and extent of ex-post mobility possibilities remains to be thoroughly examined.

LEARNING FROM EXPERIENCE. From the theoretical point of view, formal schooling decisions are only half the story in human capital accumulation and skill development. Investment does not cease after schooling: there is another sense in which it just begins. Formal schooling sets the stage for accumulation of specific skills and learning in concrete work situations, through on-the-job training. The human capital literature interprets the term 'on-the-job training' very broadly. Only a small part of the overall concept is included in formal training programmes, apprenticeships and the like. The greater part is associated with learning from experience. This broad and inclusive interpretation is supported by persistent empirical observations on the evolution of earnings over the life-cycle. The age structure of earnings shows remarkably systematic patterns. Earnings rise rapidly in the first several years of working life, but the rate of growth falls toward mid-career and tends to turn negative toward retirement. In panel data, wage rates rise throughout the life cycle, with the greatest rate of increase in the early years. An attractive interpretation of these observations is that the increase in earnings with work experience is due to increasing productivity and human capital accumulation over the entire life cycle.

A fruitful empirical approach for studying these patterns has been developed by Jacob Mincer (1974). The conception of the problem extends the education model above. A person is viewed as making human capital investment choices at each point in the life cycle. Workers can choose to invest more pay for their choice by accepting lower earnings when young and earn returns on their prior investments in the form of larger earnings when they are older. This is essentially a choice between a level experience-earnings pattern (if investments are small) and a 'tilted' one, starting at a lower point and rising to a higher one if investments are large. Mincer develops the concept of 'overtaking' to impute the total return to human capital. The basic idea extends the Smithian principle of compensation to on-the-job training investments. Suppose a person has a large variety of possible investment opportunities after completing school. If no further investments are made, the experience earnings profile is relatively flat. The slope of the earnings-experience profile is increasing and the intercept of the profile is decreasing with the magnitude of investment. Hence the investment level defines an entire family of age earnings profiles, which are spun out around a roughly common crossing point, labelled the 'overtaking' point, if in market equilibrium wealth is approximately independent of investment.

The model has a very sharp empirical prediction that in a cohort of individuals with the same schooling level and different post-school investments, the inter-personal variance of earnings should be decreasing with experience up to the overtaking point and increasing thereafter. These systematic variance patterns have been found by many investigators in a variety of data sources. The assumptions that on-the-job investments are completely equalizing and that human wealth is the same for all investment paths makes it possible to decompose total investments into formal education and on-the-job components. Mincer reports that the on-the-job components are substantial, of the order of a third of more of the total.

The complete education–experience human capital model has important implications for the analysis of poverty and income distributions. In a nutshell, human capital theory suggests that life-time earnings is the appropriate construct for understanding inequality. To the extent that age–earnings patterns are the result of rational investments in human capital, it is misleading to use unadjusted cross-section annual earnings data for inequality analysis. For those young persons who are intensively engaged in investment activities, and whose current income is therefore small at present, may be classified erroneously as poor even though they are not poor in the lifetime sense. These life cycle issues have not been given sufficient attention in the extensive literature on the social welfare consequences of inequality, in spite of the fact that Paglin (1975) conclusively shows that they have large consequences for the measurement of inequality. Taking the life cycle view yields Gini coefficient estimates of real inequality that are smaller than when only current incomes are used in the calculations.

More detailed econometric work on the dynamic structure of individual earnings based on panel data helps resolve questions of the extent to which poverty status is permanent or transitory over the life cycle. The most sophisticated study so far (Lillard and Willis, 1978) decomposes earnings into several components. One is measurable characteristics of persons, such as education and experience, which reflect human capital and other considerations. Another is a 'person effect' capturing unmeasured components of ability, health and related factors which permanently affect a person's earning power relative to his cohort. Finally, the third component reflects more transient variations, reflecting such factors as luck and other random events which may persist for a time but which eventually die out. Each component explains about one-third of the total variance of earnings. Since the measurable factors are, by human capital theory, largely equalizing on prior investments and the transitory effects have only small effects on life cycle wealth, this leaves about one-third of the total variance of life cycle earnings as attributable to permanent differences among persons or to 'pure' inequality. Certainly this is quite a difference picture than emerges from examining the cross-section distribution of current earnings.

Other approaches to understanding age–earnings profiles in the human capital framework have used a more formal capital-theoretic structure. Here human capital is associated with the latent stock of embodied skills, and investment with skill acquisition and learning. A person must give up current income to learn more and increase the stock of skills available for rental at a later date. The optimal investment programme maximizes the present value of lifetime earnings. This basic set-up of the problem was first formulated in an important paper by Ben-Porath (1967), who structured the investment control as choice of the division of a person's time between working and investing. An extension by Rosen (1972) structures it as choice among a spectrum of jobs which offer different learning environments and opportunities. The wage on a job that offers more learning possibilities is lower and the programme is implemented by a 'stepping stone' progression of positions.

This capital-theoretic formulation of the problem has virtues in demonstrating the conceptual commonalities between capital and growth theory and human capital theory. However, its generality comes at the cost of providing less robust predictions. Thus it seems fair to say that extensive work attempting to implement these rigorous ideas empirically has not met with overwhelming success in extracting information from observed age–experience trajectories. It appears that other important forces also affect these patterns. Several possibilities have been suggested. One relates to investments in information and search for enduring long job attachments. Job turnover is much larger among young workers than older ones. While this is a form of human capital accumulation and much recent work has been devoted to these issues, it has so far proven difficult to link this class of problems with the ideas reviewed here. Nor has human capital theory yet adequately come to terms with the fact that job patterns typically exhibit discrete jumps and 'promotions', where the character of human capital services rendered changes at each step. Competition for higher ranking positions is properly considered within the human capital framework, but little analysis is available so far.

Any review of human capital would be remiss in not calling attention to parallel developments and important applications in economic historians' interpretation of slavery. The work of Fogel and Engerman (1974) stands out as the primary example of the approach. Here the empirical work forcuses on direct human capital valuations rather than on earnings. The principles of capital valuation are used to examine such issues as the long-term economic viability of slavery as an economic institution in the absence of intervention. In addition, some important and fascinating agency problems must be confronted because of an inherent conflict in the master–slave relationship. The conflict arises because the owner naturally desires more effort than the slave prefers to put forth. Various institutions, involving *both* punishments and rewards, were structured to help resolve these conflicts. Mention also should be made of research on indentured servitude by economic historians (Galenson, 1981), which is analysed as a response to a capital market imperfection. A person voluntarily indentured himself for a period of years as payment for a loan to provide transportation and connections in the New World. Repayment was guaranteed by a legally binding claim on the person's services for the period of the contract.

DEMOGRAPHIC EFFECTS. Over the years there has been increasing recognition of the relationship between human capital and economic demography. This is inherent in the role of families as both producers and financiers of human capital investments. Two important recent developments strongly rest on these connections.

The first one is related to large demographic changes in the age structure of the population in the post-war period (the 'baby boom') in the United States. Rates of return on education had remained remarkably constant for a thirty-year period. This in spite of the fact that there had been an enormous increase in education over that period. However, Freeman identified a decline in the rate of return commencing in the late 1960s. The evidence currently available suggests that the rate fell by several percentage points for a 10–12 year period throughout the 1970s, but had gradually returned to its prior level. The leading explanation for this has been provided by Welch (1978) and relates to increased competition for jobs within cohorts as a function of their size.

A stable age distribution of the working population provides a naturally stable progression of work and job opportunities over a person's working life. Not only the level, but also the nature and productive role of human capital changes over the life cycle. Young workers perform different tasks and have different responsibilities than do older workers. Therefore competition and supply of human capital of various types in the labour market is strongly age related. Thus as the large birth cohorts of the 1950s began to enter the market in the late 1960s and 1970s, the increased supply of educated young workers lowered their wage rates and reduced the rate of return. These effects are diffused as the large cohort ages and works its way through the age distribution, and as the structure of work is altered to accommodate their large numbers. The weight of extensive research in this area has shown that returns and wage rates are affected by cohort size. The consequences of this research for the future development of human capital theory will be important, because it requires considering heterogeneous human capital investments and the evolution and development of different types of skills over working life. It may ultimately require analysing how work itself is organized and structured.

HUMAN CAPITAL AND DISCRIMINATION. A final important recent development proceeds on somewhat more conventional theoretical grounds. It addresses the role of human capital in observed wage differences between men and women, and is ultimately related to questions of labour market discrimination. The work in this area is firmly based on empirical calculations. The main fact to be explained is that women earn less than men, even after adjusting for differences in occupational status and hours worked. Labour market discrimination against women is one possible interpretation. However, there may be more subtle forces at work. Mincer and Polachek (1974) build an alternative interpretation on the observation that earnings–experience profiles of women are flatter and exhibit much less life-cycle growth than that of men, and tied it to the well known fact that women traditionally have exhibited less strong labour force attachments than men due to the sexual division of labour in the home and the bearing and raising of children.

The value of an investment increases with its rate of utilization. Compare two persons: one who expects to utilize an acquired skill very intensively and one who expects to utilize it less intensively. Suppose further that the costs of acquiring the skill are approximately independent of its subsequent utilization. Then the rate of return on investment is larger for the intensive user and that person will tend to invest more. The application to male–female wage differential is apparent upon connecting intensity of utilization with labour force attachments and hours worked. In so far as married women play dual roles in the market and in the household, there is a tendency to invest less in labour market skills and more in non-market skills. The opposite is true of men, given prevailing marriage institutions. These differential incentives can account for differences in age earnings patterns between men and women, as well as the larger average wages of men. Research on female labour supply supports the point by showing overwhelming evidence that labour force activities of married women are severely constrained by the presence of children in the home. Mincer and Polachek provided direct empirical support by demonstrating that earnings of never-married women closely approximate those of men.

Considerable research is in progress on these ideas (see, for example, *Journal of Labor Economics*, 1985). At a minimum, the human capital perspective shows that these issues are more complicated than appears on the surface. Yet there are some unresolved puzzles. In spite of the vast increase in female labour force participation in the past two decades, the relative wages of men and women have not changed very much in the United States, though they have come closer to parity in a number of other countries. Part of this may be due to differences in the importance of the government sector as employees of women, as well as differences in compliance with equal pay legislation. A definitive answer is not yet on the horizon.

This essay started by noting the twin origins of developments of the theory of human capital in understanding the sources of economic growth on the one hand and the distribution of economic rewards on the other. Much progress has been made on both counts. However, these two branches have not yet been clearly joined. Future progress will have to come to terms with the issue of how private incentives to acquire human capital affect the available social stock of productive knowledge, and how changes in social knowledge become embodied in the skills of subsequent generations.

BIBLIOGRAPHY

Ashenfelter, O. 1978. Estimating the effect of training programs on earnings. *Review of Economics and Statistics* 60(1), February, 47–57.

Becker, G. 1964. *Human Capital*. 2nd edn, New York: Columbia University Press, 1975.

Becker, G. and Tomes, N. 1978. An equilibrium theory of the distribution of income and intergenerational mobility. *Journal of Political Economy* 87(6), December, 1153–89.

Ben-Porath, Y. 1967. The production of human capital and the life cycle of earnings. *Journal of Political Economy* 75(4), Pt 1, August, 352–65.

Blaug, M. 1976. The empirical status of human capital theory: a slightly jaundiced survey. *Journal of Economic Literature* 14(3), September, 827–55.

Chiswick, B. 1978. The effect of Americanization on the earnings of foreign-born men. *Journal of Political Economy* 86(5), October, 897–921.

Denison, E. 1962. *The Sources of Economic Growth in the United States and the Alternatives Before Us.* New York: Committee for Economic Development.

Dublin, L. and Lotka, A. 1930. *The Monetary Value of a Man.* New York: Ronald Press.

Fogel, R. and Engerman, S. 1974. *Time on the Cross.* New York: Little, Brown.

Freeman, R. 1971. *The Market for College-Trained Manpower.* Cambridge, Mass.: Harvard University Press.

Freeman, R. 1976. *The Overeducated American.* New York: Academic Press.

Friedman, M. and Kuznets, S. 1954. *Income from Independent Professional Practice.* Princeton: Princeton University Press.

Galenson, D. 1981. *White Servitude in Colonial America.* Cambridge: Cambridge University Press.

Griliches, Z. 1970. Notes on the role of education in production functions and growth accounting. In *Education, Income and Human Capital,* ed. L. Hansen, New York: National Bureau of Economic Research.

Griliches, Z. 1977. Estimating the returns to schooling: some economic problems. *Econometrica* 45(1), January, 1–22.

Hanushek, E. 1977. *A Reader's Guide to Educational Production Functions.* Institution for Social Policy Studies, Yale University.

Kendrick, J. 1976. *The Formation and Stocks of Total Capital.* New York: National Bureau of Economic Research.

Knight, F. 1944. Diminishing returns from investment. *Journal of Political Economy* 52, March, 26–47.

Lillard, L. and Willis, R.J. 1978. Dynamic aspects of earnings mobility. *Econometrica* 46(5), September, 985–1012.

Marshall, A. 1920. *Principles of Economics.* 8th edn. London: Macmillan, 1930; New York: Macmillan, 1948.

Michael, R. 1982. Measuring non-monetary benefits of education: a survey. In *Financing Education: Overcoming Inefficiency and Inequity,* ed. W. McMahon and T. Geske, Urbana: University of Illinois Press.

Miller, H. 1960. Annual and lifetime income in relation to education, 1929–1959. *American Economic Review* 50, December, 962–86.

Mincer, J. 1958. Investment in human capital and personal income distribution. *Journal of Political Economy* 66, August, 281–302.

Mincer, J. 1974. *Schooling, Experience and Earnings.* New York: Columbia University Press.

Mincer, J. and Polachek, S. 1974. Family investment in human capital: earnings of women. *Journal of Political Economy* 82(2), Pt II, March-April, S76–S108.

Paglin, M. 1975. The measurement and trend of inequality: a basic revision. *American Economic Review* 65(4), September, 589–609.

Petty, W. 1676. *Political Arithmetic.* In *The Economic Writings of Sir William Petty,* ed. C. Hull, Vol. 1, Cambridge: Cambridge University Press, 1899.

Rosen, S. 1977. Human capital: a survey of empirical research. In *Research in Labor Economics,* Vol. 1, ed. R. Ehrenberg, Greenwich, Conn.: JAI Press.

Rosen, S. 1985. The theory of equalizing differences. In *Handbook of Labour Economics*, ed. O. Ashenfelter and R. Layard, Amsterdam: North-Holland.

Sahota, G. 1978. Theories of personal income distribution: a survey. *Journal of Economic Literature* 16(1), March, 1–55.

Schultz, T. 1961. Investment in human capital. *American Economic Review* 51, March, 1–17.

Schultz, T. 1975. The value of the ability to deal with disequilibria. *Journal of Economic Literature* 13(3), September, 827–46.

Smith, A. 1776. *An Inquiry into the Nature and Causes of the Wealth of Nations*. Modern Library Edition, New York: Random House, 1947.

Spence, M. 1973. Job market signalling. *Quarterly Journal of Economics* 87(3), August, 355–74.

Walsh, J. 1935. Capital concept applied to man. *Quarterly Journal of Economics* 49, February, 255–85.

Welch, F. 1970. Education in production. *Journal of Political Economy* 78(1), January–February, 35–59.

Welch, F. 1976. Ability tests and measures of differences between black and white Americans. Rand Corporation.

Welch, F. 1979. Effects of cohort size on earnings: the baby boom babies' financial bust. *Journal of Political Economy* 87(5), Pt II, October, S65–97.

Willis, R. 1986. Wage determinants: a survey and reinterpretation of human capital earnings functions. In *Handbook of Labour Economics*, ed. O. Ashenfelter and R. Layard, Amsterdam: North-Holland.

Willis, R. and Rosen, S. 1978. Education and self-selection. *Journal of Political Economy* 87(5), Pt II, October, S65–S97.

Inequality

ERIK OLIN WRIGHT

To speak of a social inequality is to describe some valued attribute which can be distributed across the relevant units of a society in different quantities, where 'inequality' therefore implies that different units possess different amounts of this attribute. The units can be individuals, families, social groups, communities, nations; the attributes include such things as income, wealth, status, knowledge, power. The study of inequality then consists of explaining the determinants and consequences of the distribution of these attributes across the appropriate units.

This essay on inequality has four principal objectives. First, I will propose a general typology of *forms of inequality*. This typology will help to map out the conceptual terrain of the discussion. Second, I will examine debates on the conceptual status of one particular type of inequality within this typology, inequality in material welfare. In particular, I will examine the debate over whether or not material inequalities in contemporary societies should be viewed as rooted in *exploitation*. Third, I will examine the implications of these contending views of material inequality for strategies for empirical research on income inequality. Finally, I will discuss the relationship between contending accounts of income inequality and the analysis of social classes.

1. A TYPOLOGY OF INEQUALITIES. Social inequalities can be distinguished along two dimensions: first, whether the unequally distributed attribute in question is a *monadic* attribute or a *relational* attribute; and second, whether the process of acquisition of a particular magnitude of this attribute by the individual can be considered a monadic or relational *process*.

Monadic and relational attributes. A monadic attribute is any property of a given unit (individual, family, community, etc.) whose magnitude can be defined without any reference to other units. Material consumption is a good example: one can assess how much an individual unit consumes in either real terms or monetary terms without knowing how much any other unit consumes. This does not mean that the attribute in question has no social content to it. Monetary income, for example, is certainly a social category: having an annual income of $30,000 only represents a source of inequality given that other people are willing to exchange commodities for that income, and this implies that the income has an irreducibly social content to it. Nevertheless, income is a monadic attribute in the present sense in so far as one can measure its magnitude without knowing the income of other units. Of course, we would not know whether this magnitude was high or low – that requires comparisons with other units. But the magnitude of any given unit is measurable independently of any other unit.

Relational attributes, in contrast, cannot be defined independently of other units. 'Power' is a good example. As Jon Elster (1985, p. 94) writes, 'In one simple conceptualization of power, my amount of power is defined by the number of people *over whom* I have control, so the relational character of power appears explicitly'. To be powerless is to be controlled by others; to be powerful is to control others. It is impossible to measure the power of any unit without reference to the power of others.

Monadic and relational processes. Certain unequally distributed attributes are acquired through what can be called a monadic process. To describe the distribution process (as opposed to the attribute itself) as monadic is to say that the immediate mechanisms which cause the magnitude in question are attached to the individual units and generate their effects autonomously from other units.

A simple example of a monadic process that generates inequalities is the distribution of body weight in a population. The distribution of weight in a population of adults is certainly unequal – some people weigh three times the average weight of the population, some people weight half as much as the average. An individual's weight is a monadic attribute – it can be measured independently of the weight of any other individual. And the weight acquisition process is also essentially monadic: it is the result of mechanisms (genes, eating habits, etc.) directly attached to the individual. This is not to say, of course, that these mechanisms are not themselves shaped by social (relational) causes: social causes may influence genetic endowments (through marriage patterns – e.g. norms governing skinny people marrying fat people) and social causes may shape eating habits. Such social explanations of body weight distributions, however, would still generally be part of a monadic process in the following sense: social causes may help to explain why individuals have the weight-regulating mechanisms they have (genes, habits), but the actual weight of any given individual results from these individual weight-regulating mechanisms acting in isolation from the weight-regulating mechanisms of other individuals. The empirical distribution of weights in the population is therefore simply the sum of these monadic processes of the individuals within the distribution.

Now, we can imagine a social process through which weight was determined in which this description would be radically unsatisfactory. Imagine a society in which there was insufficient food for every member of the society to be adequately nourished, and further, that social power among individuals determined how much food each individual consumed. Under these conditions there is a *causal* relation between how much food a fat (powerful) person eats and how little is consumed by a skinny (powerless) person. In such a situation, the immediate explanation of any given individual's consumption of food depends upon the social *relations* that link that individual to others, not simply on monadic mechanisms. Such an inequality generating process, therefore, would be described as relational rather than a monadic process. More generally, to describe the process by which inequalities are generated as relational, therefore, is to say that the mechanisms which determine the magnitude of the unequally distributed attribute for each individual unit causally depends upon the mechanisms generating the magnitude for other individuals.

Taking these two dimensions of inequality together, we can generate the following typology of ideal-typical forms of inequality. This typology (Table 1) is deliberately a simplification: the causal processes underlying the distribution of most inequalities will involve both monadic and relational mechanisms. Nevertheless, the simplification will help to clarify the conceptual map of inequalities which we have been discussing.

'Power' is perhaps the paradigmatic example of a relationally determined relational inequality. Not only is power measurable only relationally, but power is acquired and distributed through a relational process of competition and conflict between contending individuals, groups, nations, etc. (For discussions of power as form of inequality see Lenski, 1966; Lukes, 1974.)

Power is not, however, the only example. Social status is also generally an example of a relationally determined relational attribute. Status is intrinsically a relational attribute in that 'high' status only has meaning relative to lower statuses; there is no absolute metric of status. The process of acquisition of such high status is also generally a relational process of exclusion of rival contenders for status through competitive and coercive means. (Under special circumstances status-acquisition may be a largely monadic process. In artistic production, for example, one could imagine a situation in which each individual simply does the best he or she can and achieves a certain level of performance. There is nothing in one person's achievement of a given level of performance that precludes anyone else achieving a similar level. The status that results from that achievement, however, is still relational: if many people achieve the highest possible level of performance, then this level accords them less status than if few do, but the acquisition process would not itself be a relational one. In general, however, since

Table 1   *Typology of forms of inequality*

| | | Form of the unequal attribute | |
		Relational	Monadic
Form of the process of distribution of attributes	Relational	Power, status	Income
	Monadic	Talent	Health, weight

the process by which the level of performance itself is achieved is a competitive one in which people are excluded from facilities for learning and enhancing performance, status acquisition is itself a relational process.)

The distribution of health is largely a monadic process for the distribution of a monadic attribute. In general, as in the weight acquisition case, the mechanisms which determine an individual's health – genetic dispositions, personal habits, etc. – do not causally affect the health of anyone else. There are, however, two important kinds of exceptions to this monadic causal process, both of which imply a relational process for the distribution of health as a monadic inequality. First, infectious diseases are clearly an example of a process through which the mechanisms affecting health in one person causally affect the health of another. More significantly for social theory, where the distribution of health in a population is shaped by the distribution of medical services, and medical services are relatively fixed in quantity and unequally distributed, then the causal mechanism producing health in one person may well affect the health of another in a relational manner.

Talent is an example of a relational attribute that is unequally distributed through a monadic process. A 'talent' can be viewed as a particular kind of genetic endowment – one that enhances the individual's ability to acquire various skills. To be musically talented means to be able to learn to play and compose music easily, not actually to play and compose music well (a potential prodigy who has never seen a piano cannot play it well). Talents are caused through a monadic process since the causal mechanism which determines one person's latent capacities to acquire skills does not affect anyone else's. (Obviously, parents' talent-generating mechanisms – genes – can affect their children's through inheritance. This is identical to the effect of parents' genes in the weight example. The point is that the effectiveness of one person's genes is independent of anyone else's.) The attribute so produced, however, is clearly relational: a talent is only a talent by virtue of being a deviation from the norm. If everyone had the same capacity to write music as Mozart, he would not have been considered talented.

Income inequality, at least according to certain theories of income determination (see below), could be viewed as an example of a relational process for distributing a monadic attribute. Income is a monadic attribute in so far as one individual's income is definable independently of the income of anyone else. But the process of acquisition of income is plausibly a relational one: the mechanisms by which one person acquires an income causally affects the income of others.

2. INEQUALITIES IN MATERIAL WELFARE: ACHIEVEMENT VERSUS EXPLOITATION. More than any other kind of inequality, inequality of material welfare has been the object of study by social scientists. Broadly speaking, there are two distinct conceptualizations which have dominated the analysis of this kind of inequality in market societies. These I will call the achievement and exploitation perspectives.

Achievement models. The achievement model of income determination fundamentally views income acquistion as a process of individuals acquiring income as a return for their own efforts, past and present. The paradigm case would be two farmers on adjacent plots of land: one works hard and conscientiously, the other is lazy and irresponsible. Assuming no externalities, at the end of a production cycle one has twice the income of the other. This is clearly a monadic process producing a distribution of a monadic outcome.

The story then continues: the conscientious farmer saves and reinvests part of the income earned during the first cycle and thus expands production; the lazy farmer does not have anything left over to invest and thus continues production at the same level. The result is that over time the inequalities between the two farmers increases, but still through a strictly monadic process.

Eventually, because of a continually expanding scale of production, the conscientious farmer is unable to farm his/her entire assets through his/her own work. Meanwhile the lazy farmer has wasted his/her resources and is unable to support him/herself adequately on his/her land. The lazy farmer therefore goes to work as a wage-earner for the conscientious farmer. Now clearly, a relational mechanism enters the analysis, since the farm labourer acquires income in a wage paid by the farmer-employer. However, in the theory of wage-determination adopted in these kinds of models in which the labourer is paid exactly the marginal product of labour, this wage is exactly equivalent to the income the labourer would have received simply by producing the same commodities on his/her own account for the market. The relational mechanism, therefore, simply mirrors the initial monadic process.

In such achievement models of income acquisition genuinely relational processes may exist, but generally speaking these have the conceptual status of deviations from the pure model reflecting various kinds of disequilibria. In the sociological versions of achievement models – typically referred to as 'status attainment' models of stratification – these deviations are treated as effects of various kinds of ascriptive factors (race, sex, ethnicity) which act as obstacles to 'equal opportunity'. (The best example of status attainment models of inequality is Sewell and Hauser, 1975.) Similarly, in the economic versions of such models – generally referred to as 'human capital' models – the deviation either reflect transitory market disequilibria or the effects of various kinds of extra-economic discrimination. (The classic account of human capital theory is given by Becker, 1975; for his analysis of discrimination see Becker, 1971.) In both the sociological and economic versions, these relational mechanisms of income determination that produce deviations from the pure achievement models mean that certain kinds of people are prevented from getting full income pay-offs from their individual efforts. The inner logic of the process, in short, is monadic with contingent relational disturbances.

Exploitation models. Exploitation models of income inequality regard the income distribution process as fundamentally relational. The basic argument is as follows: In order to obtain income, people enter into a variety of different kinds of social relations. These will vary historically and can be broadly classified as based in different 'modes of production'. Through a variety of different mechanisms, these relations enable one group of people to appropriate the fruits of labour of another group (Cohen, 1979). This appropriation is called exploitation. Exploitation implies that the income of the exploiting group at least in part depends on the efforts of the exploited group rather than simply their own effort. It is in this sense that income inequality generated within exploitative modes of production is intrinsically relational.

There are a variety of different concepts of exploitation contending in current debates. The most promising, in my judgement, is based on the work of Roemer (1983). (For a debate over Roemer's formulation, see *Politics & Society*, 11(2), 1982.) In Roemer's account, different forms of exploitation are rooted in different forms of property relations, based on the ownership of different kinds of productive assets. Roemer emphasizes two types of property in his analysis: property in the means of production (or alienable assets) and property in skills (or inalienable assets). Unequal distribution of the first of these constitutes the basis for capitalist exploitation; unequal distribution of the second constitutes the basis, in his analysis, for socialist exploitation.

While Roemer criticises the labour theory of value as a technical basis for analysing capitalist exploitation, nevertheless his basic defence of the logic of capitalist exploitation is quite in tune with traditional Marxist intuitions: capitalists appropriate part of the surplus produced by workers by virtue of having exclusive ownership of the means of production. Socialist or skill exploitation is a less familiar notion. Such exploitation is reflected in income returns to skills which is out of proportion to the costs of acquiring the skills. Typically this disproportion – or 'rent' component of the wage – will be reproduced through the institutionalization of credentials. Credentials, therefore, constitute the legal form of property that typically underwrites exploitation based in skills.

Two additional assets can be added to Roemer's analysis. Unequal distribution of *labour power* assets can be seen as the basis for feudal exploitation, and unequal distribution of *organization* assets can be viewed as the basis for state bureaucratic exploitation (i.e. the distinctive form of exploitation in 'actually existing socialism'). The argument for feudalism is basically as follows: in feudal society, individual serfs own less than one unit of labour power (i.e. they do not fully own their own labour power) while the lord owns part of the labour power of each of his serfs. The property right in the serf's labour power is the basis for the lord forcing the serf to work on the manorial land in the case of corvée labour, or paying feudal rents in cases where corvée labour has been converted into other forms of payment. The flight of peasants to the cities, in these terms, is a form of theft from the lord: the theft of the lord's labour power assets. The argument for state bureaucratic societies is based on the claim that control over the organizational resources of production – basically control over the planning and coordination of the divisions of labour – is the material basis for appropriation of the surplus by state bureaucrats. (For a detailed discussion of these additional

161

types of assets and their relationship to exploitation, see Wright, 1985.) In all of these cases, the ownership and/or control of particular types of productive assets enables one class to appropriate part of the social surplus produced by other classes.

In exploitation models of income distribution, monadic processes can have some effects. Some income differences, for example, may simply reflect difference preferences of individuals for work and leisure (or other trade-offs). Some of the income difference across skills may simply reflect different costs of acquiring the skills and therefore have nothing to do with exploitation. Such monadic process of income determination, however, are secondary to the more fundamental relational mechanisms.

3. IMPLICATIONS FOR EMPIRICAL RESEARCH STRATEGIES. As one would suspect, rather different empirical research strategies follow from monadic versus relational conceptions of the process of generating income inequality. In a strictly monadic approach, a full account of the individual (non-relational) determinants of individual income is sufficient to explain the overall distribution of income. This suggests that the central empirical task is first, to assemble an inventory of all of the individual attributes that influence the income of individuals, and second, to evaluate their relative contributions to explaining variance across individuals in income attainment. In the case of the example of the two farmers discussed above this would mean examining the relative influence of family background, personalities, education and other individual attributes in accounting for their different performances. The sum of such explanations of autonomously determined individual outcomes would constitute the basic explanation of the aggregate income distribution.

It follows from this that the heart of statistical studies of income inequality within an achievement perspective would be multivariate micro-analyses of variations in income across individuals. The study of overall income distributions as such would have a strictly secondary role.

In exploitation models of income distribution, the central empirical problem is to investigate the relationship between the variability in the form and degree of exploitation and income inequality. This implies a variety of specific research tasks, including such things as studying the relationship between the overall distribution of exploitation-generating assets in a society and its overall distribution of income, the different processes of income determination within different relationally defined class positions (see Wright, 1979), and the effects of various forms of collective struggle which potentially can counteract (or intensify) the effects of exploitation mechanisms on income inequalities.

This does not imply, of course, that achievement models of income inequality have no interest in macro-studies of income distribution, nor that exploitation models have no interest in micro-studies of individual income determination. But it does mean that the core empirical agendas of each model of income inequality will generally be quite different.

4. MATERIAL INEQUALITY AND CLASS ANALYSIS. Sociologists are interested in inequalities of material welfare not simply for their own sake, but because such inequality is thought to be consequential for various other social phenomena. Above all, material inequality is one of the central factors underlying the formation of social classes and class conflict.

The two models of income inequality we have been discussing have radically different implications for class analysis. In achievement models of income distribution, there is nothing intrinsically antagonistic about the interests implicated in the income determination process. In the example we discussed, the material interests of the lazy farmer are in no sense intrinsically opposed to those of the industrious farmer. The strictly economic logic of the system, therefore, generates autonomous interests for different economic actors, not conflictual ones.

Contingently, of course, there may be conflicts of interest in the income determination process. This is particularly the case where discrimination of various sorts creates noncompetitive privileges based on ascriptive characteristics such as sex and race. These conflicts, however, are not fundamental to the logic of market economies and they do not constitute the basis for conflicts between economic classes as such.

Conflicts between classes in capitalist societies, therefore, basically reflect either cognitive distortions on the part of economic actors (e.g. misperceptions of the causes of inequality) or irrational motivations (e.g. envy). Conflicts do not grow out of any objective antagonism of interests rooted in the very relations through which income inequalities are generated.

Exploitation models of income inequality, in contrast, see class conflict as structured by the inherently antagonistic logic of the relational process of income determination. Workers and capitalists have fundamentally opposed interests in so far as the income of capitalists depends upon the exploitation of workers. Conflict, therefore, is not a contingent fact of particular market situations, nor does it reflect ideological mystifications of economic actors; conflict is organic to the structure of the inequality-generating mechanisms themselves.

These different stances towards the relationship between interests and inequality in the two approaches means that for each perspective different social facts are treated as theoretically problematic, requiring special explanations: conflict for achievement theories, consensus for exploitation theories. Both models, however, tend to explain their respective problematic facts through the same kinds of factors, namely combinations of ideology and deviations from the pure logic of the competitive market. Exploitation theories typically explain cooperation between antagonistic class actors on the basis 'false consciousness' and various types of 'class compromises' between capitalists and workers, typically institutionalized through the state, which modify the operation of the market (see Przeworski, 1985). Achievement theories, on the other hand, use discriminatory preferences and market imperfections to explain conflict.

BIBLIOGRAPHY

Becker, G.S. 1971. *The Economics of Discrimination.* 2nd edn, Chicago: University of Chicago Press.

Becker, G.S. 1975. *Human Capital.* 2nd edn, New York: National Bureau of Economic Research.

Cohen, G.A. 1979. The labor theory of value and the concept of exploitation. *Philosophy and Public Affairs* 8(4), 338–60.

Lenski, G. 1966. *Power and Privilege.* New York: McGraw-Hill.

Politics & Society. 1982. 11(3). Special issue on John Roemer's theory of class and exploitation.

Lukes, S. 1974. *Power: a Radical View.* London: Macmillan.

Przeworski, A. 1985. *Capitalism and Social Democracy.* Cambridge: Cambridge University Press.

Reich, M. 1981. *Racial Inequality.* Princeton: Princeton University Press.

Roemer, J. 1983. *A General Theory of Exploitation and Class.* Cambridge, Mass.: Harvard University Press.

Sewell, W. and Hauser, R. 1975. *Education, Occupation and Earnings.* New York: Academic Press.

Szymanski, A. 1976. Racial discrimination and white gain. *American Sociological Review* 41, 403–14.

Wright, E.O. 1979. *Class Structure and Income Determination.* New York: Academic Press.

Wright, E.O. 1985. *Classes.* London: New Left Books/Verso.

Inequality between the Sexes

E. BOSERUP

Economic theory concerning inequality between the sexes focuses upon inequality in wages, job recruitment, promotion and dismissal, for women and men with similar qualifications and availability. Neoclassical theory explains these inequalities as a result of free and rational choice, based upon the biological differences between the sexes. According to Becker (1981), women's role in reproduction makes it rational for women to specialize more in family skills, and men more in labour market skills, and parents make a rational choice for their children by preparing them for different careers. When women's reproductive role is reduced due to the decline of birth rates, women's availability for the labour market increases, and they begin to invest more in labour market skills than is the case in countries with continued high fertility. So sex-related differences in level and types of human investment and availability provide the explanation for the difference in wages, types of work and promotion.

By focusing upon the biological differences between the sexes, neoclassical theory selects the features which distinguish inequality between sexes from inequality between other discriminated groups, that is the young versus the old, or foreigners versus members of the dominant ethnic or national group. All these inequalities have been characteristic features of human societies since prehistoric times. The basic principle in the organization of societies is that only members of the superior group have adult status or civic rights, while the members of the inferior groups depend upon the benevolence of the 'adults'. In most societies, economic and social development have reduced the inequalities, but nowhere have they been completely eliminated, and the traditional power of the superior male group over the inferior female group cannot be ignored in the economic analysis of inequality between sexes. The power of the male group over the female one is supported by access to the best technology and a monopoly in learning how to use it (Boserup, 1970). Men's monopoly in the use of weapons, superior hunting equipment, and animal-drawn agricultural equipment, is of ancient origin. But even in societies where men have shifted to tractors and other industrial inputs, women often continue to use primitive hand tools for the operations assigned to them. Even in modern mechanized industries, men distribute the tasks and assign the unskilled, routine operations to the female workers.

In primitive subsistence economies, woman's reproductive role does not prevent her being assigned the most onerous tasks with incessant daily toil, and if the mother's work prevents her from taking care of young children, these are cared for by older sisters or other members of the group. At a later stage of development, when specialization of labour leads to the transfer of an increasing share of the labour power of the family to outside work, the reproductive role of women contributes to explaining why more women than men continue to work in the family and for the family, either as unpaid family members or as domestic servants. However, due to their superior status, men have the right to dispose of money incomes earned by female family members within or outside the family enterprise. There may be a regional and local differences in women's status, but in most traditional societies women cannot dispose of money or undertake monetary transactions, accept employment or move away from the locality where they live and work, without the permission of a male guardian who decides all these matters, as well as family matters, like marriage, divorce and the fate of the children. The right to take part in decisions on public matters is reserved for members of the male sex.

Gradually, as technological development transfers an increasing number of products and services from family production to production in specialized enterprises and institutions private or public, there is no need for the full labour power of all female family members in the household. Through the same process, the family economy becomes more and more dependent upon money income to purchase the products and services which the family no longer produces, and to pay the taxes which finance the growing public sector. As a result, increasing numbers of women become money earners. At this stage, women's ability to engage independently in economic and other transactions, and their lack of responsibility, becomes a handicap not only to themselves but also to their employers, creditors, customers and guardians, as well as to public authorities and male family members who must support them, if they are unable to support themselves and their dependents because of economic disabilities.

In some European countries, 'market women', who were often middle-aged women with dependents, attained adult status many centuries ago. Later, when it became customary for young girls to work for wages before their marriage, and for other single, divorced and widowed women to support themselves and their dependents by wage labour, or by self employment, these categories of women were granted 'adult' status in economic affairs; but married women continued to be denied adult status. In most industrialized countries, married women first attained adult status when further reduction of the domestic sector, together with the decline of birth rates, radically increased their participation in the labour market and made their work in the labour market an important part of the national economy. In most developing countries, women, whether married or not, are still denied adult status in economic affairs; in some countries it severely limits their labour market participation, in other cases it limits the business activities they are able to accomplish.

Human capital investment in 'market skills' becomes more and more important with economic and social development, while investment in family skills loses in importance when more and more activities are transferred from the family setting to private enterprises or public institutions. When the responsibility for physical protection is transferred from the family to the government, and formal education is introduced, educational level may replace the ability to use weapons as a status symbol for male youth. The priority given to boys over girls in formal education is not only a result of their larger labour market participation, as suggested by Becker, but also a means to preserve a higher male status, by letting men reach higher educational levels than women.

The status of parents may require that their daughters be educated as well, but that boys should not lose status by receiving less schooling than their sisters, while to preserve the superior status of the husband, the wife must not be more educated than he is. Universities were long closed to women, and in many countries the difficulties of obtaining marriage partners for educated women make both parents and daughters afraid of continuing their education. The low marriage age for girls, another means to preserve male status in the family, may also prevent continuation of the education of girls. The differences between the sexes in educational levels serve to reinforce inequality not only in the family, but also in the labour market. With economic development the difference becomes limited to the highest educational levels but it has not disappeared, even in countries with very high and uninterrupted female labour force participation.

Usually, differences in access to technical training for girls are much larger than differences in access to formal education. From the day women began to work for wages in urban activities, men have insisted on their priority right to skilled, supervisory, and other better paid work. Both in guilds, and later in industries and public service, men became apprentices and skilled workers while women remained assistants to the male workers, unskilled or semiskilled, working under male supervision. In most cases, male trade unions continued the fight of the guild members against rights for women to training, and even to membership of the organization and right to work in the trade. The inferior position of women was defended by the short stay in the labour market of young girls before they married, with no account taken of the large number of spinsters, poor married women and female heads of households, who were permanent members of the labour force both in European and in many non-European countries.

In addition to the lower position of women in the job hierarchy, female wage rates are usually much lower than male wage rates for similar work. Only in periods of great shortage of labour, for instance in wartime or in agricultural peak seasons, may female wages temporarily rise to the level of male wages. The fact that these wage differences are related to sex, and not to the burden of dependency, belies the usual explanation for them. They are a result of the principle of male superiority, and neoclassical theory has helped to make the principle acceptable. Since the theory assumes that differentials in wages equal differentials in marginal productivity of labour, the lower wage rates for women could be taken as a confirmation of the general assumption of female inferiority, which also applied to women as workers.

The superior status of men is supported when women doing similar work get lower wages; when a wife is prevented from earning as much as her husband, he preserves his superior status as principal breadwinner, even if he is too poor to enjoy the even higher status of being the only breadwinner in the family. Training girls in low-wage occupations and discriminating against women in recruitment for 'on the job training' or access to 'learning by doing' supervisory work, reduces the risk that male staff will lose status by being supervised by women.

When employers in private enterprises and public service pay males higher wages than females for similar work, they include the higher male wages in their production costs, even if that reduces the demand for products made primarily by male labour. If an enterprise or a trade has difficulties in competing, due to the payment of high male wages, employers will not reduce the wage differential, but will instead try to get the workers and the trade unions to accept the recruitment, or additional recruitment, of women. If they succeed, the trade will become less attractive to men, and the labour force will gradually become female as has happened to many trades in which trade unions were weak. The separation of the labour market into masculine and feminine trades and jobs becomes even more pronounced if the principle of equal pay for equal work is introduced by law or labour contract, since sex specialization makes it more difficult to prove that the work paid at different rates is 'equal'.

Inequalities between men and women in the labour market and in the family reinforce each other. While Becker assumes a harmony of interest between the marriage partners and an equal distribution of consumption and leisure between them, Sen (1985) uses bargaining theory to explain the observed inequalities in consumption and leisure, which in some countries include differences in coverage of calorie requirements and in access to health care between husband and wife, and between boys and girls. The wife's bargaining position is directly related to her access to the labour market and position in it, but her bargaining position is also weakened because women are likely to perceive inequalities as natural, and make no objections against them. This feature is due to the family socialization of girls from a young age. In many societies, girls are taught that they are less valuable human beings than their brothers, and virtually everywhere girls must help their mothers to provide domestic and personal services for their brothers, who are allowed much more freedom and leisure.

Even in countries with high and perpetual labour force participation by women, girls' education and training within the family focus on child care and domestic activities, and on beautifying themselves to be able to make a good match and reduce the risk of divorce and abandonment, while boys' interests are stimulated in all other fields. Usually, girls are taught to be obedient, to be modest and to do routine jobs without protest, while boys are encouraged to be enterprising, even aggressive, and more self-confident. The inferiority feelings of the girls may induce them to invest less in education and training than boys, as suggested by

Arrow (1973), but even if they have the same formal education and training as male competitors, women are likely to lose in competition with males in the labour market. Girls, who are socialized to accept routine jobs and to be modest and obedient, are unlikely to demand good jobs and advancement, or in other ways to fight actively for their interests in the labour market, even when there are few prejudices against them. Much female aptitude for routine and precision work, unsuitability for leadership and unwillingness to take responsibility results from family socialization in the first years of life. Most often, the schools continue in the same vein, but even when schools aim at abolishing inequality between the sexes, the teachers may be powerless, due to family socialization of pupils of both sexes.

In industrialized countries, the last few decades have seen an acceleration of related and mutually reinforcing changes in technology, labour participation by married women with small children, and birth rates. Decline of birth rates to below replacement level, and increasing female labour force participation provide an inducement to the improvement of household technologies, and the introduction of new products and services as substitutes for women's traditional activities and child care. These technological and social changes further induce increasing female labour force participation. A rapidly increasing proportion of married women continue their money-earning activities without reducing work hours during the period when they have small children. But the traditional sex hierarchy is dying very slowly, and although birth rates are low, female levels of education and professional training fairly high, and labour market participation high and continuous, reductions in sex differentials in earnings have been moderate, if any. Earnings in female occupations, including those requiring professional training, are lower than in male occupations with similar requirements. Except for a small female elite, women continue to occupy the positions at the bottom of the labour market within each occupation, as assistants to men, and often supervised by men, even in otherwise female occupations.

Married women with full-time work and young children have much longer working hours than men and little leisure because male patterns of work have changed very little, in spite of reduced working hours and the increasing amount of money wives contribute to family expenditure, and also because of the lack of child-care facilities in many countries. However, in spite of the differences between male and female earnings, most women in the industrialized countries have become less dependent upon male support because of the general increase of all wages and the reduction of working hours in the labour market. Therefore, women can support themselves by work in the labour market, if they choose to, and with the aid of obligatory contributions from the father, and public support to female-headed households, they can support children, although the living standards of female-headed households are usually much lower than those of male-headed households. Consequently, many young women react against unequal work burdens by demanding divorce or leaving the home, or by not entering into a formal marriage or cohabitation. Others react by reducing birth rates even further. Contrary to earlier patterns, female applications for divorce have become more numerous than male ones in some industrialized countries. These social and demographic changes serve to make young men, and public opinion in general, more inclined to consider women's demands for more equality.

In many developing countries, economic and social development are producing changes in female labour force participation and birth rates which resemble earlier changes in industrialized countries. Family legislation has been modernized, there is legal equality or less legal inequality between the sexes, access to divorce has become less easy for men and easier for women, and better access to the labour market provides women with some possibilities for self-support in case of divorce and widowhood. Age differences between the spouses are declining due to higher female marriage age, birth rates are declining, and women's position is gradually improving.

But in many developing countries, either economic changes are few, or male resistance to changes in the traditional status of women is strong. Except for voting rights to parliaments with little influence, women continue to be legally minor, and in many cases their situation has deteriorated because technological changes, or changes in land tenure, have deprived them of traditional means of self-support. In some countries, the labour market continues to be closed not only to married women, but also to deserted women, divorcees and widows, and if labour market shortages occur, they are met by large scale imports of male labour. In these countries birth rates remain high in spite of economic development. For women, economic support from sons is the only alternative to destitution, when the husband dies or ceases to support his wife, and women also desire to have many sons as a means to reduce the risk of abandonment and divorce.

BIBLIOGRAPHY

Arrow, K. 1973. The theory of discrimination. In *Discrimination in Labour Markets*, ed. O. Ashenfelter and A. Rees, Princeton: Princeton University Press.

Becker, G. 1981. *A Treatise on the Family*. Cambridge, Mass.: Harvard University Press.

Boserup, E. 1970. *Woman's Role in Economic Development*. London: Allen & Unwin; New York: St. Martin's Press, 1970.

Buvinic, M., Lycette, M.A. and McGreevey, W.P. 1983. *Women and Poverty in the Third World*. Baltimore: Johns Hopkins Press.

Cain, G. 1985. Welfare economies of policies towards women. *Journal of Labour Economics* 3(1), special issue, January, 375–96.

Sen, A. 1985. *Women, Technology and Sexual Divisions*. New York: United Nations.

Tilly, L. and Scott, J. 1978. *Women, Work and Family*. New York: Holt, Rinehart & Winston.

Inheritance

JACK GOODY

Inheritance, in the strict sense, is the transmission of relatively exclusive rights at death. Such transmission is part of the wider process of the *devolution* of rights between or within the generations (eventually always between), and particularly between persons regarded as holders and heirs. Devolution continues throughout an individual's life, involving him both as giver and as receiver, and entailing transfers *inter vivos*, between the living for education, marriage, house-purchase, etc. as well as the residuum at death. The connection between inheritance and earlier transfers is given explicit recognition in some customary systems of endowment of sons and daughters where what has already been received is deducted from the final share of the parental estate (as in the revision clause of the Paris–Orleans region from the 16th century). In the same way the trend in European and American tax laws, epitomized in the British Capital Transfer Tax, is to treat as a whole the transfers of property from an estate (in the case of an estate tax) or to one individual or donee (in the case of an inheritance tax).

In a society where production is based upon the household and where rights (whether of ownership, tenancy or use) are vested in the domestic group, then the central importance of the devolution of such rights is clear. This is the case in most sectors of pre-industrial economies, but especially in agriculture and crafts. Where individuals have no such rights in the basic means of production, being employed as wage-labourers or as salaried employees, then the productive system is involved in interpersonal transfers only through share ownership, the transmission of managerial functions having been 'bureaucratized'; the handing over of such functions takes place at retirement rather than death and involves succession to 'office' rather than inheritance to property.

Thus in industrial societies of whatever political complexion, inheritance is of less significance for individuals and for society (except as windfall income in the first instance and windfall revenue in the second) than in earlier times when, except for the landless, it involved the transfer of rights in the means of livelihood.

Even in industrial societies, the state may make special provision for family farms or firms to ensure continuity of the working group.

A radical instance of such a law was enacted in Germany by the National Socialists in 1933, provided for undivided inheritance and forbidding partition by will, the sale of the land or its encumbrance with a mortgage. The law was repealed after World War II, but in Germany as in France and other European countries, the transmission of farm property within the family is protected with the primary aim of ensuring continuity and providing an incentive to work and improve the farm for the next generation.

THE ARGUMENT ABOUT THE INHERITANCE OF WEALTH. Two divergent views on inheritance are current. On an ideological level, 'socialist' societies, parties and individuals regard inheritance as a way of transmitting inequalities and are therefore in favour of its restriction by taxation or even expropriation. Those espousing 'capitalist' theories look upon the right to transmit acquired wealth to one's offspring as part of the incentive necessary for accumulation, saving and investment. The extreme 'socialist' position is not simply a matter of recent theories of society. At the end of the 18th century the Abbé Raynal declared that at an individual's death, any land he possessed should become a free good. The theme has played a subdominant role in Christian thought over a long period. In 5th-century Gaul, the priest Salvian maintained that since all property came from God, at death it should be returned to his representatives on earth, the Church, for distribution to the poor as well as for its own purposes. Such assumptions left no room for inheritance, so the argument for the social uses of wealth depends not only on the negative case for reducing inequalities but on the positive one for assisting charities. Both positions involve an 'individualistic' view of property, 'freedom' to testate on the one hand and the reduction of the share or relatives (especially of collateral kin) on the other.

At an implicit level, we find a similar spread of ideas in simpler societies. In Africa a distinction is often made between self-acquired property, over which an individual may have a measure of freedom of disposal, and inherited property, especially land, which has come down from his forefathers. In the second case alienation is impossible because an individual is only a temporary custodian, having an obligation (as in some earlier European Laws) to hand the property down in the same line from whence it came. If it had been inherited in the agnatic line, then only agnatic relatives could benefit. In other words the property was 'corporate', or at least 'ancestral'. This notion of an heirloom runs quite contrary to the idea firstly that an individual's wealth should be confiscated in the wider interest either of the government or one of the 'great organizations'; and secondly that he should have completely free disposition over all he has accumulated. Clearly the case for inheritance is more tenable in traditional societies like those in Africa where differences in wealth were small, so that the case for redistribution (motivated either by a position notion of distributive 'justice' or a negative resentment of inequality) was hardly relevant and where the 'poor' were the responsibility of their kin group. It becomes less tenable with the greater differentiation of capital and income, especially where individuals no longer own the means of production because they are working either for an industrial corporation or for a socialized enterprise, and where it is unnecessary, and often thought undesirable from the bureaucratic standpoint, to attach the next generation to the parental enterprise.

The stress on either the 'socialist' or 'capitalist' pole obviously has some relation to the nature of the ideology and to the organization of productive enterprise. But it is also true that domestic accumulation and extra-domestic redistribution are aspects of all contemporary social systems. In 1926 the Soviet Union reversed its early positions which limited inheritance to small amounts passed on to close relatives or to the surviving spouse, providing they were in need. Later property could be left to anyone and its inheritance, listed as one of the rights of citizens in the constitution of 1936, was seen as a useful incentive to productivity. On the other hand every major 'capitalist' country levies some kind of tax at death, the proceeds of which are destined for the public purse rather than for private enjoyment.

Theories of income distribution often start by assuming normal distribution. This assumption is not adequate for all groups because of the inheritance of property at the death of the parents or other kin. But the main reason lies in the differential interest and capacity of parents to 'invest in' and encourage the abilities of their children. Such encouragement is a kind of transfer *inter vivos*, though it is part of the very process of socialization itself, one in which material gifts may play a major part in helping to provide both shelter in the form of house or apartment and, more especially, training or capital to generate income.

The ability to transfer privilege from one generation to another is, in the end, intrinsic to family life and to the reproduction process itself with its particularistic interests. Many utopian communities and ideologically based communes attempt to equalize opportunity through early 'schooling' or joint upbringing as well as wealth sharing; in the extreme case parenthood has only a physiological function, upbringing being left to the group. In the extreme case the contradictions become apparent in the longer-term development of communities like the Israeli *kibbutz* where family ties, and hence intra-familial differences, begin to manifest themselves, in limited but significant ways, after the initial period of open recruitment.

TAXATION. Whatever their ideological position, all modern societies place a progressive tax on inherited property, a tax that socialist countries see as a means of equalizing advantage, just as attempts are made to counter other benefits derived from family through a national system of education. However, many earlier and some modern taxes were primarily visualized as methods of raising income for the ruler rather than equalizing income among the citizens.

From either standpoint death provides the best moment to raise money, since future beneficiaries are unlikely to offer many objections if they have not yet taken possession. Moreover the property of the deceased often had to be listed, especially under the notarial systems of Europe, as part of the process of handing over: consequently the basis for an assessment already existed. Such forms of taxation have a long history, appearing in Rome as the *vicessima hereditatum*, the twentieth penny of inheritance. In feudal Europe the heriot, payable at the transfer of an estate, accrued to the lord; but already in 1964 a central death tax was introduced in England, taking its modern form in 1779–80. Taxes on inherited wealth thus long preceded taxes on income.

Ways of avoiding tax also had a long history. Under English law, trusts and life-estates could be set up in order to skip a generation in the transfer of property. Discretionary trusts were not available in continental Europe. But other avoidance measures including the handing over of property *inter vivos*, a long-established tradition (even extending to the farm itself), although such a practice now runs up against taxes on gifts or capital transfers: a modern alternative, that of changing one's country of residence, is more difficult to control, except by controlling the total outflow of capital from the country.

Today these possibilities remain relatively little used, and yet the revenue role of death taxes is not great. No taxes, remarks Shoup (1968, p. 559), have had a better reputation to less effect. This is partly because of avoidance and high rates of exemption, but mainly because individuals divest themselves of property to their children or use it for support in their old age, which is especially easy when personal property relates to consumption rather than to production. However, in the USA where charitable gifts are exempt, private foundations reap important benefits, while in the UK major contributions to national collections of art, buildings or land result directly from such taxes.

THE HISTORY OF INHERITANCE. The system of inheritance, involving the transmission of relatively exclusive rights over material objects, clearly varies with the mode of production. In hunting and gathering societies, rights of this kind are minimal; much of a man's property may be destroyed at his death, each individual fashioning himself or acquiring from others the tools he requires for his own use. The destruction is an aspect of the close identification of a person with the property he has created or used that is characteristic of such societies.

In simple agricultural economies, rights in land become elaborated, although with shifting cultivation access is more important their ownership. Access to the basic means of production is likely to be achieved through membership of a kin group (by descent or affiliation) rather than through an inheritance transaction. But other types of property, livestock, houses and exchange items, are transmitted in the course of long funeral ceremonies.

Where animal or other forms of non-human energy can be harnessed in the process of production, land becomes a scarcer resource, more differentiated in its distribution, with a greater complexity of rights, 'ownership' tending to be the prerogative of the dominant groups, and tenancy (or even labouring) the prerogative of others. In the case of tenancy it is landlords that tend to make the rules for the transfer of property, insisting for example on indivision (keeping the holdings intact) or on redistribution (keeping the holdings equal). The system of inheritance itself is influenced by the existence of stratified access to land, each group attempting to employ strategies of heirship to maintain or improve their position. The situation with regard to stratified access to livestock for pastoral peoples is different in certain important respects (the herd is more easily divided, increased and consumed) but tends to produce broadly similar strategies as are found in plough agriculture.

In industrial societies the situation is radically different because the vast majority of the population labour for wages rather than owning rights in the means of production. As we have seen, inheritance consequently plays a very different and more peripheral role.

Everywhere inheritance is basically a kinship transaction. While other persons may be involved, the core relationships are close 'familial' ones. In the simpler societies eligible kin are rarely, if ever, lacking since virtually all relationships are between kin. In complex ones, the definition of eligibility tends to be narrower, friendship supplements kinship, the percentage of unmarried tends to be higher and in any case other institutions, the 'great organizations' of church, state, as well as the charitable foundations, make their own demands; nevertheless the 'family' continues to dominate the process of the transfer of wealth between generations.

In kinship terms one can transmit laterally to spouses or siblings, or lineally to children or to siblings' children: the choice is one of priority since all ultimately has to go to the next generation. Downwards transmission for men can be to the sister's child (uterine inheritance) or to own children (agnatic inheritance). In simple hoe agricultural societies inheritance between spouses is rare, transmission tending to be homoparental, that is, male to male, female to female. Such is the case in much of Africa where economic differentiation is relatively small and access to land available to all or most free individuals. Historically, these forms of inheritance were usually associated with the presence of unilineal descent groups (clans or lineages) in which property is transmitted between its members of the same sex.

Patrilineal and matrilineal clans with agnatic and uterine systems of inheritance are found in all types of pre-industrial society but matrilineality is more frequent with tropical hoe agriculture (in which women often do much of the farming, continuing their role as food gatherers in hunting societies) while patrilineality predominates when agriculture is combined with the herding of large livestock (whether or not these are used for plough traction).

The alternative form of inheritance, dominant in one form or other since the advent of plough agriculture, is diverging, or bisexual, that is, with children inheriting from both parents, and parents transferring wealth to daughters as well as to sons, but not necessarily at death. One form of early transfer is the direct dowry whereby daughters are 'endowed' when they depart at marriage. While the man-to-man (homoparental) transmission of Africa excludes inheritance by spouses, diverging devolution in Eurasia tends to exclude uterine inheritance by sister's children, concentrating on passing property, after the surviving spouse has been taken care of, directly to one's own 'natural' children, and even encouraging the adoption of outside heirs before allowing property to go to collaterals. The elementary family takes precedence.

Differences in stratification associated with advanced agriculture work in favour of the identification of conjugal statuses. Transmission in such societies is usually bisexual. At marriage some kind of conjugal fund (or identity of interest) is established and the property is transmitted, though not in equal proportions, to the children of both sexes, with certain types tending to be sex-lined; for example, land may be passed down to males alone where it is associated with male status among the nobility, as under the law of the Salian Franks. Since handing down occurs not only at death but on earlier occasions, especially at marriage, questions concerning the equality of 'inheritance' have to be looked at in terms of the total process of devolving property between holder and heir throughout their lifetime. For example, a women may receive less at death because she has received a larger dowry at the time of her marriage, even as the promise of dower to maintain her as a widow.

The different treatment of siblings depending on birth order takes the form of primogeniture, ultimogeniture, or partition, known to earlier English law as Borough French, Borough English and gavelkind respectively. Rarely if ever does one find the transmission of the entire conjugal estate to a single sibling but rather the preferential treatment of one at the expense of the others. Such a preference may be tied to particular obligations, as when the inheriting child is expected to stay with the parents in their old age. In other cases the preference for one child (unigeniture) is related to the desire to keep the family estate intact, either because it will only support one family (among the poor) or because it is tied in with status consideration (among the rich). The first situation applied to pre-Revolutionary China where the poor tended to live in stem households (containing one member of each generation) while the richer lived in larger, extended ones. The poor either had less children *in toto* or the additional offspring migrated elsewhere or worked locally as landless labourers. The second situation was found in parts of 'feudal' Europe where title and position were linked to estate and income; just as one child succeeded to the title or office, so he had to inherit the bulk of the estate to which it was attached. Younger sons sought their fortunes elsewhere in the great organizations of the church or the army, to which they had access as a consequence of the political power assured by the parental estate.

DEVOLUTION, RETIREMENT AND INTERPERSONAL CONFLICT. Until the end of the 19th century (and still today in some areas of rural Europe), propertied classes endowed their daughters at marriage (and sometimes on entering a convent, on becoming 'a bride of Christ') with part of the 'portion' they would otherwise have inherited at the death of the parents. In some farming communities the parents would hand over the farm to their son or daughter on the occasion of their marriage, reserving for themselves rights to bed and board which were sometimes embodied in specific retirement contracts. One of the penalties of such an early handing over of property is that parents are placed in a King Lear situation, overly dependent upon the succeeding generation and running the danger of neglect (or 'ingratitude'). On the other hand to hang on till the end to property that is critical to status or survival leads to the opposite kind of tension characterizing the Prince Hal situation, where the son attempted to grasp his father's crown while he was still alive. These problems are of less significance in wage-earning societies where individuals are more dependent on income than on capital, and it is into training children for future employment that parents invest their time and wealth, rather than devolving property at marriage or even at death. While the state provides a minimum level of support, wealth may be invested in a pension or retained by the elderly for their support, possibly disappearing with their death in the form of annuity. Little conflict arises between holder and heir, who rarely continue to reside together (except in the case of spouse); inheritance tends to come late and to be seen as a 'windfall'. Its distribution may still give rise to conflicts within the group of potential beneficiaries, while even the prospect of a windfall produces enough underlying tension to fill the pages of many a piece of detective fiction (and 19th-century classics like *Middlemarch*), although significantly the plots are frequently located in the past when greater weight attached to rentier income.

RIGHTS TRANSFERRED. The rights transferred from the dead to the living are largely those in material property, houses, land, money, heirlooms, but they may also include rights to receive rent, interest, dividends from shares. In earlier societies they included rights to the services of other humans (of serfs and slaves), even to women as wives and to men as husbands, as in the Jewish practice of leviratic inheritance, taking on the widow of a childless brother with a view fo breeding offspring to his name. Any semblance of the inheritance of widows was rigidly excluded from the law of England at the time of the Reformation since it was on the grounds of the invalidity of such marriages that Henry VIII set aside his first wife (Catherine of Aragon, the widow of his dead brother, Arthur) in his search for a successor and an heir. Inheritance may also involve other types of right, those of non-corporeal kind, right to songs and stories (copyright), rights to armorial bearings, titles, etc., although here we touch upon the field of succession to social position, to office, to nobility or to similar benefits.

Inheritance is not only concerned with rights; duties too are involved; debts have to be paid from the estate; the acceptance of an inheritance may involve a change of name, or residence and even, especially in societies that resolve disputes by means of feud, of the specific obligation to settle a score.

A broad distinction is made in Anglo-American law between real and personal property, roughly between land and chattels, between movables and immovables. A similar distinction is found in many other cultures and is related to the special position of land within the general category of property, since it acts both as a factor in production and as a locus for all social activity. Hence different rules and practices are applied to these two categories; in England after the Norman conquest it was the royal courts that dealt with real, and ecclesiastical courts with personal property, the former emphasizing indivision, the latter allowing more testamentary freedom and alienation. Land was subject to different rules until 1926 and its transfer is still hedged about with formalities that mark it off from all other forms of property. For a hierarchy of rights is always involved; these may refer to usufruct, tenancy, mortgage, metayage, and a host of arrangements (including sovereignty itself) to which other property is not subject and some of which need to be acknowledged in the deed of transfer itself.

TESTATE AND INTESTATE. There are two types of inheritance in literate cultures, testate and intestate. The former involves making (writing) a will or testament, the latter describes what happens when there is no such statement. In nonliterate societies inheritance is automatically intestate, and 'custom' lays down how property should be distributed. There is little 'freedom' to alienate goods from the recognized heirs so that even gifts *inter vivos* have to be monitored.

The written will or testament introduces a measure of certainty in situations, reducing possible conflict or indeterminancy; where this is available, nuncupative (that is, oral) wills are considered valid only under exceptional circumstances. But in early times one of the main functions of the testament was to certify that any alienation from customary heirs was according to the wishes of the deceased. In other words its very existence assumed a degree of 'freedom', by which is meant freedom of choice for the holder, limiting the right of 'society' to say who should be the recipient. It is not surprising that the will with its corresponding freedom of testation was encouraged by the early Christian Church as a way of acquiring property to be put to divine purposes. And in more recent times it has been a central instrument for the transfer of wealth to charitable foundations. Without its intervention, inheritance goes to the family.

Testamentary inheritance occurs by means of the written will, although initially the latter term applied only to real property (land), the testament to personal property. Literacy is thus essential either on the part of the testator or on the part of the notary, lawyer or priest who draws up the will. The fact that the document has to be proven in court means that professionals tend to be employed for the purpose. Hence the whole industry of literate legal specialists involved in writing the will, in helping it to come into effect and in administering the estate, the last being currently the most profitable part of the enterprise in anticipation of which other charges may be scaled down. It is these specialists who help to ensure that the formalities are observed, not only in the words but in the witnesses, and that the will is not invalidated for other reasons. All of which tends to take the mechanics of transfer out of the hands of kin, and places the process firmly under the charge of those who engage in it for their livelihood and who tend to create their own specialist language, codes and organization.

TESTAMENTARY FREEDOM. In oral societies, little scope existed for alienation from the heirs who were regarded as the proper recipients. On the other hand testamentary freedom has disinheritance as its corollary. The problem of exclusion became acute in the early days of Christendom since some religious advisors encouraged the old to leave all to the Church and nothing to their kin. The

Church itself, and later 'hell fire' and 'charity-begins-at-home' statutes, legislated against such forms of disinheritance and indeed most contemporary systems reserve a 'legitimate' part for the spouse and the children. In this way testamentary freedom is limited by law so that close kin benefit from a portion of the estate, although not to the same extent as under intestacy. This limitation holds even in ancient Roman and modern Anglo-American law where freedom to disinherit was greater than in the civil law regimes of the continent. In England, the obligation to leave a minimum share of personal property to close kin disappeared in the course of the 17th and 18th centuries, while in 1833 the widower lost her right to a dower. In Scotland, on the other hand, rights such as the bairn's part continued. Indeed in wealthier families in England these rights were always maintained by entails, by the strict family settlement of the 18th century and by earlier devices which prevented the splitting of the estate, while parallel practices deriving from late Roman law existed on the continent. Such arrangement were the subject of objections by some because they kept land from the market and made it impossible to raise a mortgage to effect improvements. In Europe the system collapsed with the French Revolution, following which the Napoleonic Code tried to ensure partition. But in England it persisted until the Settled Land Act of 1882. More recently Family Provision Acts have restored some of the protection given to the surviving spouse and to the children, and in the Soviet Union to anyone previously dependent upon the deceased.

In fact, the beneficiaries of inheritance under a will do not turn out to be greatly different from 'intestate' inheritance, not only because of legal restrictions but because the contents of written wills follow the general sentiments of donors. Indeed because of its flexibility the pattern of testamentary inheritance may be closer to the moral climate of opinion, as in the preference it gives to the 'spouse-all' provisions of modern Anglo-American law, whereas division with the children obtains in the more conservative case of intestacy. The legal formalism connected with literacy 'tends to generalize rules that have originated in connection with special situations into applications beyond their initial scope' (Rheinstein, 1974, p. 590). At the same time the written rule tends to preserve past situations so that intestacy laws have 'frequently looked obsolete, confused, or arbitrary'.

INHERITANCE UNDER CURRENT ANGLO-AMERICAN LAW. Intestate rules in Anglo-American law usually split the property between the surviving spouse and the children. When people make wills, on the other hand, they use the testamentary freedom to leave all to the spouse, usually the wife as she is often younger and lives longer than the husband. In general it is women as widows that benefit most from inheritance. Only after the widow's death does the property drop a generation. The one exception is in the case of a remarriage where specific provision is often made in advance for the children of 'the first bed' in whose welfare the surviving spouse may have less interest.

Even here, despite the potential difference between the outcome of testate and intestate inheritance, the results are very similar since children normally hand over the portion to which they are legally entitled to their parent so that he or she can continue to lead an independent life. When the next generation eventually inherits, the property is usually split equally between children regardless of sex. However, there is one major exception to equality of partition. When one of the siblings has looked after the parents in their old age, testamentary 'freedom' or intestate adjustment is used to allocate that person a preferential share. This was one of the roles of preferential primogeniture or ultimogeniture in early English law, the last-born son being known in some parts as the *astrier*, the one who remains by the hearth. Otherwise equality is the norm both in law and in practice. Whatever discrimination operates against women in other sections of the society, little is now manifest in testamentary matters, either as spouses or as daughters (however, the 'poor' widow who did not produce a dowry can be helped from the estate, both in Justinian's law and in modern Louisiana). A wife tends to regard an inheritance as her personal peculium, a nest-egg. Given the relatively late age that most people receive legacies, these may make little difference to the lifestyles of the recipients, who sometimes use them as gifts *inter vivos* to assist their own children rather than themselves.

BIBLIOGRAPHY

Goody, J. 1962. *Death, Property and the Ancestors*. Stanford: Stanford University Press.

Goody, J., Thirsk, J. and Thompson, E.P. (eds) 1976. *Family and Inheritance: rural society in Western Europe 1200–1800*. Cambridge: Cambridge University Press.

Renner, K. 1929. *The Institutions of Private Law and their Social Functions*. Trans. from German, London: Routledge & Kegan Paul, 1949.

Rheinstein, M.Y. 1974. Inheritance. In *Encyclopaedia Britannica*, Vol. 19, Chicago: Encyclopaedia Britannica.

Shoup, C. 1966. *Federal Estate and Gift Taxes*. Washington, DC: Brookings Institution.

Shoup, C. 1968. Taxation: death and gift taxes. *International Encyclopaedia of the Social Sciences*, Vol. 15, New York: Macmillan.

Sussman, M.B., Cates, J.N. and Smith, D.T. 1970. *The Family and Inheritance*. New York: Russell Sage Foundation.

Wedgwood, J. 1929. *The Economics of Inheritance*. London: G. Routledge & Sons.

Justice

AMARTYA SEN

1. JUSTICE AND UTILITARIANISM. The concept of justice is often invoked in economic discussions. Its relevance to economic evaluation is obvious enough. However, it is fair to say that in traditional welfare economics, when the notion of justice has been invoked, it has typically been seen only as a part of a bigger exercise, viz., that of social welfare maximization, rather than taking justice as an idea that commands attention on its own. For example, in utilitarian welfare economics (e.g. Pigou, 1952; Harsanyi, 1955) the problem of justice is not separated out from that of maximization of aggregate utility. This situation has been changing in recent years, partly as a result of developments in moral philosophy dealing explicitly with the notion of justice as a concept of independent importance (see especially Rawls, 1971, 1980).

In the utilitarian formulation the maximand in all choice exercises is taken to be the sum-total of individual utilities. The approach can be seen as an amalgam of three distinct principles: (1) welfarism, (2) sum-ranking, and (3) consequentialism. *Welfarism* asserts that the goodness of a state of affairs is to be judged entirely by the utility information related to that state, i.e., by information about individual utilities. All other information is either irrelevant, or only indirectly relevant as a causal influence on utilities (or as a surrogate for utility measures when such measurement cannot be directly done). The second principle is *sum-ranking*, which asserts that the goodness of a collection of utilities (or welfare indicators) of different individuals, taken together, is simply the sum of these utilities (or indicators). This eliminates the possibility of being concerned with inequalities in the distribution of utilities, and the overall goodness or 'social welfare' is seen simply as the aggregate of individual utilities. The third principle is *consequentialism*, which requires that all choice variables, such as actions, rules, institutions, etc., must be judged in terms of the goodness of their respective consequences. The overall effect of combining these three principles is to judge all choice variables by the sum-total of utilities generated by one alternative rather than another.

2. SUM-RANKING AND EQUALITY. A theory of justice can take issue with each of the principles underlying utilitarianism, and in fact in the literature that has developed in recent decades, each of these principles has been seriously challenged (see the papers included in Sen and Williams, 1982). Some critiques have been particularly concerned with assessing and questioning the axiom of sum-ranking, and have considered the claims of equality in the distribution of well-being (see, for example, Phelps, 1973; Sen, 1973, 1977, 1982; Kern, 1978).

The summation formula can be defended either directly (e.g., in terms of attaching equal importance to everyone's 'interest': see Hare, 1981, 1982), or indirectly through invoking some model of 'impersonality' or 'fairness' (e.g., involving a hypothetical choice in a situation of primordial uncertainty, in which each person has to assume that he or she has an *as if* equal probability of becoming anybody else: see Vickrey, 1945; Harsanyi, 1955). Other routes to deriving sum-ranking involve independence or separability requirements of various kinds (see d'Aspremont and Gevers, 1977; Deschamps and Gevers, 1978; Maskin, 1978; Gevers, 1979; Roberts, 1980; Myerson, 1981; Blackorby, Donaldson and Weymark, 1984; d'Aspremont, 1985).

Whether the defences obtainable from these approaches are convincing enough has been a matter of some dispute. There have also been some interpretative discussions as to whether giving equal importance to everyone's 'interest' does, as alleged, in fact yield the formula of summing individual utilities *irrespective* of distribution, and also whether the additive formula that is obtained on the basis of hypothetical primordial choice is, in fact, a justification for adding individual utilities as they might be *substantively* interpreted in welfare economic exercises (see Pattanaik, 1971; Smart and Williams, 1973; Sen, 1982, 1985a; Blackorby, Donaldson and Weymark, 1984; Williams, 1985). It is not obvious that this debate has been in any way definitively concluded one way or the other.

3. THE DIFFERENCE PRINCIPLE AND LEXIMIN. Meanwhile, much attention has been paid to developing welfare-economic rules based on taking explicit note of inequalities in the distribution of utilities. A definitive departure on this came from Suppes (1966). Another major approach was developed in Rawls's (1971) *Theory of Justice*, even though Rawls himself was concerned not so much with the distribution of *utilities* but with that of the indices of primary goods (on which more later). The concern with the utility level of the worst-off individual has been formalized and reflected in various formulae suggested or derived in the rapidly growing welfare-economic literature on this theme. In particular, James Meade (1976) has provided an extensive treatment of this type of distributional issues, and it has also been penetratingly analysed by Kolm (1969), Phelps (1973, 1977), Atkinson (1975, 1983), Blackorby and Donaldson (1977), and others.

In fact, the Rawlsian 'Difference Principle', which judges states of affairs by the advantage of the least well-off person or group, has often been axiomatized in welfare economics and in the social-choice literature by equating advantage with utility. In this form, the 'lexicographic maximin' rule (proposed in Sen,

1970) has been axiomatically derived in different ways. The rule judges states of affairs by the well-being of the worst-off individual. In case of ties of the worst-off individuals' utilities, the states are ranked according to the utility levels of the *second* worst-off individuals respectively. In case of ties of the second worst-off positions as well, the third worst-off individuals' utilities are examined. And so on.

There is no necessity to interpret these axioms in terms of utilities only, and in fact the analytical results derived in this part of the social-choice literature can be easily applied without the 'welfarist' structure of identifying individual advantage with the respective utilities. Various axiomatic derivations of lexico-graphic maximin – 'leximin' for short – can be found in Hammond (1976), Strasnick (1976), Arrow (1977), d'Aspremont and Gevers (1977), Sen (1977), Deschamps and Gevers (1978), Suzumura (1983), Blackorby, Donaldson and Weymark (1984), d'Aspremont (1985), among others. These can be seen as exercises that incorporate concern for reducing inequality, related to recognizing the claims of justice.

While the Rawlsian approach rejects the aggregation procedure of utilitarianism (i.e., ranking by sums), a major aspect of the Rawlsian theory involves the rejection of utility as the basis of social judgements (i.e., welfarism). Rawls (1971) argues for the priority of the 'principle of liberty', demanding that 'each person is to have an equal right to the most extensive basic liberty compatible with similar liberty for others'. Then, going beyond the principle of liberty, claims of efficiency as well as equity are both supported by Rawls's 'second principle' which *inter alia* incorporates his 'Difference Principle' in which priority is given to furthering the powers of the worst-off group. These powers are judged by indices of 'primary social goods' which each person wants (Rawls, 1971, pp. 60–65).

Primary goods are 'things that every rational man is presumed to want', including 'rights, liberties and opportunities, income and wealth, and the social bases of self-respect'. The Difference Principle takes the form, in fact, of maximin, or lexicographic maximin, based on interpersonal comparisons of indices of primary goods. This rule can be axiomatized in much the same way as the other 'lexicographic maximin' rule based on utilities, and all that is needed is a reinterpretation of the content of the axioms (with the objects of value being indices of primary goods rather than utilities).

The Rawlsian approach to justice, therefore, involves rejection both of welfarism and of sum-ranking. Furthermore, consequentialism is disputed too, since the priority of liberty might possibly go against judging all choice variables by consequences only. At least, in the more standard forms, consequentialism does involve such a conflict, even though it is arguable that the problem can be, to a great extent, resolved by a broader understanding of consequences, which takes into account the fulfilment and violation of liberties and rights, and also the agent's special role in the actions performed (Sen, 1985a).

4. UTILITIES, PRIMARY GOODS AND CAPABILITIES. The claim of primary goods to represent the demands of justice better than utilities is based on the idea that utilities do not reflect a person's advantage (in terms of well-being or powers)

adequately. It is arguable that in making interpersonal comparisons of advantage, the metric of utilities (either in the form of happiness, or of desire fulfilment) may be biased against those who happen to be hopelessly deprived, since the demands of unharrassed survival force people to take pleasure in small mercies and to cut their desires to shape in the light of feasibilities (see Sen, 1985a, 1985b). The status of 'preference' may be disputed in view of the need for critical assessment (see Broome, 1978; McPherson, 1982; Goodin, 1985, among others). Also, what types of pleasures should 'count' can itself be a matter for an important moral judgement. As Rawls (1971) points out, in the utilitarian formulation, we have the unplausible requirement that

> if men take a certain pleasure in discriminating against one another, in subjecting others to a lesser liberty as a means of enhancing their self-respect, then the satisfaction of these desires must be weighed in our deliberations according to their intensity, or whatever, along with other desires (pp. 30–31).

These and other types of difficulties have been dealt with by some utilitarians through moving to less straight-forward versions of utilitarianism, for example Harsanyi's (1982) exclusion of 'all antisocial preferences, such as sadism, envy, resentment and malice' (p. 56); see also the refinements proposed by Hare (1981, 1982), Hammond (1982) and Mirrlees (1982).

Recently, it has been argued that primary goods themselves may be rather deceptive in judging people's advantages, since the ability to convert primary goods into useful capabilities may vary from person to person. For example, while the same level of income (included among 'primary goods') may give each person the same command over calories and other nutrients, the nourishment of a person depends also on other parameters such as body size, metabolic rates, sex (and if female, whether pregnant or lactating), climatic conditions, etc. This indicates that a more plausible notion of justice may demand that attention be directly paid to the distribution of basic capabilities of people (see Sen, 1982, 1985b). The approach goes back to Smith's (1776) and Marx's (1875) focus on fulfilling needs.

The achievement of capabilities will, of course, be causally related to the command over primary goods, and the capabilities, in their turn, will also influence the extent to which utilities are achieved, so that the various alternative measures will not be independent of each other. However, the basic issue is the variable that should be chosen to serve as the proper metric for judging advantages of people – the equity and the distribution of which could form the foundations of a theory of justice. On this central issue several alternative views continue to flourish in the literature.

5. FAIRNESS AND ENVY. A view of justice is not altogether dissimilar from Rawls's concerned with primary goods is captured by the literature on 'fairness', inspired by a pioneering contribution of Foley (1967). In this approach a person's relative advantage is judged by the criterion as to whether he or she would have preferred to have had the commodity bundle enjoyed by another person. This has been seen as a criterion of 'non-envy'. If no one 'envies' the bundle of anyone else,

the state of affairs is described as being 'equitable'. If a state is both equitable and Pareto efficient, it is described as being 'fair' (even though the term fairness is also sometimes used interchangeably with 'equitability').

There has been an extensive literature on existence problems, in particular whether equitability can be combined with efficiency in all circumstances. (The answer seems to be no, especially when production is involved: Pazner and Schmeidler, 1974.) There has also been considerable exploration of the effects of varying the criterion of equitability and fairness to reflect better the common intuitions regarding the requirements of justice. Various results on these problems and related ones have been presented, among many others, by Foley (1967), Schmeidler and Vind (1972), Feldman and Kirman (1974), Varian (1974, 1975), Svensson (1980), and Suzumura (1983).

It should be remarked that the fairness criterion does not provide a complete ranking of alternative states. It identifies some requirements of justice, which makes the states fair. Varian (1974) has argued, with some force, that 'social decision theory asks for too much out of the process in that it asks for an entire *ordering* of the various social states (allocations in this case)', whereas 'the original question asked only for a 'good' allocation; there was no requirement to rank all allocations' (pp. 64–5). While it is true that 'the fairness criterion in fact limits itself to answering the original question', the absence of further rankings may be particularly problematic if no feasible 'fair' allocation exists incorporating efficiency (as seems to be the case in many situations). Furthermore, while a 'pass-fail' criterion of justice may have attractive simplicity, it does not follow that two states, both passing this criterion, must be seen as being 'equally just'. Various 'finer' aspects of justice have indeed been discussed in the literature (see particularly Suppes, 1966; Kolm, 1969; Rawls, 1971; Meade, 1976; Atkinson, 1983).

It should also be noted that the 'fairness' literature deals with commodity allocations, or incomes, or some other part of the set of things that figures in Rawls's characterization of 'primary goods'. The list is, in fact, much less extensive than that of primary goods as defined by Rawls (1971), and as such it leaves out many considerations that are regarded as important in the Rawlsian framework (e.g., the social bases of self-respect). On the other hand the criticisms – discussed earlier – of the Rawlsian focus on primary goods (based on recognizing inter-individual variations in the ability to convert primary goods into capabilities) would apply *a fortiori* to the fairness approach as well.

6. LIBERTY AND ENTITLEMENTS. A different type of consideration altogether is raised by the place of liberty in a theory of justice. As was mentioned before, Rawls gives it priority. This priority has been questioned by pointing to the possibility that other things (e.g., having enough food) may sometimes be no less important than enjoying liberty without restriction by others. Rawls does, of course, attach importance to these other considerations, but in view of the priority of liberty, they may end up having too little impact on judgements regarding

justice in many circumstances, and this might not be acceptable (on this see Hart, 1973).

On the other hand, in some other theories of justice, the priority of liberty has been given even greater importance than in the Rawlsian structure. For example, in Nozick's (1974) theory of 'entitlements', rights are given complete priority, and since these rights are characterized quite extensively, it is not clear whether or not much remains to be supported over and above the recognition of rights. Nozick argues against any 'patterning' of *outcomes*, indicating that any outcome that is arrived at on the basis of people's legitimate exercise of their rights must be acceptable because of the moral force of rights as such. These rights, in Nozick's analysis, include not only personal liberty, but also ownership rights over property, including the freedom to use its fruits, to use it freely for exchange, and to donate or bequeath it to others (thereby asserting the legitimacy of inherited property).

This type of approach has been criticized partly on grounds of what has been seen as its 'extremism', since the constraints imposed by rights can override other important considerations, for example reducing misery and promoting the well-being of the deprived members of the society. In fact, it has been argued that a system of entitlements of the kind specified by Nozick might well co-exist with the emergence and sustaining of widespread starvation and famines, which are often the result of legally sanctioned exercises of property rights rather than of natural calamities (on this see Sen, 1981). Although Nozick does refer to the possibility that in case of 'catastrophic moral horrors' rights may be compromised, it is not at all clear how this theory would accommodate such waiving of rights, in the absence of formulation of other, competing bases of moral judgements. On the other hand, there cannot be any doubt that Nozick's theory does capture some notions of justice that can be found in a less clear form in the literature. Nozick's analysis gives a well-formulated and illuminating account of an entitlement-based approach to justice.

7. SOURCES OF DIFFERENCE. To conclude, theories of justice explicitly or implicitly invoked in the literature show a variety of ways in which the demands of justice can be interpreted. There are at least three different bases of variation. One source of variation concerns the *metric* in terms of which a person's *advantage* is to be judged in the context of assessing equity and justice. Various metrics have been considered in this context, including utility (as under utilitarianism and other welfarist theories of justice), primary goods index (as in the Rawlsian theory of justice), capabilities index (as in theories emphasizing what people can actually do or be, e.g., Sen, 1985b), incomes or commodity bundles (as in the literature on 'fairness', and on statistical measures of poverty, e.g., Foster, 1984), various notions of command over commodity bundles and resources (as in some notions of 'equality' developed in the literature, e.g., Archibald and Donaldson, 1973; Dworkin, 1981), and so on.

A second source of difference relates to the *aggregating* of diverse information regarding the advantages of different individuals. One approach, best represented by utilitarianism, sees nothing being needed to be ascertained other than the *sum-total* of the overall utilities of different people. Insofar as distributional considerations come into this exercise, they enter in the conversion of goods to be distributed into the appropriate metric of individual utilities. For example, inequality in the distribution of incomes may be disvalued in the approach of utilitarian justice because it may lead to a reduction in the sum-total of individual utilities, through (interpersonally comparable) 'diminishing marginal utilities'. Other approaches are more concerned with distributional properties related to the different individuals' relative positions (vis-à-vis each other). The Rawlsian lexicographic maximin is one example of such a distributional concern, and there are others that can be considered, such as adding concave transformations of the individual utility indices (e.g., the additive formula used by Mirrlees, 1971, for his taxation assessment), and using various 'equity' axioms (e.g., Kolm, 1969, 1972; Sen, 1973; 1982; Atkinson, 1975, 1983; Hammond, 1976, 1979; d'Aspremont and Gevers, 1977; Roberts, 1980).

The third issue concerns the claimed *priority* of some particular aspect of a person's advantage (e.g., Rawls's insistence on the priority of liberty), *or* non-consequentialist priority of some processes over results (e.g., Nozick's, 1974, view of rights serving as unrelaxable constraints; or ideas of exploration based on counterfactual exercises of shared rights to social resources, e.g., Roemer, 1982).

Given the diversity of moral intuitions related to the complex notion of justice, which has been extensively used over centuries to arrive at normative assessment, it is not surprising that various theories of justice have been proposed in the economic and philosophical literature. The exercise of clearly understanding what the differences between distinct theories of justice consist of (and arise from) is, in some ways, the first task. This essay has been concerned with that task.

BIBLIOGRAPHY

Archibald, G.C. and Donaldson, D. 1979. Notes on economic equality. *Journal of Public Economics* 12, 205–14.

Arrow, K.J. 1951. *Social Choice and Individual Values.* New York: Wiley.

Arrow, K.J. 1963. *Social Choice and Individual Values.* 2nd edn, New York: Wiley.

Arrow, K.J. 1977. Extended sympathy and the possibility of social choice. *American Economic Review* 67, 219–25.

Atkinson, A.B. 1975. *The Economics of Inequality.* Oxford: Clarendon Press.

Atkinson, A.B. 1983. *Social Justice and Public Policy.* Brighton: Wheatsheaf; Cambridge, Mass.: MIT Press.

Bentham, J. 1789. *An Introduction to the Principles of Morals and Legislation.* London: Payne. Reprinted, Oxford: Clarendon Press, 1907.

Blackorby C. and Donaldson, D. 1977. Utility versus equity: some plausible quasi-orderings. *Journal of Public Economics* 7(3), 365–82.

Blackorby, C., Donaldson, D. and Weymark, J.A. 1984. Social choice with interpersonal utility comparisons: a diagrammatic introduction. *International Economic Review* 25(2), 327–56.

Broome, J. 1978. Choice and value in economics. *Oxford Economic Papers* 30(3), 313–33.

d'Aspremont, C. and Gevers, L. 1977. Equity and the informational base of collective choice. *Review of Economic Studies* 44(2), 199–209.

d'Aspremont, C. 1985. Axioms for social welfare orderings. In *Social Goods and Social Organization: Essays in Memory of Elisha Pazner*, ed. L. Hurwicz, D. Schmeidler and H. Sonnenschein, Cambridge: Cambridge University Press.

Deschamps, R. and Gevers, L. 1978. Leximin and utilitarian rules: a joint characterisation. *Journal of Economic Theory* 17(2), 143–63.

Dworkin, R. 1981. What is equality? *Philosophy and Public Affairs* 10, 185–246.

Feldman, A. and Kirman, A. 1974. Fairness and envy. *American Economic Review* 64(6), 995–1005.

Foley, D. 1967. Resource allocation and the public sector. *Yale Economic Essays* 7(1), 45–98.

Foster, J. 1984. On economic poverty: a survey of aggregate measures. *Advances in Econometrics* 3.

Gevers, L. 1979. On interpersonal comparability and social welfare orderings. *Econometrica* 47(1), 75–89.

Goodin, R.E. 1985. *Protecting the Vulnerable*. Chicago: Chicago University Press.

Gottinger, H.W. and Leinfellner, W. (eds) 1973. *Decision Theory and Social Ethics: Issues in Social Choice*. Dordrecht: Reidel.

Hammond, P.J. 1976. Equity, Arrow's conditions and Rawls' Difference Principle. *Econometrica* 44(4), 793–804.

Hammond, P.J. 1979. Equity in two person situations: some consequences. *Econometrica* 47(5), 1127–36.

Hammond, P.J. 1982. Utilitarianism, uncertainty and information. In Sen and Williams (1982).

Hare, R.M. 1981. *Moral Thinking: Its Levels, Methods and Point*. Oxford: Clarendon Press; New York: Oxford University Press.

Hare, R.M. 1982. Ethical theory and utilitarianism. In Sen and Williams (1982).

Harsanyi, J.C. 1955. Cardinal welfare, individualistic ethics, and interpersonal comparisons of utility. *Journal of Political Economy* 63, 309–21.

Harsanyi, J.C. 1982. Morality and the theory of rational behaviour. In Sen and Williams (1982).

Hart, H.L.A. 1973. Rawls on liberty and its priority. *University of Chicago Law Review* 40, 534–55.

Kern, L. 1978. Comparative distributive ethics: an extension of Sen's examination of the pure distribution problem. In Gottinger and Leinfellner (1978).

Kolm, S.C. 1969. The optimum production of social justice. In *Public Economics*, ed. J. Margolis and H. Guitton, London: Macmillan.

Kolm, S.C. 1972. *Justice et équité*. Paris: Edition du Centre National de la Recherche Scientifique.

Margolis, J. and Guitton, H. (eds) 1969. *Public Economics*. London: Macmillan.

Marx, K. 1875. *Critique of the Gotha Programme*. English translation, New York: International Publishers, 1938.

Maskin, E. 1978. A theorem of utilitarianism. *Review of Economic Studies* 45(1), 93–6.

McPherson, M.S. 1982. Mill's moral theory and the problem of preference change. *Ethics* 92(2), 252–73.

Meade, J.E. 1976. *The Just Economy*. London: Allen & Unwin.

Mirrlees, J.A. 1971. An exploration in the theory of optimum income taxation. *Review of Economic Studies* 38, 175–208.

Mirrlees, J.A. 1982. The economic uses of utilitarianism. In Sen and Williams (1982).

Myerson, R.B. 1981. Utilitarianism, egalitarianism, and the timing effect in social choice problems. *Econometrica* 49(4), 883–97.

Ng, Y.K. 1979. *Welfare Economics*. London: Macmillan.

Nozick, R. 1974. *Anarchy, State and Utopia.* Oxford: Blackwell; New York: Basic Books.

Pattanaik, P.K. 1971. *Voting and Collective Choice.* Cambridge: Cambridge University Press; New York: Cambridge University Press.

Pattanaik, P.K. and Salles, M. (eds) 1983. *Social Choice and Welfare.* Amsterdam: North-Holland.

Pazner, E.A. and Schmeidler, D. 1974. A difficulty in the concept of fairness. *Review of Economic Studies* 41(3), 441–3.

Phelps, E.S. (ed.) 1973. *Economic Justice.* Harmondsworth: Penguin Books.

Phelps, E.S. 1977. Recent developments in welfare economics: Justice et Equité. In *Frontiers of Quantitative Economics*, vol. 3, ed. M.D. Intriligator, Amsterdam: North-Holland.

Pigou, A.C. 1952. *The Economics of Welfare.* 4th edn, London: Macmillan: 4th edn, New York: Macmillan, 1938.

Rawls, J. 1971. *A Theory of Justice.* Cambridge, Mass.: Harvard University Press.

Rawls, J. 1980. Kantian construction in moral theory. The Dewey Lectures 1980. *Journal of Philosophy* 77.

Roberts, K.W.S. 1980. Interpersonal comparability and social choice theory. *Review of Economic Studies* 47, 421–39.

Roemer, J. 1982. *A General Theory of Exploitation and Class.* Cambridge, Mass.: Harvard University Press.

Schmeidler, D. and Vind, K. 1972. Fair net trades. *Econometrica* 40(4), 637–42.

Sen, A.K. 1970. *Collective Choice and Social Welfare.* San Francisco: Holden-Day, and Edinburgh: Oliver & Boyd; republished Amsterdam: North-Holland.

Sen, A.K. 1973. *On Economic Inequality.* Oxford: Clarendon Press; New York: Norton.

Sen, A.K. 1977. On weights and measures: informational constraints in social welfare analysis. *Econometrica* 45(7), 1539–72.

Sen, A.K. 1981. *Poverty and Famines: An Essay on Entitlement and Deprivation.* Oxford: Clarendon Press.

Sen, A.K. 1982. *Choice, Welfare and Measurement.* Oxford: Blackwell; Cambridge, Mass.: MIT Press.

Sen, A.K. 1985a. Well-being, agency and freedom: the Dewey Lectures 1984. *Journal of Philosophy* 82(4), 169–221.

Sen, A.K. 1985b. *Commodities and Capabilities.* Amsterdam: North-Holland.

Sen, A.K. and Williams, B. 1982. *Utilitarianism and Beyond.* Cambridge: Cambridge University Press.

Smart, J.J.C. and Williams, B.A.O. 1973. *Utilitarianism: For and Against.* Cambridge: Cambridge University Press.

Smith, A. 1776. *An Inquiry into the Nature and Causes of the Wealth of Nations.* London: Dent, 1954; Indianapolis: Bobbs-Merrill, 1961.

Strasnick, S. 1976. Social choice theory and the derivation of Rawls' Difference Principle. *Journal of Philosophy* 73(4), 85–99.

Suppes, P. 1966. Some formal models of grading principles. *Synthèse* 6, 284–306.

Suzumura, K. 1983. *Rational Choice, Collective Decisions and Social Welfare.* Cambridge: Cambridge University Press.

Svensson, L.G. 1980. Equity among generations. *Econometrica* 48(5), 1251–6.

Varian, H. 1974. Equity, envy and efficiency. *Journal of Economic Theory* 9(1), 63–91.

Varian, H. 1975. Distributive justice, welfare economics and the theory of fairness. *Philosophy and Public Affairs* 4, 223–47.

Vickrey, W. 1945. Measuring marginal utility by reactions to risk. *Econometrica* 13, 319–33.

Williams, B. 1973. A critique of utilitarianism. In Smart and Williams (1973).

Williams, B. 1985. *Ethics and the Limits of Philosophy.* Cambridge: Cambridge University Press.

Labour Market Discrimination

IRENE BRUEGEL

The facts of continued discrimination on grounds of sex and race point up some of the inadequacy of neoclassical labour market theory. The idea that pay reflects value, bar peripheral imperfections, is at odds with the experience of blacks and women in the labour market. Indeed if the newly won concepts of comparable worth and equal value now embodied in the American and British equal pay legislation were truly effective, many established pay relativities would be undermined. Neoclassical labour market theory merely adds discrimination on to its existing model but discrimination, as a structural feature of the labour market, calls up a very different approach to the analysis of labour markets.

Modern neoclassical literature on discrimination takes as its starting point Gary Becker's *Economics of Discrimination*, published in 1957, and is largely couched in the framework of human capital theory. As such it is flawed from the start by an assumption that pay, productivity and value are all three accounted for by individual attributes:- specifically education, training and experience, and that relations of power, social norms and expectations are, if anything, external issues.

A perfectly competitive economy is taken as the norm, against which discrimination by sex or race is conceptualized as an unfortunate, but peripheral, aberration based on prejudice. In orthodox economists' terms the potential for wage discrimination exists wherever *equally productive* workers receive *unequal rewards*. Such a definition of (wage) discrimination does not adequately acknowledge the social determination of discrimination and the implications of this. Discrimination by sex and race are treated as essentially parallel phenomena, amenable to the same basic analysis, even though the forces which create and sustain such discrimination may in fact be very different.

There are three interrelated areas of debate in the economics of discrimination: (i) the definition of discrimination; (ii) the measurement of the scale of discrimination against any particular group; (iii) the identification of the perpetuators and beneficiaries of discrimination.

190

THE MEANING AND MEASURE OF DISCRIMINATION. There is no consensus on how discrimination is to be defined, once one goes beyond the theoretical definition to issues of policy. The first step is to confine the concept of discrimination to instances where the treatment of a person reflects his or her membership of a particular social group. But the recognition of a group as potentially vulnerable to discrimination is not unambiguous. It took organization and opposition to get the issue of women's pay and pattern of employment raised above the 'natural order of things'. In the same way, occupational and pay differences which are currently regarded as 'normal' – such as those between old and young or manual and non-manual labour, able-bodied and disabled, could usefully be placed within the context of discrimination.

In attempting to define or delineate discrimination three main issues arise; the relevance of the victim's choices, the discriminator's motivations and the meaning of equal productivity or value.

Unequal pay for equally valuable workers does not necessarily signal discrimination, because unequal pay may reflect other rewards. It has been argued that unequal pay which results from choosing a particular type of job, say one that fits with a feminine image or with domestic responsibilities, is not discriminatory. Polachek, for example, argues that women's lower pay results from a rational decision by them to opt for jobs with flat career profiles (Polachek, 1979). Other neoclassical economists dispute whether career breaks and lesser work experience do 'explain' women's poorer pay statistically (England, 1982; Beller, 1982). Feminists go further, questioning whether such choices should be characterized as rational adaptations to an immutable domestic division of labour (Dex, 1985) rather than evidence of the deep structuring of discrimination in a patriarchal society (Barrett, 1980).

Secondly, there is an issue of motivation, of direct and indirect discrimination. Sloane (1985) argues that unequal pay arising from market processes rather than a *decision* to discriminate falls outside the economists' concept of discrimination. Such a focus on intentions, rather than outcomes, would however cut out most of the indirect discrimination that the UK and US anti-discrimination legislation at least covers in principle.

The main issue is the determination of 'equally productive workers' and 'work of equal value'. Only when people are doing the same job in exactly the same circumstances is it clear whether or not they are doing work of 'equal value'. But blacks and whites, men and women are rarely to be found working alongside one another in exactly the same circumstances, precisely because of the prevalence of discrimination. There is no evidence that black people or women are inherently less productive. So the issue becomes one of identifying differences in productivity and determining which of the processes forging such differences are to be included, or controlled for, in defining and measuring discrimination.

By and large neoclassical economists identify the social processes that render different types of labour more or less valuable to capital as operating independently, and in some sense 'prior' to the labour market. People arrive on the employer's doorstep with different attributes. The neoclassical economist then analyses the pay and conditions of different groups in relation to these attributes, with the human capital theorists' focusing particularly on education and experience, to identify whether or not and how far wage discrimination exists (Mincer and Polachek, 1974; Greenhalgh, 1980; McNabb and Psacharapoulas, 1982, etc.). Alternatively discrimination is measured through *reverse regression* – establishing the scale of any qualifications gap at the same level of pay. The greater the number of prior attributes identified and measured and the more finely the place and type of work is differentiated between industries, corporations and individual workplaces, the lower the evident discrimination.

While there may be good policy grounds for trying to identify the distinct variety of processes which contribute to the poorer earnings of ethnic minorities and women, the model is flawed by its assumption that pay differentials divide nearly into two components: that due to differences in value (whether from non labour market discrimination, choices or natural attributes) and that due to discrimination. This assumes away the power relations which structure differential pay in the real world and the intertwined relationship between pre and post labour market discrimination.

In practice differences in motivation, training, domestic duties, location etc. of second-class workers reflect actual and anticipated labour market discrimination. Women and black people work in distinct industries and occupations to some degree at least because of actual and anticipated discrimination; they may also train less and have lower motivation because potential discrimination reduces the returns to them. Measuring discrimination by differences in pay between races and sexes within set occupations and industries, then ignores both these issues. It also assumes that pay differences *between* industries and occupations arise only from differences in the productivity of labour. But if employment discrimination is prevalent such an assumption is unlikely to hold. Nor does the human capital evidence – such that it is – that pay varies with experience and education negate this point. For the return from each extra year's employment may have more to do with the typical pattern of nonmanual white men's employment than with any increments to productivity.

The problem of the 'residual' view of discrimination is illustrated by Chiswick's analysis of the position of American Jews (Chiswick, 1983). Chiswick, using a standard human capital model of the type used extensively to identify the level of discrimination against blacks and women, finds that, after standardization, Jewish men earn 16 per cent more than average. He sensibly avoids a conclusion of discrimination in favour of Jews, but, short of evoking a Jewish spirit or 'X efficiency', is left without an explanation. Some refinement of the data might lower the unexplained residual below 16 per cent, but in view of the huge range of estimates of rate and sex discrimination provided by human capital models (Lloyd and Niemi, 1979; Chiplin and Sloane, 1982), the theorization must be open to question.

WHO BENEFITS? The neoclassical *explanation* of discrimination, how it arises and who benefits, is also problematic. Becker's original model (Becker, 1957) takes two forms; the first derived from international trade theory and the second from utility maximizing preference theory. In both versions discrimination is posited as a cost to the discriminator; an irrational decision within an essentially rational market. Although these are made to look like results of analysis, they really stem from the specification of the models. If, as Becker assumes, whites indulge their 'taste' for discrimination by restricting the export of capital to black 'society' (i.e. by not employing blacks) then given Becker's assumptions, standard trade theory will give the result that white 'society' will lose as a whole, even though white labour and black capital may benefit from such restrictions (Madden, 1973).

The relevance of such a model to an economy where blacks live and work amongst whites – but in inferior jobs – is clearly open to question. The application of this model to sex discrimination, where men and women live jointly in households is still more questionable. Furthermore once Becker's basic assumption – that whites/men own all available capital – is explored, it becomes clear that blacks and women are forced to accept the terms of white/male society. Including such power relations gives the result that whites/males benefit from discrimination (Thurow, 1976).

The microeconomic foundations of Becker's models are also suspect. Discrimination is said to arise from a 'taste' for discrimination (a distaste for employing blacks and women) on the part of employers, though the basis for such tastes and what might cause them to alter is never explored.

Using Becker's model with his assumptions again produces the result that discriminators lose out; employers who irrationally refuse to employ blacks or women face higher costs and lower profits. But what also follows is that discriminators would be driven out of business in a perfectly competitive market by employers with a lesser or different taste for discrimination. Thus the continued existence of discriminatory practices throws the model into question.

Developments in the model of individual-employer-based discrimination allow for employers to benefit from their actions. So-called statistical models of discrimination also allow it to be rational profit maximizing behaviour (Aigner and Cain, 1977). Discrimination arises because employers do not know the true value of 'minority' labour power. Since information costs money, it is rational to extrapolate the costs of employing a given individual from knowledge (or assumptions) about the characteristics of their group. There remains a problem, however, in explaining persistent discrimination since once one firm recognizes the value of minority labour, all others in competition would be forced to follow suit.

Madden (1973) shows how a monopsonist can exploit womens' lower elasticity of supply and thus benefit from discrimination. The persistence of sex discrimination can thus be explained as a result of women's lower mobility and lesser unionization. The monopsony model does hint at the importance of relations of power and differential power in explaining persistent discrimination for it implies that discriminatory wages arise from the inferior market power of discriminated groups. But it is neither a satisfactory model of race discrimination nor of sex discrimintion outside the context of monopsony.

An adequate theory of discrimination would be based in a model of the labour market that encompasses relations of power, not just between employers and workers or the state and workers, but also between groups of workers who for whatever reasons, differ in their immediate interests. Historical analysis (Cockburn, 1985; Hartman, 1976; Humphries, 1977) has helped to establish how differences of interest between male and female labour are created and sustained. For a variety of reasons male workers and white workers have identified their interests with the exclusion of competing groups of 'cheap' labour. That exclusionary discrimination has differentiated the labour market by sex and race. The fracturing of the working class in this way shifts the balance of class power to employers, so whatever the immediate costs of excluding cheap labour, discriminatory divisions have been pursued by white capital.

The *crowding* of 'second class' labour into a small set of specific jobs (Bergman, 1971) and the creation of a 'segmented labour market' means that women and black people are rendered cheaper labour power. This is achieved even in the absence of overt discriminatory practices through the cultural determination of 'suitable jobs'. This does not mean that powerful anti-discrimination legislation and enforcement provision can have no effect on labour market outcomes. Were they to be put into effect, they could. However, a narrow-minded focus on the 'labour market discrimination' identified through neoclassical theory is of limited relevance since it skirts over the entrenched determination of inequalities.

BIBLIOGRAPHY

Becker, G. 1957. *The Economics of Discrimination*. Chicago: University of Chicago Press.
Beller, A. 1982. Occupational segregation by sex: determinants and changes. *Journal of Human Resources* 17(3), 371–92.
Bergman, B. 1971. The effect on white incomes of discrimination in employment. *Journal of Political Economy* 79(2), 294–313.
Chiswick, B.R. 1983. The earnings and human capital of American Jews. *Journal of Human Resources* 18(3), 313–36.
Cockburn, C. 1986. *The Machinery of Domination*. London: Pluto Press.
Dex, S. 1985. *The Sexual Division of Work*. Brighton: Wheatsheaf Books.
England, P. 1982. The failure of human capital theory to explain occupational sex segregation. *Journal of Human Resources* 17(3), 358–70.
Greenhalgh, C. 1980. Male-female wage differentials in Great Britain: is marriage an equal opportunity? *Economic Journal* 90, 751–75.
Hartman, H. 1976. Capitalism, patriarchy and job segregation by sex. In *Women and the Workplace*, ed. R. Blaxall and B. Reagan, Chicago: University of Chicago Press.
Humphries, J. 1977. Class struggle and the persistence of working class families. *Cambridge Journal of Economics* 1, 241–58.
Lloyd, C. and Niemi, B. 1979. *The Economics of Sex Differentials*. New York: Columbia University Press.
McNabb, R. and Psacharopoulas, G. 1981. Racial earnings differentials in the UK. *Oxford Economic Papers* 33, 413–25.
Madden, J.F. 1973. *The Economics of Sex Discrimination*. Lexington, Mass.: Lexington Books.

Mincer, J. and Polachek, S. 1974. Family investments in human capital: earnings of women. *Journal of Political Economy* 82(2), Pt. 2, 118–34.

Polachek, S. 1979. Occupational segregation among women: theory, evidence and a prognosis. In *Women in the Labor Market*, ed. C.B. Lloyd, E.S. Andrews and C.L. Gilroy, New York: Columbia University Press, 137–57.

Sloane, P. 1985. Discrimination in the labour market. In D. Carline et al., *Labour Economics*, Harlow: Longman.

Thurow, L.C. 1976. *Generating Inequality*. New York: Basic Books.

Leisure

GORDON C. WINSTON

Leisure came into economic analysis by the back door. Even Veblen, in whose primary title (1899) leisure had the primary place, was not much interested in it except insofar as leisure embodied the idleness and waste of resources in 'pecuniary emulation' that were the motive and the trophy of the moneyed class. In the subsequent and more serious analytical business of sorting out the response of labour supply to changing real wages begun by Knight (1921) and Pigou (1920) and continued by Robbins (1930), leisure was introduced but only as a residual, the time left over when time spent working had been accounted for. Leisure became a consumption good. It needed only simple characteristics; to be sufficiently (if vaguely) pleasing that, when set against income, as all other consumption goods, it would generate a nicely behaved indifference curve in time-income space and hence a determinate allocation of time to work.

With Gary Becker's 1965 article in the *Economic Journal* and Staffan Linder's *Harried Leisure Class* (1970), recognition of the fact the consumption takes time changed all that. Leisure was no longer simply non-work, it was the time needed by the individual or 'household' to consume the goods and services bought with the money income earned by work. Leisure, no less than work, became an integral part of the economic system.

But this leisure was also less clearly 'leisure' in the sense of Veblen or Knight – time spent in idle or nonpecuniary activities. If the very act of consuming – or deriving the utility from the economic system that is its ultimate justification – is what people do during their leisure time, then the word had to carry new and different connotations.

Linder and Becker had somewhat different objectives, despite the analytical similarity of their models. Both saw utility as derived not from goods and services directly, but from the 'commodities' (Becker) or 'consumption' (Linder) the individual could produce by combining his own reified time with purchased goods and services. Time and goods, together, were necessary to the creation of utility – a cup of coffee yields little satisfaction if there isn't time to drink it. Becker set out to integrate the results of an individual's activities over the day, showing them to be the outcome of an implicitly intertemporally coherent, even optimal, choice; Linder set out to identify the large (and many small but entertaining) social implications of a secularly increasing relative scarcity of time.

The driving force of Linder's analysis was the rising real wage rates that result from historical increases in labour productivity. While most commentators had seen much increasing material affluence as a source of increased well-being, Linder argued that because 'the supply of time' was fixed, *time* and not material income would increasingly affect welfare. As material goods and services became cheaper, time would become relatively more valuable. And the result of this would be a systematic change in the things people do – an abandonment of the leisurely and contemplative activities that require a lot of time and few goods and services in favour of those frenetic activities that need a lot of goods and services and can be done in little time.

Linder's story was well told. Shortly before its US publication, *The Harried Leisure Class* was reviewed by *Time Magazine* (1969) – an honour denied to most books in economic theory – and three years later it was the focus of a special issue of the *Quarterly Journal of Economics* (1973), edited by Thomas Schelling, that included articles by Hirschman, Spence and Baumol, among others.

Time was attracted by Linder's irreverent assertions that gourmet cooking and attendance at the opera were casualties of the growing scarcity of time and that even the easy virtue of women that Linderr saw in the late 1960s was the result of the time pressures that induced them to make love quickly and get on with other things. The quality of decision-making – rationality – would suffer as people, quite rationally, spent less time backing their decisions with careful and time-intensive search, investigation, and thought. But the more serious casaulty was loss of the sense of a leisurely and controlled pace that produces genuine satisfaction:

> A slower tempo constitutes one way of spending time that, perhaps, is the best example of an activity, the yield of which cannot be increased through any addition of consumption goods. This is so by definition. 'Peace and quiet' is thus an 'inferior' way of passing time (Linder, 1970, p. 152).

Linder's leisure paradox was thus implied: rational actors were increasingly unhappy under the increasing relative scarcity of time, because they maximized utility. Linder described the hapless consumer as a Sorcerer's Apprentice who has to absorb an ever increasing volume of goods and services in a fixed amount of time – more and more and more things have to be dealt with because goods are becoming cheaper and cheaper. Those activities that use up the most goods per unit time are the ones into which he is relentlessly driven.

But though Linder's vision was powerful, it left the uneasy sense that his leisure paradox might not survive careful scrutiny; that the analysis might be flawed in some fundamental way if utility maximizing behaviour fails to maximize utility. Misery through utility maximization would appear to have problems. And it does, of three sorts.

The first problem is that it neglects the household's durable capital and with it, that most tranquil of all ways to absorb goods and services – buying and owning things that simply aren't used much of the time. His implicit Sorcerer's Apprentice assumption that *using* goods and services must take time and effort misses the fact that the consumer is in sovereign control of the prices he pays for capital service flows from the household capital stocks he owns. At will, he can vary that price-per-hour-of-use from minimum values to infinity by the simple expedient of letting things sit idle more of the time (Winston, 1982).

Instead of being compelled frantically to dash from opera to stereo store to football game to work, the affluent consumer can follow a more Veblenesque pattern and let his expensive Nikon cameras sit in the glove compartment of his Ferrari even while he spends the rare weekend on his sailboat tied up at the Newport condominium, rather than going to either his New York apartment or the empty cabin in Colarado. Rarely utilized household capital provides generous, and certainly relaxed and mellow, opportunities to absorb vast amounts of the fruits of increasing productivity.

Linder's second analytical problem lay in his classification of activities as immutably 'goods-intensive' or 'time-intensive' – a problem he shares with Becker's similar analysis. He neglected the way these input proportions would, themselves, respond to increasing incomes. So 'peace and quiet' need not be – and often is not – produced with a lot of time and little input of goods and services. Certainly it is not produced that way in mid-town Manhattan or in other urban settings, even in underdeveloped countries, where a considerable expenditure on air conditioning and devices that control light and noise are essential to producing that peace and quiet. Shift workers' low levels of night-time labour productivity in poor countries reflect meagre endowments of housing capital that deny them peace and quiet during the day. And a contemplative stroll along the beach is not an inexpensive activity if the beach is thousands of miles from home and peak-seasons rates apply to air fare and cottage.

With growing material well-being, the activities that will endure are those that best absorb increases in goods and services in their production of utility, not those that initially have the highest goods intensities. And they may well include activities with a considerable component of leisurely relaxation. Veblen would never have suggested that the rich are inadequately provided with chances to get away from it all.

But finally and most basically, Linder's former model told us that the source of utility is only the things people *do* – activities and their durations – but then his verbal descriptions told us that utility has much to do also with the *temporal density* of those activities; that we care very much about the pace of our lives and we feel harried and unhappy if that tempo is too fast. But if that aspect of our activity choices matters to us, then it surely has to be an argument of our utility functions. If it doesn't enter our utility functions, then in a coherent model we can't feel frazzled and dissatisfied because our activities are increasingly so densely packed. He slipped an implicit density variable into the verbal version of the model that didn't appear in its formal, utility maximizing statement. The result, not surprisingly, was that we maximize utility in the misspecified formal model and make ourselves miserable in the process.

But even if the logic of the leisure paradox cannot be sustained, the enduring legacy of Linder's analysis – and of Becker's – is that 'work' and 'leisure' will not again be seen by economists as an exhaustive dichotomy of human activities. Relatively few of the things people do are pure leisure activities with no extrinsic rewards: relatively few are all work, devoid of immediate intrinsic pleasures. Instead, the richer theory of activity choice that comes after Linder and Becker can recognize in most of the things we do a more complex motivational structure that combines, in different measure for different activities, some of the inherent pleasures we used to associate only with leisure and some of the extrinsic rewards attributed to work.

BIBLIOGRAPHY

Becker, G. 1965. A theory of the allocation of time. *Economic Journal* 75, September, 493–517.

Knight, F. 1921. *Risk, Uncertainty and Profit.* Chicago: University of Chicago Press, 1971.

Linder, S. 1970. *The Harried Leisure Class.* New York: Columbia University Press.

Pigou, A. 1920. *The Economics of Welfare.* London: Macmillan; 4th edn, New York: Macmillan, 1938.

Quarterly Journal of Economics. 1973. Symposium: Time in economic life. *Quarterly Journal of Economics* 87(4), November 627–75.

Robbins, L. 1930. On the elasticity of demand for income in terms of effort. *Economica* 10, June, 123–9.

Time Magazine. 1969. Leisure. August.

Veblen, T. 1899. *The Theory of the Leisure Class: An Economic Study of Institutions.* New York: New American Library, 1953.

Winston, G. 1982. *The Timing of Economic Activities: Firms, Households, and Markets in Time-Specific Analysis.* New York: Cambridge University Press.

Occupational Segregation

MYRA H. STROBER

Neither men and women nor whites and non-whites are distributed equally across occupations. This inequality by gender or race is termed occupational segregation. Occupational segregation by gender is of greater magnitude and has been more persistent over time. Also, it has been more widely studied.

Occupational segregation is generally measured by the index of segregation, I.S., defined as

$$\text{I.S.} = \frac{1}{2} \sum_{i=1}^{m} |x_i - y_i|$$

where x = the percentage of one group (e.g. women or non-whites) in the ith category of a particular occupation, and y = the percentage of the other group (e.g. men or whites) in that same category (Duncan and Duncan, 1955). The index ranges from 0, indicating complete integration, to 100, indicating complete segregation. The value of the index for segregation by gender may be interpreted as the percentage of women (or men) that would have to be redistributed among occupations in order for there to be complete equality of the occupational distribution by gender. The value of the index for segregation by race may be interpreted as the percentage of non-whites (or whites) that would have to be redistributed among occupations in order for there to be complete equality of the occupational distribution by race.

In 1981, in the USA, the index of occupational segregation by race, computed over the eleven major census occupational categories, was 24 for men (comparing white men to non-white men) and 17 for women (comparing white women to non-white women) (Reskin and Hartmann, 1986). These values reflect a considerable decline that took place during the post World War II period; in 1940 the index for the same categories was 43 for men and 62 for women (Treiman and Terrell, 1975).

It is generally agreed that in the USA the index of segregation by gender changed little between 1900 and 1960 although the changes in occupational categories over a sixty-year period make such comparisons difficult to interpret. Between 1940 and 1981, across the 11 major occupational categories, the segregation index by gender fell only slightly for whites (from 46 to 41), though somewhat more for blacks (from 58 to 39) (Treiman and Terrell, 1975; Reskin and Hartmann, 1986). The persistence of segregation by gender is seen as surprising in light of the marked increase in women's labour force participation rate in the post-World War II period, from 25.8 per cent in 1940 to 52.2 per cent in 1981. (The labour force participation rate for men was 79.1 per cent in 1940 and 77.4 per cent in 1981.)

The magnitude of the segregation index depends in part upon the degree of aggregation of the occupations: the greater the detailed specification of the occupations, the greater the level of measured segregation. For example, in 1980, although the occupational category 'professional' was gender-neutral – women were about one-half of all professionals – they were not distributed equally across the professions; about one-half of all women professionals were in two occupations, nursing and non-college teaching. For 1981, Jacobs (1983) reported the segregation index by gender at 40.0 when calculated across 10 major occupational categories, 62.7 across 426 occupational categories and 69.6 across 10,000 + categories. Bielby and Baron (1984), in their study of approximately 400 establishments in California, found that in more than 50 per cent of the establishments occupations were completely segregated by gender and that only 20 per cent of the establishments had segregation indices lower than 90.

The gender segregation index declined by about 10 per cent during the 1970s (Beller, 1984; Jacobs, 1983), mostly as a result of greater integration of occupations rather than through changes in the size of predominantly male or predominantly female occupations. The decline during the 1970s was greatest among those with more than 17 years of education, and among those 25–34 (Jacobs, 1983).

Another common way of looking at occupational segregation is to array occupations according to their percentage of female incumbents and then calculate the percentage of the female work force employed in predominantly female occupations. In 1980, about half of all employed women were in occupations that were at least 80 per cent female, while about 70 per cent of all men worked in occupations that were at least 80 per cent male (Reskin and Hartmann, 1986). For black women and men these proportions were somewhat lower (Malveaux, 1982).

Occupational segregation produces several deleterious effects. To the extent that it inhibits men and women from working in jobs that match their talents and skills and instead employs them in occupations that match societal stereotypes, occupational segregation lessens both individual satisfaction and potential economic output. In addition, occupational segregation contributes to the earnings differential between women and men. In 1970, women who worked full-time, year-round, earned approximately 60 per cent of the earnings of men who worked full-time, year-round. Based on an analysis of 499 detailed occupational categories, Treiman and Hartmann (1981) concluded that about 35–40 per cent of this earnings differential was the result of occupational segregation. (The other 60–65 per cent came from the fact that within occupations men tend to earn more than women.) Gender segregation within occupations, gender segregation by firms and job segregation within firms also contribute to the female/male earnings differential (Reskin and Hartmann, 1986). Finally, occupational segregation affects gender differences in occupational prestige and mobility as well as access to on-the-job training, job stress and vulnerability to lay-off and unemployment.

Theories to explain the existence and persistence of occupational segregation are remarkably divergent. Some sociological and psychological theories suggest that women's own behaviour – their values, aspirations, attitudes, and sex-role expectations – are the cause of occupational segregation. Similarly, human capital theory views women's choices about their educational attainment and interrupted work histories as responsible for their occupational designations and low pay rates. Other sociological theories, as well as economic theories of discrimination locate the employer, often aided and abetted by pressure from customers and/or employees or unions, as the source of occupational segregation. Although the world view of dual-labour-market or internal-labour-market theories is much less oriented toward individual choice and market processes than is neoclassical economics, these theories, too, locate the source of occupational segregation in employer behaviour. (For reviews of all of these theories see Resin, 1984 and Reskin and Hartmann, 1986). Hartmann (1976) and Strober (1984, 1986) have pointed out that in the context of the societal-wide sex-gender system, employers, male employees and female employees *all* play a role in initiating and maintaining occupational segregation.

During the 1960s and 1970s, at both the Federal and State levels, several laws and Executive orders were designed to reduce occupational segregation in employment and in education and training programmes. The laws and orders were enforced with varying degrees of stringency; indeed, in some cases, enforcement agencies lacked sufficient enforcement powers, funding and personnel. It appears that where the laws were enforced they were effective, although unevenly so: 'In general...positive effects occurred most often for black men, somewhat less so for black women, and were least evident for white women' (Reskin and Hartmann, 1986, p. 96).

It may be, however, that occupations that become integrated by gender remain so for only a brief and transient period. Bank-telling, secretarial work and teaching are all examples of formerly all-male occupations that have been resegregated as women's occupations, with concomitant losses in relative earnings and opportunities for upward mobility (Strober and Arnold, 1986; Davies, 1975, 1982; Tyack and Strober, 1981).

BIBLIOGRAPHY

Beller, A.H. 1984. Trends in occupational segregation by sex, 1960–1981. In Reskin (1984).
Bielby, W.T. and Baron, J.N. 1984. A woman's place is with other women: sex segregation within organizations. In Reskin (1984).
Davies, M.W. 1975. *Women's Place is at the Typewriter: Office Work and Office Workers, 1870–1930*. Philadelphia: Temple University Press.

Davies, M.W. 1982. Women's place is at the typewriter; the feminization of the clerical labour force. In *Labor Market Segmentation*, ed. R. Edwards, M. Reich, and D. Gordon, Lexington, Mass.: D.C. Heath.

Duncan, O.D. and Duncan, B. 1955. A methodological analysis of segregation indexes. *American Sociological Review* 20(2), April, 210–17.

Hartmann, H.I. 1976. Capitalism, patriarchy and job segregation by sex. *Signs* 1(3), Pt II, Spring, 137–69.

Jacobs, J.A. 1983. *The Sex Segregation of Occupations and the Career Patterns of Women.* Ann Arbor: University Microfilm International.

Malveaux, J. 1982. Recent trends in occupational segregation by race and sex. Paper presented at the Workshop on Job Segregation by Sex, Committee on Women's Employment and Related Social Issues, National Research Council, Washington, DC, May.

Reskin, B.F. (ed.) 1984. *Sex Segregation in the Workplace: Trends, Explanations, Remedies.* Washington, DC: National Academy Press.

Reskin, B.F. and Hartmann, H.I. (eds) 1986. *Women's Work, Men's Work: Sex Segregation on the Job.* Washington, DC: National Academy Press.

Strober, M.H. 1984. Toward a theory of occupational segregation: the case of public school teaching. In Reskin (1984).

Strober, M.H. and Arnold, C. 1986. The dynamics of occupational segregation by gender: bank tellers (1950–1980). Stanford University.

Treiman, D.J. and Hartmann, H.I. (eds) 1981. *Women, Work, and Wages: Equal Pay for Jobs of Equal Value.* Report of the Committee on Occupational Classification and Analysis, Washington, DC: National Academy Press.

Treiman, D.J. and Terrell, J. 1975. Sex and the process of status attainment: a comparison of working women and men. *American Sociological Review* 40(2), April, 174–200.

Tyack, D.B. and Strober, M.H. 1981. Jobs and gender: a history of the structuring of educational employment by gender. In *Educational Policy and Management: Sex Differentials*, ed. P. Schmuck and W.W. Charters, New York: Academic Press.

Poverty

A.B. ATKINSON

Concern for poverty has been expressed over the centuries, even if its priority on the agenda for political action has not always been high. Its different meanings and manifestations have been the subject of study by historians, sociologists and economists. Its causes have been identified in a wide variety of sources, ranging from deficiencies in the administration of income support to the injustice of the economic and social system. The relief, or abolition, of poverty has been sought in the reform of social security, in intervention in the labour market, and in major changes in the form of economic organization.

Poverty today is most obvious – and has the most pressing claim on our attention – on a world scale. The unequal distribution of income between countries, and the disparities within countries, mean that there are large numbers of people in Africa, Asia and Latin America whose standard of living would be agreed by everyone to be poor. The World Bank has suggested that there is 'a global total of close to 1 billion people living in absolute poverty' (World Bank, 1982, p. 78), of whom about 400 million are thought live in South Asia, about 150 million in China, and some 100 million in East/South-East Asia and Sub-Saharan Africa. At such levels of living, the risks of death through hunger or cold, and vulnerability to disease, are of quite different order from those in advanced countries. This has manifested itself most urgently in the occurrence of famine. Whatever the immediate cause of such disasters, whether inadequate total supply of food or whether unequal distribution, the severity of the situation in areas such as the Sahel and Ethiopia is an indicator of the precariousness of survival in many low income countries.

Such mass poverty in poor countries is quite different from poverty in advanced countries. The target of the American War on Poverty, launched in 1964, was the minority of Americans with incomes below a poverty line of $3000 a year for a family of four (in 1962 prices), which was many times the average income of India. The basis for the US official poverty line is to be found in a food consumption standard (the Department of Agriculture economy food plan), but its level reflects the prevailing living conditions in that society. It might well be argued that concern with poverty in advanced countries, at a time when other countries face disaster, is unjustified and that the term 'poverty' cannot legitimately be applied. The parallel may be drawn with rearranging the deckchairs on the *Titanic* as the ship goes down. This does not, however, seem fully apposite. A closer parallel is with the position of those on ships steaming to the aid of the stricken vessel. The overriding objective should be to get to the rescue as rapidly as possible, but those on the rescuing ships should also be concerned that their steerage passengers do not die of exposure on the way. The relief of famine, and the redistribution of income to alleviate poverty on a world scale, should have priority, but the problem of poverty in advanced countries, defined in their terms, may legitimately come next on the list of concerns.

The fact that the term 'poverty' is being used in different senses highlights the need to clarify the underlying concept, and the discussion so far has touched on several aspects which need to be elaborated. After a brief historical review of studies of poverty in section 1, we examine some key conceptual issues. What is the indicator of resources which should be employed in measuring poverty? What is the underlying notion of poverty and how is it related to inequality? These issues are discussed in section 2. The determination of the poverty standard is a crucial question. Here we need to consider approaches based on such 'absolute' concepts as food requirements and those poverty scales which are explicitly 'relative'. We must consider the treatment of families with differing needs. These topics are the subject of section 3. Once we have established the extent of poverty, its causes become a central concern. Here we are led first to ask 'who are the poor?' This is examined in section 4. Is poverty concentrated in particular classes or particular sections of society? How far is it associated with particular stages of the life-cycle? The composition of the poor provides in turn a starting point for the investigation of the underlying causes of poverty, and an analysis of policies to combat poverty. These are the subject of section 5.

1. HISTORICAL REVIEW OF STUDIES OF POVERTY. The scientific study of poverty in the Anglo-Saxon world is usually taken to date from the investigations of Booth and Rowntree at the end of the 19th century. In Britain it is true that King and others had given estimates of the number of paupers; and that *The State of the Poor* by Eden (1797) contained a great deal of material collected from over 100 parishes and giving details of family budgets. Engels and Mayhew provided insight into the condition of the poor in urban England. But it was Booth's *Life and Labour* (1892–7) survey of London, started in the East End in the 1880s, that combined the elements of first-hand observation with a systematic attempt to measure the extent of the problem. Taking the street as his unit of analysis, he drew up his celebrated map of poverty in London.

The study of Rowntree (1901) was intended to compare the situation in York, as a typical provincial town, with that found by Booth in London, but his method represented a significant departure in that it was concerned with individual family incomes and in that he developed a poverty standard based on estimates of nutritional and other requirements. The development of survey methods was taken further by Bowley (1912–13) who pioneered the use of sampling in his 1 in 20 random sample of working-class households in Reading. A great many local studies were subsequently conducted, including Bowley's Five Towns survey in 1915, replicated in the early 1920s, and the new Survey of London Life and Labour published in the early 1930s. Rowntree himself repeated his survey of York in 1936 and 1950. The latter became the standard source of information as to the effectiveness of the post-1948 welfare state, with most commentators concluding that poverty had been effectively abolished in Britain by the combination of full employment and the new social benefits. Doubt began to be cast on this conclusion by the work of empirical sociologists and came to the fore with the publication of *The Poor and the Poorest* by Townsend and Abel-Smith (1965). This showed, using secondary analysis of a national survey, that in 1960 about two million people fell below the social security safety net level. This finding was confirmed in official estimates which began to be published by the Department of Health and Social Security in the 1970s, and by Townsend's own major survey (1979).

As in many fields, the United States entered later and has taken the subject further. The definition of a poverty line was attempted by Hunter in 1904 and this was developed in a series of studies, such as the 'minimum comfort' and other budgets produced for New York City. There was the 1949 report on low income families by the Joint Committee on the Economic Report. It was not however until the 1960s that the problem of poverty received systematic study, with a few notable exceptions such as the work of Lampman (1959). *The Other America* by Harrington (1962) and *The Affluent Society* by Galbraith (1958) did much to arouse the attention of the public, politicians and academics. The 1964 report of the Council of Economic Advisers set out the $3000 poverty level, drawing heavily on the research of Orshansky (1965), and this was subsequently refined to form the official poverty line, which has been applied since that date (with modifications, such as the addition of alternative measures including the value of transfers in kind).

Similar studies have been carried out in many countries, and researchers have become increasingly interested in cross-country comparisons. The OECD made an early attempt at such comparisons and a more extensive exercise is being carried out in the Luxembourg Income Study. Any assessment of world poverty depends on the availability of information about the distribution of living standards within individual countries; and here both the World Bank and the International Labour Organization have made significant contributions. In some low income countries, there has been extensive research on poverty, India being an example, where there has been a great deal of discussion as to whether poverty has increased or decreased over time. The ILO and the World Bank have also been influential in the widespread interest, reflected in the Brandt Report (1980), in the concept of 'basic needs', or a minimum set of specific goods and environmental conditions.

2. POVERTY: LIVING STANDARDS AND RIGHTS. Concern about poverty may take the form of concern about such basic needs: for example, food, housing and clothing. In this case, we can identify clearly the items of consumption in which we are interested. This approach leads to poverty being measured in a multi-dimensional way, where a family may be deprived in one but not other respects, although particularly serious will be situations where families suffer deprivation in several dimensions, or what is referred to typically as 'multiple deprivation'.

This approach is concerned with specific depreivation, but we may also seek to record disadvantage in a single index of living standards, such as total expenditure, a household being said to be in poverty if it has total expenditure below a specified amount. This is not however the approach followed in most studies of poverty in advanced countries, which record poverty on the basis of total *income*. Income may *understate* the level of living. A family may be able to dissave or to borrow, in which case its current level of living is not constrained by current income and expenditure may be the more appropriate index. (Although in the short run there may be a divergence between *consumption* and *expenditure*, as families use up stocks of goods, etc.) The level of living may exceed that permitted by income where the family is able to share in the consumption of others. An elderly person living with his or her children may benefit from their expenditure. Income may, conversely, *overstate* the level of living. This may happen where money alone is not sufficient to buy the necessary goods: where there is rationing, or unavailability of goods. It is also possible that people choose a low level of consumption. This latter reason has led to its being argued that income *should* be the indicator of poverty, since it is a measure of the opportunities open to a family and is not influenced by the consumption decisions made.

In considering the choice between income and expenditure, it is helpful to distinguish two rather different conceptions of poverty: that concerned with *standards of living* and that concerned with *minimum rights* to resources. On the former approach, the goal is that people attain a specified level of consumption (or consumption of specific goods); on the latter approach, people are seen as entitled, as citizens, to a minimum income, the disposal of which is a matter for them. In practice, the two notions are often confounded, but the distinction is important, and it has obvious implications for the choice of poverty indicator. Income is the focus of the rights approach, but its use on a standard of living approach must be seen as a proxy for consumption.

The reference to 'rights' raises the question of the relation between poverty and inequality. Here four different schools of thought may be distinguished. There are those who are concerned only with poverty, attaching no weight to income inequalities above the poverty line. There are those who attach weight to the reduction of inequality as a goal of policy but give priority to the elimination of poverty, so that we have a lexicographic objective function. There are those who are concerned about both goals and who are willing to trade gains in one direction against losses in the other. Finally, there are those who attach no especial significance to poverty, simply regarding it as a component of the wider cost of inequality.

In this context, reference should be made to the choice of *poverty measures*. Where poverty puts survival in doubt, it is natural to take as one's measure the proportion of the population at risk. Concern for minimum rights may also make the 'head count' the most relevant measure. But we may also be concerned, particularly on a standard of living approach, with the severity of poverty, in which case measures such as the poverty deficit (the total shortfall from the poverty line) may be more appropriate. One can indeed go further, as proposed by Sen (1976), and take account of the distribution of income within the poor population: for example, with the poverty index depending on the Gini coefficient for this distribution.

3. SETTING THE POVERTY LINE. The most straightforward approach to the determination of the poverty line is to specify a basket of goods, denoted by the vector $\mathbf{x}^*$, purchasable at prices p, and to set the poverty standard as:

$$(1 + h)\mathbf{p} \cdot \mathbf{x}^*$$

where h is a provision for inefficient expenditure or waste, or a provision for items not included in the list $\mathbf{x}^*$. This was in effect the method adopted by Rowntree, whose diet for Tuesdays was porridge for breakfast, bread and cheese for lunch, and vegetable broth for dinner. It was the method followed by Orshanksky, where $\mathbf{x}^*$ represented food requirements and $h\,(=2)$ made allowance for spending on other goods. This approach is often referred to as an 'absolute' poverty standard, and contrasted with a 'relative' approach that relates the poverty line to contemporary levels of living: for example the proposal of Fuchs in the United States that the poverty line should be one-half the median family income. It is sometimes suggested that the absolute standard is less problematic than the relative approach and less dependant on value judgements.

The term 'absolute' can, however, scarcely be used in the same sense as in the physical sciences and there is scope for a great deal of disagreement about where the line should be drawn. This is most evident in the case of the rights approach, where the determination of the minimum level of income is explicitly a social judgement, but it applies also to the standard of living approach. In the case of food requirements, where a physiological basis may appear to provide a firm starting point, it is in fact difficult to determine $\mathbf{x}^*$ with any precision. There is no one level of food intake required to survive, but rather a broad range where physical efficiency declines with a falling intake of calories and protein. Nutritional needs depend on where people live and on what they are doing. They vary from person to person, so that any statement can only be probabilistic: at a certain level of consumption there is a certain probability that the person is inadequately fed. Even if these problems could be resolved, there is the difficult of the disparity between expert recommendations and actual consumption behaviour. The factor h is intended to allow for this, but the precise allowance will depend on the judgement of the investigator. Rowntree, for example, included an allowance for tea, which has little or no nutritional value but which formed a staple item of consumption.

In the case of non-food items, there is even greater scope for judgement. This applies whether we seek to include the goods in the vector $\mathbf{x}^*$ or whether we allow for non-food items via the multiplier h. For example, the procedure of Orshansky has been criticized as under-stating the proportion of income spent on food and hence overstating the value of h. More fundamentally, the role of goods in the determination of the poverty line needs reconsideration. The literature on 'household production' has pointed to the role of goods as an input into household activities, with the level of activities being our main concern rather than the purchase of goods as such. On this basis, if we denote the target level of activities by $\mathbf{z}^*$, and if there is an input-output matrix A, relating goods inputs to activity levels, then the necessary level of expenditure becomes:

$$Y = (1 + h)\mathbf{p}A\mathbf{z}^*$$

The significance of this view is that poverty may be measured in absolute terms, in the sense that the vector $\mathbf{z}^*$ is fixed, but the required bundle of goods may be changing because the intput–output matrix is affected by developments in the particular society. If the activity is 'attending school', then the demands in terms of clothing, books and equipment are quite different today from those of a century ago. This does not mean that there is no distinction between absolute and relative concepts. There is a clear difference in principle between taking the vector $\mathbf{z}^*$ as fixed and allowing it to be influenced by the living patterns of the rest of society, as in the work of Townsend (1979), who is concerned with the extent to which families can participate in the 'community's style of living'.

The notion of a fixed absolute poverty standard, applicable to all societies and at all times, is therefore a chimera. Nor is it evident that a poverty standard, once set, can be compared across time by simply adjusting by an index of consumer prices. In the case of both absolute and relative approaches, we have to face the problems of judgement. Here several lines of attack may be discerned. There are studies which take the *official* poverty standards as embodying social values, which seems natural on the minimum rights approach and which at least provides a measure of governmental performance. There are studies which base the poverty line on the views expressed in surveys of the population as a whole. In the United States, the Gallup Poll has regularly asked the question: 'What is the smallest amount of money a family of four needs to get along in this community?' These, and other approaches, will produce a range of poverty lines, and it seems unlikely that we can reach universal agreement. There are therefore strong reasons for recognizing such differences of view explicitly and using a *range* of poverty lines. This means that we may not be able to reach unambiguous conclusions – it may be that poverty will be shown to have increased according to one line but not according to another – but it will avoid a total impasse. In the same way, when making a comparison over time, we may want to compare 1950 with two alternative lines for 1980, one updated by the price index and the other adjusted to allow for rising real incomes, thus generating a 'confidence interval' around the 1980 estimate.

To this point, the poverty line has been discussed as though it were a single number, but families of different types and different sizes will receive different treatment. In Britain, for example, the social security safety net is typically some 60 per cent higher for a couple than for a single person. The relationship between the poverty lines for different family types is usually referred to as an *equivalence scale*. However, a prior question before the equivalence scales are determined is the choice of the *unit of analysis*. Here the distinction between the standard of living and rights approaches is important. In the latter case, the notion of rights must be essentially individualistic. The case for considering a wider unit must rest on there being within-family transfers which cannot be adequately observed. The family is taken when measuring poverty because we do not accept that a large number of those with zero recorded cash income are in fact without resources. At the same time, little is known about the distribution of income within the family. Certainly, it would be quite wrong to treat all married couples as having equal rights to the joint income. On a standard of living approach, the logical unit is that which shares consumption; and we may wish to go beyond the inner family to the household as a whole. This would take account of the fact that items of expenditure may have 'public good' characteristics for the family members. Again, however, it may be that there are unequal living standards within the household.

Several approaches have been adopted to the determination of the equivalence scales for different-sized units. Survey information about individual assessments of what is needed 'to get along' has been used for this purpose. More commonly, the basis had been sought for observation of actual behaviour. One of the early methods provides an illustration. By taking a commodity consumed only by adults (e.g. men's clothing), one can observe the level of income at which a family with one child, say, can attain the same level of consumption of that commodity as a family with no children. This method, and other more sophisticated implementations of the idea, have been the subject of considerable debate. The underlying difficulty is that one is assuming, in the example given, that preferences for the commodity are independent of family composition: the arrival of the child may mean that the couple go out less and spend less on clothing. With other methods based on observed consumption behaviour, identifying restrictions are similarly needed. At a more fundamental level, the ethical status of such scales is far from transparent. Not only is it impossible to draw conclusions about welfare levels with different family compositions, but also society may wish to modify the implied judgements: for example, to vary the parental evaluation to take account of the interests of the children.

4. THE COMPOSITION OF THE POOR. One of the main aims of those investigating poverty has been to establish who the poor are. Popular opinion is often coloured by vivid, but not necessarily representative, accounts of life below the poverty line. For this reason, the Council of Economic Advisers stressed at the start of

the War on Poverty in the US that poverty should not be seen as a minority phenomenon: 'Some believe that most of the poor are found in the slums of the central city, while others believe that they are concentrated in areas of rural blight. Some have been impressed by poverty among the elderly, while others are convinced that it is primarily a problem of minority racial and ethnic groups. But objective evidence indicates that poverty is pervasive... the poor are found among all major groups in the population and in all parts of the country' (1964, pp. 61–2).

Poverty in advanced countries affects a minority in terms of numbers but it is not confined to specific marginal groups. At the same time, certain groups are much more at risk. In 1983, the poverty rate for blacks in the United States was nearly three times that for whites, and that for Hispanics was more than twice. Compared with the average, the rate for families with children is nearly double, and that for families with a female head is much higher. The evidence for other countries equally shows large differences in the incidence of poverty between groups: for instance, in Malaysia, recorded poverty among Malays is much higher than among the Indian or Chinese ethnic groups. The World Bank has argued that poverty in low income countries is very much a rural problem; and the evidence from India shows poverty to be much higher in rural than urban areas.

If we seek to probe further into the composition of the poor, then the dynamics of poverty must be taken into account. Is poverty a largely transitory phenomenon, in that the families poor today will quite probably be above the poverty line next year? Is poverrty associated with particular periods of the life cycle? Transitory poverty may occur for a variety of reasons. Income may be temporarily reduced because of ill-health or unemployment or because wages are cut. It may be a bad harvest. Families may split up, leaving one parent with the family responsibilities but inadequate income. The evidence from panel surveys, where the same families are interviewed on a continuing basis (as, for example, in the Michigan Panel Study of Income Dynamics), has shown the extent of mobility in the incomes and circumstances of the poor. A sizeable fraction of those recorded as poor in one year are above the poverty line next year. This does not mean that their poverty is not a matter for concern, since low current incomes may impose severe hardship, but it means that these people do not constitute a permanent 'under class'.

Such mobility does however require careful interpretation. It may arise on account of the life cycle. In Rowntree's 1899 survey he found that the life of the labourer was marked by 'five alternating periods of want and comparative plenty', the periods of want being childhood, when he himself had children, and old age. The impact of such life-cycle factors depends on the extent to which income support is provided by state or private transfers. In this respect the situation in Britain has changed dramatically since 1899, with the introduction of state pensions, a large increase in private pensions, and the payment of child and other benefits. In other countries too there has been major growth in transfers: between 1960 and 1981 social expenditure as a percentage of GDP rose in the United States from 7 per cent to 15 per cent, in West Germany from 18 per cent to

27 per cent, and in Japan from 4 to 14 per cent (Institute for Research on Poverty, 1985). Transfers, and other programmes, such as health care, must have reduced the extent of life-cycle poverty. The incomes of the elderly in the United States, for example, are considered to have risen relative to those of the population as a whole. But there remains concern about certain stages of the life cycle, particularly among families with children; and while the poverty rate among the elderly in the US has fallen, that among the non-elderly has risen.

To the extent that poverty is a life-cycle phenomenon, this means that more people experience poverty at some point in their lives but that its duration is limited. At the same time, poverty at one stage of the life cycle may lead to poverty at a subsequent stage. Those who are hard-pressed when they are bringing up children may have little savings on which to draw in retirement. Those who grow up in low-income families may themselves be more likely to be below the poverty line, as was found in the follow-up in the 1970s of the children of the families interviewed by Rowntree in 1950 (Atkinson, Maynard and Trinder, 1983). Moreover, we should not lose sight of the fact that for some people poverty persists. Agricultural labourers, or farmers with small plots, may be in poverty even in 'good' years. Among industrial workers, there are those whose earnings are inadequate to support even themselves; there may be a problem of *low pay*. And the low paid may be more vulnerable to the transitory factors such as ill-health and unemployment.

5. CAUSES AND POLICIES. In 1913, R.H. Tawney argued for the restatement of the problem of poverty: 'the diversion to questions of social organization of much of the attention which, a generation ago, was spent on relief'. The problem of poverty, he said, was 'primarily an industrial one'. In terms of the composition of the poor described above, this means that the causes of poverty were sought not in the failure of income support but in the reasons why income was inadequate in the first place.

Tawney recognized the importance of personal factors in causing poverty, but laid principal stress on the position of groups and classes and their economic situation, factors which may equally be relevant today. Workers may be locked into low-paying industries where techniques and machinery need to be modernized; they may live in depressed regions to which private capital cannot be attracted. There may be a low level of unionization and employers may be able to hold wages down. These aspects, which have been emphasized in theories of 'segmentation' in the labour market, point to the need for government intervention. This may take the form of minimum wage legislation, to guarantee minimum levels of earnings, coupled with measures to offset any adverse effect on employment and to modernize the sectors or regions concerned. At a macro-economic level, the government has an important responsibility. Studies in the United States have identified unemployment as a much more serious problem than inflation for low income groups. There can be little doubt, for example, that the recession of the 1980s has increased the incidence of poverty in advanced countries.

The counterpart of this structural explanation in the context of less developed, primarily agricultural economies is to be found in the role of land tenure and its distribution, and in the nature of labour and capital markets. Rural poverty is high among landless labourers and those farmers with small or unproductive holdings. Their difficulties may be intensified by the terms on which they have to borrow or purchase intermediate goods. Here too policy requires government intervention, whether to redistribute land holdings, or to facilitate the introduction of new methods, or to eliminate extortionate lending practices, or to provide non-farm employment. Measures such as land reform raise major political issues, and in both developing and advanced countries it can be argued that basic changes in the form of economic system are necessary to eradicate poverty. The World Bank has noted, for example, the role played by the Chinese food security policy in the reduction of poverty and the way in which it is tied into China's collective system.

The industrial explanation of poverty may be contrasted with the 'supply side' explanation which has seen low pay as attributable to workers lacking productive skills, because they have been unable to complete education or training. This 'human capital' interpretation leads in turn to the policy recommendation that training and educational programmes should be expanded, a proposal that is congruent with the goal of reducing inequality of opportunity. Education and training had a central role in the United States War on Poverty, with schemes such as the Job Corps and the Neighbourhood Youth Corps. A characteristic of individual workers also identified in the United States is that of race. Discrimination may lead to otherwise equally qualified workers receiving lower pay, as where black workers were prevented from entering certain occupations. The civil rights legislation and the operations of the Equal Employment Opportunity Commission may have reduced the direct effect of discrimination (as well as the indirect effect via unequal opportunities in education etc.), but although the policy implications are clear in principle, experience suggests that they are not easily made effective.

Policies to improve job and earnings prospects must be central to the elimination of poverty, but they cannot succeed without complementary income maintenance provisions. The growth of transfers has not succeeded in providing a completely effective income guarantee for those without incomes from work or with additional needs. This is because of incomplete coverage, particularly where new needs develop, because of the inadequate levels of benefits (for example, those paid to people with poor employment records) and the incomplete take-up of income-tested benefits. In the last case, there is evidence that complexity or stigma deters families from claiming the transfers to which they are entitled, and hence they fall through the safety net.

To this end, proposals have been made for major reform of the transfer systems in advanced countries. One front-runner for many years in the United States has been the 'negative income tax', which would pay an income-related supplement using the income tax machinery. There are those reformers who would like to integrate fully the income tax and social security systems, as with the basic income guarantee scheme, where everyone receives a basic income and is then taxed on all income. Such a reform would mean that income maintenance largely ceased to be categorical: for example, there would not be separate treatment for the unemployed or the sick. An alternative would be to preserve the categorical nature of social insurance but to make the insurance benefits more extensive in their coverage and sufficient to avoid the necessity to depend on public assistance or other forms of means-tested benefits. In considering the feasibility of such reforms, one must have regard both to the arithmetic of the redistribution and to the reasons why they have not been enacted in the past. As the 'public choice' school of public finance economists has stressed, the actions of the government are themselves to be explained by economic and other motives. The reasons why governmens have failed to enact successful anti-poverty policies is a subject of great importance.

The policies discussed in this section are solely concerned with the poverty *within* countries, and would do nothing to redistribute between countries. Indeed, some of the policies designed to help the low paid in advanced countries may actually have adverse consequences for low income countries. The income transfers which rich countries have so far made are of miniscule size when viewed against the magnitude of the problem of world poverty, and there can be little doubt that redistribution on a world scale is of the highest priority.

BIBLIOGRAPHY

Abel-Smith, B. and Townsend, P. 1965. *The Poor and the Poorest*. London: Bell.
Atkinson, A.B., Maynard, A.K. and Trinder, C.G. 1983. *Parents and Children*. London: Heinemann.
Booth, C. 1892–7. *Life and Labour of the People of London*. 9 vols, London: Macmillan.
Bowley, A.L. 1913. Working class households in Reading. *Journal of the Royal Statistical Society* 76, June, 672–701.
Brandt, W. (Chairman). 1980. *North–South*. London: Pan.
Council of Economic Advisers. 1964. *Annual Report*. Washington, DC: Government Printing Office.
Eden, Sir F.M. 1797. *The State of the Poor*. London: Cass.
Galbraith, J.K. 1958. *The Affluent Society*. Boston: Houghton Mifflin.
Harrington, M. 1962. *The Other America*. New York: Macmillan.
Institute for Research on Poverty. 1985. Antipoverty policy: past and future. *Focus*, Summer.
Lampman, R.J. 1959. *The Low Income Population and Economic Growth*. Study Paper No. 12, US Congress Joint Economic Committee. Washington, DC: Government Printing Office.
Orshansky, M. 1965. Who's who among the poor: a demographic view of poverty. *Social Security Bulletin* 28(7), July, 3–32.
Rowntree, B.S. 1901. *Poverty*. London: Macmillan.
Sen, A.K. 1976. Poverty: an ordinal approach to measurement. *Econometrica* 44(2), March, 219–31.
Tawney, R.H. 1913. *Poverty as an Industrial Problem*. London: London School of Economics.
Townsend, P. 1979. *Poverty in the United Kingdom*. London: Penguin.
World Bank. 1982. *World Development Report, 1982*. New York: Oxford University Press.

Race and Economics

H. STANBACK

The concept of race enters formal economic theory through a range of areas primarily within labour economics. These include discrimination, inequality, human capital, labour market competition and segmentation, and class relations. The first substantive attention by neoclassical theory to the economic problems posed by race began with the work of Gary Becker in 1957 which approaches the subject from the standpoint of discrimination. (Race is addressed from a structural standpoint by Marx in *Capital*, Volume I, through his analysis of the impact of slavery and the slave trade on the working class of the United States.)

Subsequent to Becker there have been numerous theoretical advances and approaches towards an understanding of the role of race in the economy. There are three alternative formulations of the problem: (1) employer or employee discrimination; (2) labour supply; (3) competition between capital and labour.

EMPLOYER/EMPLOYEE DISCRIMINATION. I. Becker presents race as a problem of 'taste' for discrimination or a 'distaste' for physical association with a particular race (his formulation would be equally applicable to any standard physical attribute such as sex). The taste for discrimination can come from the employer or employee. Becker's employer distaste model assumes two societies; B, which is relatively labour-abundant, and W, which is relatively capital-abundant. These two societies engage in voluntary trade with each other but with the capital of W having a distaste for working in physical proximity to B labour. Given the assumptions of a pure theory of international trade and without such distaste, B and W exchange their respective relatively abundant quantities until the marginal product of each factor is equal in both societies. However, because of the distaste or subjective preference of W employers, their utility function must be augmented to include the number of B workers and $dU_W < dL_B < 0$. The capital exported by W must receive a money return greater than the return on capital domestically employed. The differences between the return on domestic vs. exported capital is the return or compensation W employers feel they must have for being physically close to B labour. Since such compensation must be positive, discrimination reduces the quantity of W capital exported and the quantity of B labour exported.

Becker's model concludes that as a result of discrimination, W labour's money income increases and W capital's net income falls because with the reduction in W capitals exported and B labour imported, W labour works with more capital and W capital works with less labour.

Since $f_{LL} < 0$ and $f_{KL} < 0$, the f_L, the wage of labor, rises under the described conditions. Since $f_{KL} < 0$, the f_{KW}, the money return to domestic capital, falls as more capital is employed (Becker, 1957).

In the absence of monopoly, discrimination would end if one employer did not have or did not exercise his distaste. This employer would reap abnormal profits thus forcing other competitors to follow, assuming the drive for profits is stronger than racial distaste.

II. A more advanced version of the employer discrimination model are 'statistical discrimination models' (Reich, 1981). Such models make discrimination by employers more 'rational' in their employee hirings than Becker's subjective preference criteria. Racial discrimination results from problems associated with the personnel costs of hiring, training and identifying productivity. Such costs give rise to discrimination in the normal pursuit of profits; consequently, discrimination persists.

Personnel costs affect racial employment in the following way. A Race A employer with few or no workers of Race B may want to employ some. However, the costs of hiring and training new workers would not be offset by Race B's lower wages. The costs are profit maximization considerations, therefore, racial inequality persists as an integral part of competition. Although marginal changes are made, the tendency is for no major overhaul in the racial composition of any employer's work force.

Prejudiced perceptions of Race B workers' productivity influence Race A employer's queueing or prioritizing workers for employment. Since it is costly to determine productivity prior to employment, employers of Race A presume that all workers of Race B are less productive than Race A workers. This presumably protects the employer because it is much more costly to hire an inefficient worker than to pass over a productive one. As a result, Race B workers are not hired or hired at a lower wage rate. Prejudiced perceptions may emerge from a variety of sources. Regardless, in this model, they provide a low cost screen in the employee search process.

III. Employee discrimination models are based on perceived and competing economic and racial interests. Such models require the ability of workers of Race A to obtain cooperation from employers and other actors in Race A to form a 'cartel' to discriminate against workers of Race B. The following characteristics describe this cartel arrangement (see Krueger, 1963; Bermann, 1971):

1. Race A capital and labour combine to discriminate against Race B's labour even though Race A labour gains while Race A capital loses (as per Becker).

2. Racial income differences can be accounted for through Race A's political control which limits inputs into Race B's schooling and, thus, skills.

3. Further discrimination against Race B takes place through the cartel arrangement by restricting hiring, occupational mobility, wage payments, access to capital markets, and through price discrimination.

4. Race B's labour is 'crowded' into certain lower paying occupations through racial discrimination. This results in a depressed marginal product because excess labour is employed and, hence, wage rates are depressed.

The results reflected in the combination/cartel arrangements require critical institutional mechanisms to assure enforcement of the 'rules' of the cartel.

LABOUR SUPPLY. Race is a component of labour supply analysis primarily in relationship to human capital theory. Differences in the quantity/quality of human capital explains racial income differences. While the subjective demand for human capital by Race B may be the same as Race A's subjective demand for human capital, the objective capacity to invest is less due to lower initial endowments which may result from discrimination. Additionally the supply of human capital, e.g., education and health care, is likely to be less (Sowell, 1975).

Labour supply analyses of racial inequality tend to locate the discrimination problem outside of the economic area, generally focusing on education as the critical form of human capital. Contemporary analyses of racial inequality have raised the question of the inequality of demand for human capital in the form of education (Sowell, 1975). Accordingly, an emerging 'underclass', disproportionately of a particular race, has a low demand for education as a result of cultural variables which reject work at the prevailing wage rate. The important cultural variables can emerge from geographic dislocation such as migration from a rural to an urban setting, or from previous experience in the labour market.

COMPETITION. All of the previously discussed approaches to race involve competition theories. Marxian economists have also approached race from the standpoint of either structural conflict between capital and labour, or between capitalists, or both. The Marxian concepts of accumulation and class struggle provide the foundation of this approach to an analysis of race. Race is examined not only to understand racial inequality as in previously discussed formulations, but also to understand competition between firms and capital-labour conflict (Baron, 1975; Harris, 1972; Reich, 1981; Sysmanski, 1975).

Racial inequality, in this framework, is the product of the pursuit of profits. Particularly, the pursuit of cheap resource markets gives economic rationality to the use of race as a means of cheapening the cost of Race B's labour. Institutional arrangements as suggested in the 'cartel' approach, and/or direct discrimination as suggested in the employer discrimination approach, may be the explicit manifestation of the pursuit of profits.

Racial inequality may also be a product of capital-labour conflict due to deliberate manipulation of Race B's access to employment by either capital or labour from Race A. In such instances, race is utilized to strengthen or weaken a particular side of the conflict. Capital may utilize cheaper labour from Race B to reduce labour's bargaining strength. Race A labour may join with Race B labour to prevent such tactics and, thereby, strengthen Race A labour's posture.

Race, in this framework, both influences and is influenced by economic processes. Often in this framework, racial inequality and the manipulation of race in competition/conflict is considered endemic to the competitive profit pursuit.

In the past 30 years there has been a dramatic increase in the attention of economic theory to race and race related issues. As indicated above, these approaches either focus on market imperfections or on the structural character of capitalism as explanations of racial discrimination and/or inequality. Most structuralist analyses also utilize race as a means of explaining the dynamics of economic processes.

BIBLIOGRAPHY

Baron, H. 1975. *The Demand for Black Labor*. Boston: New England.

Becker, G.S. 1957. *The Economics of Discrimination*. 2nd edn, Chicago: University of Chicago Press, 1971.

Bergmann, B. 1971. The effect on white incomes of discrimination in employment. *Journal of Political Economy* 71(2), March-April, 294–31.

Harris, D.J. 1972. The black ghetto as colony: a theoretical critique and alternative formulation. *Review of Black Political Economy* 2(4), Summer.

Krueger, A. 1963. The economics of discrimination. *Journal of Political Economy* 71, October, 481–6.

Reich, M. 1981. *Racial Inequality: A Political Economic Analysis*. Princeton: Princeton University Press.

Sowell, T. 1975. *Race and Economics*. New York: David McKay.

Sysmanski, A. 1975. Trends in economic discrimination against blacks in the U.S. working class. *Review of Radical Political Economics* 7(3), Fall, 1–21.

Rent Control

KURT KLAPPHOLZ

Rent control, found the world over, is an arrangement under which a governmental agency prescribes the maximum rents private landlords may charge for accommodation, as the control is intended to benefit tenants. In Section I it is argued that rent control can help existing tenants, but only if it is accompanied by additional legal measures. Since the details of these legal measures change over time, and vary across areas, only examples can be provided to illustrate the argument. Yet, whatever these legal measures, rent control can not help *potential* tenants (except in unusual circumstances, e.g. when landlords expect it to be temporary). In Section II we examine why rent control leads to inefficiency.

I. Text-book treatments of price control in competitive markets stress that, for maximum price control to be effective, the ceiling price must be below the market clearing price. This condition is necessary, but not sufficient. Consider a government enacting a law which stipulates a ceiling rent for specified kinds of accommodation, unaccompanied by any other legal provisions. Assuming landlords do not expect a future tightening of the law, its effects would be short-lived. Tenants with unexpired leases would enjoy lower rents until their leases expired. What landlords did as leases expired would depend on other provisions of the law, for example, whether *all* tenancies, or only *existing ones*, for the class of accommodation defined were subject to the control. If the latter were the case, existing tenants could be offered new leases at market rents; if the former were the case, landlords would face a number of options, among them the sale of dwellings into owner occupation, the exercise of which would imply that rent control ceased to be effective. These examples suffice to show that the mere fixing of rent ceilings below the market clearing level cannot ensure the effectiveness of rent control. Additional measures are required.

The most obvious and usual measure is to accompany rent ceilings with security of tenure, i.e. with the tenants' right to remain in controlled dwellings for as long as rent control remains in force (a period inherently difficult to predict, for political reasons), provided they pay the ceiling rent. Security of tenure is an implicit form of rationing, which renders legally null and void the expiry dates of previously signed leases. If the purpose of rent control were only the protection of existing tenants, then this measure, accompanied by effective prevention of harassment (Cullingworth, 1979, p. 68), would be sufficient to protect them at the expense of their landlords (a qualification of this is noted below, Section II).

However, sometimes rent control legislation also provides security of tenure for new tenants, as, for example, in the 1965 Rent Act in the UK. If this is done, rent control is viewed, not merely as an emergency measure, but as a '...long-term...policy for the privately rented sector' (Cullingworth, 1979, p. 67). It is important to consider what effects such a policy has, in addition to the effects just described. This can not be done in the absence of additional information about the law, in particular, about the legality of landlords charging premiums (key money) for new tenancies. If landlords are permitted to charge key money then rent control might not prevent market-clearing for new tenancies (assuming that landlords do not expect a retro-active tightening of the law, involving, e.g., a requirement to refund key money). If a market persisted, would the total rental cost be the same as that in an uncontrolled market? The answer sometimes suggested is that the cost would be the same, as key money would approximate '...the discounted present value of the difference between the expected market rent and the controlled rent over the relevant period' (Cheung, 1979, p. 28). This appears to ignore two differences between these alternative situations. First, prospective tenants would find borrowing for premiums difficult, since a tenancy is 'poor' collateral, and, if the landlord were the lender, he could not evict the tenant for non-repayment of the loan. Second, for any given premium, the cost to the tenant and the benefit to the landlord would decrease with the length of the tenant's stay. With security of tenure (see below) any agreement on the term of the tenancy would be enforceable. Landlords would know that tenants have an incentive to express dishonestly any intention to stay for a short period. Tenants would know that, should they wish to stay less long than they had originally intended, they would face bargaining problems with their landlords on wishing to terminate the tenancy (see below, Section II). These strategic considerations suggest that some mutually advantageous bargains would be inhibited, and that the outcome would not approximate the situation in which the duration of leases can be freely negotiated. It has been suggested that 'statutory law is powerless to suppress...' the taking of key money, which can be easily 'disguised' (Cheung, 1979, p. 28). This cannot be true as a general statement unless it is qualified. U.K. statutory law (as consolidated in the Rent Act 1977, Section 126) appears to have suppressed exchanges of key money for residential tenancies, since otherwise the drying up of the supply of the latter – see below – would be difficult to explain (assuming that, with key money, a market would exist).

In the absence of premiums landlords will be unwilling to offer new tenancies for the class of accommodation to which rent control applies. Text-book treatments (e.g. Le Grand and Robinson, 1984, pp. 96–99) do not stress the differential effects of rent control on existing, as against potential, tenants, and thus omit an indispensable element in the explanation of the drying up of the supply of new tenancies. That element is the legal status of security of tenure for statutory tenants (*Baxter* v. *Eckersley* [1950], 480 at 485). The kind of legislation which prevailed, e.g., in the UK from 1965–80, greatly increased the actual, and potential, number of statutory tenants. Under that kind of law a new tenant, who might be willing to pay a rent in excess of that stipulated by the legislation, and to forego security of tenure, has no legally enforceable means of assuring a landlord that he will do so, since the legislation affords tenants legally inalienable protection. Under these circumstances, if a landlord granted a tenancy, he would have to rely solely on the tenant's word. Thus, if, as was the case in the UK, the legal protection for new tenants is the same as that for existing ones, in general potential tenants will not be offered tenancies. It has been noted that 'had it been the long-term objective to kill off the private landlord, British housing policy has achieved a remarkable degree of success' (Cullingworth, 1979, p. 73). Moreover, neither existing tenants, nor the heirs who may inherit their tenancies, live for ever. When their dwellings become vacant landlords will not re-let them, but transfer them to other uses, e.g. owner occupation. In the 'long-run' (which, in the case of housing, may be long indeed) the dwellings subject to rent control tend to disappear. Then potential tenants are harmed rather than helped by rent control (Whitehead and Kleinman, 1986, ch. 6).

An equity effect of rent control, and a constitutional aspect related to it, must be mentioned. It would be a sheer fluke if the wealth transfers resulting from effective rent control conformed to any reasonable criterion of equity (Friedman, 1985, p. 460). Moreover, they do not appear in the budget and are not explicitly considered by the legislature.

II. Apart from the redistributive effects stressed in Section I rent control also has efficiency effects. One of these follows from the analysis in the previous Section, i.e. the disappearance of a service to new buyers who would wish to buy it in the absence of rent control. The extent of the resulting welfare losses depends on how close are the substitutes which remain outside control, which, in turn, depends on how comprehensively rent control is applied. To give an example, in the UK, between 1965–1974, rent control with indefinite security of tenure applied to unfurnished accommodation only, so that furnished rented accommodation remained accessible to new tenants. In 1974 tenants of furnished accommodation were accorded the same protection as unfurnished tenants, with predictable results (Maclennan, 1978; Cullingworth, 1979, pp. 71–72). It may be surmized that welfare losses increased. The persistence of this inefficiency was explained in Section I. Other inefficiencies commonly attributed to rent control can be exhaustively grouped under two headings; (i) inefficiencies in the allocation of the existing housing, of which classic examples are the immobility of 'sitting' tenants and their excessive consumption of housing space (Olsen, 1972, pp. 1096–7); (ii) inefficient maintenance, including reconstruction, of that stock. These claims about the effects of rent control are of long standing (e.g. *Rent*

Control, 1975), but the concepts which might help to explain them have been systematically introduced into economics much more recently. These concepts concern the relationship between legislative enactments, such as rent control, and the resulting changes in property rights and transactions costs.

We saw in Section I that the introduction of rent control implies a capital levy on existing landlords and a capital subsidy to existing tenants. Why should such a windfall transfer cause the inefficiencies just listed, i.e. why should it prevent the full exploitation of subsequent potential gains from trade? For example, it has been calculated that the losses to landlords from rent control in New York City were twice as high as the gains to their tenants, but what prevented the elimination of this inefficiency is not explained (Olsen, 1972). Why do existing tenants not make arrangements to transfer their tenancies to other tenants, who value them more highly, or why do they not give them up, by making appropriate arrangements with their landlords, who could then transfer the dwelling to higher valued ones?

To answer this question one needs to consider the incentives which rent control with security of tenure offers to the potential parties to the exchange, which requires us to take account of the more detailed legal specifications of the rent control legislation (Cheung, 1974, 1975, 1979).

At first sight rent control would not seem to impede transfers of tenancies from existing to new tenants, the latter paying premiums to the former, as analysed in Section 1. However, this presupposes that the law allows existing tenants to accept such premiums, which is not the case, e.g., in the UK (*Farrell* v. *Alexander* [1977]). It also presupposes that existing tenants have the right to assign tenancies without requiring their landlords' consent, which is rarely the case (Friedman, 1985, p. 460). Once the landlord's consent is required, the division of premiums is not market-determined, but is the outcome of bilateral bargaining, which raises the cost of reaching agreement between the parties. It may be noted that, *purely on grounds of efficiency*, it would be preferable if landlords could not refuse consent to the re-assignment of a tenancy – assuming tenants were allowed to accept premiums.

As regards transfers between tenants and landlords, the bargaining costs are the same as those just discussed, and whether there is a systematic bias in the direction of transfers would depend on legal influences on components of transactions costs other than bargaining. To illustrate: if security of tenure is legally inalienable a landlord cannot frame a contract which obliges the tenant to vacate the dwelling for a consideration; by contrast, if the landlord wishes to sell the property to the tenant, the transaction is an ordinary conveyance. However, landlords can offer tenants financial inducements to leave, the money being transferred to the tenant by a stake holder *after* the former has vacated the premises. These considerations do not yield any general conclusions, and it seems that the direction of transfers will depend on the circumstances.

Turning to the second group of inefficiencies it is also appropriate to ask why rent control should generate them. As regards sub-optimal maintenance, one popular answer is that landlords 'cannot afford' to maintain rent-controlled properties, but this is not a satisfactory answer (Ricketts, 1981, p. 509). The appropriate answer is that landlords certainly have no incentive to maintain the quality of the property at a level above that for which the tenant is just willing to pay the controlled rent. Indeed, the landlord might find it profitable to allow the property to deteriorate so far that the tenant quits voluntarily, leaving the landlord free to sell to an owner-occupier, unless the landlord can be legally prevented from allowing that degree of deterioration (Ricketts, 1981, p. 511). But this does not explain why tenants should not undertake adequate maintenance, since, by assumption, this would make them better off. Once again, we need to invoke the fact that, with rent control and security of tenure, both tenants' and landlords' property rights are less clearly specified that in their absence, making tenants' investment in maintenance more risky than it would be for landlords in the absence of rent control. Hence the *possibility* that rent control may even make existing tenants worse off (Ricketts, 1981, pp. 507–510).

As regards rebuilding, it is conceivable that landlords, if legally obliged to house their protected tenants at a standard stipulated by the authorities, might find it less costly to rebuild than to repair properties. In practice, this does not appear to happen. Landlords rebuild if, by so doing, they can free the building from rent control (Cheung, 1975). The question is whether the legal provisions of the rent control legislation would affect landlords' decisions regarding rebuilding. We consider only two possible legal provisions: (a) if the landlord can prove that he will rebuild, he has the right to evict his rent-controlled tenants without compensation (as was the case in Hong Kong over a certain period, Cheung, 1975); (b) the landlord may not evict tenants to re-build his property, unless he offers them 'equivalent' accommodation (as has been the case for statutory tenants in the UK since 1965 – *Hill and Redman's*, 1976, pp. 824–827, 899). One might be tempted to conclude at once that, under (a), there would not only be more reconstruction that under (b), but that there would be excessive reconstruction. This conclusion is suggested by the consideration that the private return to the landlord exceeds the social return, since the former includes a recoupment of the transfer conferred on the tenant by rent control. However, the conclusion is not yet warranted, since it ignores the incentives tenants have to bribe landlords to forego excessive reconstruction. Nevertheless, taking these incentives into account does not vitiate qualitatively the initial, albeit unwarranted, conclusion, since, given the bargaining costs with tenants, the private returns to landlords from rebuilding are likely to exceed the social returns (Cheung, 1975). By contrast, under (b) the reverse seems likely, because of the costs imposed on landlords by having to establish that they are offering tenants equivalent accommodation.

BIBLIOGRAPHY

Baxter *v.* Eckersley. [1950] 1 KB 480.

Cheung, S.N.S. 1974. A theory of price control. *Journal of Law and Economics* 17, April, 53–71.

Cheung, S.N.S. 1975. Roofs or stars: the stated intents and actual effects of a rent ordinance. *Economic Inquiry*, April, 1–21.

Cheung, S.N.S. 1979. Rent control and housing reconstruction: the postwar experience of prewar premises in Hong Kong. *Journal of Law and Economics* 22, April, 27–53.

Cullingworth, J.B. 1979. *Essays on Housing Policy.* London: George Allen & Unwin.

Farrell *v.* Alexander. [1977] All E.R. 721, H.L. (E.).

Friedman, L.S. 1985. *Microeconomic Policy Analysis.* New York and London: McGraw-Hill.

Hill and Redman's Law of Landlord and Tenant. 16th edn, London: Butterworths, 1976.

Le Grand, J. and Robinson, R. 1984. *The Economics of Social Problems.* 2nd edn, London: Macmillan.

MaClennan, D. 1978. The 1974 Rent Act – some short run supply effects. *Economic Journal* 88, June, 331–40.

Olsen, E.O. 1972. An econometric analysis of rent control. *Journal of Political Economy* 80, November-December, 1081–100.

Rent Act 1977. London: HMSO.

Rent Control – A Popular Paradox. 1975. Ed. F.A. Hayek et al., Vancouver: Fraser Institute.

Ricketts, M. 1981. Housing policy: towards a public choice perspective. *Journal of Public Policy,* October, 501–22.

Whitehead, C.M.E. and Kleineman, M.P. 1986. Private Rented Housing in the 1980s and 1990s. Cambridge, University of Cambridge Department of Land Economy, Occasional Paper 17.

Segmented Labour Markets

GLEN G. CAIN

Segmented labour markets may refer to descriptive features of labour markets or to theoretical models of the processes and outcomes of labour market behaviour. This entry emphasizes the latter, but the two aspects of the term are not neatly separable. In its descriptive uses segmentation may refer to industries, geographic areas, or to such demographic characteristics of workers as gender or race.

The term 'segment' may be usefully viewed as resting somewhere between the neutral 'separate' and the more highly charged 'stratified'. Neoclassical economists (a term used in this entry as a convenient synonym for 'conventional' or 'orthodox' economists) often discuss separate labour markets, as when they describe or analyse the market for college-trained workers and the market for unskilled labour. Stratification is a term in contemporary sociology, but when it refers to occupations it coincides with usage in economics, and the sociological concept of class stratification in industrialized societies is derived from the classical economists' three groups of the factors of production: workers, capitalist-entrepreneurs, and landowners. In modern usage in economics, the concept of segmented labour markets is imbued with more theoretical content when it moves closer to stratification and takes on political and sociological connotations.

No single theory and no single taxonomy of descriptive classification dominates the literature dealing with segmented labour markets (see Note on the Bibliography at the end of the entry). The widely used term 'dual labour market' has been referred to as a metaphor for unnumbered (but few) segments by Michael J. Piore, one of its principal advocates (Berger and Piore, 1980, pp. 2, 142), and such terms as tripartite, hierarchical, tiers, cores, peripheries, and radical abound. The only pervasive theoretical posture is that of dissent from neoclassical theories of the labour market, and segmented labour market theories are sometimes a part of radical or Marxian economics, which is a broader alternative to neoclassical economic analysis.

The first and second editions of *Palgrave's Dictionary of Political Economy* (1894–7 and 1926) contain no entries for such terms as segmented, radical, dual, or internal labour markets. *The International Encyclopaedia of the Social Sciences* (1967 edition) has an entry for just one of these terms, 'dual economy' (Werthheim, 1967), and this refers solely to preindustrialized economies that fail to achieve sustained economic growth because of stagnation in a dominant peasant (or traditional) sector. Segmented labour market theories continue to play a role in the field of development economics, but they usually apply to the industrialized or urban sectors of high-income economies.

Are there, then, new ideas in the theories of segmented labour markets? It is no disservice to their contemporary advocates to claim that there are not, and that the original editions of *Palgrave* address the major problems posed in the literature on segmented labour markets. There is merit in giving old ideas fresh and insightful applications in new settings.

Inequality is the dominant problem that motivates the analysis and policy prescriptions in the literature on segmented labour markets; specifically, inequality in wages and working conditions among various occupational, industrial, and demographic groups. To understand the segmentationists' approach to this problem, it is useful to consider the modern neoclassical restatement of the five sources of wage inequality that were originally advanced by the classical economists.

1. Compensating differentials, the theory of which is found in Chapter 10 of Adam Smith's *Wealth of Nations*, and which allow for non-pecuniary aspects of work as equilibriating sources of wage differences.

2. Human capital investments, which, although recognized already by Smith, have become increasingly important and can explain how wage differentials that are associated with different age-earnings profiles among workers can coexist with identical lifetime present values of the workers' earnings.

3. Barriers to entry in certain protected, high-paying occupations, wherein the barriers may be well-defined labour market institutions – such as trade unions or governmental regulation and licensing – or in the form of the amorphous barriers of, historically, class distinctions and class deprivation, and of, in modern times, racial, ethnic, and gender discrimination in labour markets (discussed below).

4. Transitory differentials that reflect chance factors, lags in mobility, and temporary gains or losses because of seasonal and cyclical variation in demand conditions, often associated with temporary unemployment.

5. Real differences that are in accordance with differences in preferences and abilities among workers.

John Stuart Mill ([1848], 1900, pp. 369–77) and also his follower, John E. Cairnes (1874, pp. 65–8), who coined the term 'noncompeting groups', dismissed item 1 in criticizing Smith, remarking that allowances for non-pecuniary aspects of employment would increase overall inequality in the labour market, even though the principle of compensating differentials was valid within narrow strata of skill levels. They stressed, as do the segmentation theorists, item 3, barriers to mobility. Both neoclassical and segmentation economists give attention to the institutional barriers created by certain practices of trade unions and by various laws that regulate entry and conditions of work in certain industries and occupations. The segmentationists generally have a different political and ideological interpretation of these practices, viewing them as manifestations of an employer-dominated political system that seeks to pit one group of workers against another.

Class stratification was emphasized by Mill, Cairnes, and Alfred Marshall as a deeply rooted barrier to mobility and as a source of intergenerational transmission of poverty. Marshall spoke of the inability of the poorer classes to invest 'capital in the rearing and early training' of their children because of the parents' limitations in 'resources..., power of forecasting the future, and... willingness to sacrifice themselves for the sake of their children' (Marshall [1890], 1959, pp. 467–8). Nevertheless, Marshall was characteristically optimistic about the uplifting and egalitarian results from publicly supported education and technological progress – the latter which would not only raise total wealth and reduce drudgery but facilitate the mobility of workers among industries and occupations (Marshall [1890], 1959, pp. 176–82, 214–19, 476).

Economists from all schools of thought recognize that the class stratifications producing much of today's inequality are often based on ethnic divisions and associated historical circumstances, such as the legacy of slavery among blacks in the United States or the lower economic status of immigrant groups, particularly coloured immigrants, throughout Western Europe. In addition, the unequal status of men and women in the labour market is a contemporary concern and controversy.

There is little dispute about the descriptive facts of differential wages and earnings between men and women, white and coloured groups, and certain other ethnic groups. However, the analysis of labour market discrimination, which has been abundant by both neoclassical and segmentation economists, epitomizes the latter's dissenting theories. Using a research methodology that draws primarily upon historical, institutional, and case-study materials, the segmentation economists emphasize the roles of technology, the shaping of attitudes and preferences, and certain features of bureaucratic organization – aspects of labour markets that neoclassical economists tend to place in the background.

Technology is viewed as an instrument of employers to dilute or make obsolete the skills of workers, thereby diminishing the workers' bargaining power (Braverman, 1974). This Marxian view derives consequences for inequality that are obviously the reverse of Marshall's. A second and less sinister role of technology is to necessitate within-firm, 'internal' labour markets. The complexity of modern technology and the large size of firms require firm-specific on-the-job training, internal promotion ladders, and a stable and loyal work-force. Wage rates are higher in these large and technologically advanced firms, initially to ensure a large pool of applicants and eventually as a reflection of training, tenure, and promotions. The wage rates, which tend to be rigid, are attached to jobs, not to workers.

On the supply side of the market, workers form queues for these jobs in the 'primary sector' and are selected on the basis of their trainability and future loyalty. The employers will tend to choose (discriminate) in favour of men, who are viewed as traditional career-committed workers, and in favour of workers with similar ethnic or cultural backgrounds as those of the managerial class. The rejected applicants (or non-applicants) obtain jobs in the 'secondary' or 'informal' sector, to use terms that refer to the dual labour market.

Each of the two sectors influences the worker's preferences, attitudes, and habits in ways that reinforce and shape the long-run progress, or lack thereof, of the worker's career. In the secondary sector, low wages, the lack of upward mobility, and instability in tenure – exacerbated by enervating periods of unemployment – have negative feedback effects on the worker's attitudes towards work and training. Preferences are, therefore, endogenous. The contrast with the typical neoclassical paradigm is evident, and the issue is important. Consider the problem of determining whether unemployment, or the receipt of public assistance (the 'dole'), or an initial experience of working in a 'dead-end job' has an important effect on a worker's future earnings. A change in the worker's attitudes and habits is one of several possible explanations for such an effect. Whether this explanation is admissible in neoclassical theories of labour market behaviour is less important than the formidable empirical task of ascertaining causality in these chains of events.

A dynamic model of mutual causation between tastes and labour market outcomes is unusual, but it is not a new idea. It was proposed by Gunnar Myrdal in his analysis of economic discrimination against blacks in the United States (1944, pp. 75–8, 1065–70). Two problems with its application may be responsible for its subsequent neglect. The model's dynamic properties appear to lead to explosive results which are not observed empirically. A second, related objection is that the model appears to offer implausibly easy solutions, in the form of positive interventions that set in motion the dynamics of continual progress.

Attention to institutional features of employer-employee relations and the internal labour markets of firms have also appeared in the neoclassical literature. In *Human Capital* (1964), Gary S. Becker developed theoretical models of general and firm-specific on-the-job training that provided a rigorous neoclassical explanation for internal labour markets. Becker's work shows, incidentally, that a variety of shapes of age-earnings profiles – flat to steeply rising – are perfectly consistent with neoclassical models of the investment in human capital. The flat profile is not a challenge to neoclassical theory, as some segmentationists imply, but Mill's challenge of 140 years ago remains: reconciling neoclassical models of competitive markets with persistent differences in the present values of career earnings among workers of comparable abilities and preferences.

The firm as an internalizing agent for various externalities in workers' cooperation, mutual training, and tenure longevity is another old idea in economics. A recent neoclassical application, with abundant citations, is that of Oliver E. Williamson (1975), who argues that such institutional devices as implicit contracts, collective bargaining, internal promotion ladders, and seniority rights are economically efficient when jobs and workers are heterogeneous and idosyncratic.

228

A fixed structure of wages for jobs, which is emphasized by segmentation economists, is descriptively accurate and useful for analysing short-run behaviour, but even in the short run a human capital model of supply-side productivity traits can explain the match of workers to a hierarchy of wage-fixed jobs. In the long run the human capital model can explain changes in workers' productivity traits, and neoclassical models generally would predict changes in the structure of both jobs and wages.

A discussion of empirical work and policy issues concerning segmented labour markets is beyond the scope of this entry (see the bibliography below). It should be stated, however, that the sometime claim that the neoclassical economists ignore the demand side of the market in policy discussions is unfounded.

That labour market outcomes and processes are complex and controversial is evident in the intellectual legacy of the above-listed five sources of inequality. The criticisms and empirical work of the segmented labour market economists have added to this legacy, but they, like the earlier dissenters, the Marxists and the Institutionalists, remain on the bank of the mainstream.

BIBLIOGRAPHY

The literature on segmented labour markets is extensive and diversified, and there are disputes about who are the leading theorists and which are the landmark articles. These characteristics make it difficult to provide a brief bibliography. In addition to the items cited in the text, several survey articles and books contain lengthy bibliographies: Taubman and Wachter (1986); Gordon, Edwards and Reich (1982); Wilkinson (1981); Cain (1976). The application of segmented labour market theories to development economics is not, however, covered in these sources, and the author is unaware of any survey or bibliographic sources for this application.

Becker, G.S. 1964. *Human Capital.* New York: Columbia University Press for the National Bureau of Economic Research.

Berger, S. and Piore, M.J. 1980. *Dualism and Discontinuity in Industrial Societies.* Cambridge: Cambridge University Press.

Braverman, H. 1974. *Labor and Monopoly Capital.* New York: Monthly Review Press.

Cain, G. 1976. The challenge of segmented labor market theories to orthodox theory: a survey. *Journal of Economic Literature* 14(4), December, 1215–57.

Cairnes, J.E. 1874. *Some Leading Principles of Political Economy.* New York: Harper & Brothers.

Gordon, D.M., Edwards, R.C. and Reich, M.S. 1982. *Segmented Work, Divided Workers: The Historical Transformation of Labor in the United States.* Cambridge: Cambridge University Press.

Marshall, A. [1890] 1959. *Principles of Economics.* 8th edn, London: Macmillan; New York: Macmillan, 1948.

Mill, J.S. [1848] 1900. *The Principles of Political Economy,* Vol. 1. Revised edn, The World's Greatest Classics, New York: Colonial Press.

Myrdal, G. 1944. *An American Dilemma.* New York: Harper & Row.

Taubman, P. and Wachter, M.L. 1986. Segmented labor markets. In *Handbook of Labor Economics,* ed. O. Ashenfelter and R. Layard, Amsterdam: Elsevier Science Publishers.

Wethheim, W.F. 1967. Economy, dual. In *International Encyclopaedia of the Social Sciences*, Vol. 4, New York: Macmillan and Free Press, 495–500.

Wilkinson, F. (ed.) 1981. *The Dynamics of Labor Market Segmentation*. New York: Academic Press.

Williamson, O.E. 1975. *Markets and Hierarchies: Analysis and Antitrust Implications*. New York: Free Press.

Social Security

LAURENCE J. KOTLIKOFF

Since Bismarck's introduction of social security in Germany in 1891 a large number of countries have adopted social security systems. The growth of social security in the postwar period has been particularly rapid. In some countries, such as the United States, social security has become a major, if not the major fiscal institution. Because of its scale, method of finance, and role in providing insurance, social security may be greatly influencing the performance of a number of economies, particularly with respect to their rates of saving and employment.

This brief description of social security begins by considering its principal functions, rationale, method of finance, and sensitivity to recessions and demographics. This is followed by a discussion of social security's potential impact on savings, labour supply and economic efficiency, and risk sharing. The savings discussion also includes an examination of the relationship of unfunded social security to traditional deficit finance.

PRINCIPAL FUNCTIONS. Social security is primarily involved with financing the period of retirement. Benefit payments are provided to the elderly, typically in the form of annuities which continue until the death of the recipient. In addition to old age annuities, social security systems often provide benefits to the disabled and to surviving spouses and children. These benefits are also typically paid in the form of annuities. The levels of the various social security benefits are often based on both the recipient's need and the amount previously contributed by the recipient to social security.

After old age income support, social security's most important function is the provision of insurance. In some countries, social security's disability and survivor benefits represent the public's primary source of disability and life insurance. By providing benefits in the form of annuities social security also insures against uncertain longevity; relative to receiving benefits in a one-time lump sum, receiving an annuity hedges both the risk of dying prior to spending one's lump-sum benefits as well as the risk of dying after exhausting one's lump-sum benefits.

RATIONALE FOR SOCIAL SECURITY. There are a number of possible explanations for the emergence of social security. One is simply a desire to transfer resources to a particularly needy generation of elderly, albeit at the potential expense of subsequent generations. A second rationale is paternalistic concern by the government that, left to their own devices, households will inadequately save and insure. A third rationale for social security is that the problem of adverse selection precludes the provision of certain types of insurance, particularly annuity and disability insurance, by the private market. A fourth rationale is that social security permits certain intergenerational exchanges and risk sharing arrangements that may be Pareto improving.

While determining whether social security represents a Pareto improvement is quite difficult, one can find evidence, at least in the United States, supporting each of the first three explanations. Social security was initiated in the United States during the Great Depression when the elderly were particularly hard hit by financial reverses; and the postwar dramatic United States reduction in the rate of poverty among the elderly appears largely due to the growth of social security. The paternalistic rationale for social security is supported by evidence of inadequate private saving (Diamond, 1977) and inadequate private purchase of life insurance (Auerbach and Kotlikoff, 1986). And the adverse selection problems in annuity and disability insurance market are suggested both by theory (Rothschild and Stiglitz, 1976) and by the fact that, outside of employer-provided disability insurance and old age pensions, there is essentially no private United States market in these important types of insurance.

METHOD OF FINANCE. Social security is generally financed through taxes levied on workers' earnings, part of which may be collected from the employer and the rest from the worker. Social security payroll tax rates currently range from 10 to 25 per cent in most Western economies. In some countries, such as the United States, most workers pay more in social security taxes than they do in federal income taxes and other federal taxes. Since social security benefits received are often only loosely linked to taxes paid, social security also plays a role in redistributing resources. This redistribution is both across generations, intergenerational, as well as within generations, intragenerational.

Redistribution under social security is associated with its method of finance. If social security were financed on a fully funded, individually actuarially fair basis, then each dollar contributed by a worker would be allocated by the government to provide the worker with a dollar's worth of old age annuity and other insurance benefits. In this case the government would have, at any point in time, a trust fund that would be just sufficient to meet all its future insurance obligations arising from the past contributions of all currently living workers and retirees. Dropping the requirement that workers receive back (on an actuarially fair basis) what they pay in, raises the possibility for inter- and intragenerational redistribution and also eliminates the requirement that the trust fund be of the size required for full funding.

Underfunded, rather than fully funded social security systems appear to be the rule in most countries. In the United States, for example, social security is currently essentially unfunded with the Old Age Income, Survivors, and Disability Trust Funds sufficient to cover only a few months of benefits. In contrast, a fully funded trust fund would have assets equal to roughly 30 times annual benefit payments. Rather than pay for current benefits from the principal and investment income of past contributions, unfunded social security systems use current tax contributions to pay for current benefits. The 'pay as you go' method of finance greatly benefits those 'start up' generations of the elderly who are old at social security's initiation. These 'start up' elderly receive old age social security benefits despite having paid little or no social security taxes when young. Initial young and future generations, however, do not receive the same treatment. They pay taxes to social security during their working years and receive benefits in exchange in old age. The present expected value of their tax contributions is likely to be less than the present expected value of their benefits. The reason is that a mature unfunded social security system can only pay, on average, a return on contributions equal to the rate of population plus productivity growth (plus a term of second order). If this return is less than the economy's interest rate, workers contributing to social security will receive a smaller return on their contributions than if they had been allowed to save these contributions and invest them in the economy.

To understand why social security's steady state rate of return equals the sum of the rates of population growth, denoted by m, and productivity growth, denoted by g, consider a two-period model in which individuals work in their first period when young and are retired in their second period. Suppose workers at time t in the economy's steady state contribute a fixed percentage, θ, of their labour earnings, W_t, to social security. When the worker is old he or she will receive benefits at time $t + 1$ equal to $\theta W_t(1 + m)(1 + g)$ in social security benefits, since there are $(1 + m)$ workers for every beneficiary in period $t + 1$ and the earnings of each worker in period $t + 1$ are $(1 + g)$ times larger than they were at time t. Note that if the worker in period t had been permitted to save the amount θW_t, the principal plus interest in period $t + 1$ on this saving would have been $\theta W_t(1 + r)$, where r is the steady state interest rate. Hence, if r exceeds $m + g + mg$ the worker is worse off under social security. This discussion has so far concentrated on social security's redistribution in partial equilibrium and has ignored the possible general equilibrium effects of social security on factor rewards, particularly the wage rate and the interest rate. If unfunded social security depresses long-run savings and capital formation as suggested by Feldstein (1974), it will make capital relatively scarce in comparison with labour and reduce the wage earned by workers and raise the interest rate. This means a further reduction in the welfare of future generations because of social security. Ignoring issues of economic distortions, one can show that if economic losses to young and future generations do arise from unfunded social security, these losses will equal, in present value, the economic gains to initial elderly start up generations. This is not to suggest that social security necessarily makes future generations worse off in improving the lot of the start up elderly. If $m + g + mg$ exceeds r, the introduction of an unfunded social security system can be Pareto improving (Samuelson, 1958), i.e., all generations can benefit from this 'chain letter' system that involves each new generation passing resources to the previous generation.

Unlike a chain letter or Ponzi scheme with a finite number of participants in which the last participants are made worse off, unfunded social security, when $m + g + mg$ exceeds r, can make all participants better off because there are an infinite number of participants, namely all future generations. As long as $m + g + mg$ exceeds r the growth in the number and earnings capacity of the new chain letter participants exceeds the cost of waiting for them to arrive on the scene. Of course, if capital formation is reduced by social security the interest rate will begin to rise. Once r equals $m + g + mg$, further increases in social security are no longer Pareto improving.

SENSITIVITY OF UNFUNDED SOCIAL SECURITY TO RECESSIONS AND DEMOGRAPHICS. As mentioned, under an unfunded social security system current benefits are financed by current tax contributions. Hence, any increase in the number of beneficiaries relative to the number of workers or any decline in the earnings and, thus, tax contributions of workers requires either a reduction in benefit levels of an increase in contribution rates. The adjustments required of social security to changing demographics and economic conditions can be substantial. For example, in the United States the fraction of adults over age 64 is projected to rise from a value of about one-fifth in the 1980s to a value of two-fifths by 2040. To avoid a doubling or more of social security tax rates by the early part of the 21st century, legislation was enacted in 1983 to raise gradually social security's normal age of retirement from 65 to 67, and to accumulate over the period 1985–2010 a huge trust fund that would be available to finance benefits after 2010.

SOCIAL SECURITY AND SAVINGS
A. Savings effects in the Keynesian and Barro models. The impact of social security on savings is quite sensitive to one's theoretical model of saving. In the simplest Keynesian model in which each household consumes the same fraction of its disposable income, transfers from young to old households under social security have no effect on aggregate consumption and aggregate saving (assuming no social security induced changes in aggregate labour earnings).

Another saving model in which social security is not predicted to reduce savings is Barro's (1974) model of intergenerational altruism. In this neoclassical model each household is altruistically linked to all its future descendants. Interestingly, this altruistic linkage to future descendants can arise even if households do not directly care about their future descendants, but simply care about their own children. The fact that their children care in turn about their own children and the grandchildren care about the great grandchildren, etc., is sufficient to establish altruistic linkages to all future descendants. In making current consumption decisions such intergenerationally altruistic households consider the welfare as well as the economic resources of all of their descendants. Indeed, current households effectively act as if they were going to live forever and were maximizing an infinite horizon utility function of the consumption of themselves and all their progeny. The budget constraint in this maximization problem is that the present value of current and future consumption of the household and its descendants (1) equals the household's current net worth, plus (2) the sum of their own and their descendant's human wealth, less (3) the sum of their own and their descendant's present value of tax payments net of transfers made to the government.

Note that if the government redistributes intergenerationally between the current household and its descendants, the infinite horizon budget constraint is unaffected since the present value change in the current household's net taxes will exactly equal minus the present value change in the net taxes of the household's descendants; since the budget constraint involves the sum of the present values of net taxes of the current household and its descendants, the budget constraint is unaltered, and, *pari passu*, the household's current consumption is unaltered. Thus in the Barro model, unfunded social security's intergenerational redistribution has no affect on current household consumption (ignoring any associated redistribution between different infinite horizon Barro families).

B. Savings effect in the life cycle model. In the life cycle model of saving developed by Modigliani and Brumberg (1954) and Ando and Modigliani (1963), unfunded social security is predicted to reduce savings and, in a closed economy, the capital stock. Simulation studies (Kotlikoff, 1979; Auerbach and Kotlikoff, 1987) suggest that unfunded social security systems of the scale observed in the 1980s in many developed economies could reduce the long-run capital stock of these economies by 20 to 30 per cent, assuming, of course, that these economies adhere to the life cycle model. To date, the results of numerous empirical analyses of social security's impact on savings have been mixed (e.g. Feldstein, 1974; Barro, 1978).

Since the life cycle model has such strong predictions concerning unfunded social security it is worth illustrating this model in some detail. Consider, for simplicity, a two period model in which both the utility and production functions are Cobb-Douglas:

$$U_t = C_{yt}^{\beta} C_{ot+1}^{1-\beta} \tag{1}$$

$$Y_t = K_t^{\alpha} L_t^{1-\alpha} \tag{2}$$

Equation (1) expresses the lifetime utility of a member of generation t as a function of consumption when young, C_{yt}, and consumption when old, C_{ot+1}. The economy's production function relates output per young worker, Y_t, to capital per young worker, K_t, labour per young worker, L_t. L_t is exogenously supplied by each young worker and is measured in units such that $L_t = 1$. We ignore productivity growth here and assume that the population grows at rate n. Equation (3) gives the lifetime budget constraint of an individual who is young at time t.

$$C_{yt} + C_{ot+1}/(1 + r_{t+1}) = W_t(1 - \theta_t) + B_{t+1}/(1 + r_{t+1}) \tag{3}$$

where W_t is the wage earned in period t, θ_t is the social security tax rate at time t, B_{t+1} is the social security benefit paid at $t + 1$, and r_{t+1} is the period $t + 1$ return on savings. Equation (3) states that the present value of consumption equals the present value of labour earnings. It can also be expressed as:

$$C_{ot+1} = A_{t+1}(1 + r_{t+1}) + B_{t+1}, \tag{3'}$$

where A_{t+1}, the assets (net wealth) of the old at time $t + 1$, equals the saving done by these elderly when they were young, $W_t(1 - \theta_t) - C_{yt}$. Maximization of (1) subject to (3) yields consumption demands. In particular, $C_{yt} = \beta[w_t(1 - \theta_t) + B_{t+1}/(1 + r_{t+1})$, and the supply of capital by the household sector, A_{t+1}, can be written as:

$$A_{t+1} = W_t(1 - \theta_t) - \beta[W_t(1 - \theta_t) + B_{t+1}/(1 + r_{t+1})] \tag{4}$$

Since the social security system is assumed to be financed on a 'pay as you go' basis, social security revenues per young worker must equal benefit payments per young worker:

$$B_t = \theta_t W_t(1 + n) \tag{5}$$

Using (5), rewrite (4) as:

$$A_{t+1} = W_t(1 - \theta_t) - \beta[W_t(1 - \theta_t) + \theta_{t+1} W_{t+1} \times (1 + n)/(1 + r_{t+1})] \tag{4'}$$

Profit maximization by representative firms in the economy implies the following expressions relating factor demands to factor returns:

$$W_t = (1 - \alpha)K_t^\alpha \tag{6}$$

$$r_t = \alpha K_t^{\alpha - 1} \tag{7}$$

The condition for equilibrium in the market for capital is given by:

$$K_t = A_t/(1 + n), \tag{8}$$

where (8) reflects the fact that K_t is capital per young worker and A_t is assets per old retiree.

Substituting for W_t, r_t, and A_{t+1} in (4') from (6), (7), and (8) yields a nonlinear first order difference equation in K_t. This equation determines the transition path of the economy's capital stock and, via (6) and (7), the general equilibrium changes in the wage and interest rate. Denoting steady state values by $\hat{}$, the steady state value of $\hat{K}$ is implicitly defined by:

$$(1 + n)\hat{K} = \hat{W}(1 - \hat{\theta}) - \beta\left[\hat{W} - \frac{(\hat{r} - n)\hat{\theta}\hat{W}}{1 + \hat{r}}\right], \quad \text{or:} \tag{9}$$

$$(1+n)\hat{K}^{1-\alpha} = (1-\alpha)\left[(1-\hat{\theta}) - \beta(1+n)\hat{K} = \hat{W}(1-\hat{\theta}) - \beta\left[\hat{W} - \frac{(\hat{r}-n)\hat{\theta}\hat{W}}{1+\hat{r}} \right], \text{ or:}$$

$$(9')$$

Differentiating $(9')$ at $\hat{\theta} + 0$ yields:

$$(1+n)\frac{\partial \hat{K}^{1-\alpha}}{\partial \hat{\theta}} = -(1-\alpha)\left[1 + \beta\frac{(n - \alpha\hat{K}^{\alpha-1})}{1 + \alpha\hat{K}^{\alpha-1}} \right] \tag{10}$$

i.e., introducing unfunded social security reduces ('cowds out') the steady state capital stock.

The intuitive explanation for this crowding out of savings and the capital stock is as follows: If, starting at time t, B_t is raised from zero to a positive value $\bar{B}$, the consumption of the elderly at time t, $C_{0,t}$, rises by $\bar{B}$ since the marginal consumption propensity of the elderly is unity. Ignoring for the moment changes through time in benefit levels, tax rates, and factor rewards, the present value loss to the initial young from this policy is $\bar{B}(r-n)/(1+r)$, since they pay $\bar{B}$ when young, but receive $\bar{B}(1+n)$ when old. The young, whose marginal propensity to consume is less than unity, will reduce their consumption by a fraction of this present value loss. Hence, in the initial period in which social security is introduced each elderly individual increases his or her consumption, measured per young person, by $\bar{B}/(1+n)$, while each young person reduces his or her consumption by a fraction of $\bar{B}(r-n)/(1+r)$. Total private consumption in the initial period therefore increases, and saving is crowded out.

While each future generation suffers a loss in present value of $\bar{B}(r-n)/(1+r)$, at any point in time there will always be future generations who have yet to arrive on the scene and experience this resource loss. Thus, at any point in time the initial period increase in private consumption will not yet have been fully offset by reduced consumption of future generations. This explains why the economy ends up in a new steady state with a permanently lower stock of savings.

Adding general equilibrium effects to this partial equilibrium story only reinforces the intergenerational transfer away from future generations. As the capital stock is crowded out, the wage falls and the interest rate rises. Those generations who are elderly when interest rates rise benefit from the greater return on their savings, while the corresponding young and future generations are worse off because the concomitant fall in their wages is more detrimental to their economic welfare than the reduced price of old age consumption reflected in the higher interest rate. In the case of a two-period model in which the social security tax rate is levied at time t at a given rate and kept constant thereafter, the first generation of young workers benefits from the general equilibrium changes in factor returns; since the crowding out takes one period to get under way, the interest rate is high when they are old, but the wage received by this first set of young workers is unaffected by the introduction of social security. In contrast, generations born after the first generation, while benefiting from higher interest rates, receive lower wages during their initial working period.

C. The relationship of unfunded social security to traditional deficit finance. The 'crowding out' of capital has often been associated with deficit finance. It is worthwhile, therefore, in the context of this simple model to point out that unfunded social security could easily be run as an explicit government debt policy. Suppose that at the initiation of social security the government chooses to label its initial benefit payments as transfer payments, but labels its initial and subsequent social security receipts from young workers as 'borrowing' from young workers rather than as 'taxes'. In addition, the government labels benefit payments, with the exception of those made in the initial period, as 'principal plus interest payments' on the government's borrowing. Let the government also levy a special tax (possibly transfer) on each elderly generation reflecting the fact that social security benefits do not correspond precisely to tax payments when young plus interest.

With the new language exactly the same model, after the initial period, can be described in the following five equations:

$$C_{o,t} = A_t(1 + r_t) - T_t \tag{11}$$

$$C_{y,t} + C_{o,t+1}/(1 + r_{t+1}) = W_t - T_{t+1}/(1 + r_{t+1}) \tag{12}$$

$$K_{t+1} = [(W_t - C_{y,t}) - D_t]/(1 + n) \tag{13}$$

$$T_t = \Theta_t W_t(1 + r_{t+1}) - \Theta_{t+1} W_{t+1}(1 + n) \tag{14}$$

$$D_t = \Theta_t W_t \tag{15}$$

where T_t is the special old age tax, and D_t is the stock of official government debt owed to the public by the social security system. A_t is still private assets, but A_t now equals $W_{t-1} - C_{y,t-1}$ rather than $W_{t-1}(1 - \Theta_{t-1}) - C_{y,t-1}$, and capital per retiree equals assets per retiree, A_t, less debt per retiree, D_t. Comparison of the above five equations with equations (3), (3'), (4), (5), and (8) shows that the economy's real behaviour is not altered by the relabelling. However, the relabelling makes explicit the debt policy associated with running unfunded social security; i.e., the relabelling increases from zero to D_t the level of officially reported debt in period t.

For the United States such a change in the labelling of social security taxes and benefits would have enormous implications for the level of government debt reported to the public. In this case, the amount of additional government debt that would show up on the United States books equals the sum over all cohorts of the accumulated (at historic interest rates) amount of social security taxes paid less benefits received. Formulae presented by Kotlikoff (1979) suggest that this number for 1986 could be as large as $8 trillion (30 × social security tax revenues), which is more than 4.5 times larger than the 1986 official stock of United States debt. Calculations of this kind should make one wary of relying on official government debt numbers as indicators of the government's true policy with respect to intergenerational redistribution.

SOCIAL SECURITY, LABOUR SUPPLY AND ECONOMIC EFFICIENCY. Social security can influence labour supply both through income and substitution effects. The transfers to start up generations represent potentially large windfalls that could induce early retirement, assuming that leisure is a normal good, i.e., leisure increases with income. In addition, social security's payroll tax may reduce work incentives, leading individuals to substitute more leisure for consumption, especially if future social security benefits are not linked at the margin to tax contributions. A third potential inducement to leisure is the earnings testing of social security benefits that occurs in some countries. Earnings testing refers to the fact that social security benefits may be reduced if recipients earn too much. In the United States social security recipients have often been permitted only to earn small amounts, beyond which they lose as much as 50 cents in benefits for every dollar they earn, until their benefits are exhausted. This earnings test effectively constitutes a 50 per cent marginal tax rate which, when combined with federal and state income and sales taxes, may leave many recipients in very high effective marginal tax brackets.

The postwar period in the United States saw a very considerable acceleration of the trend towards early retirement. For example, between 1950 and 1985 the labour force participation rate of males 65 and older declined from 45 per cent to 16 per cent. A number of studies (e.g. Boskin and Hurd, 1984) suggest that the United States social security system is in large part responsible for this decline in the labour supply of the elderly. The size of effective marginal labour taxation arising from social security is critically important for determining potential economic inefficiencies caused by social security. As is well known, the degree of economic inefficiency associated with the distortions from taxation rises with the square of the tax rate (ignoring second best considerations). Thus if social security's effective marginal tax on labour supply is 10 per cent and the effective marginal tax from other forms of taxation is 30 per cent, social security may be almost doubling the excess burden (economic inefficiency) arising from taxing labour. The extent to which social security's payroll tax raises effective labour taxes depends on the linkage between tax payments and benefits received and how that linkage is perceived by workers. In some countries there is a strong link between marginal benefits and marginal taxes, but the formulae determining this linkage are so complex that workers are not likely to understand the degree of linkage and may simply assume it is zero.

Even if marginal linkage were correctly understood there would still be considerable labour supply distortion in many instances. For example the United States in the postwar period has permitted wives (husbands) to receive dependent and survivor benefits based on their husbands' (wives') social security contributions if such benefits exceed what the wife (husband) could receive based on her (his) own history of contributions. This means that spouses who will elect to collect benefits as dependents or survivors receive nothing back at the margin for their own contributions to social security. For such spouses their effective marginal tax on labour earnings includes the entire social security payroll tax. For primary married earners the failure in many cases of social security to require additional contributions to pay for survivor and dependent benefits means that such earners may face negative effective taxes from social security at the margin since their additional contributions mean additional benefits both to themselves, their spouse, and often their children. Parenthetically, the fact that social security often provides dependent and survivor benefits to spouses and children without requiring additional contributions from the worker means that married couples with only one working spouse may fare much better under social security than either two earner couples or single individuals. In the United States the difference in lifetime treatment of one earner and two earner couples by social security has often been of the order of a year's earnings; i.e., social security's intragenerational redistribution has often been quite substantial.

SOCIAL SECURITY AND RISK SHARING. Social security's improvement in risk sharing may make the introduction of a funded and possibly even an unfunded social security system Pareto efficient. In addition to potentially improving annuity and disability insurance arrangements, social security may play a role in pooling the risk of the return on human as well as non-human capital across generations. Finally, social security may be pooling economic risks, such as the risks of recession, across generations in ways that are not available to private markets. Social security's improvement in insurance may not only affect the efficiency of risk pooling, but it may also have implications for saving. In the absence of such insurance precautionary savings might be considerably larger (Kotlikoff, Shoven and Spivak, 1986).

The risks associated with uncertain longevity which are hedged with annuities can be quite substantial. Kotlikoff and Spivak (1981) suggest that risk averse older individuals with no other source of annuity insurance might be willing to give up as much as a third to one half of their economic resources in order to gain access to an actuarially fair annuity market. While risk sharing within families may be providing a considerable amount of implicit annuity insurance, social security has undoubtedly improved annuity insurance considerably.

Insurance for disability appears particularly difficult for the private market to insure since certain types of medical conditions, such as back pain and fatigue, associated with ageing cannot be objectively identified. The government can insure disability without subjecting itself to widespread fraudulent claims by earnings testing disability benefits. Such earnings testing may be quite difficult for private insurance companies since private companies, unlike the government, do not have access to earnings information. Hence, the government may be the most efficient provider of disability insurance, and social security's earnings tests may be viewed as the deductible for this type of insurance (Diamond and Mirrlees, 1978).

Under pay as you go social security unexpected declines (increases) in labour earnings and social security tax revenues may lead to reductions in benefits. In this case retirees will share some of the human capital risk of younger workers. In addition, other elements of the tax structure may spread the riskiness of retirees' returns to their savings to workers. Thus if there is a consumption tax in place, reduced capital income means less revenues from retirees and higher required revenues from young workers. Merton (1983) has shown that by appropriately structuring social security and other elements of the tax structure, the government can potentially efficiently diversify human and non-human capital risk across young workers and old retirees.

Another aspect of social security's insurance provision is the pooling of risks across generations. One interpretation of the growth of unfunded social security in the United States in the postwar period is that the government elected to redistribute to a generation that had suffered from the depression in the 1930s and had made significant contributions to the nation during World War II. As described above, the burden for paying for these transfers is likely to fall on future generations both in the form of receiving a lower than market return on their social security contributions and in the form of receiving lower wages in their working years because of the crowding out of the capital stock. Clearly, the sharing of risks of wars and recessions across generations cannot be accomplished by the private insurance market if only for the simple reason that future generations are not yet alive to sign private insurance contracts.

BIBLIOGRAPHY

Ando, A. and Modigliani, F. 1963. The 'life cycle' hypothesis of saving: aggregate implications and tests. *American Economic Review* 53, March, 55–84.

Auerbach, A.J. and Kotlikoff, L.G. 1986. Life insurance of the elderly: adequacy and determinants. In *Work, Health, and Income Among the Elderly*, ed. Gary Burtless.

Auerbach, A.J. and Kotlikoff, L.J. 1987. *Dynamic Fiscal Policy*. Cambridge: Cambridge University Press.

Barro, R.J. 1974. Are government bonds net wealth? *Journal of Political Economy* 82(6), November/December, 1095–118.

Barro, R.J. 1978. Social security and private saving – evidence from the U.S. time series. In *Studies in Social Security and Retirement Policy*. Washington, DC: American Enterprise Institute.

Boskin, J.M. and Hurd, M. 1984. The effects of social security on retirement in the early 1970s. *Quarterly Journal of Economics* 99(4), November, 767–90.

Diamond, P.A. 1977. A framework for social security 'analysis'. *Journal of Public Economics* 8, 275–98.

Diamond, P.A. and Mirrlees, J.A. 1978. A model of social insurance with variable retirement. *Journal of Public Economics* 10(3), 295–336.

Feldstein, M. 1974. Social security, induced retirement, and aggregate capital accumulation. *Journal of Political Economy* 82(5), Part 2, September/October, 905–26.

Kotlikoff, L.J. 1979. Social security and equilibrium capital intensity. *Quarterly Journal of Economics* 93(2), May, 233–54.

Kotlikoff, L.J., Shoven, J.B. and Spivak, A. 1986. The effect of annuity insurance on savings and inequality. *Journal of Labor Economics* 4(3), Part 2, July, 183–207.

Kotlikoff, L.J. and Spivak, A. 1981. The family as an incomplete annuities market. *Journal of Political Economy* 89(2), April, 372–91.

Merton, R.C. 1983. On the role of social security as a means for efficient risk-bearing in an economy where human capital is not tradeable. In *Financial Aspects of the U.S. Pension System*, ed. Z. Bodie and J.B. Shoven, Chicago: University of Chicago Press.

Modigliani, F. and Brumberg, R. 1954. Utility analysis and the consumption function: an interpretation of cross-section data. In *Post-Keynesian Economics*, ed. K.K. Kurihara, New Brunswick, NJ: Rutgers University Press.

Rothschild, M. and Stiglitz, J. 1976. Equilibrium in competitive insurance markets: an essay on the economics of imperfect information. *Quarterly Journal of Economics* 90(4), November, 630–49.

Samuelson, P.A. 1958. An exact consumption-loan model of interest with or without the social contrivance of money. *Journal of Political Economy* 66(6), December, 467–82.

Trade Unions

HENRY PHELPS BROWN

When they formulated their classic definition of a trade union, Sidney and Beatrice Webb had in view the long struggle of groups of English workers to maintain associations that could stand up to employers and gain acceptance by the community. 'A trade union,' they said, 'is a continuous association of wage earners for the purpose of maintaining or improving the conditions of their working lives' (1894, p. 1). An economist starting from the assumption of the ultimate rationality of decisions is likely to see the trade union as a cartel or monopoly intended to maximize the benefits of its members. An intermediate view recognizes that men and women join trade unions for reasons that arise out of imperfections of the labour market. Because of the slow response of employment to lower labour cost, the job seekers in any one district will be confronted at a given time with a limited number of jobs: if then they exceed that number, even by one, and compete with each other by underbidding, the wage can be brought down to a limit set by bare subsistence or the level of support in unemployment.

But even suppose that the numbers of vacancies and applicants match exactly: then if the employer and an individual applicant cannot reach agreement on the rate for the job, so that for the time being the employer lacks a workman and the applicant has no job or pay, which is in the greater trouble? As Adam Smith said, 'In the long run the workman may be as necessary to his master as his master is to him; but the necessity is not so immediate.' The applicants here are evidently unable to move away readily to other employers: those with whom they are dealing are monopsonists or oligopsonists. Against this, they try to maintain a monopoly. They agree to hold out for a minimum in common. They want to keep up the price of their work by limiting the supply. They also want to safeguard their jobs against a drop in demand – they aim to establish a property in jobs. To these ends they defend lines of demarcation, within which they have the sole right to work, or they allow only approved entrants, in limited numbers, to acquire certain skills, or to be recruited for certain purposes. The defensive object of preventing their rates being undercut or their labour being displaced by outsiders merges here into the calculated purpose of pushing up their earnings by restricting supply.

In modern Western economies, trade union membership has also been maintained or extended, especially among white collar workers; by the need to renegotiate the pay of all employees to compensate for changes in the cost of living; the addition of an improvement factor in real terms has also been regarded as defensive from the point of view of any one group, which would otherwise fall behind the others. Beyond these issues of the rate of pay and job security are those that arise at the place of work. People join trade unions to secure protection against discrimination and arbitrary treatment by management, and the negotiation and observance of a code governing discipline, grievance procedure, promotion, redundancy, the pace of work, and the like.

FACTORS AFFECTING MEMBERSHIP. These forces making for trade union membership have arisen and taken effect only in certain conditions. Where trade unions emerged, their form and function differed widely in different societies. In the Western democracies, the proportion of employees unionized has varied widely over time and between countries (Bain and Price, 1960); sometimes it has fallen even against the trend of economic growth, notably in the USA since the 1960s. In full employment, and in places where the individual had access to a number of alternative employers, or to natural resources like the American open frontier, he would feel able to fend for himself. The absence of observed falls in wage rates down the centuries (Phelps Brown and Hopkins, 1981) implies that custom and tacit understandings can maintain rates in the absence of overt trade unionism. Individuals whose qualifications, temperaments, and entries into employment interest them in personal advancement are not likely to become trade unionists; but these factors deterring clerical, administrative and managerial employees from membership have been offset by the growth of offices in size and impersonality, and the need of staff to negotiate frequent salary rises to offset inflation. The ability of manual workers to form their own trade unions has depended upon leaders coming forward from their ranks who were literate, upright, and skilful in administration; the workers themselves must be able to keep up a subscription, and have the discipline to sustain a stoppage. Where those conditions are lacking, as in much of the Third World, trade unions tend to be organized by outsiders, often a political party.

In all countries, the ability of trade unions to maintain themselves and function depends on the provisions of the law and their application in the courts: landmarks here were the immunity from civil liability conferred on British trade unions in 1906, and the promotion of trade unionism and collective bargaining by American legislation in the 1930s. Linked with this is the attitude of the employers: whereas those in France, Germany and the United States generally felt themselves justified, down to 1914 and sometimes later, in resisting trade unionism, many British employers had come to accept it as a means of stabilizing industrial relations. In the Soviet-type economies, discontent with the conditions of employment leading to combined action can result only in a political revolt; trade unions exist by name, but only to administer social benefits and maintain the control of the party within the establishment.

Trade unions thus have to be viewed in their local variety and historical setting. 'Where we expected to find an economic thread for a treatise,' the Webbs wrote in the Preface to their *History of Trade Unionism* (1894), 'we found a spider's web; and from that moment we recognized that what we had first to write was not a treatise, but a history.'

TRADE UNIONS AS MONOPOLIES. None the less, there are economic threads to be followed through. One is the effect of the trade union on the relative pay of its members. Here the theory of the monopoly power of the trade union directs attention to the elasticity of substitution between the members' labour and other factors of production, and to the elasticity of demand for the product. Substantially, much depends on the possibility of the labour being replaced by equipment, and of the trade union gaining control of this if it were introduced. It is in the firms and industries themselves most strongly placed in the market, and able to retain ample margins, that trade unions are likely to maintain levels of pay above those obtaining elsewhere for similar grades of labour. The employers concerned are thus paying what seems more than the supply price of labour to them, and the differences found in surveys in the rates paid even in adjacent firms suggest that this is so; the trade unions may be said to share in the monopoly power of the employers. They may also acquire monopoly power directly by restricting supply and by forcing demand.

Craft unions have restricted supply by limiting the numbers of apprentices; when a trade is being organized for the first time, attacks on non-members who are continuing to work for less than the union rate serve either to exclude or recruit them; and this shades into the general purpose of the rule that no one shall undertake work of a certain kind unless he or she holds a union card, which serves more for recruitment than for exclusion. The pre-entry closed shop provides the most complete control. A trade union that organizes all the existing workers in an industry has to reckon with the possibility of the market being invaded by the products of non-members newly employed elsewhere – except in those cases where of its nature the produce must be supplied in the place where it is consumed.

Trade unions force demand by rules preventing work being taken away from their members, such as compositor's work being done by advertisers, or builder's work by the makers of pre-fabricated components; by stopping other workers doing jobs in the territory to which they claim exclusive rights; and by resisting the application of labour-saving equipment to their own work. Many restrictive prices are intended to maintain or increase the input of labour per unit of output.

The monopoly power of a group of workers who form an essential link in a chain of production but account for a small part of the whole cost, appears great. Adam Smith instanced the half dozen woolcombers who were needed to keep a thousand spinners and weavers at work. Marshall asked why the bricklayers of his day did not get 'an enormous rise' by pushing their own rate up. This power is in fact limited by the employer's powers of resistance. He may redesign process or product, so as to by-pass the labour in question; he may put the work out to subcontract, or import components; at the limit, he may move the whole operation to a location where the trade union is not in control. His resistance to a claim by the union will also be stiffened by his knowledge that other groups in his employ will have regard to relativities, and will base their own claims on concessions he makes to the union.

COLLECTIVE BARGAINING. The most widely available use of monopoly power is the pushing up of the rate of pay by bargaining, which leaves it to employers to restrict the supply by the limitation of the number they engage at the higher rate. If we consider in the first place a negotiation whose effects are largely confined to the immediate parties, bargaining power proper may be defined as the power to inflict loss by withholding consent. It is understandable that if two parties cannot agree upon the terms of an agreement to work together, they should suspend operations meanwhile. But this suspension is not a merely negative act, for it puts each part into difficulties. Workers are left without pay. Craft unions have often had funds from which to issue strike pay; other unions, needing to keep subscriptions low, pay none, but have sometimes been able to maintain long strikes none the less with the aid of contributions from other unionists and the public. There has been a risk of the vacant places being filled by disloyal members of the union, or by imported blacklegs who will be kept on when the dispute is settled. These difficulties increase the longer the stoppage goes on. But so do those of the employer. There is the immediate loss of profitable operation, and in some industries this cannot in the nature of things be made good by increased output when work is resumed. There is the likelihood that customers will resort to other suppliers meanwhile, and the possibility that some of them will never return. Firms that have been unprofitable, though on that account they cannot easily afford a rise, may not however be able to hold out against settling for one, because of their attenuated cash flow. The actual experience of increasing difficulty makes the parties willing to modify the terms for which they stood out when the stoppage began: there is convergence, and they reach agreement. Such at least is a natural interpretation of the observation that most stoppages have ended in a compromise. Reflecting on this, J.R. Hicks inferred (1932, chapter 7) that if the parties estimated each other's powers of resistance accurately beforehand, there would be no stoppage, but agreement would be reached at once on the terms reached only at the end of a stoppage that occurs when the parties do not know those powers, or misconceive them, and find out the facts by painful experience.

That most agreements are reached without a stoppage does not mean that bargaining power is not exerted. But more enters into the reaching of an agreement than bargaining power. The matter to be negotiated is the terms and conditions on which a joint activity is to be carried on by the parties in future, and this is not, like the price of a horse, to be haggled over between two people who may never deal with each other again: the relation between parties who continue to be indispensable to one another is more nearly matrimonial. The parties are therefore open to influence by the thought of what is fair and reasonable in the terms on which they can work together. Trade unionists may be moved by the aim, not of receiving the greatest possible gain, but of obtaining what is justly due to them, or of righting a wrong. Where justice is at stake they will fight without weighing the cost against the gain.

Another consideration in their conduct of a negotiation is their determination to avoid subservience. They refuse to accept the force of the remark that the improvements in terms achieved by a strike will not make good the wages lost in the strike until after many years: for that is an argument to show that the employer's superior resources should always oblige the workers to accept his terms. Bargaining may turn again into warfare, in which trade unionists whose blood is up will make sacrifices according to no maximizing calculus, and will attack blacklegs with patriots' hatred for a traitor.

So far, the bargaining power of the trade union has been considered as if it were exerted by one of two parties facing each other in isolation; but the power of many unions is enhanced by the impact of their strikes on third parties and on the community. The third parties who are most likely to be disturbed by the stoppage of the employer's activity, and interest in his reaching an early settlement, are the firms who supply him with substantial parts of their own output, and those who depend on him for supplies that they cannot readily replace from stock or from other sources. A trade union that can withhold the supply of an essential product or service from a whole region can force the intervention of the government.

In 1893 the power of the English Miner's Federation to cut off much of the country's heat, light and inland transport brought about what was unthinkable a short time before – the intervention of Government to effect a settlement. When the French railwaymen went on strike the Government broke the strike by mobilizing them for military service. A strike of the British miners that threatened to bring the whole country to a halt in 1912 was settled by an Act of Parliament that gave the miners much of what they had claimed. Where the Government has to settle a national emergency dispute, it cannot force the trade unionists to resume work on terms that they reject as unfair and unreasonable, but it can apply a substantial coercive force to the employers.

Control of essential supplies and services offered certain trade unions great power in this way, and the Triple Alliance of miners, transport workers and railwaymen was formed in Great Britain to exploit it; but the Government for its part built up a detailed organization, held in reserve against an emergency, for the maintenance of supplies. In the USA, the Taft–Hartley Act of 1947 provided that in a strike that creates a national emergency the President might take the business concerned into public possession for eighty days, during which the employees must return to work while a fact-finding board reported on the circumstances of the dispute. With the extension of trade unionism in the public sector and in services in Great Britain, the object of strikes has shifted from inflicting loss on the employer to demonstrating discontent by disrupting the activities of the community, and inflicting hardship on the parents of schoolchildren or on invalids or commuters.

TRADE UNIONS AND THE LAW. The bargaining power of trade unions depends upon legal privilege. Employers may refuse to recognize a trade union unless the law obliges them to do so. In a strike, labour is commonly withdrawn in breach of the individual workers's contract of employment; losses are usually inflicted on third parties. In the USA, employers were able to inhibit many forms of trade union action by obtaining injunctions against them from the courts, until the Norris–La Guardia Act of 1932. If those who suffer damages are able to bring civil actions to recover them, most strikes will be impossible: British trade unions have operated under the shelter of immunities that were given outright statutory form by the Trade Disputes Act 1906. Many strikes, again, will not be effective unless pickets are posted to turn back men and women who want to go on working, or stop supplies moving: the effectiveness of legal provisions designed to regulate picketing depends on the possibility and practice of enforcement. Not only the activities but the very existence of a trade union, as a combination in restraint of trade, are anomalous in a country whose common law protects the freedom of the individual to use his labour and property. In these countries the law has found a place for the trade union by way of large exception, rather than by the conferment of delimited rights.

The close bearing of the law on trade union activities has led the trade unions to bring pressure to bear on the legislature. The entering of representations on particular measures was the original purpose of the British Trades Union Congress, and the policy of the American Federation of Labour under Gompers. In later years the British trade unions have become the principal financial support of the Labour Party, and the American leadership has become associated with the Democratic Party. A main reason for association between European trade unions and a political party is the sharing of social principles and ideals, and in France and Italy different groups of trade unions are linked with different parties.

THE BARGAINING AREA. Bargaining power cannot be considered apart from the bargaining area within which it is exerted. What that area shall be in a given case is the outcome of historical factors. Sometimes the initiative in shaping the present area has been taken by employers, sometimes by trade unionists. American employers, perhaps because they were highly individualistic and competitive, have generally been loath to associate, even for the legitimate purpose of collective bargaining, and the plant contract has predominated. The British tradition has been that of the craft union that has tried to make one rate obtain for all engagements, and maintain it through times of slack trade; here the wider the front that could be held, the better, and trade union policy drew together the major employers of each district. Through World War I this extended to industry-wide bargaining. 'Putting a floor under competition' throughout an industry in that way was a step towards turning it into a cartel. It might seem to offer the trade unions concerned the opportunity to push up their pay as far as the elasticity of demand for the products of the industry would let them. The difference between wages in the 'sheltered' and 'unsheltered' industries in the interwar years suggests that some effect of that kind did come about, if only in resisting downward pressure. More positive effects are less likely because employers' resistance will be based on their expectation of price rises stimulating competition from fresh sources at home as well as abroad.

Ideally, trade unions use establishment bargaining (the plant contract) to combine central control of 'the rate for the job' in all establishments, with whatever extra benefits can be extracted from the profitability of particular firms; but in hard times the local or union branch may prefer job security to maintenance of rates, and make concessions. Whereas industry-wide agreements are limited to simple provisions capable of general application, the American plant contract is generally voluminous, and provides rules for all manner of working practices and procedures in the plant. The trade union can therefore undertake to submit any dispute arising during the currency of the contract to arbitration, as the arbitrator can interpret and apply the relevant rule to the facts of the case.

TRADE UNIONISM AT THE PLACE OF WORK. Whether or not the trade unionists working in an establishment negotiate their own agreement with management, they are concerned with issues arising within its walls. Such issues include the allocation and pace of work; discipline; promotion; redundancies; and the processing of grievances. Under the law of the USA, the sole negotiating rights for all the manual workers of an establishment can be vested in one union; the officers of its local branch will then represent them on all these issues. In a British establishment the workers may belong to a number of unions, but the shop stewards elected by the members of the different unions come together in a council, which provides unified representation in meetings with management; its convenor may be wholly occupied with administrative business. Where the roots of trade unionism run back to handicrafts, the workshop is the arena in which the issues arise which bind the member to the union and over which sterner battles have been fought, as new machines and methods have come in, than have been caused by disputes about pay.

It has long been the aim of some trade unions in Europe, but not in the USA, to transcend the adversary system which opposed their members to management at the place of work. Many have sought to do this by a political revolution that would abolish capitalism; but equally in the social democracies, part of the case for nationalization has been that it would substitute public appointment for the irresponsibility of the private employer. Some trade unions have been more concerned with the substance of face-to-face relations, and the possibilities of workers' control and self-management. Interest has therefore attached to the statutory provision in the laws of some European countries, especially Germany, for works councils and the appointment of directors to represent the workers on supervisory boards. The general verdict on the German provisions is that the works councils – where the franchise extends to all employees, but the representatives are in practice the trade unionists – are greatly valued by the trade unions as a means of consultation and joint consideration of management issues; but the appointment of 'worker directors', though a mark of status whose removal would be resented, is not found to confer benefits that are actively felt.

THE IMPACT OF THE TRADE UNION ON PAY. Some estimate of the effects that trade unions have taken can be made by comparing the behaviour of pay in periods of trade union activity and at other times. In a number of Western countries there was a rapid extension of membership, for example, in the years following 1890; in Great Britain membership doubled during World War I; in many Western countries again, but not in the USA, membership rose in the years of full employment after World War II. When such indications as these of trade union strength and activity are set against the economic record, certain inferences suggest themselves about the extent to which trade unions may have changed the course of events, at large and in detail.

It appears that their effect on the general level of money wage rates has been in part to reinforce the ratchet effect which stops those rates dropping back and which has long been present even in the absence of combination: the much smaller reductions of wages in the organized trades in the USA in the great depression of 1929–34 is particularly striking. Generally it was observed that when the falling phase of the eight-year cycle brought wage cuts, the trade union deferred them or even staved them off altogether. Correspondingly, in the rising phase trade unionists were able to get a rise earlier than unorganized workers in their place would have done. But it has not appeared that even widespread and solid trade unionism has been able to push up the general level of money wage rates in a hard market environment, that is, when employers generally have not been able to pass higher costs on in higher prices. The case has been different when the expectation of the employers, reinforced by the commitments of government, allow the negotiation of wage rises needed to keep the workers concerned in line with others, even though product prices must be raised in consequence: in these conditions associated with full employment the trade unions decide the course of the price level jointly with that of money wage rates.

The effect of trade unions on the level of real wages depends on their effect in the first place on productivity, or output per head, and then on their effect on distribution, or the share of output that accrues to the worker. That the 'restrictive practices' enforced by those unions whose control of employment is close enough to serve to reduce productivity is evident from their nature, and from the willingness of managers to pay for their removal; but there are understandings about stints and working practices among unorganized workers too, and management must accept some understanding about these issues in any negotiated agreement with its workforce – the question is where the line shall be drawn. If changes in the strength of trade unionism have affected changes in productivity over time, it has been as only one among other and stronger influences: though the activity and spirit of the New Unionism in Great Britain were held responsible for the check to productivity that became conspicuous there at the beginning of the 20th century, the extension of trade union membership, and of trade union activity at the place of work in the 1950s and 1960s occurred at a time when the rise of productivity was exceptionally fast and sustained.

The effect of trade unions on distribution is illuminated by the evidence from a number of countries of trends that have kept real wages proportionate to productivity, that is, to real output per head (Phelps Brown and Browne, 1986). Whatever the course of money wages, and whatever trade unions may have done at certain times to make them rise faster, the prices of products must have been adjusted so as to maintain a given ratio of wage to product; and in periods such as 1874–89 and 1923–37 in Great Britain, when money wages did not rise at all from end to end but productivity rose, the real wage was raised by a fall in prices. A further implication is that the proportionate division of the product between pay and profits has been constant. But this division, and the stability in the ratio of the real wage to productivity, has been subject to occasional displacement, in which that ratio has been raised. In depression and deflation, the power of the trade union to resist cuts compresses profit margins, and it appears that when the upheaval is sufficiently thoroughgoing, as after World War I, norms and expectations are permanently shifted, and the previous share of profits may never be restored.

Evidently the rise in the standard of living which has transformed the condition of the working population of the western world since 1850 seems to owe nothing directly to trade union pressure for higher wages. Trade unions appear to have taken more effect on distribution as anvil than as hammer. But these inferences from the behaviour of the general level of wages are compatible with substantial influence of the trade unions on the structure of pay. Particular groups may have gained by unionization. One effect of unionization is that it reduces the dispersion of rates for labour of the same type of grade, which otherwise is commonly wide, even in the same locality. Inquiries have also agreed in finding that unionization lifts the organized relatively to the unorganized. Collectively, this shows itself in the rise obtained when a group first bargains; but this is only an impact effect. There has been a cyclical pattern of variation between the wages of organized and unorganized workers, but not progressive divergence. Whether trade unions have changed the differential for skill depends on whether the skilled grades are organized and negotiate separately, or, if they belong to a general union, on their political influence within it. In Sweden in the 1950s and 1960s the pay structure was compressed by agreements made at the national level in pursuance of the egalitarian philosophy of the Landsorganisationen, the national trade union organization; but differentials were restored by wage drift on the shop floor. Statistical studies have shown that individuals who belong to trade unions earn substantially more than non-members when allowance is made for the factors making up personal earning capacity: the difficulty is to be sure that all such factors have been taken into account.

COST PUSH, STAGFLATION AND INCOMES POLICIES. The ability of trade unions to push up the general level of pay when employers are not constrained from raising prices became an engine of cost inflation in the 1960s, when trade unionists sloughed off the cautious expectations formed in harder times, and began raising their claims. Various forms of incomes policy were devised to persuade or require the trade unions to accept rises in money wages that did not outrun the prospective rise in productivity. But for the individual trade unionist, a rise in the money wage was equally a rise in the real wage at the time it was given; and experience showed that the tolerance of trade unionists for policies that required them to accept less than full compensation for rises in the cost of living, was limited. When in the 1970s recession brought back constraints on employers, the trade unionists' expectations and claims persisted, and the combination of unemployment and cost inflation was known as stagflation. It was widely recognized that in these circumstances an expansion of demand would be effective in reducing unemployment only if it was not used by trade unionists in jobs to push their pay up, and that it would therefore have to be accompanied by some form of agreement on restraint between the government and the trade unions.

BIBLIOGRAPHY

Bain, G.S. and Price, R. 1960. *Profiles on Union Growth.* Oxford: Blackwell.

Hicks, J.R. 1932. *The Theory of Wages.* 2nd edn, London: Macmillan, 1963.

Phelps Brown, E.H. and Hopkins, S.V. 1955. Seven centuries of building wages. *Economica* 22, August, 87. Reprinted in E.H. Phelps Brown and S.V. Hopkins, *A Perspective of Wages and Prices,* London and New York: Methuen, 1981.

Phelps Brown, E.H. and Browne, M.H. 1968. *A Century of Pay: the course of pay and production in France, Germany, Sweden, the United Kingdom, and the United States of American, 1860–1960.* London: Macmillan.

Smith, A. 1776. *An Inquiry into the Nature and Causes of the Wealth of Nations.* Ed. E. Cannan. Reprinted, London: Methuen, 1961; New York: Random House, 1965.

Webb, S. and B. 1894. *The History of Trade Unionism.* 2nd edn, London: Longmans, 1920.

Urban Economics

PETER MIESZKOWSKI

Large cities and urban areas exist because it is advantageous to pursue production and consumption activities in a spatially concentrated fashion. Cities are characterized by high population densities, congested intra-city movement, expensive land and the substitution of capital for land. Since persons and firms interact in high density concentrations, the essence of urban economics is the analysis of externalities, neighbourhood effects and related forms of market failure. Traffic congestion, agglomeration economies, pollution, racial segregation, and the provision of public goods all involve externalities and jointness in consumption or production.

Urban economics addresses two central positive issues. First, it explains the internal form, or the density gradient, of a city vis-à-vis a centralized place of employment, the central business district (CBD); and second, it analyses the determinants of relative city size.

The density gradient is a measure of the rate at which population or employment density declines in space as a function of commuting distance from the CBD. The declines in these densities are non-linear, approximately exponential; absolute densities, and land rents, decline very rapidly as distance from the CBD increases. Historically, urban density gradients have become flatter, cities have become much less dense, more decentralized, more suburbanized. This rapid development of suburban areas has eroded the fiscal bases of central cities, and in the United States, large portions of older central cities have become racially segregated low-income ghettoes. A basic concern of social policy is with the effects of this spatial concentration on the poor themselves, and on the general community.

The analysis of urban hierarchies, or the system of cities, abstracts from the internal structure of cities and studies the determinants of the size of different cities. Recent studies have emphasized the relationship between city size and productivity. Economies of scale in production are either localization economies, which are external to the firm but internal to the industry, or urbanization or agglomeration economies, which depend on the size of the metropolitan area. These economies of scale interact with various diseconomies to produce varying levels of utility, or real income, at different levels of population. An important policy issue is whether decentralized migration and firms' location decisions result in an efficient system of cities. Some countries, such as the United Kingdom and France, have evidently decided that they do not. In response to externalities such as pollution and congestion, they have restricted the growth of their largest cities and have built new towns as part of their policies to decentralize urban development.

Urban economics analyses the spatial distribution of the population and the policies designed to change the distribution of the population within cities, between cities, and between urban and rural areas. The basic objective of this branch of economics is to study market failures, and to help design public policies to improve upon the shortcomings of non-coordinated allocative decisions in urban areas.

HISTORICAL REVIEW. As structures are durable and can be maintained indefinitely, the structure of a city at a particular point in time will strongly reflect its historical development. Variations in average residential densities across American cities are highly correlated with the size of the city and average age of the housing stock. Although the typical densities of new suburban development in older metropolitan areas (Boston) and new metropolitan areas (Houston) may be similar, the overall structure of these two cities is quite different because of cumulative urban development. A historical perspective is therefore very important for understanding variations in urban structure within metropolitan areas and across cities.

In the 19th century intra-city movements of persons and goods were very expensive, and cities were relatively small and very compact. Virtually all employment was located within one to three miles of the central business districts with workers' residences often located close to their places of employment. Within cities, freight was transported by horse and wagon, and communication between firms was either through messages or face-to-face meetings. The horse-drawn carriage and rail-guided horse and wagon were expensive means of transportation relative to earnings and were used primarily by higher income groups.

In the late 19th century the development of electric traction permitted the running of clean subways and trolley cars. This technological change led to an increase in city size and the decentralization of urban areas. A more dramatic, far-reaching transportation innovation was the development of the automobile and the truck. The effects of this innovation continue to the present day as automobile ownership becomes more ubiquitous throughout the world. In the United States over 90 per cent of adults drive cars and the vast majority of households, including the poorest quintile group, own automobiles.

The truck was first used in intra-city movements of freight and then increasingly for inter-city transportation, after the more recent development of interstate highways and outer-circumferential routes. Improvements in the long-distance truck and intra-city automobile transportation permitted firms to draw workers from a wider area, and to locate in less expensive, less dense surburban locations in more efficient one-storey continuous process operations. Industries and residences have decentralized in cities throughout the world.

EXPLANATIONS OF INTRA-METROPOLITAN DECENTRALIZATION. In the United States, and in some other industrial countries, the decentralization of activity within urban areas has been accompanied by an increased concentration of low income groups in central cities. In 1983 the median income of families resident in American central cities was 70 per cent of the median income of suburban communities. A large portion of the growing income disparity between the central city and suburbs is explained by the increased concentration of poor black families in central cities. The median income of suburban black households is 45 per cent higher than that of black families residing in central cities.

Two somewhat conflicting explanations have been offered for suburbanization of metropolitan areas. One, based on the monocentric model of urban areas, stresses technological change, decreasing transportation costs, the increased use of the automobile, rising real incomes, and population growth. The alternative explanation stresses lower suburban tax rates and a variety of central city social factors: high crime rates, congestion, smog, poor schools and neighbourhood blight. According to this explanation middle income families move to the suburbs to escape these problems.

To formulate appropriate public policies it is important to identify the relative contributions of different factors causing intra-metropolitan decentralization. If suburbanization is largely explained by technological changes that permitted the transformation of a compact, highly dense city to a more sprawling city form, and if the success of the suburbs is explained by the revealed preference of more affluent households for new housing and land-intensive residential patterns, the case for public intervention in rebuilding the central cities is weak. Intervention and fiscal aid to central cities need to be justified primarily on distributive grounds, to improve the level of public services and the general quality of life for poorer residents of the central city.

If, on the other hand, fiscal distortions, crime and the quality of education are important causes of decentralization, the case is much stronger for a broad set of policies to stem the potentially unstable cumulative decline of central cities. Fiscal distortions decrease the overall level of national income by dissipating production and consumption economies. The case for public intervention will rest on considerations of allocative efficiency, as well as redistributive objectives.

The monocentric model of urban areas assumes that employment is concentrated at the CBD and that households make residential location decision by trading off commuting costs and higher housing costs close to the CBD. If households are identical in terms of income and preferences, an equilibrium set of housing prices must yield the same level of real income at all residential locations. Housing services are produced with inputs of land and capital and it is possible to substitute capital for land by building multi-storey residential structures. The substitution of capital for land explains the rapid decline of both density and land values close to the CBS, and the less rapid declines at more distant locations.

A key concept in this analysis of urban form is the bid rent function, or the rent offer curve. Firms and households bid for land at different locations. The equilibrium structure of land rents requires that firms have no incentive to move; they earn zero profits at all locations or in the case of households achieve an equal level of utility (real income). Although there is no well-developed theory on intra-urban employment location, some firms, even if they ship all of their output for sale at the CBD, will have an incentive to move to the suburbs to take advantage of lower land prices and lower wages. As employment decentralizes, a negative wage gradient will evolve as suburban residents will accept lower wages in suburban employment to offset commuting costs to the CBD.

It is important to note that the monocentric model as developed by Mills (1972) and Muth (1969) is an equilibrium model. The capital (housing) stock is assumed to be malleable so that in effect the city is 'rebuilt' in each period. Under certain simplifying assumptions, the monocentric model yields a negative exponential density function of the form.

$$D(u) = D_0 e^{-\gamma u}$$

where $D(u)$ is the residential density, u miles from the CBD, and D_0 is the density next to the CBD. The model predicts that as the population of the metropolitan area increases D_0 will increase, but there is no prediction on the relationship between city size and the density gradient γ. However, it can be argued that larger cities will be more decentralized, and γ will be smaller in absolute size as large metropolitan areas will support more subcentres for shopping and employment.

The effects of rising real income on urban structure are ambiguous. Rising real incomes will increase the demand for housing and land and will lead to suburbanization. However, as rising real incomes increase the time costs of commuting, it is uncertain whether increases in real income, other things equal, will result in a more decentralized urban structure. The empirical evidence indicates that the income elasticity of the demand for housing is only slightly larger than the income elasticity of commuting costs. Also there is no empirical evidence that the rent offer curves get flatter as the incomes of households increase. Consequently the location of high income groups in suburbs *cannot* be explained by a high income elasticity of demand for housing relative to increases in commuting expenses. In fact, there is some evidence that, other things equal, high income groups will outbid lower income groups for high quality surburban sites with better access to central city employment.

The long-run equilibrium portrayed in static models of urban spatial structure may, in fact, never be achieved. Anas (1978) and Harrison and Kain (1974) have developed models based on the assumption that residential capital is very durable and non-malleable. According to this model, the city does not develop by being 'rebuilt' in every period; rather, urban form depends on a set of incremental investment decisions. City development takes place in rings moving outwards from the city centre. Each ring represents a historical period of growth. The development process is assumed to be myopic, so housing of a particular vintage incorporates the income and transportation conditions that prevail at the time of construction.

One implication of this formulation is that urban development is a cumulative process and that two cities of the same size and income levels may have very different density structures depending on their historical pattern of development. The cities that had substantial population in 1900 will be of a different form than the new cities developed after the widespread introduction of the automobile.

The most striking implication of the assumption of durable, non-convertible capital is that rising incomes or declining transportation costs will lead to the obsolescence of central city housing and to abandonment. As development proceeds outwardss from the city centre, the oldest housing will be small, reflecting lower real income in the past. With increases in real income, rental income on the older housing will fall, and if income growth is large enough the oldest housing will ultimately become economically obsolete.

However, as Wheaton (1982) noted, this conclusion forgets that older sites can be redeveloped. Wheaton showed that reconstruction will occur at the most central locations and that the densities of the redeveloped sites will be greater than that of replaced use. According to this formulation, the central city is developed first, and for a long period new construction occurs at the fringe, but as the city continues to grow, central redevelopment will displace at least some new construction in the suburbs. Even in the absence of different income groups then, the urban developmment process will go through stages in which a central city first declines and is then reconstructed.

Wheaton has also shown, in a perfect foresight model, that for a growing city it will be efficient to withhold some land from premature development. For example, some land close to the CBD that will be especially valuable in the future as high density business development will not be developed currently as lower density residential property. This result illustrates the social value of land speculation, and partially counters criticism of urban sprawl. Land markets do not work perfectly, but city planning designed to curb urban sprawl and proposals to impose differentially high taxes on vacant land may by myopic and inefficient. Similarly, abandonment of certain housing units, or even whole neighbourhoods, is not necessarily evidence of market failure even when redevelopment occurs after a long lag. The current value of the cleared land may simply be less than demolition and clearing costs.

A vintage model of a durable housing stock assuming myopic foresight has been developed by Cooke and Hamilton (1984) to explain the tendency for high income groups to reside in suburban areas. These authors assume a demand function for housing based on income and price and a particular distribution of income. According to this model, in the decade beginning in 1900 a housing stock was built to house the population, and the characteristics of the houses built during that decade reflected income and price conditions at that time. A variety of housing types accommodated persons of different incomes. In the next decade, 1910, a new distribution of income determined an updated housing demand distribution. This new demand distribution then set the rents on the first period's stock of housing. Units in excess supply filtered down the income distribution to low income groups.

New units were built on the periphery of the city as income grew over time, leaving smaller houses in high density neighbourhoods in the central city. These older, less desirable units tended over time to be occupied by low-income groups, while more affluent households lived in larger, newer housing in the suburbs. This version of the filtering model of housing predicts a growing income disparity between the central city and the suburbs solely in terms of the age and characteristics of the housing stocks. According to this analysis, the fiscal and social problems of central cities caused by high concentrations of low-income population in these areas may be largely a reflection of the way housing markets operate.

Some writers have stressed changes in transportation modes as the basis of central city revival or redevelopment. Historically, when everyone walked to work the centre of the city was an area of high prestige. However, upon the successive development of the omnibus, the commuter tram, the streetcar, and finally the automobile, all expensive modes of transportation relative to earnings at their time of introduction, the suburbs became the prestigious areas. Only recently, when the cost of car ownership relative to income has fallen and the ownership of cars for housholds in the lowest income quintile in the United States has increased to over 60 per cent, are lower income groups able to commute to suburban properties. The more equal access to the most effective means of transportation suggests that more affluent households will move back to the central city and low and moderate income groups will move increasingly to the suburbs.

Most empirical investigations of the factors behind decentralization have utilized cross-section data for American cities. Muth (1969) estimated density gradients for 46 American cities in 1950 and found car registrations, the intra-metropolitan distribution of employment and the proportion of the central city population which was black to be the most consistent variables in explaining variation in density gradients across cities. Muth also concluded that the physical characteristics of the central city, such as the age and condition of the housing stock, do not have a significant effect on decentralization. A careful study by Mills and Price (1984) explaining a cross section of density gradients to 1970 also concluded that a set of measures of central city social problems – race, crime, and taxes – adds almost nothing to the explanation of suburbanization.

Several other studies, using other measures of decentralizations and different time periods, concluded that the net fiscal surplus received by middle-class families in central-city versus suburban locations does affect their residential location. Also, there is evidence for the 1970s that school desegregation led to a sharp drop in white enrolments in central city schools. A significant majority of affluent households that continue to reside in the central city do not have school-aged children.

Evidence of racial prejudice also appears from empirical work on white-black housing cost differentials. Studies based on 1970s data show lower housing prices and rents in black neighbourhoods. These differentials, approaching 20 per cent, confirm models of prejudice that predict whites are willing to pay a premium to maintain a distance from racial integration.

The most persuasive evidence that recent governments transportation and housing policies, racial tensions and other central city problems are *not* the primary explanations of suburbanization is historical evidence on declining density gradients throughout the world. Mills and Tan (1980) have assembled evidence on the flattening of density functions, a measure of decentralization for a large number of developed countries. Some of the evidence goes back into the early 19th century. The evidence for European and American cities shows that decentralization is *not* a post-World War II phenomenon and there is relatively little variability from one decade to the next at the rate at which decentralization has occurred.

The demonstration that density gradients have been decreasing throughout the world for a hundred years is an important achievement. This result shows that suburbanization has occurred in countries without the social problems characteristic of American cities. Decentralization must be rooted in technological changes, the interaction between employment and residential decentralization and the growth of real income. Cities have simply changed form, and there is little reason for public policy to try to change the less dense, more decentralized urban structure.

Yet our understanding of urban decentralization, past and future, remains imperfect. First, relative transportation costs have not been directly introduced into the econometric investigations of density gradients. Second, there are difficulties with dismissing the role of social and racial factors in explaining suburbanization. A summary statistic, the density gradient, may be too aggregative a measure to capture the effects of fiscal and related neighbourhood effects. Moreover, the idea that rich households have a high income elasticity of demand for the newest, most desirable housing that is located in the suburbs is a very short step away from the idea that the same households have the same high income elasticity of demand for the best schools and the safest, low density neighbourhoods, which are also located in the suburbs. Nevertheless, existing empirical research provides very partial support for the importance of social factors as determinants of intra-metropolitan decentralization.

THE SIZE DISTRIBUTION OF URBAN AREAS AND OPTIMAL CITY SIZE. The distribution of city sizes is skewed to the right as there are many small cities and few very large ones. Early explanations of the size distribution of cities emphasized specialization of economic function and the role of cities as central market places. The foundation of this theory is the number of rural residents that can be served by cities of the smallest size. The rural residents buy a variety of goods and retail and personal services produced by these cities. One step higher in the city hierarchy are towns that provide more specialized functions to their own populations, and to urban areas of the next smallest size. City size increases as cities become more specialized, and the more specialized the functions, the smaller the number of cities. Beckmann (1958) has shown that the simple model, grounded in the idea that urban areas are service areas for the farm population, can be used to generate the rank-size rule where the second largest urban area has half the population of the largest city and the third largest has one-third the population of the largest and so on.

In contrast to traditional considerations of specialization and exchange, recent work on city size has emphasized amenity characteristics, such as climate, and the interaction between economies and diseconomies of scale. This analysis seeks to explain the level of per capita real income, or utility, as a function of a city's total population. In the simplest versions of these models there are two production activities and two consumption goods, a manufactured good and housing services. The production of the export good is subject to increasing returns to scale while the production of housing services, which requires land space and involves commuting, is subject to decreasing returns. At low population levels it is postulated that the economies of scale outweigh the diseconomies and that real income increases with increases in population. As the city grows it becomes more spread out, more congested, and at larger population levels diseconomies of scale outweigh at the margin additional economies, and utility per capita reaches a maximum and declines with further increases in population. The relationship between individual utility and population size is bell-shaped.

The economies of scale can be consumption economies as well as production economies. One example of a consumption economy is a non-rival public good whose price or cost per person is inversely proportional to the size of the population. Also the variety and quality of various private consumption goods increases with population size. Increases in city size are associated with a variety of subtle advantages as well as a number of more obvious disadvantages.

Interaction between economies and diseconomies of scale and the implied differences in relative prices and differences in consumption bundles across cities explain differences in money wages across cities, and the co-existence of the same industries in cities of varying size. The higher money wages paid to workers in larger cities are made possible by higher labour productivity in these cities. Different industries will be subject to varying economies of scale, and city size will vary according to the industries in which they are specialized. The existence of consumption economies also decreases the likelihood that maximum per capita utility is determined at a unique population level.

As a particular city grows, congestion and related diseconomies may outweigh production economies and per capita at medium population levels and utility will decrease. However if growth continues the larger population generates a number of consumption economies (lower per-capita costs for public services, more varied recreation), per-capita utility will again rise with population. Similarly, the growth and development of a particular city may occur very rapidly over a short period of time as increases in population improve the quality of life in the city. This improvement leads to further in-migration of population, and growth continues until it is slowed by diseconomies of scale.

For some policy purposes it is important to determine whether production economies are economies of localization, which are internal to each industry in a particular city, or are economies of urbanization, or agglomeration economies, which are external to individual industries. These reflect the advantages of operation in cities with larger labour forces, diverse suppliers and customers. Empirical research indicates that external economies of scale are primarily those of localization, not urbanization, and they peter out as city size increases. This finding suggests that cities should be specialized and that smaller cities will be specialized, and it enhances the case for coordinating firm location decisions. For example, if a city becomes too large it will be difficult to develop secondary production centres as dispersal will require coordination by industry.

Localization economies also explain why industrial activity in less developed countries is typically concentrated in a primary city. In these countries business, financial services and quality public services are initially very scarce. As industrialization begins it is quite natural for new manufacturing firms to establish themselves in the largest city, and the advantages of newly developed localization economies acts as a magnet for new firms. Coordination at the early stages of industrialization might be needed to avoid the disadvantages of future industrial concentration.

The United Kingdom and France have actively pursued policies to disperse employment and population away from their principal economic regions, London and Paris. These policies were designed to counteract the concentration of manufacturing investments in the capital regions. Although economic activity continues to shift to southeast England, the population of greater London has declined, and manufacturing in England and France has been dispersed. The benefits of population dispersal have not been quantified, but these polices are relatively non-controversial and remain in effect.

In contrast, the United States has not attempted to limit the size of its largest cities, and there is little support for a national policy on population distribution. This is explained by the greater degree of political decentralization in the United States and by the very rapid decrease in primacy. Between 1940 and 1980 the population of the New York metropolitan area as a percentage of total US population fell from 18.6 per cent to 10.2 per cent. A number of the largest metropolitan areas grew very slowly or declined during the 1970s. Much of the growth of the US population occurred in the South and Southwest, regions with smaller cities and less urbanization. Market forces appear to be controlling the growth of the largest cities and promoting a more diversified national urban structure.

Regional income differentials have narrowed in the United States and, after adjusting for cost-of-living differences, differences in real incomes across broad regions have virtually disappeared. Migration into the high-income West coast region has decreased incomes there while migration of unskilled farm population from the South to the industrial North and of capital and skilled white collar labour into the South have eliminated North-South income differentials.

These equalizing trends may be unique to the United States. Some anti-neoclassical writers have described European regional development as highly unstable and leading to an extremely skewed urban structure because of a highly unstable process of cumulative causation. Whatever the case may be for European development, this process clearly does not apply to the US. In fact, post-war regional trends and urban development in the US are basically consistent with neoclassical considerations of comparative or differential costs, along with internal migration towards warmer, more rapidly growing areas.

A fundamental reason for questioning the advisability of restricting the size of the largest cities is Tolley's (1974) result that large cities may be too small relative to their optimal size when their internal organization is inefficient because of the existence of pollution and congestion externalities.

Tolley argues that pollution and congestion decrease amenity values in a city, decrease the supply of residents and increase nominal wages. In the absence of taxes on pollution and congestion the real income or utility of a city is below its optimal level for any given population level. This result implies that the primary policies of dealing with inefficiencies in large cities should attack the problems at their source, and regulate or price externalities. Pollution and congestion are related to population size, but the technological links may be quite weak and indirect. The efficient, direct solution to the externality problems is to modify polluting production processes and to change commuting patterns, and/or the structure of the transportation network.

This argument, with its conclusion that inefficiently organized cities may be too small, does not rule out the need for a coordinating national population policy to achieve a first best outcome. In general, decentralized policies initiated by local governments to deal with pollution and congestion, though necessary for efficiency, are not sufficient to achieve full efficiency in the distribution of a nation's population.

The general condition for the efficient allocation of population between cities or regions, *given that the internal organization of each city is efficient*, is the difference between social marginal product (SMP) and the social marginal cost (SMC) of maintaining a person at a given level of utility equalized across cities. To illustrate, for large cities L, and small cities S.

$$SMP_L - SMC_L = SMP_S - SMC_S.$$

If large cities are over-populated relative to small cities then

$$SMP_L - SMC_L < SMP_S - SMC_S.$$

One model with non-rival public goods illustrates that free migration between cities will not be inefficient when utility is equalized across cities and each city is efficiently organized. There are two cities each with a finite amount of land space. One city has more land, supports a larger population, and has a lower tax price per capita for public goods. Some writers conjecture that the advantage would result in an excessively large population in the larger city. It has been shown that a non-coordinated or decentralized equilibrium will be inefficient unless per capita taxes are equalized across cities, and this will occur only in very special circumstances. Also empirical evidence supports the expectation that the large city will be overpopulated relative to the social optimum.

A very similar result obtains when Pigovian taxes are imposed by local governments to control pollution. The outcome is suboptimal relative to a first best national policy which adopts different tax rates in cities of varying size but which requires equal transfers per capita. When capital and labour are the production inputs and pollution is harmful to labour but not to capital, the optimal solution requires the conservation of labour and a high wage rate. A decentralized equilibrium undermines the optimal solution when larger per capita taxes are collected in the larger, more heavily polluted communities, and are transferred to local labour. The condition of equal per capita transfers requires a nationally administered pollution policy.

Variability in the quality of urban sites also results in coordination problems in a developing country undergoing urbanization. The first cities will be developed on superior sites, often on the coast. Interior sites will not be developed until the coastal cities are large, polluted and congested. Interior development will begin when real income in the two regions is equal. Because of economies of scale, real incomes in the interior cities and in coastal cities will increase as the population migrates from the congested coast to the emerging interior cities.

The improvement in welfare throughout the nation establishes that the development of interior sites occurred too late, i.e., the urban population of the nation became large enough and real income low enough so pioneers began trickling into the interior. One policy superior to laissez-faire development to coordinate migration into the interior is to guarantee residents a certain level of real income. This policy, if timed correctly, will not require fiscal transfers between cities. The first best policy will require a still earlier development of the interior and will require fiscal transfer between cities (regions).

The need for coordination in the development of cities arises from economies of scale and variations in the quality of urban sites, which result in a lumpiness problem. J.V. Henderson (1985) has argued that if there exist a large number of cities and cities can be replicated, the lumpiness problem becomes less significant. In the extreme case where the number of cities becomes very large and individual cities approximate their efficient size, a constant returns-to-scale world is approached. This result suggests that the importance of intervention in the shaping of the system of cities will vary from country to country. The spontaneous development of new, efficient cities in a relatively short period is much more likely in a large country with a varied urban structure than in countries with small populations, such as Australia, Argentina and Canada, or in countries with large populations but with an underdeveloped urban system consisting of a small number of large cities.

263

CONGESTION AND OTHER FORMS OF MARKET FAILURE IN URBAN AREAS. The principal urban externality is congestion, which is related to peak-hour work-trips made to the CBD. Commuters take account of the average level of congestion in deciding whether and when to travel, but do not account for the additional congestion costs they impose on other commuters. The divergence between marginal and average congestion cost is large, and calls for congestion tolls that would vary according to time of day. The tolls would finance highway construction, and it can be shown that when the long-run marginal cost of highway capacity is constant, the optimum congestion toll will just finance a road system that has been carried out to the optimum level.

There are administrative problems in setting tolls and, more significantly, there is no political support for them. Consequently, there is too much commuting to the CBD by automobile, the rent gradient is flatter than it would be with congestion tolls and residential location is more decentralized. The absence of congestion tolls distorts land values, and market prices of land close to the CBD are below their social value. The use of distorted land values by highway planners to determine highway capacity will lead to an excessive allocation of land to roads. Without congestion tolls, attempts to alleviate congestion in certain bottleneck situations by increasing capacity will have little social value as additional traffic simply fills the increased capacity of the bottleneck. Also because of the increased reliance on the automobile, congestion, especially in the largest cities such as New York, has gotten worse over time.

These conclusions notwithstanding, the principal solution to urban congestion is the expansion of the highway system. In the United States 90 per cent of work trips and 95 per cent of all trips in urban areas are made by private automobile. Due to the decentralization of employment within metropolitan areas, only 15 per cent of work trips are towards the CBD. Public transit is relatively inconvenient for reverse-direction and circumferential commutes.

During the 1970s the US Congress established new grant programmes to subsidize operating expenses of local transit systems and provide 80 per cent of the construction costs of new subway systems. Passenger contributions fell to 38 per cent of operating expenses, and new rail systems were built in Washington, San Francisco and several southern cities with relatively low population densities. While the real value of transit taxes decreased, the subsidy programmes failed to increase transit travel significantly on existing systems. The ridership on new rail systems was overprojected by a factor of two, these expensive systems ran large operating losses and the cost per auto trip avoided was very high.

As expressways near the centre of CBDs are very expensive, peak-hour users are also heavily subsidized, although as a group urban highway users provide more in highway tax revenues than is spent on highway expenditures. Further subsidies to local transit to offset the subsidy to peak-hour highway users will increase travel in general, thus misallocating resources. A more appropriate step might be to decrease federal subsidies to all forms of local transportation.

Even in the absence of congestion tolls, evidence has accumulated that highways are underbuilt in metropolitan areas. Some urban travel-demand models have found very high values of travel time and very high willingness to pay for the benefits of the private automobile. Benefit-cost analyses have concluded that additional lanes of highway could pay for themselves in one year alone. And a study on the benefits of urban roads concluded that an expanded all-auto system would also yield substantial benefits.

In very large cities such as New York a significant expansion of the highway system is not feasible because of high construction costs and social disruption. For very dense cities, congestion tolls seem to be essential instruments of policy as congestion is most pronounced and extension of highway capacity most difficult. Given the diversity of city type and differences in density across cities, there is a strong case for decentralized urban transportation policies and solutions tailored to the needs of specific cities. Congestion tolls represent an important financial instrument in effecting decentralization.

Unpriced accessibility poses problems similar to unpriced congestion. Koopmans and Beckmann (1957), in a classic paper, argued that if there are *n* indivisible plants to be assigned to *n* sites, and if plants sell intermediate products to one another, no price system will sustain any assignment of plants to sites. Subsequent research reveals that this theorem is incorrect and there are cases where land markets will clear. The explanation of the problem is that firms differ in their preferences for sites first *qua* sites, and second because of transportation costs resulting from interplant trade. The market breaks down because it fails to price accessibility to other plants, *and* the locational preferences of firms for sites *qua* sites is not strong enough to establish locational stability by overcoming these externalities.

Firms and households also may not account for negative externalities in making locational decisions; the glue factory may choose to locate in a high-quality residential neighbourhood. Empirical studies on the effects of non-conforming land uses on residential property value have generally found that they are very small or affect only a small number of adjacent properties, a finding which undermines the traditional basis for land use regulations (zoning). Evidence has also accumulated that, rather than improving the efficiency of land markets, regulations have distorted development and are used to exclude low-income groups from many suburban communities. By restricting the amount of land for apartments, they increase the cost of moderate income housing.

Reliance on the residential property tax for local finance results in exclusionary zoning, but the incentives to exclude and to limit new development go well beyond fiscal considerations. For instance, the residents of a partially developing community have a high incentive to restrict development since they rarely own the undeveloped land in the community and have no interest in the value of this land. Furthermore, they may also have a preference for low density development, open space and ecological protection. Finally, they do not have to compensate the owners of the undeveloped land and by restricting development they increase the value of their properties. One empirical study has concluded that in a metropolitan area with highly concentrated zoning authorities, development controls have increased housing prices by 50 per cent.

Another example of public intervention in the United States was the urban renewal programmes introduced in the 1950s and 1960s. The local agencies, heavily subsidized by the federal government, bought buildings in blighted neighbourhoods, cleared the land and auctioned the land to private developers. The market value of cleared land was well below the original cost plus demolition.

The justification for public intervention in redevelopment is the existence of neighbourhood effects and interdependencies between property owners. Efficient redevelopment is more likely to be undertaken if coordinated. Fragmented ownership of properties complicated the assembly of a number of neighbourhood properties because of the possibility of price gauging by a small number of holdouts.

The criticism of past urban renewal programmes is that they were operated without any relevant criteria for expenditures as they were heavily subsidized. Yet local authorities should use eminent domain to assemble properties when benefits of coordinated redevelopment exceed costs.

POVERTY AND RACE. A significant social problem in many industrial countries is unemployment and poverty among the youth who are concentrated in the central cities. In the United States the poor are disproportionately black, and residential patterns in American cities are highly segregated by race. Only a small portion of the observed patterns of segregation can be explained by income and family structure. Social concern over urban decentralization is closely related to the fiscal problems of central cities and to racial equality. Suburbanization in housing and employment diminishes the employment, housing and educational prospects for minorities who are concentrated in central cities.

The income gap between individual black workers and whites has narrowed significantly, but many black families have not shared in these gains because an increasing number of black families are headed by women. The incidence of poverty in many central city neighbourhoods has increased over time and there is evidence of the bifurcation of black America as more successful blacks move out of ghetto areas. There is little understanding of the causes of the increased instability of black families, though the compensatory welfare programme has had little effect on changes in black family structure.

Existing patterns of racial segregation are explained by the prejudice of whites. There are many empirical studies on the effects of prejudice and discrimination on black/white housing price differentials. The studies with data for the 1960s, when substantial numbers of blacks migrated to northern areas, showed that blacks paid 10–15 per cent more for housing of the same quality. During the 1970s black urbanization slowed and the weight of the empirical evidence shifted as 1970s data showed that housing prices in black neighbourhoods were 20 per cent lower than comparable housing in white areas. This research supports the view that whites are prejudiced and will not rent or buy in largely black residential areas. Thus, even if open housing laws were rigorously enforced, residential segregation would remain as blacks would find it cheaper to live in black areas.

One argument for opening up the suburbs to blacks at all income levels is the importance of neighbourhood effects on the quality of life and on individual behaviour. A small minority of individuals victimize all of the residents of lower income black areas. A specific benefit of greater racial and class integration resulting from suburbanization might be higher educational attainment by low achievers. The results of empirical studies on the importance of peer-group effects on educational achievement are mixed. One study found that students of all levels of achievement gain by being in classes with higher levels of average achievement. Other studies found peer-group effects to be small, or insignificant.

As employment has decentralized to the suburbs, residential segregation may diminish the employment and income prospects of minorities. Some empirical evidence for the 1960s was developed which linked the employment rate of blacks in an area to residential location and to distance of the location from major black ghettoes. The results were used to argue that the dispersal of black settlement would increase the employment of blacks.

More recently, there are reports of severe labour shortages of unskilled workers in affluent suburban areas at a time when the unemployment rate of black youth has increased absolutely, and relative to the unemployment of white youth. This seems to confirm the importance of the link between housing segregation and deteriorating employment prospects for non-whites. But systematic research on this topic, though limited in quantity, has not established the importance of residential location as a determinant of earnings. One study, after controlling for education, occupation, experience and other factors, found the income difference of black residents in the suburbs and in the central city to be no larger than five per cent. This is a small effect relative to the estimate of the racial discrimination effect of 15 per cent and relative to the 20 per cent difference in black-white earnings that is attributed to differences in education and related human capital endowments.

A special survey of the employment problems of inner-city youth confirms the weak evidence for the spatial mismatch hypothesis. In Chicago, where some residential areas are close to clusters of factories and jobs and other residential areas are not, it was found that proximity to jobs does not help non-white youth. Even when the jobs were nearby, white youths got them.

The general subsidization of public transit is a cost-ineffective method of increasing the mobility of the poor as this group accounts for only 25 per cent of transit trips and low-income ridership is concentrated on short trips in the central city. Also the diversity of origins and destinations of the poor who commute to the suburbs makes *existing* public transit an ineffective transportation system for their needs. However, if transportation access is the primary cause of the employment problems of central-city minority residents, the solution would be straightforward and relatively inexpensive. Special programmes could be introduced where public transit could be restructured by providing more individualistic door-to-door service with smaller vehicles. Furthermore, if labour shortages in the suburbs exist and there is unemployment in the central city, firms should have the incentive to transport workers to suburban job sites.

CONCLUDING REMARKS. Urban economics has developed rapidly, and a large theoretical and empirical literature now exists. The work on urban structure is perhaps most advanced as this knowledge is based on both theory and quantitative research. There have been substantial advances in research sub-areas such as transportation, housing markets, and urban public finance. The work on optimal city size and system of cities has advanced theoretically, but considerably more empirical research is needed on the contributions of various economies and diseconomies of scale to economic welfare.

Despite the vast literature on the subject, little is known about the most effective solutions to urban poverty and related social pathologies such as crime and the unstable structure of low-income families. One important conclusion, though based on a very small number of empirical studies, is that the spatial isolation of the poor is not a primary determinant of their employment and income.

Perhaps the most significant contribution of urban economics is that is has demonstrated, despite outward evidence of sprawl, blight and racial segregation, that decentralized market forces do a reasonably good job in allocating resources. Sound rationalizations can be provided for sprawl and land speculation, and for abandonment of housing in the growing, changing cities. Governmental intervention in the allocative process should be used sparingly, given the history of past mistakes and the inefficiencies of existing land-use regulations. The theoretical basis for various forms of public intervention exists but poverty is the primary cause of the most acute urban problems, not the lack of governmental planning of urban structure.

BIBLIOGRAPHY

Anas, A. 1978. Dynamics of urban residential growth. *Journal of Economics* 5(1), January, 66–87.

Beckmann, M.J. 1958. City hierarchies and the distribution of city size. *Economic Development and Cultural Change* 6, April, 243–8.

Cooke, T.W. and Hamilton, B.W. 1984. Evolution of urban housing stocks: a model applied to Baltimore and Houston. *Journal of Urban Economics* 16(3), November, 317–38.

Harrison, D. and Kain, J.F. 1974. Cumulative urban growth and urban density functions. *Journal of Urban Economics* 4(1), January, 113–17.

Henderson, J.V. 1985. *Economics Theory and Cities*. 2nd edn. New York: Academic Press.

Koopmans, T.C. and Beckmann, M. 1957. Assignment problems and the location of economic activities. *Econometrica* 25, January, 53–76.

Mills, E.S. *Studies in the Structure of the Urban Economy*. Baltimore: Johns Hopkins Press.

Mills, E.S. and Tan, J.D. 1980. A comparison of urban population density functions in developed and developing countries. *Urban Studies* 17(3), October, 313–21.

Mills, E.S. and Price, R. 1984. Metropolitan suburbanization and central city problems. *Journal of Urban Economics* 15(1), January, 1–17.

Muth, R.F. 1969. *Cities and Housing*. Chicago: University of Chicago Press.

Tolley, G.S. 1974. The welfare economics of city bigness. *Journal of Urban Economics* 1(3), July, 324–45.

Wheaton, W.C. 1982. Urban spatial development with durable but replaceable capital. *Journal of Urban Economics* 12(1), July, 53–67.

Value of Life

THOMAS C. SCHELLING

It is not identified lives but statistical lives – the reduction of some mortal hazard to some part of the population – whose value is our topic. But the prolongation of individual lives is getting increased attention, and it deserves some of ours before we get on with the main business.

'Our society values life', a California judge commented when he ordered force-feeding for a quadriplegic woman who wished to die and had asked the hospital's help in starving to death. Medical technology now provides, and medical institutions often require, procedures that prolong lives expensively and indefinitely even when the life is of dubious quality to the patient. These are procedures that the deciding institutions either cannot deny or will not permit to be withdrawn, and they are independent of any assessment of value of the life extension procured. In some cases rejoicing is unanimous when death mercifully terminates an effort to prolong life.

Even assessing the value of statistical lifesaving – reducing some small carcinogenic hazard – is not universally considered properly subject to a comparison of costs and benefits. In the US government there has been controversy whether the cost per life saved should be a consideration in occupational-safety decision: even the courts have had difficulty construing the legislation to permit taking costs into account. Nor is it generally accepted that hazardous activities should always be relocated to less densely populated areas where fewer would be at risk. Marginal outlays per expected life saved vary among agencies by two orders of magnitude.

In economics, valuing life means the prevention of death, not the creation of people who might never have existed. The economics of overpopulation can draw an economist's attention, but nobody measures the welfare gain to sterile parents of a steady supply of births for adoption. Economies of scale to population size in a sparsely populated area are easy to handle; but the value of simply having more 'lives' – more people born to enjoy life – is rarely discussed in our profession. It is only philosophers (Parfit, 1984, pp. 351–454, 487–90), and few of them, who write about 'whether causing someone to exist can benefit this person'. Our topic is therefore asymmetrical. I confine this essay to the value of preventing deaths because that is what the subject has been, but we can hope that the next Palgrave may have a more symmetrical topic to pursue.

WORTH TO WHOM?

The first principle that ought to bear on what it is worth to save a statistical life – to reduce a mortal risk to some part of the population – is that there ought to be some person or collection of persons to whom it is worth something. To whom is it worth something to reduce the risk of death to some identified part of the population? We can begin with the people at risk. They may not be good at calculating risks and handling probabilities and expected values; they may give exaggerated emphasis to risks that are mysterious or sensational; but if they are susceptible, they care; and unless their attitude is wholly superstitious they are likely to recognize that reducing statistical risks to their own and their families' lives is worth paying for. What is at stake is not only life itself but grief and the permanent loss of parents, children and spouses.

Many of the people targeted for risk reduction will be financially responsible for others. The family has an economic interest in the parent's continued living. The importance of the parent's livelihood, in contrast to his living, will depend on the private and public insurance and other arrangements to care for his dependents.

Social and private insurance, charities, and all the claims that the deceased's family will exercise introduce another set of interests – all the people and institutions that are sources or recipients of transfers on account of the death. The fact that in one respect the transfers cancel out – the dependents of the deceased showing receipts equivalent to the public and private payments to them – does not make them uninteresting. The transfers change and broaden the answer to the question, to whom is it worth something that these deaths be prevented.

Transfers can go in either direction. Some of the current discussions of health policy neglect this important fact. It is often alleged that people who smoke impose costs on the health-care system and should be penalized through higher cigarette taxes or health insurance premiums. But the typical lung cancer victim enriches the society he leaves behind. The median age for lung cancer is 65 and most victims are dead within a year; the median male retirement age in the United States is about 63; a 65-year-old male victim loses an expected fifteen years of life. Discounting at 5 per cent, if he is without dependents he relinquishes upwards of $50,000 in social security benefits, and if he was at the median income level during his pre-retirement years he may relinquish a like amount in private pensions. His terminal illness inflicts a small fraction of that on the health insurers (and he will not be around to be hospitalized again later in life).

Lung cancer reminds us that our financial stakes in the continued living of those among us who are at risk can be positive or negative. Aggregating the financial interests, positive and negative, that different people may have in the demise or longevity of some segment of the population is simpler than distinguishing local and national tax payer interests, occupational interests in shared retirement funds, or policyholder interests in the claims exercised on a life insurance company. For policy purposes the question of who has interest in reducing (or not reducing) some mortal risk may be as important as how big the algebraic sum of those interests is.

So far we have identified two sources of 'value' for enhanced survival, the 'consumer interest' of a family in its own survival and the externalities that take mainly the form of transfers to or from the consuming unit. Whether it makes sense to add up the transfers into a net figure and add that figure to the consumer's own value will depend on the purpose for which some calculation of worth is desired. If the purpose, for example, is to see whether there are enough votes to support a programme that may save lives there may be jurisdictional constraints on the components that go into one's estimate of worth.

There are other interests. One that has received attention is the Gross National Product that is lost when a person dies (Rice, 1967; Hartunian, Smart and Thompson, 1981, pp. 41–56). The 'value' of the lives lost in motorcycle accidents that could have been saved with helmets has been approximated by the discounted lifetime earnings of the kinds of people who die in motorcycle accidents – mostly young men without dependents. But it is difficult to identify anyone to whom this loss accrues. The motorcyclist dies and this piece of the GNP disappears, but so does the person who was going to consume most of it. The economy does not miss him. He could as well have moved to another country. We can of course consider the taxes he paid and the exhaustible public benefits that he consumed, but we did that already in considering those transfers. It is not worth anything to the economy to spare his life. (The point can be reduced to absurdity by observing that a modest extension of this methodology discovers that abortions in the United States are 'costing the economy' a quarter of a trillion dollars every year.)

CONCERN FOR OTHERS' LIVES

To this point I have looked at selfish interests. What about our compassionate interest in the longevity of fellow citizens, or our charitable interests in the lives of those who are especially at risk because their poverty exposes them to hazards? What is the government's obligation for the safety of its citizens and how should it assess the worth of a programme, regulatory or budgetary, that may save some expected number of lives?

The question especially arises because many of the activities that promise to reduce mortality are public goods. We can find motorcycle helmets, smoke detectors and seatbelts in the market, but if we want more effective treatment for coronary heart disease we have to expect publicly financed medical research to carry the burden. (The research, of course, does not have to be financed by our own government to benefit us, as rescue and regulation would.)

How should the government, then, evaluate the lifesaving consequences of an activity that requires budgetary outlays or imposes regulatory costs on its citizens? Take the question on two assumptions, first that all families share equally in the

271

potential benefits and, second, that programmes discriminate in their benefits by age, wealth, occupation, health status, or geographical location. 'Sharing equally' could mean either of two things: equal reductions in some risk of dying, or equal extensions of life expectancy, the difference depending mainly on age. If we take families as the sharing units, age differences will average out somewhat (and we can avoid the questions whether or not to count a foetus as a child). For simplicity assume that if citizens share equally in the expected reduction of mortality they also share equally in the associated transfers. This assumption is certainly false and is introduced only to reduce the scope of this essay.

In a first approximation I see no reason why a legislator or administrator should not approach mortal-risk-reducing activities in the same way he approaches activities that raise productivity, save time, reduce annoyance, provide entertainment, or reduce the discomforts of nonfatal illness (Schelling, 1968; Mishan, 1971; Zeckhauser, 1975). Specifically, one considers how the beneficiaries value the reduced mortality compared with what they could have procured with lower taxes or prices. It is always the case that some citizens value these things differently from others even when they benefit equally; that is in no way peculiar to risk reduction.

A way in which mortal-risk reduction differs from other benefits is in the lesser likelihood that the beneficiaries of reductions in small risks can articulate what it is worth to them or even discuss it reasonably when the issue arises. Traffic lights that reduce congestion are more susceptible to public hearings to establish their money values than lights primarily intended to save children's lives. On the other hand there is an economy of information to be enjoyed in connection with lifesaving if the principle can be adopted that, where all the citizens share equally in the reduced mortality, all benefits will be measured proportionately to the lives saved. (Or, if people so choose, life-years saved; see below.) If lifesaving is valued identically for traffic lights, cancer research, and police protection, one good determination of the 'value of lives saved' can be used repeatedly within any jurisdiction in which the character of the population has not changed much since that determination was made. This kind of determination has rarely if ever been done in any jurisdiction, but the same can probably be said of the value of noise reduction. The problem is not in the theory.

The hard issues arise when the benefits are not shared equally, and especially when the beneficiaries of a risk-reducing activity will be poor, or the innocent victims of the location of some hazardous activity. The debate in this case is familiar. Economists usually argue that if the beneficiaries are going to pay for the activity it is their valuations that should govern the decision. And even if it is difficult to penetrate their valuations it can be concluded that the poor will value risk reduction, compared to the other things that money will buy, less than the well-to-do.

It is only one step to the corollary that when the poor are to be provided greater safety at the expense of the well-to-do it should still be their privilege to request cash instead that they can spend as they please on other things they value more than the reduction in some life-threatening hazard. Institutionally, however, it is usually not the case that funds available for reducing mortal hazards can be transferred to procurement of whatever the beneficiaries want even more.

There is an argument here that economics cannot resolve. In the days when the *Titanic* hit an iceberg there were lifeboats for first class and tourist, steerage was expected to go down with the ship. The economic efficiency of that arrangement does not necessarily make it appealing; and even letting the poor travel cheaply on densely packed separate ships with no first class and no lifeboards can be objected to on grounds that are not easily dismissed by mere reference to economic efficiency.

SOME TECHNICAL ISSUES

Life vs. risk. Despite emphasis that our topic is *risk reduction*, there is temptation to talk about the value of a *life* saved. If an individual will pay annually (or forego in wages) $100 to reduce some mortal risk to himself from 1:10,000 annually to 1:20,000 – a reduction of 1:20,000 – it is convenient to say that he 'values his own life' at $2 million. That sounds as if, confronted with certain death, he would come up with $2 million to stay alive. But that is not what we meant, and it does not follow from the small-risk calculation. (In particular, there would be income effects if the risk-eliminating payment rose from $100 to $100,000.) What we mean is that 20,000 identical individuals identically at risk would collectively pay $2 million for each yet unidentified averted death among themselves. A terminological proposal is suggested by the unit of measure in part-time hiring, the FTE, 'full-time equivalent'; we can say that our subject values reducing the risk to his own life at $2 million per FLE, 'full life equivalent'.

Years of life saved. 'Saving a life' by reducing some mortal risk means only prolonging it; death eventually ensues. An alternative to the worth per life 'saved' would be the worth per 'year of life' saved. And not all years are worth the same. Some index of 'quality-adjusted life-years' has been proposed. These approaches are alternatives: we can impute more value to young lives than old, or measure benefits in life-years to the same effect.

Insurance. The availability of life insurance should have a powerful influence on the value of risk reduction to the person who provides for a family. Just as one might make heroic and uneconomic investments in fire safety to protect a home or farm that represented all of one's assets if insurance were unavailable, extreme precautions against the risk of death might appear necessary for the young parents of triplets if life insurance could not be procured. Thus any of the institutions that insure the welfare of dependent survivors can help to avoid inefficient investments in longevity. Similarly, older people without dependants might make collectively inefficient investments in longevity out of wealth that they would lose if they died; life annuities are a contractual solution.

Risk and anxiety. The elimination of certain mortal risks, besides saving lives, can reduce anxiety. Fear can afflict those who survive as much as those who die, so it is not double counting to include reduced anxiety among the benefits. But anxiety or concern, according to some studies, is not proportionate to the risk (Starr and Whipple, 1980). Some of it appears due to the stimuli that remind people of the danger, for example stories of violence on the streets at night. Two policy questions result. One is whether governments might wisely and properly give disproportionate emphasis – pay more per life actually saved – where the risks generate extraordinary anxiety, on grounds that the anxiety is commensurate in its impact on welfare with the actual incidence of death. (This would be like weighing nonfatal illness along with the fatal.) The second is whether a responsive government should deploy its resources toward those risks that citizens express most concern about, even when the government has evidence that those concerns are based more on imagination than on fact.

There are two possibilities here. One is that citizens grossly exaggerate some risk – a food additive, radioactivity, night-time violence – and the government knows that the public is simply wrong. The other is that citizens have preferences that are not confined to the arithmetic of life expectancy and consider certain horrors – perhaps those that their minds insist on dwelling on – more worth eliminating than others.

Discounting. Many policies entail current investment in future safety or reduced future mortality. (The two are not the same: exposure to asbestos or radiation increases the likelihood of cancer some decades later.) The question of discounting arises: is a death averted twenty years hence, or a hundred, worth less than a death averted today? Again: 'worth' to whom? People today who would bear the cost of averting that death a century hence can be expected to be less interested than they would be in averting a death that could be their own or their families', i.e. a death today, just as people who might bear the cost of saving lives in some remote part of the world, not being potential beneficiaries, would have to think of it as charity, not personal safety, and might be less interested.

But many programmes for health and safety are charitably motivated, that is, the expenses are incurred by people who do not expect to benefit. Should they discount future lives saved? There are economic arguments for discounting not the 'lives' but the money value imputed to a future life saved by some expenditure today. (1) Money spent today to save lives in the future could be invested instead to yield a larger lifesaving budget when the time comes, saving more lives. (2) Technological progress may make lifesaving cheaper in the future; wait and take advantage of the lower prices. (3) There is uncertainty about what hazards may disappear in the interim or cease to be lethal, and some of today's outlay will have procured no benefit. (4) And people may be richer in the future and better able to spend their own money to save their own lives. If one does not discount lives saved, the first two arguments together imply a higher marginal productivity in future lifesaving, and that all lifesaving resources should be channelled toward future lives until the marginal costs of future lifesaving have risen to that of current lifesaving. That that is not done is probably evidence that people do discount future lives whether or not they realize that they do.

Implicit valuations. It is sometimes argued that we should look at the implicit valuations expressed in social policy to 'discover' what 'our society' considers lives to be worth. In the United States there are tens of thousands of coronary bypass operations per year at a cost of $25,000 each. Most are undertaken in the hope of prolonging life. Since this surgical technique has been around for only a decade the data on its contribution to life extension are indecisive but suggest that the contribution is at most a year. (Some studies dispute any positive contribution.) Americans apparently acquiesce in the procurement of extended life at $25,000 or more per year. At that rate an averted lung cancer in a 65-year-old is worth (discounted at 5 per cent) upwards of $250,000, a youthful motorcycle fatality upwards of $500,000. These may not be bad numbers; but they do not reflect any explicit determination that the cost of bypass surgery is a reasonable price to pay for the life extension that on average it produces.

Market evidence. Some investigators have examined the relation of wage differentials among occupations or industries to the risk differentials, as measured by accidental deaths and work-related fatal illnesses (Viscusi, 1983). Econometric analysis leads to estimates of implicit own-life FLEs – the income workers forego to work in safer occupations. In 1980 prices, implicit FLEs are obtained over the range from roughly one to five million dollars, with workers in the extremely risky occupations 'revealing' implicit FLEs under one million. The different estimates are partly due to different data and methodologies but probably reflect also individual differences in willingness to trade money against risk of death, and some consequent sorting into the more and the less risky occupations.

BIBLIOGRAPHY

Hartunian, N.S., Smart, C.N. and Thompson, M.S. 1981. *The Incidence and Economic Costs of Major Health Impairments*. Lexington: Lexington Books.

Mishan, E.J. 1971. Evaluation of life and limb: a theoretical approach. *Journal of Political Economy* 79, 687–705.

Parfit, D. 1984. *Reasons and Persons*. Oxford: Clarendon Press.

Rice, D. 1967. Estimating the costs of illness. *American Journal of Public Health* 57, 424–40.

Schelling, T.C. 1968. The life you save may be your own. In *Problems in Public Expenditure Analysis*, ed. S.B. Chase, Jr., Washington, DC.: The Brookings Institution.

Starr, C. and Whipple, C. 1980. Risks of risk decisions. *Science* 208, 1114–19.

Viscusi, W.K. 1983. *Risk By Choice*. Cambridge, Mass.: Harvard University Press.

Zeckhauser, R.J. 1975. Procedures for valuing lives. *Public Policy* 23, 419–64.

Welfare State

I. GOUGH

The term 'welfare state' first entered the English language in 1941 when Archibishop Temple coined the phrase to differentiate wartime Britain from the 'warfare' state of Nazi Germany. It quickly entered the vocabulary associated with the Beveridge Report (1942), which propounded state responsibility for individual welfare 'from the cradle to the grave'. Paradoxically, however, it was Germany which pioneered both modern social insurance in the 1880s and the concept of *Wohlfahrstaat* in the 1920s. It is not easy to define the welfare state; for one reason the term refers both to goals (the idea of state responsibility for welfare) and to means (the institutions and practices through which the idea is given effect). Let us begin with goals and a well-known definition by Briggs (1961, p. 228):

> A 'Welfare State' is a state in which organized power is deliberately used (through policies and administration) in an effort to modify the play of market forces in at least three directions – first, by guaranteeing individuals and families a minimum income irrespective of the market value of their property; second by narrowing the extent of insecurity by enabling individuals and families to meet certain 'social contingencies' (for example, sickness, old age and unemployment) which lead otherwise to individual and family crises; and third by ensuring that all citizens without distinction of status or class are offered the best standards available in relation to a certain agreed range of social services.

This has the merit of defining the welfare state as one form of state intervention in a capitalist, market economy. It then specifies those interventions which have as their aim the elimination of poverty and insecurity, and the guaranteeing of 'best available' standards of certain services in kind. Dispute still ensues, however, as to whether those are the defining goals of a welfare state. Some argue that it normally refers only to the provision of a minimum income 'floor' or minimum standards in certain areas of need (e.g. Wilensky and Lebeaux, 1965). Others argue that social policies can serve other goals; for example, meritocratic education policies (Flora and Heidenheimer, 1981). Gough (1979, pp. 44–5) goes further and defines the welfare state as 'the use of state power to modify the reproduction of labour power and to maintain the non-working population in capitalist societies'. Hence a wide range of goals, motives and functions is attributed to the contemporary welfare state, but perhaps there is general agreement that the welfare state signifies the responsibility of the state for the well-being of all individuals on the basis of citizenship rights.

Turning to means, the minimum range of services included within the rubric of the welfare state is that adopted by the ILO, which comprises all cash benefits to individuals (social insurance, social assistance and universal benefits) together with public health services. As Wilensky suggests above, however, this list is usually extended to include education, personal social services and housing. Beyond this core the boundaries of the welfare state are disputed. Mishra (1984) would include full employment policies; Titmuss (1963) the range of tax expenditure he calls 'fiscal welfare' and even the occupational welfare schemes of corporations; Gough (1979) the state regulation of private activities of individuals and corporate bodies which affect the conditions of life of individuals and groups.

Notwithstanding these grey areas, there is general agreement that the welfare state was inaugurated in the mid-19th century with the provision of public elementary education, and more specifically in 1883 when the first of Bismarck's social insurance schemes was enacted. Before this time public assistance and poor relief existed but was based on the punitive criterion of 'less eligibility' and/or was coupled with the loss of citizenship rights (see Rimlinger, 1971, for the 'prehistory' of the welfare state). Developments since this time have been charted by Flora and Heidenheimer (1981) for selected Western countries (Table 1). Two general conclusions can be drawn from this survey of landmarks. First, except

Table 1

Year of Introduction of:	Germany	UK	Sweden	France	Italy	USA	Canada
Social insurance for:							
Industrial accidents	1884	1906	1901	1946	1898	1930	1930
Sickness insurance	1883	1911	1910	1930	1943	—	1971
Pensions	1889	1908	1913	1910	1919	1935	1927
Unemployment insurance	1927	1911	1934	1967	1919	1935	1940
Family allowances	1954	1945	1947	1932	1936	—	1944
Health insurance/service	1880	1948	1962	1945	1945	—	1972
General personal income tax operated uninterruptedly from:	1920* (1873)	1918	1903	1960	1923	1913	N/A
Education:							
Adult illiteracy first <20%	1850	1880	1880	N/A	N/A	1870	N/A
Secondary school enrolment first >10%	1925	1923	1937	N/A	N/A	1915	N/A
University enrolment first >10%	1975	1973	1968	N/A	N/A	1946	N/A

Notes: 'Social insurance' refers to compulsory state insurance, not employer's liability laws or social assistance schemes for specific groups.
* Introduced in Prussia in 1873.
Source: Flora and Heidenheimer (1981), tables 3.1, 6.1, 8.1–4.

for elementary education and some pioneering legislation, the welfare state is essentially a product of the 20th century. Second, countries display marked variations in the vintage and scope of their welfare systems; compare, for example, the exceptional position of the USA as pioneer in education yet laggard in the rest of social policy. This will be returned to below.

The scope of the welfare state has expanded dramatically in the 20th century as measured by the share of social service spending in GNP. In Britain social service spending as a share of GNP rose from 4 per cent in 1910 to 29 per cent in 1975, notably in bursts after the two world wars followed by a prolonged period of expansion from the early 1960s to the mid-1970s. This third state of growth was near-universal in OECD countries, the elasticity of growth rates of expenditure to GDP for the OECD as a whole over this period being 1.75 for health, 1.42 for income maintenance and 1.38 for education. The welfare state has been the most dynamic postwar factor increasing the share of the public sector as a whole in GDP. In all major OECD countries except the UK social expenditure exceeded 50 per cent of total public expenditure in the late 1970s. Despite attempts by many governments to stop or reverse this trend after 1973, it continued to rise into the 1980s. By 1981 social expdenditure exceeded one-third of GDP in the Netherlands, Denmark, Sweden and West Germany amongst others. Similar results are found by measuring social service employment and the share of household income accounted for by public transfers and employment.

At the same time national variations in the size of the welfare state are wide and persistent: there is no tendency towards convergence over time (Alber, 1983). On all rankings, Japan and the USA come near the bottom whilst Sweden, the Netherlands and Denmark are at the top. The UK is now below average in social expenditure among OECD countries. In Eastern Europe social expenditure exhibits a slower growth and a somewhat lower claim on resources than in Western Europe (though higher than in the USA and Japan).

In the face of such a massive transformation of capitalist economies, it is not surprising that the *causes* and *consequences* of the modern welfare state are disputed. Nor is it surprising that a shift in the respective roles of the economy, the state and civil society has attracted the attention not only of economists but also of sociologists and political scientists amongst others. Theories of the causes of welfare state development can be grouped into three: collective choice theories, modernization theories and Marxist theories.

The economic theory of politics as applied to the welfare state has not been spelt out in definitive form, but Mishra (1984) provides a good overview. It explains the universal growth of welfare spending in terms of political competition for votes, the lack of a cost constraint on voters' behaviour due to the low salience of taxes, the pressure of interest groups outside the state, notably trade unions and professionals, and the operation of budget-maximizing bureaucracies within the state. These forces, buttressed since World War II, by Keynesian economic theory, have exerted an upward 'ratchet' effect on welfare programmes and expenditure, which in turn are predicted to expand faster than tax resources. The theory would appear to explain the expansion of the welfare state since World War II, but is less sucessful in explaining the wide national disparities in welfare provision noted above.

By contrast, sociological theories (e.g. Wilensky and Lebeaux, 1965; Wilensky, 1975; Flora and Heidenheimer, 1981) have interpreted the welfare state as a response to the structural requirements of modernization. Economic development increases the division of labour and undermines the 'security functions' previously performed by families and communities; this generates new societal problems and requirements which call forth the widening responsibility of the state. Two schools of thought can be distinguished within this theoretical framework. The first emphasizes the role of social policy in adapting the labour force and other social institutions to the requirements of the economy; for example, via changes in the education system. The second, following Durkheim, emphasizes the need for new modes of social integration and explains the welfare state as the response to this societal need. T.H. Marshall's (1963) theory in which the welfare state is perceived as the culmination of citizenship rights, is the most notable example of this school. Both variants of modernization theory are able to theorize the universal expansion of the welfare state, but they suffer from two related problems. First, they offer 'functionalist' explanations of the process which are now discredited, on the familiar grounds that one cannot explain the origin or persistence of a policy in terms of its consequences – whatever they are (Goldthorpe, 1962). Second, they cannot satisfactorily explain historical and contemporary disparities in welfare state development – why, for example, Germany introduced national sickness insurance in 1883 yet the USA (at the time of writing) still has not followed suit.

Marxist theories relate the form and development of the welfare state to the structure and development of the capitalist mode of production. Offe (1975) has shown how the capitalist state is constrained by the fact that it does not control investment decisions and the process of accumulation, yet depends on a healthy capitalist sector for its tax revenues. Hence, whatever the nature of the party in power, it is constrained from pursuing welfare policies harmful to broad capitalist interests. In the hands of some writers, this has resulted in a Marxist version of functionalist modernization theories. Others, however, stress the existence of exploitative class relations and endemic class conflict which generate the modern labour movement which seeks to utilize the state to modify market processes. Thus O'Connor (1973) argues that the state must try to fulfil two basic and often contradictory functions: accumulation and legitimation (the latter to maintain the conditions for social harmony). Gough (1979) interprets the welfare state as the outcome of two sets of forces: on the one hand, the ability of the capitalist welfare state to adapt the population and policy framework to the changing requirements of capital; on the other hand, the pressure exerted by the working class to modify the play of market forces to improve need-satisfaction and levels of welfare. Stephens (1979) and Therborn (1984) argue that measures of labour movement strength correlate well with national and temporal variations in social expenditure. Thus Marxist theories offer some explanation of contemporary welfare variations; nevertheless, they lack an explanation of the citizenship-rights *form* of contemporary welfare policies.

Lastly, we turn to different interpretations of the *consequences* of the welfare state for modern capitalist economies. We can distinguish two interpretations here which we shall label the compatibility and the incompatibility theses. The first has been argued by Keynesian economists (the welfare state as an agency of demand management), and by modernization theorists and radical functionists, both of whom stress the economic and integrative roles of the welfare state. The view that the welfare state and capitalism form a harmonious partnership was widespread over the postwar decades of economic growth and political stability. The onset of economic crisis in 1973 however has undermined this position.

The opposing incompatibility thesis is argued on the right and left of the political spectrum. On the right it is argued that the extent of contemporary welfare activities has led to government 'failure' and 'overload'. Among the unintended consequences of government action are cited increasing inflation, the failure of social programmes to meet their goals and the erosion of individual responsibility and independence. The responsibilities of the welfare state expand alongside the expectations of citizens, and the result is the political destabilization of democracies (summarized in Mishra, 1984). This version of the incompatability thesis was one foundation of the Thatcher and Reagan governments' adoption of monetarist and supply-side economic policies designed to reduce government welfare expenditure and taxation. On the left the incompatability thesis is argued by O'Connor (1973), Offe (1984) and Habermas (1976). Systemic failures result from the central contradiction of capitalist welfare states: the necessity of the welfare state to both commodify and decommodify the economy. 'Commodification' is necessary to permit market mechanisms to operate to ensure economic growth, but 'decommodification' (collective regulation) of the economy isalso necessary to cope with the ensuing problems of an economic system which it cannot control.

Though popular since the mid-1970s, incompatability theories have been critized on theoretical and empirical grounds. The former essentially reiterate the positive consequences of welfare state activity noted earlier. An empirical survey of the impact of the welfare state by George and Wilding (1984) concludes that its negative economic consequences have been much exaggerated and may be outweighed by its positive effects, whilst the welfare state is also a positive source of political stability.

Incompatability theories have predominantly been articulated and their policy implications implemented, within the English-speaking countries. In Europe, countries such as Sweden and Norway continued to pursue both full employment and expansionary welfare policies after the mid-1970s (Himmelstrand et al., 1981). Future research is needed on the comparative differences between capitalist socio-economic systems, their welfare states and their economic performance. It is likely to demonstrate, first, that incompatability theories are not generalizable, and second, that the welfare state signals an historic, irreversible and progressive transformation of advanced capitalist societies.

BIBLIOGRAPHY

Alber, J. 1983. Some causes of social security expenditure development in Western Europe, 1949–1977. In *Social Policy and Social Welfare*, ed. M. Loney et al., Milton Keynes: Open University Press.

Beveridge, W.H. 1942. *Social Insurance and Allied Services.* Cmnd 6404, London: HMSO.

Briggs, A. 1961. The welfare state in historical perspective. *Archives européennes de Sociologie* 2(2), 221–59.

Flora, P. and Heidenheimer, A.J. (eds) 1981. *The Development of Welfare States in Europe and America.* New Brunswick: Transaction Books.

George, V. and Wilding, P. 1984. *The Impact of Social Policy.* London: Routledge & Kegan Paul.

Goldthorpe, J.H. 1962. The development of social policy in England, 1880–1914. *Transactions of the Fifth World Congress of Sociology* 4, 41–56.

Gough, I. 1979. *The Political Economy of the Welfare State.* London: Macmillan.

Habermas, J. 1976. *Legitimation Crisis.* London: Heinemann.

Himmelstrand, U. et al. 1981. *Beyond Welfare Capitalism.* London: Heinemann.

Marshall, T.H. 1963. Citizenship and social class. In T.H. Marshall, *Sociology at the Crossroads and Other Essays*, London: Heinemann.

Mishra, R. 1984. *The Welfare State in Crisis.* Brighton: Wheatsheaf Books.

O'Connor, J. 1973. *The Fiscal Crisis of the State.* New York: St. Martin's Press.

Offe, C. 1975. The theory of the capitalist state and the problem of policy formation. In *Stress and Contradiction in Modern Capitalism*, ed. L. Lindberg et al., London and Lexington, Mass.: D.C. Heath.

Offe, C. 1984. *Contradictions of the Welfare State.* Ed. J. Keane, London: Hitchinson.

Rimlinger, G.V. 1971. *Welfare Policy and Industrialization in Europe, America and Russia.* New York: Wiley.

Stephens, J.D. 1979. *The Transition from Capitalism to Socialism.* London: Macmillan.

Therborn, G. 1984. The prospects of labour and the transformation of advanced capitalism. *New Left Review* (145), May-June, 5–38.

Titmuss, R. 1963. The social division of welfare. In R. Titmuss, *Essays on 'The Welfare State'*, 2nd edn, London: Allen & Unwin.

Wilensky, H.L. 1975. *The Welfare State and Equality.* Berkeley: University of California Press.

Wilensky, H.L. and Lebeaux, C.N. 1965. *Industrial Society and Social Welfare.* New York: Free Press.

Women's Wages

J. RUBERY

Women's average wages are consistently lower than men's average wages in all countries, even after adjustments for differences in working hours. These lower wages cannot be simply explained by differences in the productivity of women workers, or by the segregation of women into different jobs: they are related to the role of women in the social reproduction sphere, that is to their expected contributions to domestic labour and to family income. However, women's wages should not be identified as a separate issue; to do so suggests that it is women's wages that do not conform to a competitive norm and therefore require separate analysis as an anomaly. Women form too large a segment of the labour force for this 'anomaly' not to affect the other segment, 'male labour', and men's role in social reproduction has an equal and specific impact on their characteristics as wage labour. There is nevertheless an argument on social and political grounds for singling out women's wages for special study. Women's wages are not only low at the average or macro level, but also are consistently lower than men's at the micro level of the occupation, firm or industry. Women account for overwhelmingly the largest share of low-paid adult workers in the UK, so that ten years after the Equal Pay Act it is still reasonable to talk of a separate set of wages for women to that available to the majority of men.

NEOCLASSICAL EXPLANATIONS OF WOMEN'S WAGES. There are three different types of hypotheses that have been put forward within a neoclassical framework to explain women's lower wages. The first is the wage discrimination hypothesis, associated with Becker's (1971) work on racial discrimination, under which women are paid less than their marginal products to compensate either employers or co-workers for their distaste for female workers. The second and third hypotheses assume that women are paid relative to their actual marginal products; according to the second hypothesis women are less productive employees than male employees, and under the third hypothesis, women are employed in less productive jobs than men, but not necessarily because they are inherently less productive workers. The discrimination hypothesis of Becker was found to be rather difficult to reconcile with neoclassical theory unless one could assume all employers were equally discriminatory. A less or non-discriminating employer would be able to compete successfully against the established group of discriminating employers.

The second hypothesis is associated with human capital theory; women's lower wages are attributed to lower levels of educational training and perhaps more significantly, to their lack of continuous work experience which develops skills and also renews and updates them. Pre-market discrimination, in-market discrimination or personal and household preferences could all account for these different patterns of human capital acquisition, but whatever the cause the lower wages are taken to result directly from women's lack of skills relative to men's. Women's role as wives and mothers may have an indirect effect on productivity through lowering human capital acquisition, but there may also be a direct effect if women take prime responsibility for the family and they behave in ways which make them less committed and less productive workers, such as working only part-time hours or having a higher tendency to absenteeism or to voluntary quits.

One of the consequences of such characteristics might be that women are in fact confined to lower-productivity jobs, because of the difficulties of adjusting all jobs to meet different behaviour patterns and characteristics of workers. This 'confinement' may be a demand side phenomenon, employers making assumptions about women's behaviour patterns, or a supply-side phenomenon, women choosing jobs which allow them to carry out their domestic responsibilities. The origins of these different preferences or 'tastes' are taken either to be exogenous to the economy and outside the sphere of economics, or as in the New Household Economics, to arise out of the process of welfare maximization for the household, instead of for the individual. Thus one explanation of the third hypothesis, job segregation, is women's role in social reproduction.

Segregation may also be held to result because of either prejudice, based on custom and practice, about which jobs are suitable for women, or thirdly, because women have essentially different attributes or skills to those of men. All three versions of the job segregation hypothesis are compatible with a view that the jobs women do are low skilled, low productivity jobs, but with the latter two versions it could be the over-supply of women to a relatively narrow range of jobs which results in lower supply prices, more labour-intensive technology and consequently lower-marginal products (Mill, 1848; Bergman, 1971). According to these two versions if demand for labour in these types of jobs rose, women's wages would be expected to rise accordingly, but under the first social reproduction hypothesis, an increase in demand for labour in these type of jobs could stimulate substitution of women by more 'committed' and 'productive' workers. The hypothesis of job segregation through prejudice is open to the same objections as were raised against Becker's hypothesis; unless the basis for segregation is real differences in skills then it would be broken down eventually by non-prejudiced employers. The 'economics of information costs' has helped to restore this hypothesis by suggesting that it may be rational for employers to use cheap 'screens' such as sex in their recruitment decisions, to avoid hiring and firing costs. Women may be excluded from a segment of the labour market either because on average women have less desirable characteristics than men (Phelps, 1972), or because no women think it worthwhile to acquire the skills for entry into this segment, so the employers' beliefs remain untested (Spence, 1973).

It is, nevertheless, more comfortable for neoclassical economists to attribute low wages for women to supply-side characteristics, to differences in attributes or preferences arising out of biological or social and cultural factors, than to place the burden of explanation on demand-side imperfections which prevent the equalization of returns to productivity. Under neoclassical analysis the forces of competition will always be working towards undermining these demand-side constraints, but as economists offer no analysis of the forces of social and biological change, persistence of inequality can be more readily accounted for, and changes in the economic status of women can be attributed to exogenous changes in tastes. However it is this procedure that also reveals the weakness of neoclassical analysis (Humphries and Rubery, 1984); by eschewing the need to develop an analysis of the historical relationship between the organization of production and the organization of social reproduction, neoclassical theorists make adjustments to the preference functions in their models, not to take account of changes they have identified in the organization of social reproduction but to find a better fit for their model when the previous preference function fails to perform adequately. There is thus no theoretical basis for making these changes (Tarling, 1981). This critique of neoclassical methodology suggests that it may be more appropriate to consider women's preferences in the labour market as conditioned by past historical experience and responses to current opportunities than as an independent cause of low wages.

A second major problem with the neoclassical analysis of women's wages arises from its assumption that relative wages reflect relative marginal products, so that the issue to be explained is why women workers have low marginal products. Clearly, therefore, all the critiques which apply to the marginal productivity approach to wage determination also apply here to the specific issues of women's wages. However this issue also highlights some of the deficiencies of the neoclassical approach. For example, the analytical framework is based on competitive wage determination, with market clearing, but historical and cross cultural empirical evidence suggests that the female wage labour market is rarely if ever cleared. Surveys indicate a high level of hidden unemployment amongst economically inactive women, so that there are still large supplies of labour available at current wage rates. Secondly, the neoclassical approach implies that wage relativities should reflect relative skills and relative efficiencies of labour. Women's wages are in practice remarkably uniform, displaying much lower dispersion at micro and macro levels than male wages. The exclusion of women from more skilled work only provides a partial explanation, as the usual practice is to place all women's jobs whatever their characteristics, and all women, regardless of their skill or experience, within a narrow band of pay at the bottom of the pay hierarchy (Craig et. al. 1985). Thirdly, if marginal products influence wages, changes in the ratio of female to male pay should come about as a result either of a change in the distribution of women within the labour market, or as a result of changes in demand or supply in the female labour market. In practice changes in the ratio have been associated, at least in Britain, more with social and institutional forces than with changes in labour market opportunities.

These considerations suggest that women's lower wages may be determined to some extent prior to the allocation of women to jobs, and independently of their characteristics and attributes. This proposition is taken up by two of the three non-neoclassical theories examined below, that is the patriarchy theory and the family wage theory. This type of approach was rejected by neoclassical theorists because it is not easily compatible with theories of competitive equilibrium. Segmentation theory, the other non-neoclassical perspective examined below, argues that there is in fact no necessary tendency for the system of competition to bring about equalization of returns to productivity for the labour employed.

NON-NEOCLASSICAL EXPLANATIONS OF WOMEN'S WAGES. Patriarchal theories of women's wages start from the assumption that the fundamental explanation of women's inferior position in the economic system is their inferior position in the social and cultural system. Patriarchal social relations existed prior to capitalism and capitalism has had to adapt to a patriarchal system (Hartman, 1979). Women earn lower wages than men in order that there should be no challenge to the system of authority within the family and the social and political structure. Employers share the patriarchal values of society, so that the system is not subject to challenge by profit-seeking entrepreneurs. Inequality in pay may be reinforced by the subordination of women in inferior or 'feminine' jobs, but the low wages do not arise out of the characteristics of the jobs but out of the characteristics of women's position in a patriarchal society.

In contrast, the labour market segmentation approach, in its simple form, locates the causes of female inequality in the process of uneven development of the capitalist economy. Women are concentrated in particular sections of the labour market, but unlike the neoclassical model of dualism, the origins of the division between the so-called 'primary' and 'secondary' sectors are not social and institutional imperfections which distort the market, but the requirements of the economic system itself (Doeringer and Piore, 1971). Primary employment sectors develop in order to maximize advantages from operating at efficient levels of capacity with a stable and fully-trained labour force. Fluctuations in demand are dealt with by subcontracting to secondary employment sectors. In addition, whole industries are located in the secondary sector if the demand for the product is generally variable and unstable. The explanation of the divergence between returns to labour in the two sectors is rooted in the operation of the economic system, but in this dual labour market model, the explanation of why women are concentrated in the secondary sector has to be looked for elsewhere. The radical version of labour market segmentation theory (Edwards, Gordon and Reich, 1975) provides an explanation both of the structuring of the labour market

285

into primary and secondary sectors and of the allocation of women to the secondary portion. To forestall the development of class consciousness, capitalists, it is argued, segmented or divided the labour force by creating 'artificial' hierarchies or divisions. In orderr to minimize the likelihood of alliances being formed across these divides, workers with different social characteristics were allocated to different segments: hence the concentration of women and ethnic minorities in secondary segments.

In the family-wage approach the analysis of women's position in the family and social system is linked directly to the analysis of the forces of production (Humphries, 1977; Beechey, 1978). Reliance simply on Marx cannot provide an adequate theory of women's wages because of the absence of a theory of the family. In contrast to the predictions of Engels, the nuclear family failed to 'wither away' to produce a wage labour market of undifferentiated individuals. Instead individuals on the labour market are still reproduced within a sex-differentiated social and family system and within a social reproduction system which provides forms of income support to non-wage labour. It is the differences in men's and women's relationships to the social reproduction system that leads to their labour being supplied on different terms. Men's wages are based on the cost of their own social reproduction and that of their dependents, but women's wages are based on only part of the cost of their own reproduction, on the assumption that they have access to support from either their husbands or their fathers, an assumption which is reinforced by social security systems which deny married women access to income support in their own right.

The tendency for women's labour to be supplied at below the value of labour power (that is below the average cost of reproduction) has specific consequences for the mobilization and utilization of female labour within the productive system. Female labour will tend to be mobilized at times when there are strong competitive pressures on capital to restore the falling rate of profit and female labour will tend to be concentrated in those sectors where capital is under particular pressure to force the cost of labour down below the value of labour power. Individual households do not in fact exercise 'choice' over their sexual division of labour as women are confined to jobs which offer wages below the cost of average adult subsistence. Thereby the structure of wages in the productive sphere serves to reinforce the system of social organization on which it is founded.

Under this family wage hypothesis, therefore, the lower wages that women are paid derive primarily from their own social characteristics, in particular from their position in the family income system, and not from the characteristics of the jobs that they perform. Women's low wages are thus assumed in some sense to be independent of the jobs the perform, as in the patriarchy argument. However, contrary to the simple patriarchy notion, women's lower wages are identified as having a materialist base which relates both to their role in social reproduction and to their role in production. The lower wages are used not simply to reproduce patriarchal values but to serve competitive objectives. Thus even though low wages for women are not caused by different patterns of job allocation they may themselves lead to different patterns of female labour throughout the economy.

In order to develop a fully adequate theory of women's wages it is necessary to combine the insights of the family-wage hypothesis with the perspectives on job segregation offered respectively by the patriarchy and labour market segmentation approach. There is now a considerably body of empirical research which suggests that, at least in the UK, women's low wages cannot be explained by the characteristics of the jobs they perform. Many women's jobs require skills and experience, but these factors are not reflected in pay or grading of the jobs (West, 1982; Craig et al., 1985). Moreover, work carried out within the context of the labour process debate suggests that there is no direct relationship between the skill of a job, however measured, and its pay and status. The characteristics and the bargaining power of the workers employed are more important explanatory variables. Indeed in order to 'deskill' a job it may be necessary to employ workers of lower status and bargaining power. However the substitution of women for men in order to deskill jobs has not been a universal process, so we need to understand the limits to this process. It is here that patriarchal relations may play an important role in setting up boundaries between men's work and women's work which are only breached when economic or other social forces are strong enough to break down the customary division of labour by sex. Moreover when the old division of labour is broken down and a new division established, newly feminized jobs are quickly redefined as only suitable for women, and the new division of labour is rigidified by these social values and by the continuing differentials in male and female pay.

Segmentation theory helps to explain why the utilization of women within the production sphere is concentrated in specific areas. Within this approach, it is argued that capitalism is subject to a process of uneven development, with different systems of competition prevailing in and between different sectors of the economy. As competition cannot be reduced to simplify cost minimization, there is no necessary tendency for the incentives to substitution to be such as to ensure equalization of wage costs between firms or categories of labour. However, once a firm or sector becomes organized around low wage labour that cost structure becomes built into its system of organization.

The incentive to substitute low wage labour for higher paid labour is constrained by the firm's other objectives; such substitution might endanger the overall efficiency of the firm, by increasing the likelihood of instability among the experienced labour force or by reducing overall cohesion and cooperation. Moreover labour markets are also regulated by trade union organization and government employment policy which reduce firms' discretion in both wages and employment decisions. The actual form of trade union organization and government labour regulations differ considerably between countries and have a major impact both on the established norm for female wages and on the specific ways in which female labour is utilized in the economy. Thus trade union wage policies, the type of legal minimum wage system and the employment protection and benefits associated with part-time work have an impact on the terms and conditions under which women are employed which is relatively independent of the characteristics of the jobs that they perform in any particular country.

Women's wages cannot be explained solely by reference to women's family position, as the wage levels are also influenced by the system of wage determination and employment protection that prevails in the labour market. It is significant that it is countries with more egalitarian trade union wage policies or more effective minimum wage policy that tend to have a higher earnings ratio for women to men although these always stop short of unity.

These higher ratios automatically raise women's contribution to family income, and as these higher pay levels become permanently established, so the dependence of the family on women's income is strengthened. However it is not clear whether differences in systems of family organization between countries are themselves a cause of differences in labour market earnings for women or an outcome of these differences. This issue raises important questions over the ways in which women's pay inequality could be reduced. It could be argued that as women's inferior economic status can be attributed primarily to their historical role as dependents in the family system, then it is to changes in family organization that we must look before any real progress in women's position can be made. If women were to become reliant on their own earnings for their subsistence, the 'natural price' of female labour would change in theory; however it is possible that this change would reduce the standard of living of many women unless there are mechanisms by which the necessary real wages to maintain current consumption standards could be secured in the labour market. Indeed it could be argued that increasing numbers of American women have been thrown into poverty because a change in family organization towards more single parent families has preceded the development of any effective mechanisms for women to improve upon the wage levels which relate to an outdated system of family organization. If instead gains for women are secured through trade union organizations, government labour market regulations or other means, then these are likely to be relatively easily and quickly translated into a new family budget structure which then becomes a material basis for changes in women's social and family roles.

BIBLIOGRAPHY

Becker, G. 1971. *The Economics of Discrimination.* 2nd edn, Chicago: Chicago University Press.

Beechey, V. 1978. Women and Production: a critical analysis of some sociological theories of women's work. In *Feminism and Materialism*, ed. A. Kuhn and A.M. Wolpe, London: Routledge and Kegan Paul, 155–97.

Bermann, B.R. 1971. The effect on white incomes of discrimination in employment. *Journal of Political Economy* 71(2), Mar-Apr., 294–313.

Craig, C., Garnsey, E. and Rubery, J. 1985. *Payment Structures in Smaller Firms: Women's Employment in Segmented Labour Markets.* Department of Employment Research Paper no. 48, London.

Doeringer, P. and Piore, M. 1971. *Internal Labour Markets and Manpower Analysis.* Lexington, Mass.: D.C. Heath.

Edwards, R., Reich, M. and Gordon, D.M. (eds.) 1975. *Labour Market Segmentation.* Lexington, Mass.: D.C. Heath.

Hartman, H. 1979. The unhappy marriage of Marxism and feminism: towards a more progressive union. *Capital and Class* 8, Summer, 1–33.

Humphries, J. 1977. Class struggle and the persistence of the working-class family. *Cambridge Journal of Economics* 1(3), September, 241–58.

Humphries, J. and Rubery, J. 1984. The reconstitution of the supply-side of the labour market: the relative autonomy of social reproduction. *Cambridge Journal of Economics* 8(4), 331–46.

Mill, J.S. 1848. *Principles of Political Economy.* 1st edn, London.

Phelps, E.S. 1972. The statistical theory of racism and sexism. *American Economic Review* 62(4), September, 659–61.

Spence, A.M. 1973. Job market signalling. *Quarterly Journal of Economics* 87(3), August, 355–74.

Tarling, R. 1981. The relationship between employment and output: where does segmentation theory lead us? In *The Dynamics of Labour Market Segmentation*, ed. F. Wilkinson, London: Academic Press, pp. 281–90.

West, J. (ed.) 1982. *Work, Women and the Labour Market.* London: Routledge & Kegan Paul.

Contributors

A.B. Atkinson Thomas Tooke Professor of Economics and Statistics, London School of Economics and Political Science. Fellow, British Academy. *Poverty in Britain and the Reform of Social Security*; *The Economics of Inequality* (1975; 2nd edn 1983); *Lectures on Public Economics* (with J.E. Stiglitz, 1980); *Poverty and Social Security*.

Robin Barlow Professor of Economics, University of Michigan. *The Economic Effect of Malaria Eradication* (1969); 'Efficiency aspects of local school finance', *Journal of Political Economy* 78 (October 1970); 'Policy analysis with a disaggregated economic-demographic model', (with G. Davies) *Journal of Public Economics* 3 (February 1974); 'A test of alternative methods of making GNP comparisons', *Economic Journal* 87 (September 1977); *A Resource Allocation Model for Child Survival* (with H. Barnum, L. Fajardo and A. Pradilla, 1980); 'City population and per capita city government expenditures', in *Research in Population Economics* 4 (ed. J. Simon, 1982).

Gary S. Becker University Professor of Economics and Sociology, University of Chicago. Honorary degrees from Hebrew University, Jerusalem; Knox College; University of Illinois, Chicago; W.S. Woyinsky Award; John Bates Clark Medal; Frank E. Seidman Distinguished Award in Political Economy; MERIT Award; John R. Commons Award; President, American Economics Association, 1987; Member, National Academy of Sciences; American Philosophical Society; American Academy of Arts and Sciences; National Academy of Education. *The Economics of Distribution* (1957); *Human Capital* (1964); *Economic Theory* (1971); *The Allocation of Time and Goods over the Life Cycle* (with G. Ghez, 1974); *The Economic Approach to Human Behavior* (1976); *A Treatise on the Family* (1981).

Richard A. Berk Professor, Department of Sociology, Program in Social Statistics, University of California, Los Angeles. *Water Shortage: Lessons in Water Conservation Learned from the Great California Drought, 1976–77* (with T. Cooley, C. LaCivita and K. Sredl, 1981); 'Capitalizing on nonrandom assignment to treatments: a regression discontinuity evaluation of a crime control program', (with D. Rauma) *Journal of the American Statistical Association* (March 1983); 'Supply-side sociology of the family: the challenge of the new home economics', (with S. Berk) in *Annual Review of Sociology* 9 (ed. R. Turner, 1983); 'Renumeration and recidivism: the long term impact of unemployment compensation on ex-offenders', (with D. Rauma) *Quantitative Criminology* (March 1987); 'Police responses to family violence incidents: an analysis of an experimental design with incomplete randomization', (with L. Sherman) *Journal of the American Statistical Association* (March 1988); 'Causal inference for sociological data', in *The Handbook of Sociology* (ed. N. Smelser, 1988).

Francine D. Blau Professor of Economics and Labor and Industrial Relations, University of Illinois, Urbana-Champaign. Executive Board-Member, Industrial Relations Research Association, 1987–9; Vice-President, Midwest Economics Association, 1983–4. *Equal Pay in the Office* (1977); 'Causes and consequences of layoffs', (with L. Kahn) *Economic Inquiry* (April 1981); 'The use of transfer payments by immigrants', *Industrial and Labor Relations Review* (January 1984); *The Economics of Women, Men and Work* (with M. Ferber, 1986); 'Discrimination: evidence from the United States', (with M. Ferber) *American Economic Review* (May 1987); 'Trends in earnings differentials by gender: 1971–1981', (with A. Beller) *Industrial and Labor Relations Review* (July 1988).

Ester Boserup Author and consultant. Honorary degrees in Economics, University of Copenhagen; Agricultural Science, University of Wageningen; Human Letters, Brown University. *The Conditions of Agricultural Growth* (1965); *Women's Role in Economic Development* (1970); *Population and Technological Change* (1981).

Irene Bruegel Chief Economic Development Officer, London Borough of Ealing. 'Women as a reserve army of labour', *Feminist Review* (1979); 'Women's employment', in *Women's Welfare: Women's Rights* (ed. J. Lewis, 1983).

Glen G. Cain Professor of Economics, Department of Economics, University of Warwick. *Married Women in the Labor Force* (1966); *Income Maintenance and Labor Supply: Econometric Studies* (ed., with H. Watts, 1973); 'Estimation of a model of labor supply, fertility, and wages of married women', (with M. Dooley) *Journal of Political Economy* (August 1976); 'The challenge of segmented labor markets to orthodox theory', *Journal of Economic Literature* (December 1976); 'The economic analysis of discrimination: a survey', in *Handbook of Labor Economics* volume 1 (ed. Ashenfelter and Layard, 1986); 'A reanalysis of marital stability in the Seattle–Denver income maintenance experimen'' (with D. Wissoker) *American Journal of Sociology* (1989).

Robert L. Clark Professor, Department of Economics and Business, North Carolina State University. Senior Fellow, Center for the Study of Aging and Human Development, Duke University; Senior Research Associate, Center for Demographic Studies, Duke University. 'Economics of aging', (with J. Kreps and J. Spengler) *Journal of Economic Literature* (September 1978); *Economics of Individual and Population Aging* (with J. Spengler, 1980); 'Individual mobility, population growth and labor force participation', (with S. Cantrell) *Demography* (May 1982); *Inflation and the Economic Well-Being of the Elderly* (with G. Maddox, R. Schrimper and D. Sumner, 1984); 'Earnings and pension compensation', (with A. McDermed) *Quarterly Journal of Economics* (May 1986); 'Unions, pension wealth, and age-compensation profiles', (with S. Allen) *Industrial and Labor Relations Review* (July 1986).

Ansley J. Coale Senior Research Demographer, Office of Population Research; Emeritus Professor of Economics and Public Affairs, Princeton University. Member, National Academy of Sciences; American Academy of Arts and Sciences; American Philosophical Society; Corresponding Fellow, British Academy. Honorary Degrees: Universities of Pennsylvania, Louvain and Liege. *Population Growth and Economic Development in Low-Income Countries* (with E. Hoover, 1958); *New Estimates of Population and Fertility in the United States* (with M. Zelnik, 1963); *Regional Model Life Tables and Stable Populations* (with P. Demeny, 1966); 'Age patterns in marriage', *Population Studies* 25 (July 1971); *The Growth and Structure of Human Population* (1972); *Human Fertility in Russia since the Nineteenth Century* (with B. Anderson and E. Harm, 1979).

James S. Coleman University Professor, University of Chicago. Member, American Philosophical Society; American Academy of Arts and Sciences; National Academy of Sciences; Royal Swedish Academy of Sciences. *Equality of Educational Opportunity* (with E. Campbell, C. Hobson, J. McPartland, A. Mood, F. Weinfeld and R. York, 1966); 'Inequality, sociology, moral philosophy', *American Journal of Sociology* 80(3), (November 1974); 'What is meant by "An equal educational opportunity"?', *Oxford Review of Education* 1(1), (1975); *Individual Interests and Collective Action* (1986); 'Social capital in the creation of human capital', *American Journal of Sociology* 94 (supplement), (1988); 'Equality and excellence in education', in *Surveying Social Life: Papers in Honor of Herbert H. Human* (ed. Herbert J. Gorman, 1988).

Richard A. Easterlin Professor of Economics, University of Southern California. President, Population Association of America, 1978; President, Economic History Association, 1979–80; Fellow, Econometric Society, 1983; American Academy of Arts and Sciences, 1978; Guggenheim Foundation, 1988. *Population Redistribution and Economic Growth, United States 1890–1950*, 2 vols, (with S. Kuznets, D. Thomas, E. Lee, A. Miller and C. Brainerd, 1957, 1960); *Population, Labor Force, and Long Swings in Economic Growth: The American Experience* (1968); *American Economic Growth: An Economist's History of the United States* (ed., with L. Davis and W. Parker, 1972); *Population and Economic Change in Developing Countries* (ed., 1980); *The Fertility Revolution: A Supply-Demand Analysis* (with E. Crimmins, 1985); *Birth and Fortune: The Impact of Numbers on Personal Welfare* (1987).

Isaac Ehrlich Professor of Economics and Director of the Institute for the Study of Free Enterprise Systems, University of Buffalo, State University of New York. Melvin H. Baker Chair of American Enterprise. 'Market insurance, self-insurance and self-protection', (with G. Becker) *Journal of Political Economy* 80(4), (July/August 1972); 'Participation in illegitimate activities – a theoretical and empirical investigation', *Journal of Political Economy* 81(3), (1973); 'The deterrent effect of capital punishment – a question of life and death', *American Economic Review* 65(3), (1975); 'Asset management, allocation of time and returns to saving', (with U. Ben-Zion) *Economic Inquiry* 14(4), (1976); 'On the usefulness of controlling individuals: an economic analysis of rehabilitation, incapacitation, and deterrence', *American Economic Review* 71(3), (1981); 'The derived demand for advertising: a theoretical and empirical investigation', (with L. Fisher) *American Economic Review* 72(3), (1982).

Victor R. Fuchs Henry J. Kaiser, Jr. Professor of Economics, Stanford University. *The Service Economy* (1968); *Who Shall Live? Health, Economics, and Social Choice* (1974); *Economic Aspects of Health* (ed., 1982); *How We Live* (1983); *The Health Economy* (1986); *Women's Quest for Economic Equality* (1988).

Jack Goody Professor of Economics, St John's College, Cambridge. Fellow, British Academy. *Death, Property and the Ancestors* (1962); *Technology, Tradition and the State in Africa* (1971); *Production and Reproduction* (1976); *The Development of the Family and Marriage in Europe* (1983); *The Logic of Writing and the Organisation of Society* (1986); *The Oriental, the Ancient and the Primitive* (1989).

Christopher A. Gregory Lecturer, Department of Prehistory and Anthropology, Australian National University. *Gifts and Commodities* (1982); *Observing the Economy* (with J. Altman, 1989).

Peter J. Hammond Professor of Economics, Stanford University. Fellow, Econometric Society; Guggenheim Fellow, 1986–7. 'Charity: altruism or cooperative egoism?' *Altruism, Morality and Economic Theory* (ed. E. Phelps, 1975); 'Overlapping expectations and Hart's conditions for equilibrium in a securities model', *Journal of Economic Theory* 31 (1983); 'Project evaluation by potential tax reform', *Journal of Public Economics* 30 (1986); 'Consequentialist social norms for public decisions', *Social Choice and Public Decision Making: Essays in Honor of Kenneth J. Arrow* Vol. 1 (ed. W. Heller, R. Starr and D. Starrett,

1986); 'Consequentialist foundations for expected utility', *Theory and Decision* 25 (1988); 'Market as constraints: multilateral incentive compatibility in continuum economics', *Review of Economic Studies* 54 (1987).

Olivia Harris Senior Lecturer in Anthropology, Goldsmiths College, University of London. 'Conceptualizing women', (with F. Edholm and K. Young), *Critique of Anthropology* 9/10 (1977); 'Households as natural units', in *Of Marriage and the Market* (ed. K. Young, C. Wolkowitz and R. McCullagh, 1981); 'Households and their boundaries', *History Workshop Journal* 13 (1982); *La Participacion indigens en los mercados surandinos* (ed., with B. Larson and E. Tandeter, 1987).

Susan Himmelweit Lecturer in Economics, Open University. 'Domestic labour and capital', (with S. Mohun) *Cambridge Journal of Economics* 1(1), (1977); 'Production rules OK? Waged work and the family', in *What is to be done about the family?* (ed. L. Segal, 1983); 'Value relations and divisions within the working class', *Science and Society* 48(3), (1984); 'The real dualism of sex and class', *Review of Radical Political Economics* 16(1), (1984); 'More than a right to choose', *Feminist Review* 29 (1988); *New Reproductive Technologies* (1989).

Kurt Klappholz Reader in Economics, London School of Economics and Political Science. 'Methodological prescriptions in economics', (with J. Agassi) *Economica* (1959); 'Identities in economic models', (with E. Mishan) *Economica* (1962); 'Value judgements and economics', *British Journal for the Philosophy of Science* (1964); 'Economics and ethical neutrality', in *The Encyclopedia of Philosophy* (ed. P. Edwards, 1967); 'Equality of opportunity, "fairness" and efficiency', in *Essays in Honour of Lord Robbins* (ed. M. Peston and B. Corry, 1972).

Laurence J. Kotlikoff Professor of Economics, Boston University; Research Associate, National Bureau of Economic Research. 'The family as an incomplete annuities market', (with A. Spivak) *Journal of Political Economy* (April 1981); 'The role of intergenerational transfers in aggregate capital formation', (with L. Sumners) *Journal of Political Economy* (August 1981); *Pensions in the American Economy* (with D. Smith, December 1983); *Dynamic Fiscal Policy* (with A. Auerbach, 1987); *The Wage Carrot and the Pension Stick: Retirement Benefits and Labor Force Participation* (with D. Wise, 1988); *Determinants of Savings* (1989).

Peter Mieszkowski CLINE Professor of Economics, Rice University. 'On the theory of tax incidence', *Journal of Political Economy* 74 (June 1967); 'The effects on unionization of the distribution of income', (with H. Johnson) *Quarterly Journal of Economics* 84 (1970); 'The property tax: excise tax or profits tax', *Journal of Public Economics* 1(1), (1972); 'Public goods, efficiency, and regional fiscal equilization', (with F. Flatters and Vernon Henderson) *Journal of Public Economics* 3 (1974); 'The returns to investment in language: the economies of bilingualism', (with Albert Breton), in *The Political Economy of Fiscal Federalism* (ed. W.E. Oates, 1977); 'The new view of the property tax: a reformulation', (with George Zodrow) *Regional Science and Urban Economics* 16 (1986).

Peter Mueser Assistant Professor, Department of Economics, University of Missouri. 'The effects of noncognitive traits', in *Who Gets Ahead? – The Determinants of Economic Success in America* (ed. C. Juecks et al., 1979); 'The Wisconsin model of status attainment', (with C. Jeucks and J. Crouse) *Sociology of Education* (1983); 'A note on simultaneous equations models of migration and employment growth', *Southern Economic Journal* (1985); 'Patterns of net migration by age for U.S. Counties 1950–1980: the impact of increasing spatial differentiation by life cycle', (with M. White and J. Tierney) *Canadian Journal of Regional Science* (1988); 'Implications of boundary choice for the measurement of residential mobility', (with M. White) *Demography* 25 (1988); 'The spatial structure of migration', *Regional Studies* (forthcoming).

Edmund S. Phelps McVickar Professor of Political Economy, Columbia University. Member, National Academy of Sciences; Vice-President, American Economic Association, 1983; Honorary Doctorate, Amherst College, 1985. *Microeconomic Foundations of Employment and Inflation Theory* (with others, 1970); *Inflation Policy and Unemployment Theory* (1972); *Studies in Macroeconomic Theory* 2 vols (1979, 1980); *Individual Forecasting and Aggregate Outcomes*, (with R. Frydman, 1983); *Political Economy* (1985); *The Slump in Europe*, (with J. Fitoussi, 1988).

Henry Phelps Brown Fellow, New College, Oxford, 1930–47; Professor of the Economics of Labour, London School of Economics and Political Science, 1947–68. Fellow of the British Academy, 1960. *The Framework of the Pricing System* (1936); *The Growth of British Industrial Relations* (1959); *A Century of Pay* (1968); *The Inequality of Pay* (1977); *The Origins of Trade Union Power* (1983); *Egalitarianism and the Generation of Inequality* (1988).

Sherwin Rosen Bergman Professor of Economics, University of Chicago. Fellow, Econometric Society; Member, American Academy of Arts and Sciences. 'Hedonic prices and implicit markets: product differentiation in pure competition', *Journal of Political Economy* 82 (1974); 'The value of saving a life: evidence from the labor market', (with R. Thaler) *Household Production and Consumption*, NBER Studies in Income and Wealth No. 40 (ed. N. Terleckyj, 1976); 'Human capital: a survey of empirical research', *Research in Labor Economics* 1 (ed. R. Ehrenberg, 1977); 'Rank-order tournaments as optimal labor contracts', (with E. Lazear) *Journal of Political Economy* 89(5), (1981); 'The economics of superstars', *American Economic Review* 71(5), (1981); 'Implicit contracts: a survey', *Journal of Economic Literature* 23(3), (September 1985).

Amartya Sen Drummond Professor of Political Economy, Oxford University; Lamont University Professor, Harvard University. President, Econometric Society 1984; Fellow, British Academy; numerous honorary degrees. *Choice of Techniques: an aspect of planned economic development* (1960; 3rd edn, 1968); *Collective Choice and Social Welfare* (1970); *On Economic Inequality* (1973); *Poverty and Famines: an essay on entitlements and deprivation* (1981); *Choice, Welfare and Measurement* (1984); *Resources, Values and Development* (1984).

Howard Stanback Commissioner of the Department of Education, Chicago.

Hillel Steiner Senior Lecturer in Political Philosophy, University of Manchester. 'Individual liberty', *Aristotelian Society Proceedings* 75 (1975); 'The natural right to the means of production', *Philosophical Quarterly* 27 (1977); 'The structure of a set of compossible rights', *Journal of Philosophy* 74 (1977); 'Liberty and equality', *Political Studies* 29 (1981); 'Exploitation: a liberal theory amended, defended and extended', in *Modern Theories of Exploitation* (ed. A. Reeve, 1987); *An Essay on Rights* (forthcoming).

Myra H. Strober Associate Professor, School of Education, Stanford University. 'Towards a general theory of occupational sex segregation: the case of public school teaching', in *Sex Segregation in the Workplace: Trends, Explanations, Remedies* (ed. B. Reskin, 1984); 'The percentage of women in public school teaching: a cross-section analysis, 1850–1880', (with A. Lanford) *Signs: Journal of Women in Culture and Society* (Spring 1986); 'The scope of microeconomics: implications for economic education', *Journal of Economic Education* (Spring 1987); 'Integrated circuits/segregated labour: women in three computer-related occupations', (with A. Carolyn) *Computer Chips and Paper Clips: Technology and Women's Employment* vol. 3 (ed. H. Hartmann, R. Kraut and L. Tilly, 1987); 'The dynamics of occupational segregation among bank tellers', (with A. Carolyn) *Gender in the Workplace* (1987); *Feminism, Children and the New Families* (ed., with Dornbusch, 1988).

Gordon C. Winston Professor of Economics, Orrin Sage Professor of Political Economy and Provost, Williams College. 'Addiction and backsliding: a theory of compulsive consumption', *Journal of Economic Behavior and Organization* (December 1980); *The Timing of Economic Activities: Firms, Households and Markets in Time-Specific Analysis* (1982); 'The economics of academic tenure: a relational perspective', (with M. McPherson) *Journal of Economic Behaviour and Organization* (1983); 'Introduction' and 'Three problems with the treatment of time in economics', in *The Boundaries of Economics* (ed. W., G. and R. Teichgraeber, 1988); 'The time-shape of transactions', *Applied Behavioral Economics* (1989); 'Activities in time: a new approach to work and consumption', *Journal of Economic Behavior and Organization* (forthcoming).

G.D.N. Worswick Fellow and Tutor in Economics, Magdalen College, Oxford, 1945–65; Director, National Institute of Economic and Social Research, London, 1962–82. Fellow, British Academy; President, Royal Economic Society, 1982–4. *The Economics of Full Employment* (contributor, 1944); *The British Economy 1945–50* (joint editor, 1952); *The British Economy in the 1950's* (joint editor, 1962); *The Uses of Economics* (ed., 1972).

Erik Olin Wright Professor of Sociology, University of Wisconsin. *Class, Crisis and the State* (1978); *Classes* (1985); 'Marxism and methodological individualism', (with Elliot Sober and Andrew Levine) *New Left Review* 162 (1987); 'The transformation of the American class structure, 1960–1980', (with Bill Martin) *American Journal of Sociology* (1987), 'Exploitation, identity and class structure: a reply to my critics', *Critical Sociology* (1988); 'Women in the class structure', *Politics and Society* (1989).